MANAGEMENT ACCOUNTING

MANAGEMENT ACCOUNTING

By
DR. NISAR AHMAD
M. A. (Eco), M. Com., Ph. D.
Dept. of Commerce and Business Studies
Jamia Millia Islamia
New Delhi

ANMOL PUBLICATIONS PVT. LTD.
NEW DELHI-110 002 (INDIA)

ANMOL PUBLICATIONS PVT. LTD.
4374/4B, Ansari Road, Daryaganj
New Delhi - 110 002
Ph.: 23261597, 23278000
Visit us at: www.anmolpublications.com

Management Accounting

First Edition, 1997

Second Edition, 1998

ISBN 81-7488-412-2

Reprint, 2004

PRINTED IN INDIA

Published by J.L. Kumar for Anmol Publications Pvt. Ltd., New Delhi - 110 002 and Printed at Mehra Offset Press, Delhi.

Dedicated

to

The Sweet Memory of My Brother

Contents

Preface

With the increase in the nature and size of business undertakings and fastly changing business environment, the business complexities have assumed such a shape that the sound decision-making has become a difficult proposition. The role of intuition and subjective considerations in decision-making process has considerably declined and the management needs data and other informations for understanding the business problems in their right perspective and take rational decisions for the achievement of business objectives. Management also needs the understanding and application of the tools and techniques which are used in the presentation, analysis and interpretation of data for pragmetic decisions. Management Accounting has been developed to help solve the managerial problems of business by those who are concerned with various types of decisions of far reaching consequences.

Management Accounting is taught in commerce and management courses in almost all the universities in India with a view to develop necessary skill and knowledge for being used in the development of industry and other spheres of economic activities. The present text book duly meets the requirements of the syllabi of various universities and other academic institutions imparting knowledge in Management Accounting. The book has been written primarily keeping in view the standard of the Indian students persuing M.Com., M.B.A. and Diploma courses in management. It will also be immensely helpful to the students persuing courses such a Chartered Accountancy, Cost and Works Accountancy, company secretaryship, etc. The book will be equally helpful to modern managers in planning, execution and evaluation of business operations of their undertakings. There is sufficient material in the book to encourage the serious readers to think further on the subject as it is a growing subject and it cannot be regarded as finished in its present form.

I take this opportunity to thank all my friends and well-wishers who have always encouraged me to complete the present work at an early date. My wife and children deserve special thanks for the cooperation they extended during the course of the completion of the book. I appreciate the contribution of my daughter—Humra Nisar B.Sc., M.S.W. (Jamia Millia Islamia). Last but not the least, I congratulate Anmol Publications Pvt. Ltd., Darya Ganj, New Delhi for showing keen interest in the publication of the book and bringing out the same so correctly and neatly in a short period of time.

Suggestions to further improve the book are most welcome.

Dr. Nisar Ahmad

1

Nature and Scope of Management Accounting

Introduction

According to need, every business enterprise adopts a particular system of book-keeping and accountancy which is largely influenced by the nature and size of the enterprise. The system of accountancy followed in a small scale enterprise is, generally different from the system used in a large scale firms and joint stock companies. The need of a petty business man is satisfied by the maintenance of incomplete records consisting of a cash book and personal accounts of debtors and creditors for the simple season that the number of mercantile transactions in such an enterprise is so small that there is no need for an elaborate and expensive system of recording transactions. Besides, the account books of petty and small scale business units are not governed by any law and they are also not required to give account of their performance and economic position to outsiders. The need for a complete system based on scientific principles increases with an increase in the nature and size of business in which many internal as well as external parties become interested for various reasons. A partnership firm being run fairly on large scale has to keep complete records of its business transactions for obtaining different informations for running the business more effectively. The maintenance of complete business records is absolutely essential in case of a company form of business organisation in which management and ownership is divorced and the management has to render true account to its shareholders and comply with the provisions of the Act under which the company is set up. The complete record of business transactions in an organisation serves the following purposes:

1. The preparation of a complete set of primary books help the preparation of ledger accounts which enable the proprietor to know the following on a given date:

(a) How much money has been spent on the purchases of raw materials goods, payment to workmen and various direct and indirect expenses from time to time?
(b) How much money has been received from the sale of goods and income from other sources such as interest from investments, discounts, commission, etc.
(c) What is the position of cash in hand and balances with banks?
(d) How much money the customers owe to the proprietor?
(e) How much money is payable to the supplies of raw materials, goods, machinery and for other items of credit purchases?
(f) What is the position of different asset being used in the enterprise?

2. The accurate preparation of Final Accounts, i.e. the Manufacturing/Trading and Profit & Loss Accounts and Balance Sheet is only possible when the records in all respects are complete and nothing has been left to be brought in the primary books and ledger. The Profit & Loss Account enable the entrepreneurs and other interested parties to know the performance of an undertaking during a financial period and the economic state of business affairs on a given date.

3. The proprietors can determine their tax liability only when they have come to know the profit or loss for a financial year.

4. The complete and systematic records is the only record which is reliable and can be produced in support of the claims by the proprietor, whenever necessary.

5. Scientific maintenance of financial records form the bases for further analysis and interpretation of accounting data for decision-making.

Above explanation clearly shows that the proper maintenance of account of financial transactions or financial accounting is of great practical value to a business enterprise. But, it is of limited use in its original form in assisting the management in the discharge of managerial functions. The management is, no doubt, benefitted by financial accounts to the extent it is able to exercise control over properties and assets of the business under their charge. The scope of the functions of management has so widened that the financial accounting can serve only limited purpose.

Limitations of Financial Accounting

Financial accounting was developed to meet the requirements of trade, industry and commerce. The basic need was to know the amount of profit earned or loss suffered for a particular period and also to know the position of assets and liabilities at any point of time. The financial accountants paid very little attention to improve the operating results with the help of the accounting system. No doubt, the financial accounting is a basic necessity and we cannot do away with it but it fails to answer the following questions which are of vital importance for the development of any enterprise.

1. What is the nature and direction of change over a period of time, relating to sales, gross profit, expenses, incomes, net profit, etc. of the undertaking?

2. Whether the undertaking is in a solvent position i.e., whether it is able to meet out fixed business charges and honour its short-term and long-term liabilities?

3. Whether working capital is adequate to maintain operational efficiency?

4. Why the business firm is experiencing shortage of funds despite promising sales and profits as shown by the profit and loss account?

5. What are the causes for the increase or decrease in the per unit cost of product?

6. Is the enterprise running on optimum level of efficiency?

7. How much cash the enterprise will need in a particular month of the year to meet its business obligations?

8. What should be the level of output for a desired profits under the given conditions of production?

9. What will be the profit if a particular level of production is attained?

10. What is the impact of price level changes on the economic position of the enterprise?

11. What should be the reasonable cost per unit of output?

The financial records are based on certain conventions and concepts. Few of these are not relevant in decision-making by management of any undertaking. The financial accountancy deals only with those events which have financial aspects and are capable of being measured in monetary units. Any event, however important it might be is not considered in financial accounting if it does not involve money. This is in tune with the money measurement concept of recording transactions according to which only those transactions which can be interpreted in monetary terms are brought into financial records. For example, the change in the commercial and industrial policy of the government might influence the enterprise considerably but an accountant is not required to estimate the probable effects of such changes and make entries in the books of accounts. Another important concept is 'Cost cocept according to which the actual amount involved in a transaction is brought into books although a different real value may be attached to it. For instance, if an entrepreneur has succeeded in buying a plant for Rs. 50,000 only, he will show the same in financial books at Rs. 50,000 despite the fact that the plant can fetch Rs. 80,000 on immediate disposal in the market. The management of an enterprise cannot loose sight of such important events in the life of an undertaking. It has to adjust its policies in accordance with the dynamism of economic opportunities and change in its organisational structure. For the purpose of exchange of shares on amalgamation and absorption of companies, the management has to calculate the real value of shares which is based on the intrinsic worth of the company. In calculating the intrinsic worth, the assets are not taken at cost or book values but at estimated realizable value which might be quite different from the former.

Financial Accountancy takes into account only those mercantile transactions which have taken place and provide for the known expenditure and incomes. Thus financial records project the past and tells nothing about the future. Owing to this characteristic feature, the financial accounting is also known as historical accounting. Since it is the oldest system based on certain, concepts and conventions, it is also termed as traditional accounting. The Profit and Loss Account of a concern includes the items of costs, incomes and expenditure and shows the profit or loss for the period for which it is prepared. The profit earned and declared rate of dividend can be known from this document but it gives no idea about the future expected earnings and rate of dividend. This is one of the serious limitation of financial accounts from the view point of management who has to forecast for future to run the enterprise on most profitable lines.

Meaning and Definition of Management Accounting

Owing to the limitations of financial accounting as an effective tool of management, we need some system of accountancy which may help the management in the successful discharge of its important duties of planning, implementation of plans, controlling and evaluation of business performance etc. As the name suggests, Management Accounting is any form of accounting which is helpful to management in the discharge of its managerial functions for efficient utilization of business resources to achieve the fundamental objective of optimising profits. In fact, there is no formal method or system of accounting which may be given the name of management accounting. This is the reason that the ICA England and Wales defines Management Accounting as "Any form of accounting which enables a business to be conducted more efficiently can be regarded as management accounting."

Decision-making is a difficult process which requires a lots of accounting and other information for understanding the problem in right perspective and then take decision for future. Intitution and subjective considerations find secondary place in a modern complex business environment for the simple reason that important business decisions by a large-sized industrial enterprise cannot be left to the prejudices of a manager. Under management accounting system, any problem concerning production, financing or marketing is analysed on the basis of relevant facts and figures and a report prepared for the consideration of the management. In the opinion of Brown and Howard, "Management Accounting is concerned with the efficient management of a business through the presentation to management of such information as will facilitate efficient and opportune planning and control." The main source of informations in a running business enterprise is the internal record of financial transactions which consists of Income

Statements, Balance Sheets, Flow of Funds statements and other reports prepared for managerial uses.

Such accounting informations forms the basis of management accounting. R.N. Anthony has defined Management Accounting as, "Management Accounting is concerned with accounting information which are useful to management." It may be clearly understood that mere collection of accounting and other informations is not Management Accounting. It may best be called a step in the direction of management accounting. The process of management accounting involves so many things such as collection of accounting data, analysis and interpretation of data and presentation of the same in an intelligible form for submission to management for managerial action to achieve business objectives. Management Accounting provides a framework to a manager who can use the same using his own knowledge, experience and skill for desired results. It simply suggests an action in a particular direction but without any particular prescription. Accounting to J. Batty, "Management Accounting is the term used to describe the accounting methods, system and techniques which, coupled with special knowledge and ability, assist management in the task of maximising profits or minimising losses."

Similar views have been expressed by the American Accounting Association which apines, "Management Accounting is the application of appropriate techniques and concepts in processing historical and projected economic data of an entity to assist management in establishing plans for reasonable economic objectives in the making of rational decisions with a view towards these objectives." The definition as given by the Association of Certified and Corporate Accountants, U.S.A. seems exhaustive. In the words of ACCA, "Management Accounting is the application of accounting and statistical techniques to the specific purpose of producing and interpreting information designed to assist management in its functions of promoting maximum efficiency and in envisaging, formulating and coordinating their execution." This definition emphasises the following points in its efforts to define Management Accounting:

(a) The basic objective of Management Accounting is to assist the management to make it more efficient.

(b) Management Accounting makes use of various accounting and statistical measures to represent the accounting and other informations in the most suitable form for the convenience of management.

(c) Under Management Accounting the accounting informations are further analysed for better understanding and decision-making.

(d) Management Accounting helps the management in envisaging and formulating realistic plans. Coordination is also effected with the help of this technique.

(e) Management Accounting is not only concerned with plan formulation and decision-making but also deals with measuring the execution of the plans so as to know whether or not the desired efficiency has been achieved.

After having considered various definitions, the Management Accounting may be defined in our own words as under : "Management Accounting is a system of presentation and analysis of historical accounting data and other information to draw logical conclusion for the purpose of efficient formulation, execution and appraisal of business plans." Management Accounting may also be considered "as a discipline which deals with the collection of relevant financial data and other informations for the purpose of analysis and interpretation to arrive at some conclusion which may be used in developing necessary business plans and finally evaluate the effectiveness of those plans and take corrective action, wherever required."

Tools and Techniques of Management Accounting

Management Accounting makes use of various accounting and statistical tools and techniques in the discharge of its basic functions of analysis of data, formulation of business plans and efficient implementation and appraisal of plans. Following are some of the important techniques and accounting and statistical tools which form the subject-matter of Management Accounting:

1. Budgeting

It consists of capital budgeting and operational budgeting. Long-term investment decisions are made with the help of capital budgeting technique which is concerned with the development of capital budgets and evaluation of capital expenditure proposals with a view to choose the one which is more profitable. Operational budgeting deals with the preparation of different types of budgets such as cash budget, raw materials budget, sales budget, etc. These budgets are used as an effective means of communication and control of business activities.

2. Accounting Ratios

Technique of accounting ratios is widely used to evaluate the operational performance and judge the liquidity and solvency of an undertaking.

3. Flow of Funds Statement

These are used to know the sources of funds and application of funds during a financial period. The projected Funds Flow Statements help in the better management of available funds.

4. Standard Costing and Variance Analysis

This technique suggests setting up of standard for different items of expenditure and incomes, comparison of actuals with specified standard, determination of variance and taking corrective action in cases of adverse variances. Thus, the technique aims at controlling costs and achieving maximum efficiency in production.

5. Break-even Analysis

This tool of management accounting is applied in planning costs, volume of sales and profits of an enterprise.

6. Responsibility Accounting

It is a system that recognises various divisions or responsibility centres throughout the organisation and traces costs to the individual managers who are primarily responsible for making decisions about the costs.

7. Management Reporting

An efficient management reporting system is vital for smooth running of various segments of any undertaking. It is used to meet the informational needs of different levels of management.

8. Statistical Analysis

Statistics is an important tool which is frequently used in accounting analysis. The measures of central tendency, dispersion and sampling are mostly used in the analysis of accounting and other informations for drawing dependable conclusions.

Scope of Management Accounting

Any form of accounting which contributes in effective management itself implies the vast scope of management accounting. It seeks to study not only the financial and cost accounting data for planning and control purposes but it derives tools and techniques of other disciplines such as economics, mathematics, statistics, operation research, etc. There is hardly any aspect of business which is not covered by management accounting. A study of different tools and techniques and their application in the solution of business problems falls within the scope of management accounting. Following areas are, generally covered by Management Accounting:

1. Financial Accounting

Financial Accountingfurnishes basicinformation which is useful to management. The knowledge of principles and practice of financial accounting is essential to a management accountant.

2. Cost Accounting

It is one of the specialized areas of accounting which deals with preparation of cost accounting records for cost analysis and cost control. Management Accounting borrows the tools of budgeting, standard costing and marginal costing from cost accounting for cost and profit planning and control purposes.

3. Revaluation Accounting

This is the technique which is concerned with placing real current values on different assets with a view to show current economic position of an enterprise. Since inflation has been persistent during the last 4-5 decades, the technique is also known as Inflation Accounting. It forms an integral part of management accounting system.

4. Tax Accounting

Tax planning, computation of tax as per tax laws, filing return and making payment are the activities which are taken care of by management accounting.

5. Budgeting

Preparation of capital budget and various operating budgets and using the same as a means of coordinating and controlling business activities are the important functions of Management Accounting.

6. Management Reporting

Management Accounting realizes the important of reports relating to different segments of a business entity. Accordingly, the reports covering a particular time period are prepared at regular intervals to keep the management informed of the status of work and performance in the enterprise. Preparation of business reports for the consideration of management is an essential element in any system of management accounting.

7. Auditing

In order to check the accounting errors and frauds and detect the same in time, internal auditing is absolutely important for an undertaking. The effectiveness of the final audit depends to a great extent on the efficiency of internal auditing which is always dear to a management accountant.

8. Statistical Techniques

Management Accounting is intimately related to statistics in the sense that the statistical measures such as averages, dispersion, correlation, regression, probability and sampling are widely used in the analysis and enterpretation of accounting and other informations for decision-making. A study of statistical methods and their application in understanding business problems falls, very much within the scope of management accounting.

9. Law

Management Accounting takes into accounts the provisions of various laws which affect business decisions. The knowledge of the laws like Companies Act, and business laws is essental to a management account.

10. Economic and other Social Sciences

An economic institution operates under somekind of economic environment and social set up. The proper knowledge and understanding of the economic and social environment is highly important to management for being successful in the achievements of business objectives. Management accounting covers the study of these social sciences to the extent they are able to help the management in decision-making.

Distinction Between Management Accounting and Financial Accounting

Management Accounting is entirely new area of accounting which has gained importance, for the last 4 to 5 decades. Financial accounting is a very old system of accounting which was developed to meet the requirements of business for recording, classifying and summarising mercantile transactions. For quite a long period in the history of accounting, the financial accounting was used by managers in the discharge of their managerial functions. Management Accounting has been specially designed to meet the special needs of management. It is closely related to financial accounting as it is heavily reliant for relevant informations on financial accounting. However, a distinction is drawn between the two types of accounting on the basis of the following points:

1.Objective

Basic objective of financial accounting is to keep proper records of all the mercantile transactions which take place in an organisation so that the profit or loss for a particular period may be determined and the economic position on any point of time ascertained. On the other hand, the objective of management accounting is to design the accounting system in such a manner that it is helpful to management in decision-making.

2. *Nature*

Financial Accounting is historical in nature, as it deals with mercantile events which have taken place in an organisation. On the other hand, Management Accounting in futuristic in nature as its main concern is planning and control of business activities.

3. Sources of Data

In financial accounting, the sources of information are the journal, sub-journals and ledger accounts which form the basis for drawing

Income Statement and Balance Sheet. Thus, the source of information is internal. But the management accounting draws informations both from internal as well as external sources. The external sources of information may be the magazines, newspapers and other publications. Sometimes, the intuition of decision-maker exert powerful influence in Management Accounting.

4. Degree of Accuracy

In keeping records of mercantile transactions, our effort is to remain as exact as possible.All mercantile transactiosn are recordd at cost values which help us to achieve objectivity. In certain cases such as inventary valuation and depreciation accounting, the management decides the policy which is consistently followed by the financial accountign office. But, in Management Accounting, we are not conscious of precision which is neither desirable nor possible.the decision-makers are satisfied with the information if they are correct to a large extent. Thus, the effort in Management accounting is to achieve a reasonable degree of accuracy.

5. Legal Requirements

Financial accounting is legally required in case of a company form of organization. The Indian Companies Act prescribes the guidelines according to which the accounts have to be maintained by companies. The management is required to keep proper records of its business activities and publish the same in the form of Profit and Loss Account and Balance Sheet for the information of shareholders and others. On the other hand, the setting up of management accounting system is purely voluntary.

6. Users

Financial accounts in the form of Profit and Loss Account and Balance Sheet, Flow of Funds statement and other schedules of information published by companies are extensively used by various interested parties, especially by the existing and potential shareholders, debenture holders and financial institutions. The management accounting system is exclusively for internal use of the management for policy formulation and control purposes. Management Accounting office collects and preserves important informations but the outsiders have no access to such informations.

7. Adherence to Accounting Principles

Financial Accounting is based on certain well-recognized accounting principles and conventions which are generally followed by all orgnaisations in the same letter and spirit. For example, the cost principle and convention of conservatism are ordinarily followed in all business houses. But, Management Accounting has no such principles to be followed. Since, it is concerned with decision-making for future, it has to adapt itself according to need warranted by the changes in the economic conditions which have great bearing on business policies. For instance, Management Accounting duly recognises the impact of price level changes and suggests suitable changes in Income Statement and Balance Sheet. Such a provision is against the time-honoured cost principle which is very dear to financial accountants.

8. Coverage

Financial accounting takes into account each and every transaction which involve money or money's worth with a view to know the ultimate result of the business activities. It treats the business as one entity and presents the macro view of the same through Balance Sheet. On the other hand, Management Accounting treats every department as a separate entity for the purpose of control and decision-making. The business as a whole may show profits despite loss in certain department. The management is more concerned about the department or product which has shown losses. Thus the management accounting may suggest continuance or closure of a department which has shown loss. In Management Accounting, each activity is considered separately.

9. Treatment of Data

Financial accounting presents and publish accounting information in a systematized manner in accordance with the rules of the law. Management Accounting collects and presents the accounting informations in a form which is more suitable to management. It is also concerned with the analysis and interpretation of data as no scientific decision is possible without it.

From the above the distinction between financial accounting and management accounting becomes quite clear. However, it may be remembered that the two systems are not entirely different. Management Accounting pre-supposes the existence of financial accounting and most of the information needed by management are drawn from financial records.

Sometimes, a distinction is also drawn between Management Accounting and Cost Accounting. We have already examined the nature of Management Accounting. Cost Accounting is a specialised branch of accounting, which deals with maintenance of cost records for various inputs of costs, ascertainment of cost per batch or per unit of output, specification of standard cost for cost-control and cost-reduction, marginal costing as a method of cost, volume and profit planning, etc. Management Accounting is closely related to cost accounting as it uses cost accounting tools for management purposes. There appears to be no difference between Cost Accounting and Management Accounting in so far as the nature of costing tools and their object and methods of application is concerned. The only difference between the two lies in the fact that Cost Accounting exclusively deals with cost data whereas Management Accounting takes into account cost data, financial data and all other necessary information in its process of decision-making. Infact, the scope of Management Accounting in wider than all other forms of accounting.

Functions of Management Accounting

Financial accounting performs the functions such as recording mercantile transactions, preparation of ledger accounts and construction of Final Accounts as per the concepts, conventions and standard practices and Cost Accounting deals with cost data for pricing of products and cost control. Unlike it, Management Accounting is concerned with the use of variety of data and information which is eventually required by management in the discharge of its managerial functions. Basic functions of Management Accounting are :

1. Collection of Data

Management requires dependable data and other information for taking objective decisions on their basis. Management Accounting gather relevant facts and figures from all possible sources. Main source. of such information, however, remains the financial and cost accounting. Qualitative information influencing the problem in question are also ascertained for consideration of management.

2. Modification and Presentation of Data

The data as collected from different sources are not fit for comparison and further analysis. Management Accounting tests the authenticity and modify the data to suit the managerial requirements. Data are presented in columns and rows to facilitate the understanding of management.

3. Analysis of Data

Analysis of data is pre-requisite for interpretation of any problem rightly. Management Accounting tools and techniques are applied in the analysis of data.

4. Planning and Forecasting

Management Accounting is primarily concerned with planning business activities. Collection, modification and analysis of data is done to understand a problem in its right perspective with an ultimate object of deciding about the future and the strategy to be followed to achieve the targetted figures. Management Accounting attempts to forecast for future by using various statistical and economic methods of business forecasting.

5. Control

Necessary control is desired in the implementation of plans to achieve the targets. Management Accounting performs the control function through different tools and techniques. For example, the cost control is effected through standard costing and Budgetary control system. Control also implies proper coordination and communication among the various segments or departments of the business entity. Management accounting reports are helpful in achieving coordination among the departments. They also serve the purpose of communication alongwith other tools of management accounting.

6. Reporting

Reporting is an important function of management accounting under which different types of reports are prepared to meet the requirements of different levels of management. Reports regarding budgeted activities, techniques of implementation of budgets and performance reports are periodically prepared to communicate to the concerned department for necessary action.

7. Decision-making

Ultimate object of management accounting is to assist the management in their task of decision-making relating to pricing, production, marketing, financing, etc. Management Accounting through its processes of analysis and interpretation of data suggests a particular managerial action. Objective and realistic business decisions are possible only by the application of the tools of management accounting.

Importance of Management Accounting

Management Accounting has emerged as an important subject of great practical value in the modern complex business world. Any subject assumes special significance only when it contributes significantly in understanding and solving problems for achieving desired results. Management Accounting is very useful to a large scale business enterprise which is confronted with so many business complexities of far-reaching consequences. The importance of management accounting can be realized in the light of the functions it performs and its contribution in the achievements of business objectives of an enterprise. The question as to why management accounting is important can be answered as under:

1. Efficient Planning

Planning helps in the development of proper strategy to achieve the planned targets. The success of an enterprise is largely influenced by the nature of its plans. Management Accounting is important became it seeks to develop realistic business plans. Capital expenditure planning and working capital estimation are done by capital budgeting and working capital management techniques of management accounting. Functional budgets such as sales budgets, production budgets, cash budgets, raw materials budgets, etc., are prepared to plan business operations. Planning becomes efficient if it is done by properly using the tools and techniques of management accounting. All the available financial and physical resources at the option of the management can be put to maximum use through efficient planning.

2. Efficient Business Operations

Measurement of performance and reporting to management brings efficiency in business operations as the departmental heads become more conscious of achieving planned targets and bring maximum efficiency in their work. Techniques of Accounting Ratios, Budgeting and standard costing and Variance analysis are used in performance appraisal which provides basis for further improvement in business operations.

3. Efficient Control

Management Accounting contributes greatly in developing efficient control mechanism in an organisation. Better planning, efficient method of communication and coordination, performance appraisal, etc., bring about an efficient control system which is very important for the growth and development of an enterprise.

4. Optimum Labour Efficiency

Labour is an active factor of production which can show miracles, if properly dealt with by management. Management Accounting aims at improving labour productivity through its proper education and training and developing in it a sense of high degree of responsibility through variety of its measures such as standard labour costing, linking bonus with productivity, workers participation in management, etc. Fixation of reasonable labour standards develop confidence among labourers and generate a climate condusive for healthy industrial relations.

5. Satisfaction of Customers

The customers are better served if the management accounting tools and techniques are rightly applied in controlling production—its volume, cost and quality. The customers are able to receive better quality of products at reasonable rates with assured supplies. This contributes in maintaining good public relation which is important for enhancing future sales and profitability of the business.

6. Efficiency of Management

Management is said to be efficient if it is able to develop realistic plans, implement plans as per schedule and evaluate the performance which is in true with the planned targets. Management Accounting helps the management to maintain and improve efficiency by the provision of variety of tools and techniques. It replaces to a great extent intuitive decision-making by a scientific methods of analysis, interpretation and decision-making. Management audit which forms a plart of management accounting is helpful in evaluating the effectiveness of business policies which are envisaged by managed.

Limitations of Management Accounting

In order to understand the exact nature and importance of Management Accounting, it is necessary to understand the limitations under which it has to perform its functions. Main limitations may be mentioned as under:

1. Dependence an Historical Data

Data provided by financial accounting and cost accounting from the basis of decision-making. Accuracy of decisions arrived at on the basis of such data depends on the accuracy of data itself. Thus the success of management accounting is governed by the efficiency and accuracy with which the financial and cost records are maintained in an organisation.

2. Lack of Desired Skill

It has been generally observed that the management accountant or any other officer dealing with management accounting tools for decision purpose lack necessary skill and experience due to which a high degree of managerial efficiency cannot be expected. We have yet to develop a cadre of professional management accountants who could better took after the management accounting processes in large-sized public companies.

3. Scope for Subjectivity

Though Management Accounting attempts to replace intuition by objectivity and scientific reasoning yet it is not possible to do away with subjectively as the decision-makers utilise non-quantitative informations which provide a lots of scope for subjectivity in decision-making. This limitation can be overcome if the management uses personal judgment with great care and tries to remain as objective as possible.

4. Management Indifference

Sometimes the indifference of management limits the use of management accounting. Many managers do not like that there exists any formal system of accounting to guide them in decision-making. Resistance and non-cooperation of labour also hinder the application of standard labour costing technique on the pretax of their exploitation. Indifference of management and opposition from within the organisation limit the application of Management Accounting.

5. Costly Affair

Management Accounting is a costly affair as its installation requires heavy investment in physical facilities and trained man-power. It is quite unsuitable for a Small Scale business enterprise. Large-Scale undertaking can only afford to bear to costs and run the management accounting system.

6. Imperfect Tool

Management Accounting is a growing subject. Its tools and techniques are not fool proof. Two different management accountants while treating a similar problem may draw different conclusion from the same set of figures. For example, the technique of accounting ratios provides an indication towards a particular situation but it does not give precise answer to the problem. The profitability ratio (ratio of profit to sales or capital employed) tells nothing if it is not interpreted in the light of some specified profitability ratio. Management Accounting has yet to perfect its tools through intensive research and experience.

7. No Substitute for Management

Management Accounting is a means to an end; the end being the efficient business operations for achievements of business objectives. It cannot replace management as it is simply a tool in the hands of management and the ultimate success in business depends upon the will and dedication of management.

Management Accountant

Large scale business enterprises utilise the services of management accountants who are equipped with extensive knowledge of financial accounting, cost accounting, economics, finance, statistical tools, etc.

A management Accountant occupies a unique position in an organization as he is in staff relationship with other executives and in line relationship with the top management. He is known by different names in different organisations.

Popular names given to a management accountant in India are the controller of Accounts and Finances, Financial Controller, Financial Advisor or Chief Accounts Officer. The term 'Comptroller' or controller is used in the united states of America for the top management accountant executives in a firm. Whatever may be the status or designation of management accountant in an organisation, his main function to facilitate decision-making by top management remains the same. In order to assist management in proper manner, a management accountant discharges the following functions:

1. Control of Operations

Planning and Control of business operations is essential to help achieve the business objectives. Planing is basic function in which a management accountant contributes by doing exercises such as profit planning, capital investment planning, budgeting, forecasting, specification of cost standards, etc. As planning is not fruitful without proper control, he has also to develop necessary procedure for the success of planning.

2. Measurement of Performance

A management accountant is not only involved in planning and developing necessary procedures to make planning a success but he is also required to measure performance and compare the same with operating plans and standards.

3. Reporting

Management Accountant analyse and interpret the operational performance of business and report to all levels of management to keep them informed of the manner in which the work is going on in different segments of the business entity. He also prepares special reports on the basis of data collected both from within and outside the organisation to meet the special requirements of the management.

4. Consultations

In order to be successful, he has to consult all segments of management responsible for policy or action on issues such as effectiveness of policies, organisation structure, procedures. etc.

5. Appraisal of External Forces

External forces like government economic policies pressures of social institutions in industry, international political and economic events, etc. exert a great influence on the functioning of an industrial enterprise. A management accountant is required to continuously appraise economic and social forces and government influences and interpret their effect on business.

6. Tax Administration

Administration of tax policies and procedure is one of the important functions of a management accountant.

7. Assets Protection

Management accountant is required to assure fiscal protection for the assets of the business through adequate internal control and proper insurance coverage.

8. Preparation of Reports

An undertaking has to submit reports to government, financial institutions and share-holders. Management accountant supervises and coordinates the preparations of reports for timely submission to concerned quarter.

From the above, it may be realized that the functions of management accountant touch almost all aspects of a business where some kind of managerial action is needed. It may, however, be noted that a management accountant may be authorised to deliberate on any issue concerning business management.

QUESTIONS

1. Why is management accounting needed in a large scale business enterprise? Explain.

2. Discuss the nature and scope of Management Accounting.
3. Explain, briefly, various tools and techniques of management accounting.
4. Explain the role of management accounting in a modern complex business enterprise.
5. What are the limitations of Management Accounting? How should a management accountant work in order to be successful in the discharge of his functions?
6. How does Management Accounting contribute in the solution of business problems? Explain clearly.
7. Write an explanatory note an "Management Accounting as an aid to management."

2

Analysis and Interpretation of Financial Statements

Meaning of Financial Statements

Every business organisation keeping the complete records of its mercantile transactions on double entry book-keeping principles prepares two important statements namely, Profit and Loss Account (Income Statement and Balance Sheet (Position Statement) at the end of every financial year which is generally a period of one calendar year. These statements are known as financial statements or Annual Accounts which are based on the balances of ledger accounts. A financial statement may be defined as a statement which provides financial informations relating to an organisation's economic activities in a condensed and orderly form for the guidance of the interested parties. The Profit and Loss Account or Income statement contains the items of revenues and expenditure and the net result in the form of profit or loss for a given period of time. On the other hand, the Balance Sheet or Position Statement provides information relating to assets, liabilities and owner's equity on a given date. Sometimes, certain schedules explaining critical items are attached to the financial statements. For example, an insurance company in India is required to append "Classified Summary of Assets' in a prescribed form which is considered as a part of Balance Sheet. In the recent years, some progressive companies have started preparing statement of changes in financial position and publish the same alongwith their annual accounts with a view of providing informations regarding changes in the position of Fund which is not clear from the traditional Balance Sheet. Thus, by financial statements, we mean the Income Statement and Balance Sheet and any other schedule or statements attached thereto to explain the informations contained in these statements.

Purpose of Construction

The financial statements — Income statement and Balance Sheet are constructed primarily to know the operating results and state of economic affairs of any concern. In case of sole proprietory concerns and partnership organisations, the construction and publication of financial statements is not compulsory as is the case with joint stock companies which are compulsorily required under law to maintain the records of their transactions and publish the statements for the information of the investors, creditors and others. Generally, the sole traders and partnership firms also keep proper records and prepare the Profit and Loss Account and Balance Sheet because these documents serve much purpose. The construction of the financial statements is advantageous to the business houses in the following manner:

1. The Profit and Loss Account shows the profit or loss position for a given period of time. The management can manage the income only when it becomes known to them through the preparation of the Income Statement.
2. The operating expenses are brought into the Income Statement to determine the net profit. The management can know the position of administration expenses and take steps to control them if they are excessive.
3. The figures of sales, gross profits and net profit, if compared for the last few years, show the direction of change, the knowledge of which is very important for the management. Such information is readily available from the Income Statement.
4. The management can exercise better control over properties, assets and liabilities by the preparation of Balance Sheet which provides an aggregate view of assets, liabilities and owners' equity.
5. The statement of changes in financial position which is published by some companies is a very useful statement for managerial decision-making. It reveals those changes which cannot be understood from the Balance Sheet.
6. Financial statements can be produced in courts in support of owners claims for income tax, insurance claims, etc.
7. The lending institutions ask for the annual accounts when an

entrepreneur approaches them for financial accommodation. Thus, the annual accounts facilitate the task of borrowings by an undertaking.

8. An existing company, when raising additional capital by issuing its unissued capital, has to publish the information relating to the position of its capital, reserves, profits, dividends, etc. for the last few years. The financial statements provide such informations to the management without any inconvenience.

Parties Interested in Financial Statements

Apart from the management, there are many other parties who are interested in the financial statements of public companies. Following parties, directly or indirectly, become interested in the annual published financial statements of companies:

1. Shareholders

Shareholders are the real owners of joint-stock companies. Since the management and ownership is divorced in a company form of organisation, the shareholders have no access to the internal records of their companies and they have to depend upon the published statements for their decision-making. The shareholders are interested in the study of the profit earning capacity and solvency of the company in which they have made investments. The Profit and Loss account and Balance Sheet read alongwith the director's Report and Chairman's speech throw sufficient light on the issues, such as profitability and solvency and future prospects of an undertaking. The financial statements provide an objective basis for the potential shareholders to invest or not in a particular company.

The financial statements are of great help to a company which intends to acquire controlling interest in any other company. The company desirous of purchasing majority of shares of another company is not as much interested in the declared rate of dividend, as in the future earning capacity of the latter. A critical study of the financial statements for the last few years guide the holding companies in their decision for purchase of controlling interest in subsidiary companies.

2. Debenture-Holders

The debenture-holders are the long-term creditors who are interested in the safety of their funds and the regularity of the payment of interest by the company. Generally, debentures enjoy floating or fixed charge on the assets of the company and the company can provide safety to debentureholders only if it is able to maintain its fixed assets. The maintenance of assets and payment of fixed charge in the form of interest depends upon the profit-earning capacity of the company. Any organisation can enjoy long and continued life if it grows steadily. An intelligent study of the financial statements can guide the debenture-holders about the existing financial condition and future prospects of a company.

3. Creditors

The creditors of a company are the persons who have supplied materials on credit or rendered some service to the company. They are interested that the debtor company remains solvent atleast in the short-period, so that their claims are paid in time. Short-term solvency of a company can be judged with the help of the data contained in the Balance Sheet.

4. Trade Unions

Trade Unions effort is to raise the wages of their fellow workmen. They have to keep an eye on the profits of the company in their efforts of wage-maximisation. Where there is profit-sharing scheme, the workers are entitled to share in the profits of the company. The trade unions have to see the profit position which becomes clear from the Income Statement of the company. If the bonus is linked with productivity or profits, the Income Statement in the hands of the trade unions is a very useful document to determine the share of bonus accruing to the workers.

5. Parliamentarians

Parliamentarians and legislators are specifically interested in the financial statements of public undertakings. They study the published and other accounts of public enterprises with a view to know the operational efficiency and solvency of such enterprises. The financial statements provide them necessary informations for raising issues on the working of public enterprises in the parliament and state legislatures.

6. Tax Authorities

Tax authorities are interested in the Income Statement of the enterprises which come within the purview of income tax. They ask the tax-paying enterprises to submit the detailed statement of their income for the financial year. It is the Income Statement which provides the basis for assessing the taxable income by tax authorities.

7. Research Scholars

Research scholars and academicians also make use of financial statements of companies to understand their growth and development. The data contained in the annual published accounts are a good source of secondary data which are extensively used in research studies.

8. Lending Institutions

Bankers and specialised financial institution are always interested in the financial statements of those companies which approach them for financial accommodation. On the basis of financial statements for the last few years, the lending institutions decided about the earning capacity and large-term solvency of the borrowing units.

9. Government and Controlling Agencies

In order to know how far an industrial enterprise is discharging its social responsibility, the state and central government departments dealing with the industry also study the financial statements of concerning companies. Controlling Agency like SEBI is obviously interested in the financial statements of companies for exercising better control over them to serve and protect the interests of investors. Similarly, stock exchanges are specifically interested in the listed companies financial statements.

Objective of Analysis

The analysis of financial statements means a critical examination of statements for better understanding and drawing fruitful conclusions. It is only an analytical study of statements which can help draw dependable conclusions. Therefore, analysis becomes a pre-requisite for interpretation of financial data in the form of annual accounts and statements. The technique of analysis depends upon the objective of analysis. Different persons have different objectives. For example, the object of short-term creditors is primarily to know.about the short-term solvency and the long-term creditors, such as debenture holders and financial institutions aim at knowing the long-term solvency of the enterprises to which they have lent money. There are investors who are interested in the declared rate of dividend; other investors, such as holding companies are interested in the earning capacity and growth and development of the enterprise. Thus, different persons will analyse the financial statements from different objects in mind.

Accuracy of Financial Statements

The analyst should first ensure that the financial statements which form the basis of his crucial decisions are accurate, adequate and fit for the purpose of analysis. Generally, the audited Profit and Loss Account and Balance Sheet are considered dependable statements. If the analyst is compelled to use the un-audited accounting statements, he should first ascertain their truth. It is very difficult to verify the correctness of the Income Statement and Position Statement without the basic information in the form of ledger accounts and other records. However, a comparative study of the important items such as depreciation, reserve for bad and doubtful debts, goodwill, un-written off capital expenditure, statutory reserves, etc. will reveal the trend and the causes for any unusual change in the trend may be enquired into by the financial analyst. Sometimes, the companies change the method of charging depreciation and valuation of inventory items. In such a case the data of different years loose their comparability. Similarly, the revaluation of assets remarkably change the net worth of the enterprise. The financial analyst should try to find out all such and other similar unusual changes which are brought out by managerial action. The joint stock companies are required to prepare their published accounts on the prescribed proforma and in accordance with the guidelines provided in the Acts. The financial analyst should see that the final accounts have been drawn up according to law and nothing has been left or concealed. Once the analyst is satisfied about the accuracy of published final accounts and statements, he can safely proceed to further analyse them for the purpose of drawing conclusions. However, he should always keep in mind the limitations of financial statements.

Limitations of Financial Statements

The main financial statements are Profit and Loss Account and Balance Sheet. They suffer from certain limitations such as,

1. Concept of Accounting period is not technically correct. The Profit and Loss Account is prepared for an accounting year which is generally a period of one year. This gives rise to the problem of cost and income allocation. In fact, real profit or loss can be calculated only at the end when the unit is closed down. The annual accounts can best be considered as interim reports.

2. The profit or loss figure as shown by a Profit and Loss Account is not necessarily a correct figure which is influenced by the personal judgement of the management regarding depreciation, inventory valuation and provisions for various reserves and contingencies. The management can manipulate profit/loss figure to serve their interests. The financial analyst should see that the income has been rightly computed by following consistent accounting policies.

3. The financial statements do not show qualitative changes which undoubtedly affect greatly the performance of an undertaking. The financial accounts do not account for events such as change in management, labour strikes, changes in government policies affecting enterprise, etc. The financial analyst should try to assess the impact of qualitative changes on the profitability of the concerning enterprise.

4. Cyclical fluctuations affect the working results of an undertaking. For example, the money incomes of an enterprise may go up without any increase in the volume of its business due to inflationary pressure. Under such a situation an increase in money income is not meaningful and the enterprise cannot be said to have grown at all. But the financial analyst may draw a different conclusion if he does not take into account the impact of inflation on money incomes which is not clear from the traditional final accounts. The consideration of physical quantities of production and sales will be useful for drawing logical conclusions under conditions of inflation.

5. Balance Sheet is a static document, which means, a document showing the economic position of an enterprise on a given date. The Balance Sheet is prepared on the last day of a financial year, i.e., on 31st

December, 31, March or 30th June. Generally, the Balance Sheet is prepared and published very late after the close of the accounting year. The Balance Sheet looses much of its significance and practical utility due to a long time-gap between the close of an accounting year year and the actual publication of the same. A financial analyst should always bear this limitation in mind.

6. Assets shown in the Balance Sheet might not be shown at their fair or current values. Goodwill is an item which is closely related to profits. If a company suffers loss continuously for the last few years, it clearly means that it no more enjoys the goodwill as shown in the books of the company. But the companies continue to show goodwill at the usual figure despite continuous losses. Similarly, companies in general do not account for the impact of inflation on their fixed assets and liabilities and show them at cost values. The financial analyst should take precaution and give due recognition to the assets valuation as done by a company.

7. Financial statements are historical in nature. They tell nothing about future. Since the financial analyst is concerned with analysis and interpretation for formulation of future business policies, he should re-structure the statements in such a manner, that they become more intelligible and useful for projections for future.

The management is, generally, not in a position to understand readily the financial statements in their traditional form. But, when the statements are presented to management in an analytical form with brief explanations on critical items, it becomes easier to understand them to take decision without inconvenience and loss of time.

Method of Construction

Financial statements are the summaries of the mercantile transactions for a specified period of time. They are based on the balances of ledger which contains various types of accounts according to the nature of enterprise. The mercantile transactions are first recorded in the primary book, i.e. journal which is divided into sub-journals or subsidiary books, such as Cash Book,Purchases Book, Sales Book, Bills Book, Purchases Returns Book, Sales Return Book, Journal Proper, etc. Entries in the journal are made according to the set rules of book-keeping and accounts. The entries as recorded in the sub-journals or subsidiary books are transferred to Ledger which shows the classified summary of all the accounts. Ledger is a principal book of accounts which contains different types of accounts relating to purchases, sales, incomes, expenditure, personal accounts of Debtors and Creditors, accounts of properties and assets, etc. At the end of the financial year or at the time when the construction of final accounts is desired, a trial balance is prepared with a view to judge the arithmetical accuracy of account books and facilitate the task of preparation of Final Accounts. A trial Balance is a statement of debit and credit balances of different types of accounts which are in operation on a particular date. The Final Accounts show the ledger balances or balances as collected in the form of a Trial Balance in an orderly and systematic from in accordance with the requirements of the law under which the enterprice is set up. Thus the accounting cycle which started from journalising the mercantile transactions ends with the preparations of Final Accounts, which represent the recorded facts. The recorded facts form the basic raw materials for the construction of Final Accounts.

Final Accounts of a concern depends not only on the recorded facts which provide objectivity but also on the personal judgements of management and accounting conventions which introduce subjectivity in accounting. For a student of management accounting, it is important to understand the concepts, principles and conventions underlying the accounting informations which are presented in the form of Income statement and Balance sheet.

Accounting Principles

Accounting is an organisation is done by following certain principles which are the result of long experiences of those who have been associated with accounting theory and practice. Accounting principles provide general guidelines for measurement and recording mercantile transactions. They also guide in the preparations of Final Accounts to ensure objectivity and comparability of accounting data. There are certain accounting principles which are generally accepted by all accountants and professional bodies and institutes. Generally accepted principles of book-keeping and accountancy may be studied under two categories viz. (a) Accounting Concepts and (b) Accounting Conventions.

Accounting Concepts

Accounting concepts means the ideas, assumptions or conditions upon which the accounting system is based. A brief explanation of different accounting concepts is provided hereunder:

1. Separate entiry concept

According to this concept, the entity of business is different from that of its owners for the purpose of maintaining records of business activities. It means the private incomes, expenditures, properties and assets of proprietors are kept separate and not mixed up with business transactions. Accordingly, the Income statements and Balance sheets of an undertaking will show exclusively the trading results of that undertaking. The separate entity concept may be expended to different segments of a concern for knowing the operating results of each segment separately. A company within the same group always enjoys separate legal entity and its success or failure has nothing to do with the progress and performance of other group companies.

2. Money measurement concept

This concept treats money as a unit of measurement of all the transactions which take place in an organisation. All those transactions which can be measured in terms of money or money's worth are brought into books of accounts and other events which cannot be interpreted directly in monetary units are excluded from the purview of accounting. This concept assumes that the value of money as a measuring rod remains stable. A management accountant,while analysing the financial statements should bear in mind the inplications of the concept as there are so many events like change in managements, strikes and lock-outs, change in government fiscal and monetary policies, international economic and political events, etc., which considerably influence the operational performance of any organisation. The assumption of stable money value is also not realistic under the changing business scenario all around.

3. Cost concept

Cost concept suggests that a transaction should be recorded

with the actual cost involved though an entirely different value may be placed on it. If, for example, an asset is acquired for Rs.50,000 or exchanged with any other asset which is valued at Rs.50,000, then it should be shown in account books at Rs. 50,000, despite the fact that its real value to the organisation is more than this value. This concept provide objectivity in accounting by preventing the arbitrary values for recording purposes. However, there are implications of recording transactions at cost values, and a management accountant should clearly understand them as his job is to analyse and interpret financial statements for decision-making. He should realize that the cost values of assets rarely correspond with their market or current values and as such the Balance Sheet fails to reflect the current economic position of an enterprice which has not changed the post-acquisition costs of assets. Similarly, cost values are not relevant when acquisitions and mergers takes place. Estimated realizable values forms the basis to calculate the purchase considerations in cases of amalgamation and absorption of companies.

4. Going-concern concept

It is based on the assumption that the business concern will continue to functions in the foreseeable future or there is no chance of its being liquidated in the near future. Such an assumption help the management to design long-term accounting policies regarding income generations and cost expiration. The principle of continuity implies the utilization of resources whereas liquidation is concerned with sale of assets or disposition of resources. According to going-concern concept, the assets in a Balance Sheet are shown at cost less depreciation as against realisable values' in case of a "quit concern." A financial analyst should check up whether or not the final accounts have been drawn up following the going-concern concept.

5. Dual aspect concept

Every business transaction has dual or two aspects and both the aspects should be taken into account if book-keeping has to be done an scientific basis. The dual aspects are the receiving aspects (debit) and giving aspect (credit) and a scientific system of book-keeping takes into account both the aspects in recording the mercantile transactions. In raising loans by issue by debenture, the two aspects involved are the cash receipt and the debentureholders who have subscribed the debentures of the company. Entry for this transaction will be made on the receipt side of Cash Book and also an the credit side of the debenture Account in the ledger. Cash is an asset and debenture a liability carrying same value. Thus assets of any concern will be equal to its liabilities. Double Entry system of book-keeping is a scientific system based an dual-aspect concept of accounting. Large scale business firms keep their accounts an Double Entry principle of book-keeping, which enable than to prepare Final Accounts. Small business firms and petty shop-keepers may instead maintain records of their transactions on single entry basis (incomplete or unscientific system) when a Cash Book and personal accounts of debtors and creditors are desired to be kept. Financial analysts are concerned with the analyses of accounts of large firms which maintain records on the principles of double entry which rightly recognises the dual-aspect concept of accounting.

6. Accounting period concept

This concept presumes that the performance of any undertaking can be measured at short intervals during its long life. The period for which income measurement is done and Balance Sheet prepared is termed as an accounting period' which is usually a period of twelve months, the management accountant should note the length of Accounting period while making comparison of financial statements for two or more years. If the accounting period is not the same in all the cases, he should express the performance on an uniform annualised basis. The accounting period for internal reporting may be even shorter, say a period of one month or three month may be choosen for the preparations of interim reports. In case of Joint ventures which are the partnerships for a short period, the accounting period terminates with the completion of joint venture business.

7. Matching principle

Correct measurement of profit for an Accounting period is possible only if the Matching principle is rightly applied in the measurement of profit. According to this principle, expenses incurred in an accounting year should be matched with the revenues recognised in that year. For the purpose of accounting, revenue from sales is considered as having been realized when the sales transaction has been finalised between the seller and buyer and necessary entry made in the account books. All expenses relating to such a sale should be brought in the income statement according to the requirements of matching principle. It would be incorrect if all sales are shown as revenue but the commission is shown only on the collected sales. Matching principle makes a clear distinction between expired costs and unexpired costs. Expired cost is the cost which is consumed to generate revenue in the same accounting year whereas unexpired costs belong to the future years and as such all expired costs are debited to Income Statement and unexpired costs are excluded any carried forward. Similarly, cost of a fixed asset expired as a result of wear and tear (depreciation) is shown as expense and asset at cost less depreciation is shown in the Balance Sheet

Application of the matching principle is not always an easy jobs. Some costs like depreciation cannot be precisely measured; it can be estimated in the light of the depreciation policy being adopted in the organisations. Financial analyst,while ascertaining the accuracy of financial statements, should see that the matching principle has been properly followed.

Accounting Conventions

Accounting conventions means the traditions or customs which are in use in the construction of Final Accounts. The conventions are so powerful that they are generally accepted and followed by all financial accountants. Following are most important accounting conventions:-

1. Material Disclosure

This convention implies that all material facts should be shown in the Final Accounts. A material fact is one which is likely to effect the decision of a financial analyst. Method of valuation of inventory and investments, provision for bad debts and expected losses, unrealised profits due to revaluation of assets, loss of foreign markets due to international competition or tariff restrictions, change in accounting policies, etc., are some of the examples of material informations which are vital for decision-makers. The informations may be shown in the body of financial statements or by way of notes attached thereto.

2. Consistency

The convention of consistency suggests that the accounting practices and methods should be consistently followed or they should not be allowed to change from one year to another in the interest of comparability of accounting informations. For example, method of changing depreciation should remain the same in different accounting years. It may, however, be noted that consistency does not mean rigidity, and the management is bound to follow a particular practice or method for an indefinite period. A desired change may be incorporated but it should be properly indicated to enable the users to understand the financial statements in the right perspective.

3. Conservatism

According to this convention, an accountant is required to provide for all expected losses and ignore the expected gains till they are actually realised in the measurement of income for a particular accounting period. Provision for bad and doubtful debts and valuation of inventory at cost price or market price, whichever is less are the practices which are in tune with the convention of conservatism. Conservative approach in accounting may result in the under estimation of profits and creation of secret reserves in the Balance Sheet, which are against the principle of full disclosure. The idea of conservative accounting practice is to play a safe game under conditions of risks and uncertainties. However, the convention should be followed cautiouly as it may mislead the users of accounts by presenting a picture which does not depict the true and fair view of operating results and economic position of the enterprise. The financial analyst should check whether the assets have been under-valued and liabilities over-stated in the Balance Sheet for a realistic analysis and interpretation of the same.

Recording Transactions

Double entry system of book-keeping and accountancy is the only system which provides a scientific basis for recording mercantile transactions to understand the operating results and economic state of affairs of any enterprice. According to this system, the dual aspect of every transaction is recognised and entries are accordingly made in relevant accounts. For the purpose of recording, the transactions have been classified into three broad categories of accounts namely: (1) Real Account, (2) Personal Accounts, (3) Nominal Accounts, and rules for making entries in account books specified.

1. Real Accounts

Real accounts are those accounts which are concerned with things such as goods, cash, machinery building, furniture etc.

2. *Personal Accounts*

There are the accounts which are related with the names of persons. A person may be a natural person like—Ram, Raheem, Anthony or an artificial person such as State Bank of India, Life Insurance Corporation, Reliance Industries Limited, which are the creatures of law, sometimes an account represents aperson and hence called a representative personal account. For example, capital Account is a representative personel account which represents a body of shareholders who have contributed towards the equity capital of the company.

3. Nominal Accounts

Nominal Accounts deals with the items of revenue income, expenditure, profits and losses, Wages A/c, Rent A/c, Advertising Expenditure A/c, Commission A/c, Dividend A/c, Interest A/c, etc., are the examples of nominal accounts.

Recording of Transactions

There are two set of books which are maintained to keep record of all the transactions which take place in an organisation. First set consists of the primary books of accounts. Journal is the primary book which is further sub-divided into many sub-journals or subsidiary books. Following sub-journals or subdsidiary books are generally kept in a large scale business enterprise:

1. Cash Book
2. Petty Cash Book
3. Purchases Book

4. Purchases Return Book
5. Sales Book
6. Sales Return Book
7. Bills Receivable Book
8. Bills Payable Book
9. Journal Proper.

Entry made in any of the above account books also finds corresponding place in the Ledger which forms another set of books. Ledger contains detailed summary of transactions relating to a particular accounts. For example, all the transaction concerning Ram may be seen under Ram's Account in the ledger.

Double Entry Book-Keeping

The entries in the primary books i.e. journal are made according to the set rules of journalising transactions. Every transactions involves two accounts and entries are to be made in both the accounts. For every debit, there is a corresponding credit entry. The general rule to make an entry is,

Debit what comes in credit what goes out	For Real Accounts
Debit the Receiver Credit the Giver	For Personal Accounts
Debit Expenses & Losses Credit Incomes & Gaines	For Normal Account

The Book-keeper has to identify the two accounts involved in a transactions. It is possible that a transaction may involve both the real accounts, one real account and another personal account, one nominal account and other personal account, one real and other nominal account, etc.

Illustration—1

Enter the following transactions in the books of a proprietor:

1995		*Rs.*
Jan. 1.	Introduced capital	80,000
" 5.	Purchased goods for cash	25,000
" 10.	Purchased furniture	5000
" 12.	Sold goods for cash	5000
" 13.	Cash sales	3000
" 15.	Credit Sales to Ram	8000
" 20.	Received cash from Ram	5000
" 22.	Deposited cash in Central Bank	20,000
" 25.	Purchased good an credit from Singh & Sons	15,000
" 28.	Paid to Singh & Sons	10,000
" 31.	Paid Rent of office building	1,000
" 31.	Bank Interest received	500
" 31.	Wages paid	3,500

Journal

Date	*Particulars*	*Ledger Folio*	*Debit (Rs)*	*Credit (Rs)*	*Kind of Account*
1	*2*	*3*	*4*	*5*	*6*
1994					
Jan 1	Cash Account Dr		80,000		Real A/c
	To Capital A/c			80,000	Personal A/c
" 5	Goods(Purchases) A/c Dr		25,000		Real A/c
"	To Cash A/c			25,000	Real A/c
" 10	Furniture A/c Dr.		5,000		Real A/c
	To Cash			5,000	Real A/c
" 12	Cash A/c Dr		5,000		Real A/c
	To goods (sales)			5,000	Real A/c
" 13	Cash A/c Dr		3,000		Real A/c
	To goods(sales)			3,000	Real A/c
" 15	Ram's Account Dr		8,000		Personal A/c
	To goods(sale)			2,000	Real A/c
" 20	Cash A/c Dr.		5,000		Real A/c
	To Ram			5,000	Personal A/c

1	2	3	4	5	6
" 22	Central Bank A/c Dr.		20,000		Personal A/c
	To cash			20,000	Real A/c
" 25	Goods(Purchases) A/c Dr		15,000		Real A/c
	To Singh & Sons			15,000	Personal A/c
" 28	Singh & Sons A/c Dr		10,000		Personal A/c
	To cash			10,000	Real A/c
" 31	Rent Account Dr		1,000		Nominal A/c
	To cash			1,000	Real A/c
" 31	Cash Account Dr		500		Real A/c
	To Interest			500	Nominal A/c
" 31	Wages A/c Dr		3,500		Nominal A/c
	To cash			3,500	Real A/c

Ledger

Individual accounts of persons, property & assets, expenses, incomes, etc. are opened in another book called ledger. An Account depicts the summary of transactions which have taken place at different time periods and the net effect of those related transactions for a given period of time. Ledger is a principal book which helps in the preparations of annual accounts to know the net result of the business and the position of assets and liabilities. There are two sides of an accounts namely Debit side and Credit side. Debit side is on the left hand side and credit is on the right-hand side.

Illustration—2

Prepare ledger accounts on the basis of the journal entries of the previous illustrations:

CAPITAL ACCOUNT

(Dr.) (Cr.)

Date	*Particulars*	*J.F*	*Amount*	*Date*	*Particulars*	*J.F*	*Amount*
1994 Jan. 31	To balance c/d		80,000	1994 Jan. 14	By cash		80,000
			80,000				80,000

CASH ACCOUNT

1994			1994		
Jan. 1	To Capital	80,000	Jan. 5	By Goods	25,000
Jan. 12	,, goods	5,000	Jan.10	" Furniture	5,000
Jan. 13	,, goods	3,000	Jan. 20	" Ram	5,000
Jan.31	,, interest	500	Jan. 22	" Central Bank	20,000
			Jan. 28	" Singh & Sons	10,000
			Jan. 31	" Wages	3,500
			Jan. 31	" Rent	1,000
			Jan. 31	" Balance c/d	24,000
		88,500			88,500

GOODS (PURCHASES) ACCOUNT

1994			1994		
Jan. 5	To Cash	25,000	Jan. 31	By Balance c/d	45,000
Jan. 25	" Singh & Co	20,000			
		45,000			45,000

GOOD (SALES) ACCOUNT

1994			1994		
Jan. 31	To Balance c/d	16,000	Jan. 12	By Cash	5,000
			Jan. 13	By Cash	3,000
			Jan. 15	By Ram's A/c	8,000
		16,000			16,000

FURNITURE ACCOUNT

1994			1994		
Jan. 10	To cash	5,000	Jan. 31	By Balance c/d	5,000
		5,000			5,000

RAM'S ACCOUNT

1994			1994		
Jan 15	To goods (sales)	8,000	Jan. 20	By Cash	5,000
				" Balance c/d	3,000
		8,000			8,000

CENTRAL BANK ACCOUNT

1994			1994		
Jan. 22	To Cash	20,000	Jan31	By balance d/d	20,000
		20,000			20,000

SINGH & SONS ACCOUNT

1994			1994		
Jan. 28	To Cash	10,000	Jan. 25	By goods (purchases)	15,000
Jan. 31	To Balance c/d	5,000			
		15,000			15,000

RENT ACCOUNT

1994			1994		
Jan. 31	To Cash	1,000	Jan. 31	By Balance	1,000
		1,000			1,000

INTEREST ACCOUNT

1994			1994		
Jan. 31	By Balance	500	Jan.31	By Cash	500
		500			500

WAGES ACCOUNT

1994			1994		
Jan. 31	To Cash	3,500	Jan. 31	By Balance	3,500
		3,500			3,500

Trial Balance

A Trial Balance is a schedule of debit and credit balances of ledger accounts. It is prepared to check the arithmetica accuracy of accounts and facilitate the task of preparation of Final Accounts. The two sides of a Trial Balance must tally if there is no accounting error in the books. However, there are some errors which do not affect the agreement of a trial balance. The errors which are not disclosed by a Trial Balance are as under:-

1. Errors of Principle

These are the errors which are caused due to the violation or wrong application of the rules of making entries in the primary books of accounts. For example, if an expenditure of capital nature is treated as revenue expenditure and entry made accordingly, then it will not make any difference and the two sides of Trial Balance would agree.

2. Errors of Omission

If a transaction has been left to the entered in the primary books, then also it will not affect the agreement of the Trial Balance

3. Errors of Commission

If a wrong amount is entered in the journal, it would not have any effect in the Trial Balance. Similarly, if a wrong account is debited or credited, than also the Trial Balance would not disagree.

4. Compensatory Errors

A compensatory error is one which neutralises the wrong effect of any other error, and thus does not affect the agreement of a Trial Balance. For example, if X's account is debited by Rs 150 instead of Rs 50 and simultaneously another account say Y's account is posted on credit side by Rs.50 instead of entering with the same amount on the debit side of Y's Account. These are the accounting errors but their affect on Trial Balance will be nil.

Preparation of Trial Balance

Trial Balance is prepared with the balances of accounts as shown in the ledger. The balance of an account is said to be a debit balance if the debit side is bigger than the credit side. The balance is the credit balance if the credit side is bigger than the debit side. Debit balances of individual accounts are brought in the Debit column of the Trial Balance. Similarly, the credit balances are shown in the credit column. The agreement of the total of Debit balances and credit balances of accounts appearing in a Trial Balance is generally a proof of the arithmetical accuracy of books.

Illustration—3

Using the ledger balances from the illustration No 2 prepare the Trial Balance as on 31st January 1994.

TRIAL BALANCE AS AT 31ST JAN. 1994

	Debit Balance	*Credit Balance*
Capital A/c	—	80000
Cash A/c	24000	—
Goods (Purchases)A/c	45000	—
Goods (Sales)A/c	—	16000
Furniture A/c	5000	—
Central Bank A/c	20,000	—
Ram's A/c	3000	—
Singh & Son's A/c	—	5000
Rent A/c	1,000	—
Interest A/c	—	500
Wages A/c	3500	—
Total	1,01,500	1,01,500

Unsold stock Rs. 35000
Stationary bill unpaid Rs.300

Preparation of Final Accounts

Final Accounts—Profit & Loss Account and Balance Sheet may be prepared any time the management desires to know the operating results and economic position of the enterprise. The Profit & Loss Account shows the profit earned or loss suffered for a given period of time but the Balance Sheet depicts the economic portion at a point of time.

Trading or Manufacturing Account may be separated to know the gross profit. Other part of the P.& L. A/c will show the net results in the form of profit or loss. The companies also prepare a separate account to show the appropriation of profits. The Profit & Loss Account may be prepared either in an account form or in horizontal form. If the Account is prepared in an account form, then all the items of costs, expenses and losses are shown on the left-hand side or debit side and all items of income and gains are represented on the right hand or credit side.

Strictly speaking, the Balance Sheet is not an account but it is a statement of assets and liabilities. It has two sides right hand side to show assets and left-hand side to represent liabilities. The two sides of a Balance Sheet are always equal. The assets and liabilities in a Balance are shown either according to fixity or liquidity of assets and liabilities. The companies are required to prepare their Balance Sheets in accordance with the prescribed performa under the Act.

Illustration—4

Prepare the Profit & Loss Account to measure the profit for one month and the Balance to show economic position as at 31st Jan. 1994 from the Trial Balance of illustration no.3.

Trading And Profit & Loss Account
For The Month Ending at 31st Jan.1994

Expenditure	*Rs.*	*Income*	*Rs.*
To Opening Balance	nil	By goods (sales)	16000
" Good (Purchase)	45000	" unsold stock	35000

" Wages	3500		
" Gross Profit c/d	2500		
	51000		51000
To Rent	1000	By Gross Profit b/d	2500
" Stationary bill payable	300	" Interest	500
" Net Profit carried to Balance Sheet	1,700		
	3000		3000

BALANCE SHEET AS AT 31ST JAN, 1994

Liabilities	*Amount*	*Assets*	*Amount*
Capital A/c	80,000	Furniture	5,000
Profit & Loss (cr.)	1,700	Unsold stock	35,000
Singh & Sons A/c (creditors)	5,000	Ram (debtor)	3,000
		Central Bank (cash with Bank)	20,000
Stationary bill (outstanding Exp.)	300	Cash in hand	24,000
	87,000		87,000

The above case to explain the accounting cycle is a simple one as it has taken into account few transactions for a month only. In actual practice, more elaborate final accounts are prepared. It will be useful to consider items of assets and liabilities which usually appear in the Balance Sheet of a large scale business enterprice organised in the form of a public limited company.

Liabilities		*Assets*	
- Share capital		Land & Buildings	—
Equity share capital	—	Plant & Machinery	—
Preference share capital	—	Furniture and Fixtures	—
- Share premium A/c	—	Patent & trade marks	—
- General reserve	—	Goodwill	—
- Dividend equalisation	—	Capital works in progress	—

Fund	—	Investments	—
- Investment fluctuation fund	—	Stock in trade	—
- Debenture redemption	—	Work in progress	—
Reserve A/c	—	Sundry debtors	—
- Workmen compensation	—	Accrued Incomes	—
Fund	—	Bill receivable	—
- Contingency reserve A/c	—	Advance with suppliers	—
- Profit & Loss A/c	—	Cash and Bank balances	—
Revaluation reserve	—	Miscellaneous expenditure	—
Loans	—	(to the extent not written off)	
Public deposits	—	Profit & Loss Account	—
Debentures	—		
Sundry creditors	—		
Bill payable			
Bank overdraft			
Unclaimed dividend	—		
Tax payable	—		
Outstanding expenses	—		
Receipts in advance	—		

Nature of Assets and Liabilities

The assets of an organization may be classified as under:

Fixed Assets. Fixed assets are the assets which are acquired not for re-sale but for keeping them permanently. The consumption of such assets is gradual and they give service for fairly.. long-period of time, Land & building, plant and machinery, furniture, etc. are the good examples of fixed assets, Intangible assets like goodwill is also a fixed asset.

Current Assets. Current assets are also termed as floating assets. These are the assets which keep on changing their shape and volume. Cash in hand and bank balances, stock-in-trade, sundry debtors, work-in-progress, bills receivable, etc., are the examples of current assets. Current assets may be classified into. (a) liquid Assets, and (b) Non-liquid assets. A liquid asset is one which is in the form of cash or near-cash current asset. A near-cash asset is defined as an asset which is convertible into cash with convenience and without loss at a very short-notice. Cash Balances, very good debtors, marketable securities bills receivable are the examples of liquid assets. Non-liquid assets consist of all those current assets which cannot be converted into cash at a short notice. These consist of stock-in-trade, work-in-progress, debtors which remains outstanding for more than six months. Current assets are needed to meet the usual expenditure of business.

Miscellaneous Expenditure (to the extent not written off). Technically speaking, an expenditure not represented by any tangible or intangible asset cannot be an asset. When expenditure on any item is heavy, it is capitalized instead of showing the total as a business expense in the Profit & Loss A/c of the year in which it is incurred. For example, heavy expenditure on massive advertising campaign in any year is capitalised and the portion of expenditure not written off is shown on the asset side of the Balance Sheet under the head 'Miscellaneous Expenditure.' Similarly, pre-operative and preliminary expenses are capitalised and written off gradually over a period of 3-5 years.

Profit and Loss Account (Debit Balance). Technically speaking, Debit Balance of Profit & Loss Account cannot be an asset but it is treated so for technical reasons. A company is required to show its capital at paid up value which means the loss in any year cannot be deducted from the capital. Thus the alternative is either to deduct the loss from general reserve or show it as an asset. Generally, the Profit & Loss (debit) is shown on the asset side for the time being. It is written off against the profit of the subsequent years.

Nature of Liabilities

A company's owings to its equity shareholders and other creditors may be termed as liabilities which are classified into three broad categories as under:

1. Owners equity

It represents paid up share capital and reserves and surplus. According to separate entity concept, these are the liabilities of a company to its owners-shareholders. However, these are not such liabilities which call for payment during the life time of the company. These become payable to shareholders only in the event of winding up of the company. Reserves and surplus can, however, be used for writing down capital loss, if any, and payment of bonus to shareholders by its capitalization.

2. Long-time liabilities

Outsiders' claims to be paid after more than one year's time constitute long-term liabilities. Debentures, loans from specialised financial Institutions and public deposits are the long-term liabilities which are repayable after 2-5 years in future.

3. Current liabilities

These are short term financial obligations which arise due to dealing with the outsiders in the usual course of business. Sundry creditors, bills payable, outstanding expenses, tax payable, etc., are all short-term or current liabilities as they arise in the normal course of business and are to be paid within a year's time.

Contingent liabilities

Contingent liabilities are not the actual liabilities but they become actual liabilities on the happening of a certain unfavourable event in the future. Debts not acknowledged as debt for which the case is lying in the court, is a glaring example of a contingent liability. Since, the contingent liabilities are not actual liabilities, they are shown in the Balance Sheet by way of footnotes only.

Sometimes, liabilities are also recognized as Internal and External liabilities. Owners Equity including all free reserves and credit balance of profit and loss A/c is Internal liability as it has not to be paid to any outsider but to the shareholders of the company. On the other hand, External liabilities represent the claims of outsiders. All long-term and current liabilities as explained above constitute external liabilities.

PRESENTATION OF FINANCIAL STATEMENTS

Income Statement

An Income statement may be presented either in horizontal form ('T' form) or in vertical form (single-column form). Part I of Schedule VI of the Indian Companies Act has laid down the proforma for presentation of Final Accounts by companies incorporated under the Act. The idea is that the companies highlight maximum informations and a uniformity is maintained for better understanding and comparison of accounting data. Presently, the Indian companies prepare and publish their final accounts in verticular form and the necessary details are shown in the schedules attached thereto. An idea can be formed from the Balance Sheet and the Income Statement of an Indian Company (URC (India) Limited) for the year 1989

STATEMENT CONTAINING SALIENT FEATURES OF BALANCE SHEET AND PROFIT & LOSS ACCOUNT ETC. AS PER

SECTION 219 (1) (B) (IV)

USHA RECTIFIER CORPORATION (INDIA) LIMITED

ABRIDGED BALANCE SHEET AS AT 31ST DECEMBER 1989

Particulars	*Figures as at the end of*	
	Current Financial Year (Rs. 000)	*Previous Financial (Year Rs. 000)*
1	*2*	*3*
I Sources of Funds		
1. Shareholders Funds		
(a) Capital		
(i) Equity	135993	55971
(ii) Preference	—	—
(iii) Share Application Money	—	32365
(b) Reserves & Surplus		
(i) Capital Reserve	2530	2500
(ii) Revenue Reserve	90152	26590
(iii) Revaluation Reserve	46527	43832
(iv) Share Premium A/c	43625	—
(v) Surplus in Profit and Loss Account	74249	30313
2. Loan Funds		
(a) Debentures	890143	120475
(b) Public deposits	3417	4881
(c) Secured Loans (other than debentures)	41706	165931
(d) Unsecured Loans	4814	76

1	*2*	*3*
(e) Debenture Application Money	152768	11650
	1439158	494584
II. Application of Funds		
1. Fixed Assets		
(a) Net Block-(Original cost less depreciation)	242744	233601
(b) Capital work in progress	530654	29567
2. Investments		
(a) Government Securities	170905	—
(b) Investment in subsidiary companies		
(a) Quoted	—	—
(b) Unquoted	123810	8821
(c) Others		
(a) Quoted	—	—
(b) Unquoted	101	1
3. (i) Current Assets, Loan and Advances		
(a) Inventories	160710	185372
(b) Sundry Debtors	353865	114072
(c) Cash and Bank Balance	33938	18312
(d) Other current assets	—	—
(e) Loans and Advances		
(i) To subsidiary companies	8663	1385
(ii) To others	64382	52563
	621558	371704
Less:		
(ii) Current Liabilities and Provisions		
(a) Liabilities	189060	137874
(b) Provisions	65041	15255
	254101	153129
Net Current Assets (i-ii)	367457	218575
4. Miscellaneous expenditure to the extent not written off or adjusted	3487	4019
5. Profit and Loss Account	—	—
	1439158	494584

USHA RECTIFIER CORPORATION (INDIA) LIMITED

ABRIDGED PROFIT AND LOSS ACCOUNT FOR THE PERIOD ENDED 31 DECEMBER 1989

	Particulars		*Figures as at the end of* Current Financial Year Rs. 000	Previous Financial Year Rs. 000
I.	**Income**			
	Sales		1313390	441505
	Other income		6264	16883
		Total	1319654	458388
II.	**Expenditure**			
	Cost of goods consumed / sold			
	(i) Opening Stock	93011		40904
	(ii) Purchase	1101561		379931
	Less : closing stock	93616		93012
			1100956	327823
	Manufacturing expenses		34291	30571
	Selling expenses		5989	6796
	Salaries, Wages and other employee benefits		11933	12367
	Managerial remuneration		714	136
	Interest		27874	15466
	Depreciation		11297	7348
	Auditor's remuneration		124	85
		Total	1193178	400592
III.	Profit/Loss before Tax (I-II)		126476	57796
IV.	Provision for taxation		1500	1500
V.	Profit after Tax		124976	56296
VI.	Proposed Dividend:			
	-Equity Shares		61103	17944
VII.	Transfer to Reserves and Surplus		63873	54380

Note: In the financial year ended on 31st Dec., 1988 a sum of Rs. 16028 thousands has been written back to that year's profits from Investment Allowance Reserve.

Analysis of Financial Statements

Analysis of financial statement is a technical job which can be performed properly only by a knowledgeable and experienced financial analyst. In order to he successful in his analysis and interpretation, a financial analyst must possess thorough knowledge of accounting theory and practice and he must understand various tools and techniques of accounting and their application in the analysis and interpretation of data. The knowledge of the requirements of the law relating to the organisation is must for a financial analyst. In addition to this, he must also understand the industry environment in which the unit is operating. His personal qualities such as penetrating vision and insight, tectfulness alertness, leadership qualities, etc., help him greatly in the successful discharge of his functions as financial analyst.

Techniques of Analysis

There are various techniques which are used to understand the financial statements in a comprehensive manner. Following are the methods which are generally employed to analyse the financial statements:

1. Comparative statements
2. Common size statements
3. Trend analysis
4. Technique of accounting ratio.

Comparative Statements

Joint stock companies are required to provide in their annual published accounts the corresponding figures for the year immediately preceeding the current financial year so as to provide a comparative picture of their business affairs. The decision-makers prefer to study the picture of not only for one or two years but for few more year in the fast. The Income Statement and Balance Sheet in their usual form are not much useful from management point of view. Therefore, the analysts re-arrange the information in different group as the group study alongwith the individual items is more meaningful for the purpose of interpretation and decision-making. If two or more companies have to be compared (inter-firm comparison), the analyst should take care that the group are homogeneous. He should also bear in mind the size of the enterprise in terms of capital investment and turnover. A comparative financial statement may be presented in any one of the following forms:

A. Absolute figures for the years of comparison
B. Absolute figures alongwith variations (in absolute figures)
C. Absolute figures alongwith variation in terms of pecentage or ratio.
D. Individual items as percentage of a base year.

It may be noted that the absolute figures, especially when they represent large amount are not easy to remember; therefore, it is advisable that the figures are expressed as a percentage or ratio.

Illustration—5

On 31st December 1994, the Profit and Loss Account and Balance Sheet of Jay India Ltd. stood as under:

PROFIT & LOSS ACCOUNT FOR THE YEAR ENDED AT 31ST DECEMBER, 1994

1993	*Expenditure*	*1994*	*1993*	*Incomes*	*1994*
20,000	To opening Stock	20,000	280,000	By Sales	4,00,000
1,20,000	To Purchases	1,50,000	20,000	By Closing Stock	50,000
10,000	To Carriage Inward	15,000			
50,000	Direct wages	90,000			
20,000	Gas, water and Power	50,000			
80,000	To Gross Profit	1,25,000			
3,00,000		4,50,000	3,00,000		4,50,000
8,000	To Salaries	9,000	80,000	By Gross Profit	1,25,000
2,500	To Rent and Taxes	3,000			
1,000	To Printing and stationery	1,500			
800	To Advertising	1,000			
2,000	To Interest on loans	1,000			
65,700	To Net Profit	1,09,500			
80,000		1,25,000	80,000		1,25,000

You are required to compare the performance of the company by re-arranging the data suitably and give your comments on the operational performance of the enterprise.

COMPARATIVE INCOME STATEMENT

Particulars	*1993*	*1994 decrease (±)*	*Increase/ decrease (±)*	*Increase*
1	*2*	*3*	*4*	*5*
1. Sales	2,80,000	4,00,000	+ 1,20,000	+ 43%
2. Purchases	1,20,000	1,50,000	+ 30,000	+ 25%
Carriage inward	10,000	15,000	+ 5,000	+ 50%
Direct wages	50,000	90,000	+ 40,000	+ 80%
Gas, water and power	20,000	50,000	+ 30,000	+ 150%
3. Direct cost of Production,	2,00,000	3,05,000	1,05,000	52%
Opening stock	20,000	20,000	—	—
	2,20,000	3,25,000	1,05,000	+ 52%
Less closing stock	20,000	50,000	30,000	+ 150%
4. Cost of sales	2,00,000	2,75,000	75,000	+ 37%
5. Gross margin	80,000	1,25,000	+ 45,000	+ 56%
6. Operating expenses:				
Sales ...	8,000	9,000	+ 1,000	+12½%
Rent and taxes	2,500	30,000	+ 500	+ 20%
Printing & stationery	1,000	1,500	+ 500	+ 50%
Advertising	800	1,000	+ 200	+ 25%
Total operating Expenses	12,300	14,500	+ 2,200	+ 18%
Net operating Income	67,700	1,10,500	+ 42,800	+ 63%
Less interest charges	2,000	1,000	1,000	- 50%
Profit after Interest but Before taxes	65,700	1,09,500	+ 43,800	+ 67%

Comments

An analysis of the Income statement in the above form clearly shows the variations in the individual item of 1985 on compared to their corresponding figures in 1984. An increase of 43% in sales has led to an increase of 56% in gross Margin which represent an ecouraging position. The operating cost has gone up only by 18% which shows an efficient control over a overhead charges. A study of the compisition of direct cost reveals that the increase in direct wages and gas water and power has been 80% and 150% respectively. Such an increase seems disproportionatety high as compared to increase in the volum of sales. The increase in these items need to be further investigaged in order to ascertion real causes for such an abnormal increase in these direct expenses of production. However, the over-all performance of the enterprise in 1985 as compared to 1984 is quite satisfactory.

Comparative Balance Sheet

Comparative Balance Sheet can be prepared in the same manner as the income statement as shown in the above illustration. The management accountant while presenting a comparative Balance Sheet under suitable heads, should be very clear about that structure of different assets and liabilities. The assets may be grouped under four major heads viz. (a) Liquid assets, (b) Non-liquid assets, (c) Fixed assets, and (d) pre-operative expenses not written off. Similarly, the liabiblies may be grouped into trade liablities and long-term liablities. The break-up of Balance Sheet in this manner will provide a better picture of the state of affair of an enterprise:

Illustration —6

On 31st December 1995, the Balance Sheet of Perfect Engineers (India) Ltd. stood as under:

BALANCE SHEET AS ON 31ST DECEMBER 1995

1994 (Rs.)	*Capital and Liabilities*	*1995 (Rs.)*	*1994 (Rs.)*	*Property and Assets*	*1994 (Rs.)*
4,00000	Share capital	5,00,000	2,50,000	Land and Building	2,95,000
60,000	General Reserve	80,000	4,50,000	Plant and Machinery	4,05,000
8,000	Investment Fluct-uation Fund	10,000	50,000	Furniture and Fixtures	75,000

6,000	Workmen compensation fund	15,000	1,00,000	Investments	1,50,000
			1,25,000	Stock in trade	2,00,000
2,00,000	15% Debentures	3,00,000	58,000	Sundry debtors	1,50,000
2,00,000	Loans from IDBI	1,50,000	30,000	Bills Receivable	56,000
2,00,000	Fixed Deposit	3,00,000	20,000	Marketable securities	40,000
80,000	Sundry creditors	1,00,000	25,000	Cash Balances	50,000
4,000	Rent outstanding	6,000	50,000	Pre-operation Exp.	40,000
11,58,000	14,61,000		11,58,000		14,61,000

You are required to re-cast the above Balance Sheet so as to reflect the financial position move clearly.

Solution

COMPARATIVE BALANCE SHEET AS ON 31-12-1995

	1994	*1995*	*Increase/ decrease*	*Increase/ (%)*
1. Fixed Assets:				
Land and Building	2,50,000	2,95,000	+ 45,000	+ 18%
Land and Machinery	4,50,000	4,05,000	45,000	10%
Furnitures	50,000	75,000	+ 25,000	+ 50%
Total Fixed Assets	7,50,000	5,75,000	+ 25,000	+ 33%
2. Investment	1,00,000	1,50,000	50,000	+ 50%
3. Current Assets:				
(a) Liquid Assets:				
— Cash balances	25,000	50,000	+ 25,000	100%
— Debtors	58,000	1,50,000	+ 92,000	159%
— Bills Receivable	30,000	56,000	+ 26;000	+ 87%
— Marketable Securities	20,000	40,000	+ 20,000	+ 100%
	1,33,000	2,96,000	+ 1,63,000	+ 123%
(b) Non-liquid Assets:				
— Stock-in-Trade	1,25,000	2,00,000	+ 75,000	+ 60%
Total Current Assets	2,58,000	4,96,000	+ 2,38,000	+ 92%
4. Pre-operative expenses	50,000	40,000	- 10,000	- 20%
Total Assets	11,58,000	14,61,000	3,03,000	+ 26%
1. Capital and Internal liabilities				
— Share capital	4,00,000	5,00,000	+ 1,00,000	+ 25%

— General Reserve	60,000	80,000	+ 20,000	+ 33%
— Investment Fluctuation Fund	8,000	1,000	+ 2,000	+ 25%
— Workmen Compensation Fund	6,000	15,000	+ 9,000	+ 15%
Total Capital	4,74,000	6,05,000	+ 1,31,000	+ 28%
2. Long-term liabilities				
— Debentures	2,00,000	3,00,000	1,00,000	+ 50%
— Loans from IDBI	2,00,000	1,50,000	- 50,000	- 25%
— Fixed Deposit	2,00,000	3,00,000	+ 1,00,000	+ 50%
Total long term liabilities	6,00,000	7,50,000	+ 1,50,000	+ 25%
3. Current liabilities:				
— Sundry creditors	80,000	1,00,000	+ 20,000	+ 25%
— Rent Outstanding	4,000	6,000	+ 2,000	+ 50%
Total current liabilities	84,000	1,06,000	+ 22,000	+ 26%
Total Liabilities	11,58,000	14,61,000	3,03,000	+ 26%

Comments

A comparative study of assets structure reveals that there has been negligible increase of 3.3% in the total fixed assets in 1995 in comparison with 1994. The investments have gone up by 50% and there has been considerable increase in liquid and non-liquid assets as they have gone up by 123% and 60% respectively. Whether such an increase in current assets (92%) truely shows the liquid position is an issue which should be decided in the light of the current liabilities of the company. The decrease in the preparation expenses clearly shows that the company has written of such expenses to the tune of 20% during the current year.

As regards the liabilities, the shareholders funds as represented by capital and other reserves have gone up by 28%. These has been marked increase of 150% in the workmen compensation Fund due to transfer of Rs. 9000 in the current year, long-term liabilities and current liabilities have increased by 25% respectively. The management should further investigate the causes for marked variations in current assets and workmen's compensation fund with a view to review their credit policy and the policy for building up of the workmen compensation fund.

Common Size Statements

The Profit and Loss Account and Balance Sheet can also be presented in the form of Common-size statements. A statement in which individual items are expressed as a per centage of same common base is termed as an common-size statement. In a common-size Profit and Loss Account, the sale figure is generally taken as base (sale - 100) to calculate the proposition of other items figuring in the Profit and Loss a/c and a common size Balance Sheet expresses individual assets and liabilities as percentage of total assets/liabilities. Common-size comparative statements provide a better historical perspective of an undertaking. Any significant departure from the normal trend need further investigation to as certain the reasons for unusual movement in the figures so that due care is taken in the formulation of future plan.

The Profit and Loss Account as Balance Sheet as given previously are presented below in the from of common-size statements.

COMMON-SIZE PROFIT AND LOSS ACCOUNT

	1994		*1995*	
	Amount	*% to sales*	*Amount*	*% to sales*
Sales	2,80,000	100	4,00,000	100
1. Cost of production	2,00,000	71.4	3,05,000	100
2. Cost of Sales	2,00,000	71,4	2,75,000	68.7
3. Gross Margin	80,000	28.3	1,25,000	31.2
4. Operating Expenses	12,300	4.4	14,500	3.6
5. Net Operating Profit	67,700	24,2	1,10,500	27.6
6. Profit after interest	67,500	23.4	1,09,500	24.9

COMMON SIZE BALANCE SHEET

Items	*1994 Amount*	*% of total assets*	*1995 Amount*	*% to total Assets*
A. Land and Buildings	2,50,000	21.6	2,95,000	20.2
Plant and Machinery	4,50,000	38.8	4,05,000	27.7
Furniture and Fixtures	50,000	4.4	75,000	5.2
Fixed Assets	7,50,000	64.8	7,75,000	53.1

B. Investments	1,00,000	8.6	1,50,000	10.2
C. Cash Balances	25,000	2.2	50,000	3.4
Debtors	58,000	5.0	1,50,000	10.4
Bills Receivable	30,000	2.6	56,000	3.8
Marketable Securities	20,000	1.7	40,000	2.7
Liquid Assets	1,33,000	11.5	2,96,000	20.3
Stock-in-trade	1,25,000	10,.8	2,00,000	13.7
(Non-liquid asset)				
Total current assets	2,58,000	22.3	14,61,000	34.0
D. Pre-operating Exp.	50,000	4.3	40,000	2.7
Total Assets	11,58,000	100	14,61,000	100
Capital and liabilities:				
Share capital	4,00,000	34.5	5,00,000	34.2
General Reserve	60,000	5.2	80.000	5.5
Investment Fluctuation Fund	8,000	0.7	10,000	0.7
Workmen Çompensation Fund	6,000	0.5	15,000	1.0
Total Shareholders fund	4,74,000	40.9	6,05,000	41.4
Long Term liabilities:				
Debentures	2,00,000	17.3	3,00,000	20.5
Loans	2,00,000	17.3	1,50,000	10.3
Fixed Assets	2,00,000	17.2	3,00,000	20.5
Total long term liabilities	6,00,000	51.8	7,50,000	51.3
Current liabilities:				
Sundry creditors	80,000	6.9	1,00,000	6.8
Rent Outstanding	4,000	0.4	6,000	0.4
Total current liabilities	8,4000	7.3	1,06,000	7.2
Total Liabilities	11,58,000	100	14,61,000	100

Observations

The common-size Balance sheet shows the assets and liabilities structure in relation to total assets/liabilities. As is evident from the above, the fixed assets in 1995 formed 53.1% of the total asset in the same year. The current assets accounted for 34% which consisted of liquid and non-liquid assets of 203% and 13.7% respectively. Preoperative expenses were only 2.7% of the total assets. It may be understood that the asset structure of any enterprises defends upon its very nature. In a capital intensive industry, the proportion of fixed assets is much more than that of the current assets. Against it, the labour-intensive industries have lower proportion of fixed assets and higher percentage of assets is devoted to working capital in the form of current assets. Therefore, the position of the constituents of total assets should be interpreted in terms of the very nature of industry. In the above case the structure of assets in 1995 has substantially changed. The fixed assets which were 64.8% in 1994 had gone down to 53.1% despite additions to land and building and furniture. The decline seems due to decrease in the value of assets due to depreciation. The liquid position of the company has significantly improved from just 22.3% to 34.0% but this may be rightly interpreted in relation to corresponding current liabilities.

As regards liabilities, the shareholders funds represented by capital and reserves accounted for 40.9% and 41.5% at the end of 1994 and 1995 respectively. The long-term liabilities were 51.8% and 51.3% at the same point of time. Current liabilities constituted 7.3% and 7.2% at the end of the same periods. Thus the liabilities structure in 1995 is not much different from that at the end of the year 1994. From this type of observation, one may be tempted to conclude that the company has not grown over a period of one year as the percentage constituents of different liabilities is more or less the same. This type of conclusion will be erroneous. It may be realized that the common size statements present vertical representation of facts at a point of time and the comparison in the above form may mislead the analyst. Therefore, the consideration of absolute figures of assets and liabilities alongwith their percentages is highly important before any conclusion is drawn.

Trend Analysis

The absolute figure of an activity is not much useful in decision-making. Therefore, a set of figures for purposes of comparison is necessary. The accounting figures relating to sales, production, profit, overheads, working capital, etc., for the last few years expressed as a percentage of some figure in a base period give trend which throw more light on the related problem. Generally, the figures for the last 3 to 5 years should be considered for better understanding of an economic phenomenon. The trend indicates general tendency or direction of change in which management is more interested, but the fact that a trend is more influenced by the base year figure, should always be borne in mind. The analysis and interpretation will not be fruitful if the base year figure is unusually high or low. Therefore, the selection of the base year should be done carefully. It should be the year of normal conditions. The trend can be rightly interpreted if the effect of inflation on different years figures of money income is neutralized. Another method of proper analysis would be to calculate the percentage of physical quantities, wherever possible, by the use of index numbers technique. The percentage of current year may be calculated as under:

$$\% \text{ for current year} = \frac{\text{Current year figure}}{\text{Base year figure}} \times 100$$

The trend analysis may be understood by perusing the following financial statement based on imaginary figures of few important items of Income and position statements of an hypothetical firm.

Items	*1982*		*1983*		*1984*		*1985*		*1986*	
	Amount	*%*	*Amount*	*%*	*Amount*	*%*	*Amount*	*%*	*Amount*	*%*
Sales	20,000	100	22,000	110	30,000	150	25,000	125	32,000	160
Direct Cost	8,000	100	10,000	125	14,000	175	11,000	137	13,000	163
Factory overheads	1,000	100	1,200	120	1,400	140	1,200	120	1,500	150
Administration overheads	800	100	800	100	1,000	125	1,000	125	1,000	125
Selling overheads	200	100	250	125	300	150	250	125	350	175
Gross Margin	12,000	100	12,000	100	16,000	133	14,000	117	19,000	158
Profit before tax	10,000	100	9,750	97	13,300	133	11,550	115	16,150	161
Gross working Capital	40,000	100	45,000	112	45,000	112	50,000	125	80,000	200
Current liabilities	20,000	100	25,000	125	25,000	125	30,000	150	35,000	175

Precautions in Financial Statement Analysis

The objective of analysis of financial statement is achieved only if the analysis is rightly done. In order to be successful the analyst should be well-versed in the art of analysis, he should take the following precautions in the analysis of financial statements:

1. He should see that the financial statements have been prepared by following the same concepts and conventions of book-keeping and

accounting. If there has been any change in the depreciation policy, inventory valuation method or any other variable affecting profit figure and assets and liabilities, the analyst should first make the data comparable by making necessary adjustments in the concerning items.

2. If two or more companies are being compared, it should be seen that their nature and size do not widely differ.

3. In the computation of trend the base year, with which the data of other years are compared should be selected carefully. The base year in any case should be a normal year.

4. Sometimes a percentage figure is misleading. Therefore, the analysis of statements submitted to management should contain absolute figures alongwith their percentages.

6. The relationship should be established only between the relevant figures. For example, the profitability should be interpreted only in terms of sales or capital employed.

Ratio Analysis

The ratio analysis is one of the important and widely used techniques of financial analysis. It has gained a lot of popularity as a tool of financial analysis in the recent years Many companies in India compute important accounting ratios and publish the same in their annual reports in order to show the performance and financial position in the most simple and effective manner. A ratio expresses relationship of one figure with any other relevant figure. It is simply defined as one number expressed in relation to another number Thus an accounting ratio signifies numerical or mathematical relationship between two relevant items contained in the Income Statement and / or Balance sheet. There are many items in a Income Statement and Balance Sheet which are closely related to each other. For example, gross profit and sales have a close relationship in the sense that the volume of sales directly affects the amount of gross profit if other variables such as cost of sales, selling price and inventory valuation method remain more or less the same. Higher the volume of sales, higher will be the gross profit and vice versa. Similarly, the profitability is affected by the availability of capital for employment in the venture. The accounting ratio technique of financial analysis attempts to compute relevant relationship between two items of financial statements and interpret them for the purposes of decision-making.

Methods of Expression

A ratio can be expressed in a number of ways. We can present a ratio in the form of quotient, percentage or proportion. If the gross profit on a sale of Rs. 1,50,000 is 50,000 then this relationship can be expressed in the following forms.

As a quotient, $\frac{\text{Gross Profit}}{\text{Sales}} = \frac{50,000}{1,50,000} = 0.33$

The ratio of 0.33 shows that for a sale of Re 1, the gross profit is 33 paise.

As a percentage, $\frac{\text{Gross Profit}}{\text{Sales}} \times 100; \quad \frac{50,000}{1,50,000} \times 100 = 33.3\%$

The percentage figure of 33.3 shows that the gross profit is 33.3% of sales.

As a proportion, 50,000 : 1,50,000 or 1:3

It means the gross profit is one-third of sales.

Significance of Ratio Technique

1. The significance of ratio technique lies in the fact that it reduces the huge related accounting figures to a single figure which is easy to understand and remember relationship. It is always convenient to remember that gross profit is 1/3rd of sales than to remember the absolute figures of gross profit and sales.

2. The ratio analysis technique is a better technique as compared to other methods of financial analysis. It tells us the relative importance of accounting date. The absolute figures are not as much relevent and meaningful as the ratio between them.

3. The technique of ratio analysis is very important to management in the discharge of its functions of planning, communication, coordination and control. Future business activities can be planned with the help of historical trend of accounting ratios. The accounting ratios can be used to communicate effictively the business plans, performance and economic position to the concerned persons. The ideal ratio may be used for the

purposes of comparison and take corrective action, wherever necessary.

4. The management can make inter-firm comparison more realistically with the help of accounting ratios keeping in view the hetrogenity between the firms.

5. The accounting ratios are equally important to the outside world. The investors, creditors and debenture holders employ various profitability and solvency ratios to assesse the efficiency of management while taking decisions with regard to their investment or disinvestment in the companies. Similarly the provider of funds—banker and financial institutions make use of accounting ratios in their financial decision-making.

Limitations of Ratio Analysis

The Financial analyst should clearly understand that the ratio analysis is not perfect in itself. It suffers from many limitations which should be properly recognised in the computation and application of ratios for interpretation and decision-making. It is most likely that wrong ratios may be computed and erroneous results drawn if proper pre-caution is not taken in the computation of accounting ratios and developing future plans on their basis. Following are some of the serious limitations with which the ratio analysis technique suffers.

1. A ratio is based an historical informations and as such indicates the past history and tells nothing about future with which the management is specially concerned.

2. The correctness of the ratios depends upon the reliability of the informations contained in the financial statements. If the statements have been window-dressed, then the ratios will be misleading.

3. Ratios are calculated for the purpose of comparison with similar ratios in the past or with some standard ratio specified by the management. The specification of a standard ratio is a difficult task and a single standard cannot be prescribed for all firms in an industry. Thus inter-firm comparison becomes difficult.

4. A single ratio has limited role to play in the financial analysis of a firm because there are so many ratios which can be used to understand the same problem.

5. Generally, there is a time lag between the dates of data presentation and actual computation of ratios for decision-making. A ratio losses much of its practical utility if it is based an obsolete figures.

6. Accounting ratios cannot reveal the qualitative changes underlying them due to this limitation ratios fail to explain the problem in right perspective.

7. The accounting ratios cannot be said to be fit for the purpose of comparison if the price level changes have not been incorporated in the financial statements. The incorporation of price level changes in financial statements is itself a problem.

8. Accounting ratios as a tool of financial analysis cannot replace the original data on which they are based. sometimes, the consideration of absolute figures is highly important for understanding the underlying problem in proper form. Thus, the ratios can best he used as a complimentary tool and not as a substitute to the basic information.

9. The success of computation and interpretation of accounting ratios basically defends upon the knowledge and experience of the analyst. If the analyst lack the knowledge of accounting, auditing and financial management, he cannot be a good analyst because be has to first ascertain the correctness and reliability of the information and understand the nature and size of firms if inter-firm comparison is discussed. Interpretation of ratios is a technical and sensitive job which can be performed only by an experienced financial analyst.

Interpretation of Ratios

Financial analyst should understand the ways in which the accounting ratios can be interpreted. Following are the usual ways in which ratios are interpreted.

1. Individual Ratio Interpretation : An individual ratio does not throw much light on the nature and significance of the problem under study. A current ratio of 1.5 : 1 indicates that a firm is able to pay off its current liabilities and also leave some amount for meeting its working capital requirement but the ratio does not provide any ideas about the structure of current assets. Therefore, individual ratios should be interpreted with reference to other related ratios.

2. *Study of Group Ratios:* The study of related ratios is more useful for drawing dependable conclusions. For correct understanding of the current economic position of any enterprise, it would be advisable to follow the group ratios approach and use the Acid Test ratio, Assets-Turnover and Debtors-Turnover ratios, simultaneously.

3. *Trend of Ratios:* In this type of ratio interpretation, the ratios for the past few years are compiled and presented in a tabular form. The table so constructed reveals the trend which gives a better idea about the problem under consideration. Interpretation of ratios based on trend is more dependable than the one based on individual ratio approach.

4. *Comparison of Inter-Firm Ratios:* A ratio may also be interpreted in terms of the related ratio of other similar nature firms. Industry ratios can be used as the model for the comparison with ones own firm's ratios.

For the interpretation of ratios, it would not be proper to follow any one approach but simultaneously other approaches should also be tried for understanding the true meaning underlying the ratios.

Classification of Ratios

Financial analyst come across a large number of ratios which are used for analysing different types of problems. Ratios have been classified in various groups according to statements, time, importance, functions, users or purpose as shown below:

1. *Statements as Basis of Classification:* According to statement basis of classification, the ratio are grouped into categories such as (a) Income Statement Ratios which are derived from the data of Income statement alone. (b) Balance Sheet Ratios which are the accounting ratios of Balance Sheet only and (c) Inter-statement ratios which use one figure from the Income Statement and another from the Balance Sheet.

2. *Time Base Classification:* According to time as a basis of classification, the ratios may be put into two groups—(a) structural ratios which are for the same point of time such as ratios based on the income statement and Balance Sheet for a particular period of time and (b) Trend ratios which relate to past years and show trend over those years.

3. *Importance as Basis of Classification:* Importance as the basis of classification suggests two types of ratios (a) Primary ratios which serve

the primary purpose of understanding the profitability on turn-over or capital employed, (b) Secondary ratios which are computed to understand rightly the primary ratios. These are also known as subsidiary or supporting ratios. To understand profitability in its right perspective ratios of cost of sales to sales, operating expenses to sales, etc. are also computed. Such ratios may be called secondary ratios.

4. Purpose or Tests Satisfied as basis of Classification: Accounting ratios are computed to serve certain purpose or to test some fundamentals about the firm in which the analyst is interested. Generally, the concerning parties are interested to test the profitability, liquidity, solvency and activity of their enterprises. Accordingly, the ratios are classified into (i) Profitability Ratio, (ii) Liquidity Ratios, (iii) Solvency Ratios and (iv) Activity Ratios.

Computation of Accounting Ratios and Their Interpretation

The classification of accounting ratio according to purpose or test satisfied is more realistic as it is intended to serve the purpose of different parties who are interested in financial statement analysis. We know that the short-term creditors are more interested in the liquidity and short-term solvency whereas the long-term creditors are more concerned with the profitability and long term solvency of the debtor organisation. The management examines various aspects of the firm as its main concern is the growth and long-term financial stability of the organisation. If we scrutinize the interests of various parties, we will find that the interests of all the parties are more or less the same because the interests of everybody is better served only if the enterprisegenerates adequate surplus, maintain liquidity and grow steadily to enjoy long-term financial soundness. Therefore, we will concentrate on the calculation of profitability ratios, liquidity ratios, solvency ratios and activity ratios.

Profitability Ratios

Profit earning is the ultimate aim of business firms which direct their resources towards the achievements of that objective. Profit generation is essential for the survival of an enterprise in the long-run. The business firms review their performance periodically and calculate estimated profits. The public limited companies in India publish their income statements in the abridged from in the middle of the year for the information of their members and others. Profit in absolute term is not of much importance for a decision-maker. Therefore, we use profitability ratio which expresses profits in a relative sense. Profitability ratio measures profits in relation to sales or capital employed. Profitability depends upon the volume of sales, cost of sales, operating expenses, capital investment, etc. All these factors have therefore to be taken into consideration while interpreting profitability. Following ratios are calculated to measure profitability.

1. Gross Profit Ratio (GP Ratio)

Gross profit is defined as the profit before the recovery of operating expenses. It is the difference between the sales and cost of sales. The gross profit is directly related to sales as it directly varies with the volume of sales if cost of sales remains the same. Generally cost of sales does not show significant fluctuations in the short-run. The Gross Profit Ratio is computed by the use of the following formula:

$$\text{Gross Profit Ratio} = \frac{\text{Gross Profit}}{\text{Sales}} \times 100$$

Interpretation of Gross Profit Ratio

Absolute G.P. Ratio does not tell anything about the adequacy or otherwise of the gross profit. Therefore, the G.P. Ratio has to be compared with standard ratio, if any. The study of the G.P. ratios for the past few years will throw sufficient light on the performance of the enterprise. A comparison of G.P. ratios of two similar nature companies will clearly highlight the differences in the profitability of the concerns. If there is a difference in the G.P. ratios for two different periods of the same firm, then the financial analyst should identify the reasons for differences and report to management. A higher or increasing G.P. ratio is considered as a sign of improving profitability. Financial analyst should understand that an increase in the Gross Profit Ratios may be due to one or more of the following reasons.

1. An increase in the selling price without any increase in the cost of sales.
2. A decrease in the cost per unit of output due to efficient management of production facilities whereas selling price has not changed.
3. An over-valuation of unsold stock due to change in the methods of inventory valuation.

4. Goods with higher profit margin might have been sold in larger quantity as compared to previous period.
5. Accounting errors such as inclusion of sales both in sales and closing stock if goods sold remained undelivered. Similarly, goods purchased excluded from Purchases Account but included in unsold stock increase the gross profit.

A decrease in the Gross Profit Ratio is a clear sign of poor performance if it has not been effected by accounting error or window dressing by the management. The decrease in G.P. ratio is caused by the following:

1. Decrease in selling.price without any change in cost of sales.
2. Increase in cost of production without any change in selling price.
3. Undervaluation of unsold stock due to change in the policy of inventory valuation.
4. Goods with low profit margin sold in larger quantities as compared to previous year.
5. Accounting error such as exclusion of sales both from sales account and closing stock. Similarly, goods purchased but left to be included in closing stock.

The financial analyst must realize that the G.P. Ratio gives a rough idea of profitability and no definite and fruitful conclusion can be drawn on this basis without regard to the operating expenses of the enterprise. A higher G.P. Ratio is meaningless if the operating expenses are also quite high. Therefore, the Net Profit Ratio need to be calculated.

2. Net Profit Ratio

Net Profit may be defined as profit after the recovery of all operating expenses. Thus Gross profit minus operating expenses equals the net profit. It is the net profit which is relevant from management, stockholders and employees point of view as it governs the long-term survival of the enterprise to serve everybody's interests All the parties are more interested in the net profits than in gross profit of their concerns. Net Profit measures the net effect of business transactions for a financial year. It can be calculated with reference to sales, capital employed, total assets or shareholders finds, etc. Before attempting the calculation of net profit ratio, it is important to ensure that the net profit has been rightly calculated. Special attention should be given to the following:

a) All operating incomes and expenditure have been brought into the Income statement.
b) Depreciation has been rightly provided.
c) Reasonable provision for bad debts and expected losses has been made.
d) Consistent policy with regard to writing off capitalized expenditure has been followed.

For the purpose of comparison of net profits of different years, it is to be ensured that non-operating expenses and gains should be ignored in the calculation of profit for the purpose of comparison. A company may inflate its profits by not charging depreciation in one year but show loss in another year by not only charging depreciation of that year but also the depreciation of earlier years. Such a situation should be reconcited before taking profit for calculating the ratio.

There are various concepts of profit such as profit after interest and taxes (PAIT), Profit before interest and taxes (PBIT) Profit after interest but before taxes (PAIBT), etc. Which concept of profit be adopted for the purpose of ratio analysis is an issue which should be resolved carefully. The profit after interest and taxes (PAIT) is more important from shareholders point of view as they are more concerned with disposable profit whereas profit before interest and taxes (PBIT) is considered more practical from management's point of view, because the management is keenly interested in the earning power of company under their control. Net Profit Ratio based an sales may be calculated in the following manner.

A — Profit - after - interest and Taxes (PAIT) = $\frac{\text{PAIT}}{\text{Sales}} \times 100$

B — Profit - before - interest but before Taxes (PBIT) = $\frac{\text{PBIT}}{\text{Sales}} \times 100$

C — Profit after interest but before Taxes (PAIBT) = $\frac{\text{PAIBT}}{\text{Sales}} \times 100$

Illustration—7

The Trading and Profit and Loss Account of International Telecommunications Ltd. for the year ended on 31 March 1995 stood as follows:

To Opening Stock	2,50,000	By Sales Less Returns	28,00,000
To Purchases Less Retunrs	25,50,000	By Closing Stock	8,00,000
To Direct Expenses	1,00,000		
To Gross Profit c/d	7,00,000		
	36,00,000		36,00,000
To Administration Exp.	1,50,000	By Gross Profit	7,00,000
To Selling and Distribution Expenses	50,000		
To Interest on Loans	1,00,000		
To Net Profit	4,00,000		
	7,00,000		7,00,000
To Provision for Tax	1,60,000	By Net Profit	4,00,000
To General Reserve	50,000		
To provision for dividend	1,00,000		
To Profit carriedto Balance Sheet	90,000		
	4,00,000		4,00,000

Calculate the profitablity ratios if the standard G.P. ratio and N.P. ration (after interest & taxes) are 25% and 10% respectively, comment on the adequency of profitability in the current year.

Solution

$$\text{Gross Profit Ration} = \frac{\text{G.P.}}{\text{Sales}} \times 100 = \frac{7{,}00{,}000}{28{,}00{,}000} \times 100 = 25\%$$

Net Profit after Interest & Taxes (PAIT)= Net Profit 4,00,000

Less taxes (40% assumed) 1,60,000

2,40,000

$$\text{Ratio of Net Profit After Int. \& Taxes} = \frac{2{,}40{,}000}{28{,}00{,}000} \times 100 = 8.57\%$$

Comments

As compared with the standard G.P. ratio of 25% the realised G.P. Ratio is exactly 25%; hence the gross profitablity is maintained. However, the actual net profit ratio of 8.57% is lesser than the standard ratio of 10%, therefore, the net profitability isomit meagure which, obviously is due to higher operating cost.

Profit to Capital Employed

Capital investment is one of the important variable with which the profit is intimately related. Profits in an organisation accrue because of employment of capital. There is positive correlation between capital investment and volume of profits. Higher the capital investment higher the volume of profit. Therefore, it is quite reasonable that the profitability of an organisation is judged in relation to the capital which has helped in the earning of those profits. An absolute figure of profit is not meaningful till it is read with reference to capital employment. In this connection, it is essential to clearly understand the meaning of the terms 'Profits' and 'Capital employed' as any change in the meaning of these will affect the rate of profitability.

Meaning of Profit

There are number of concepts of profit such as Gross Profit, Net Profit, Profit Before Interest and Taxes (PBIT), Profit After Interest and Taxes (PAIT), Disposal Profits, etc. Profit simply means excess of revenue over expenditure. Gross Profit is defined as the difference between Sales and Cost of sales. It may also be defined as the profit before the recovery of operating expenses, depreciation and necessary provisions. Net Profit is the net gain after all expenses have been charged against the income for a particular period. The concepts of PBIT and PAIT are also used in decision-making. Whatever is left to the shareholders for distribution as dividend after necessary transfer to reserves and provision for taxes, etc., is the disposal profit. Shareholders who prefer regular income in the form of dividend are more concerned with the disposable profits of their companies.

So far as the profit figure for management purpose is concerned, it should be a different figure, which should exclude all exceptional losses and gains.

Meaning of Capital Employed

Capital denotes the amount introduced by the proprietors to run an enterprise. It increases or decreases with an increase or decrease in profits. In case of a company, the capital is shown at its paid up value and the Profit and Loss Account is represented separately. Different types of free reserves are nothing but retained earnings or profits. Capital is paid back to the shareholders only in the case of winding up of a company. Similarly, all reserves and Profit & Loss balance are credited to shareholders account to determine their claim while closing books on liquidation of company. In case of a continued company, capital employed is not only the paid up capital but also all other reserves and surplus which are profits retained for bringing financial stability, growth and development of the company. For calculating the profit rate on capital employed, any one of the following concepts may be used. Selection of a particular concept is however, depends upon the object of profitability analysis:

1. Gross Capital

It is represented by total resources in the form of fixed assets and current assets. Preliminary or pre-operative expenses to the extent not written off and the debit balance of Profit and Loss account are deducted from total of the Balance sheet to arrive at Gross Capital employed. Thus,

Gross Capital = Fixed Assets + Current Assets.

2. Net Capital

Gross Capital minus current liabilities is equal to Net Capital. It may also be calculated by adding together the paid up capital, outstanding long-term debts and all free reserves and Profit and Loss (cr.). Thus,

Net Capital = Gross Capital — Current liabilities.

Or

Net Capital = Paid up Capital + Long-term debts + Reserves + Profit and Loss A/C credit balance.

3. Proprietors Capital

Other names given to Proprietors Capital are, Shareholders Funds, Owners Equity and Net Worth. It is found out by deducting from the gross capital all liabilities belonging to trade creditors, debentures, financiers and deposit-holders, etc. Thus,

Proprietors Capital = Gross Capital — (Trade creditors + debenturs + loans + fixed deposits)

Which one of the three concepts should be taken into account for calculating the profitability rates? This issue should be resolved in the light of the object of analysis. If the objective is to know the effectiveness of the use of total resources, the Gross Capital concept will be most appropriate. In case the return on proprietors funds is desired to be known, then the proprietors capital is to be used for the purpose of calculating the profitability rate. The rate of profit can be calculated as under:

% Profit to Capital employed = or Return an Capital Investment $\dfrac{\text{Profit}}{\text{capital employed}} \times 100$

Illustration—8

Calculate the capital employed according to its different versions from the Balance Sheet as shown as page No. 56-57.

Gross Capital Employed = Fixed Assets + Current Assets

Land and Building	2,95,000	
Plant and Machinery	4,05,000	
Furniture and Fixtures	75,000	
Investment	1,50,000	9,25,000
Stock in trade	2,00,000	
Sundry debtors	1,50,000	
Bills Receivable	56,000	
Marketable Securities	40,000	
Cash Balances	50,000	
		4,96000
Total		14,21,000

Net Capital Employed: = Gross Capital — Current liabilities

Gross Capital = 1421000

Less Current liabilities:

Creditors	1,00,000	
Rent outstanding	6000	
		1,06,000
	Total	13,15,000

Proprietory Capital:

Share capital	5,00,000
General reserve	80,000
Investment fluctuation fund	10,000
Workmen compensation fund	15,000
	6,05,000
Less Pre-operative Exp.	40,000
Total	5,65,000

Alternatively, Proprietory Capital = Gross Capital — (outsiders. funds + Current liabilities)

= 14,21,000 – (3,00,000 + 1,50,000 + 3,00,000 + 1,00,000 + 6,000)

= 14,21,000 – 8,56,000 = 5,65,000.

Illustration—9

Supposing, the company earned a profit of Rs. 1,20,000 after charging interest and depreciation but before income tax in the same year, you are required to calculate the profitability rate and comment on the same if the budgeted profitability rate on total resources was 15% (using illustration on page 56-57).

Solution

Profitability rate on

Gross Capital employed = $\dfrac{1,20,000}{1,42,1000} \times 100 = 8.44\%$

Profit rate on
Net Capital = $\dfrac{1,20,000}{13,15,000} \times 100 = 9.12\%$

Profit rate on
Proprietors funds = $\dfrac{1,20,000}{5,65,000} \times 100 = 21.23\%$

Thus profitability rates are different according to different concepts of capital employed. As compared to budgeted 15% profit rate, the realized profitability of 8.44% is much less and as such the company has performed poorly.

Earning Per Share (EPS)

Investment managers make use of the concept of EPS in evaluating profitability. EPS is computed by calculating the profit after tax and preference dividend and dividing the same by number of share outstanding. Thus

$$\text{EPS} = \frac{\text{Profit after tax and preference dividend}}{\text{Number of equity shares outstanding}}$$

In order to have a fair idea of the profitability in an organisation, the EPS for the last few years may be compared. An increasing upward trend is an indication of steady performance whereas a declining tendency is a danger signal for management. The EPS may also be compared with industry EPS and the earnings per share of other similar nature companies.

Dividend per Share. Generally the whole of the profit earned by a company during a year is not distributed by way of dividend. A part of the profit is retained for re-employment and meeting future contingencies. Thus the dividend per share depends upon the amount of profit which is meant for distribution in the form of dividend. The Dividend Per Share (DPS) is arrived at by dividing the profit allocated for dividend by the number of equity shares.

$$\text{DPS} = \frac{\text{Profit available for dividend}}{\text{Number of equity shares}}$$

Those shareholders who are more conscious of the declared rate of dividend prefer to make investment in the companies which are liberal in the payment of dividend. An analyst would recommend investment for such investors in the companies which have paid dividend at increasing rates in the past. The DPS is lesser than EPS as a part of profit earned is retained for future use.

Percentage yield. It may be noted that the dividend per share is calculated on the nominal value of shareholders paid up capital.

In order to understand the effective rate of return (yield), the dividend per share is to be interpreted in terms of market value which is different from the nominal value of a share. Percentage yield on high value shares is low. It is calculated as per the following formula:

$$\% \text{ yield} = \frac{\text{Dividend per share}}{\text{Market value per share}} \times 100$$

Illustration—10

Following information pertain to a limited company. You are required to calculate dividend yield and comment on the same if the desired yield of an investor is 5%.

Nominal value per share = Rs. 10

Market value per share = Rs. 60

Dividend 20% or Rs. 2 per share

Solution

$$\% \text{ Dividend yield} = \frac{\text{Dividend per share}}{\text{Market value per share}} \times 100$$

$$\% \text{ D.Y.} = \frac{2}{60} \times 100 = 3.33\%.$$

Since the dividend yield of 3.33% is lower than 5% desired yield the purchases of shares at Rs. 60 cannot be recommended.

Price-earning multiple (P/E Ratio). It establishes relationship between market price and earnings per share. Thus,

$$\text{P/E Ratio} = \frac{\text{Market price of a share}}{\text{Earning per share}}$$

This ratio is widely used to know whether a share is over-priced, under priced or reasonably priced. Standard P/E ratio vary from industry to industry. A comparison of P/E ratio for a company's share with industry P/E ratio will properly guide the investors in making investment decisions.

Illustration—11

You are furnished the following information and asked to comment on the price of the share:

EPS = 6

Market Value of a share = 60

Industry P/E ratio = 15

Satisfactory P/E ratio = 12

Solution: P/E ratio = $\frac{\text{Market price}}{\text{Earning per share}}$

$$= \frac{60}{6} = 10$$

It means the market price of the share is 10 times the earnings per share. The industry P/E ratio is much higher and the P/E ratio which an investor considers satisfactory (12) is also higher than the prevailing P/E ratio of 10. Thus, the share at Rs. 60 is under-priced and may be recommended for buying from the market.

Liquidity Ratio

Liquidity means the availability of liquid assets to pay off the current liabilities at any point of time. Liquid assets are the assets which are in the form of cash and near-cash assets. The near-cash assets may be defined as all those assets which can be converted into cash conveniently without any loss at a short notice. Cash balances, bills receivable, marketable securities and good debtors are the liquid assets which can be used to pay off the current obligations. Liquid assets are also known as Quick Assets as they are quickly convertible into cash.

Liquidity Ratio or Quick Ratio measures a firms ability to honour its very short-term business commitments. The application of liquidity ratio is also known as Acid Test since it tests a firms immediate or market period solvency. The liquid ratio is calculated by dividing the liquid Assets by liquid or current liabilities.

$$\text{Liquid Ratio/Quick Ratio/Acid Test} = \frac{\text{Quick Assets}}{\text{Current liabilities}}$$

Interpretation of Liquid Ratio

Generally, a LR of 1 : 1 is considered satisfactory as it enables a firm to pay off all the current liabilities out of liquid assets at any time. It means, at any moment of time, a firm must have liquid assets equal to its current liabilities. It may be clearly understood that a too high or too low a liquid ratio is bad from financial point of view. A higher LR implies idle cash balances and a low LR means poor liquid position. Efforts should therefore, be made to maintain liquid assets equal to current liabilities which are required to be paid in the short period. This is a difficult task and requires regular monitoring of the changes in the quality of current assets.

The liquidity Ratio of 1:1 is a rule of thumb or crude measure to judge the liquidity in an organisation. A firm can afford to work with a low ratio if its non-liquid assets like inventory is readily saleable. Similarly, a low ratio can work during off-season when the demand for cash balances declines. Liquidity Ratio is also affected by the nature of current liabilities. Any current liability which is more or less of permanent nature, should be excluded from the calculations of Liquidity Ratio. If the Bank overdraft is a permanent feature in the firm, then it shall be excluded from the computation of Liquidity Ratio.

Current Ratio

It is a measure of a firm's short-term solvency. A firm is said to be in a short-period solvency if it is able to honour its short-term liabilities and left with adequate working capital to meet normal business expenditure. A current ratio is the ratio between current assets and current liabilities. Generally a current ratio of 2 : 1 is considered as satisfactory for the purpose of evaluating short-term solvency of a firm. It means current assets should be twice the current liabilities if a firm want to enjoy short-term solvency.

For the purpose of computing a reliable Current Ratio, a financial analyst should be clear about the current assets and current liabilities. Any asset which is convertable, in the normal course, into cash in a year's time is considered as current asset. Similarly, any liability which is to be paid during the same period is taken as current liability. Usual items of current assets and current liabilities are as under:

Current Assets = Liquid Assets + Non Liquid Assets

Or

Current Assets:	Cash in hand
	Balances with Banks
	Bills recoverable
	Debtors less doubtful debts
	Marketable investment
	Prepaid expenses and advances
	Unsold stock
	Work-in-progress
Current liabilities:	Trade creditors
	Bills payable
	Outstanding expenses
	Tax payable
	Bank overdraft
	Proposed dividend
	Short-term loans.

It may be noted that, if in any year a company wishes to liquidate its long-term liability, then such a liability may be considered as a current for that year. Current Ratio is arrived at simply by dividing the current assets by current liabilities.

$$\text{Current Ratio} = \frac{\text{Current Assets}}{\text{Current liabilities}}$$

A ratio of 2 :1 is fairly a good indicator of a firm's short-term economic stability. Both high and low current ratios are bad as the former implies an excessive investment in current assets and the later means inadequate liquidity. Consideration of quality of current assets, especially inventories is important in the evaluation of short-term financial position. A firm will fail in meeting its current liabilities even if it maintains a current ratio of more than 2 : 1 if its inventories which form a high proportion of current assets are not easily saleable.

On the other hand, a firm will feel comfortable if the proportion of inventory is low and there is no selling problem. Thus, the Current Ratio should be interpreted in the light of the quality of current assets.

Long-Term Solvency Leverage Ratios

Long-term solvency is concerned with a firm's ability to honour its long-term debts as and when they fall due for repayment. It is also related with the regular payment of fixed interest charges so that the debt-holders do not compel the debtor company for liquidation of its business affairs. Earning power or profitability and its sound management determine solvency and exert powerful influence on the long-term survival of any undertaking.

We know that a company introduces financial risk by employment of debt capital in its total resources. The degree of risk varies with the amount of debt in the total finds. It is truely said—Higher the debt, higher is the financial risk. Therefore, the degree of financial risk may be measured by measuring the proportion of long-term debts in the capitalisation of any company. Debenture holders and financial institutions are interested in the long-term solvency of debtor companies. They prefer that the debt-content in the capital structure is lower or within manageable limits. Investors like to make investment in equity shares of companies in which promoters stake in the form of equity capital is far more than the loan capital.

There are a number of accounting ratios known as Leverage Ratios which are used to judge the long-term solvency of large business concerns as explained below:

(i) Debt-equity ratio

It is the ratio between debt and equity. Debt consists of all long-term liabilities which are in the form of debentures, loans from the financial institutions, public deposits and any other long-term business obligation. And equity stands for paid up equity and preference share capital and retained earnings in different forms such as Profit and Loss (cr.) general reserve and other free reserves. The debt to Equity ratio is calculated simply by dividing the long-term debts by the shareholders equity as follows:

$$\text{Debt-Equity Ratio} = \frac{\text{Long-term Debts}}{\text{Shareholders Equity}}$$

As a general rule, debts should not exceed shareholders equity. Thus a debt-equity ratio of 1 : 1 is considered reasonable from the view point of long-term solvency. An increasing debt-equity ratio beyond one is considered as a sign of increasing financial risk and a danger to the long-term solvency. However, the ratio may be interpreted in the light of the prevailing business practice and the economic conditions under which the firm is operating. A firm can easily afford to work with a high debt-equity ratio if it is experiencing a phase of prosperity under which the earnings ratio is more than the rate of interest or cost of borrowed funds. In an effort to raise the disposable profit to equity shareholders, the companies prefer to work with a debt-equity ratio of 2 : 1. Though a low debt-equity ratio representing a low debt content in capital plan may be viewed as safer yet it may not be profitable. A low ratio will imply that the company has not rightly recognised the importance of debt capital in harnessing the profitable business opportunities. Therefore, the management can decide a workable debt-equity ratio after considering external and internal factors such as existence of profitable business opportunities, legal requirements, availability of funds at a reasonable rate, control considerations, etc.

(ii) Proprietary Ratio

With the help of this ratio we can understand the manner of financing of total assets and also the exposure of an undertaking to financial risk. This ratio expresses relationship between shareholders funds and total assets.

$$\text{Proprietary Ratio} = \frac{\text{Shareholders Funds}}{\text{Total Assets}}$$

The meaning of shareholders fund is the same as explained in case of debt-equity ratio and total assets means the total of fixed, current and other assets or simply the total of the Balance Sheet. The calculation and interpretation of this ratio may be explained below:

Suppose, total assets in a company on any given date is 120

crores and the shareholders funds amount to Rs. 72 crores. In this case the proprietory ratio is 0.6 or 60% (72 - 120). It shows that shareholders funds represent 60% of the total assets or 60% of the assets have been financed out of proprietors funds and the remaining 40% money has come from external sources (debts). A higher proprietory ratio is better from long-term solvency point of view, but it will suffer from the same limitation as the Debt-Equity Ratio suffers as the former ratio is a variant of the later one.

(iii) Capital-Gearing Ratio

The capital-gearing ratio is calculated to measure the proportion of fixed-charges-bearing securities in relation to owners equity.

We know that the preference share capital and debentures are the fixed charges-bearing securities which are paid at a fixed rate before anything can be paid to equity shareholders. There is no particular rate at which the equity shareholders will receive the dividend which depends upon the availability of profits in the company. The capital-gearing ratio is expressed as under:

$$\text{Capital-gearing Ratio} = \frac{\text{Preference capital + debentures}}{\text{Equity capital + Reserve and Surplus}}$$

As a general rule, the proportion of preference capital + debenturers should not exceed the equity capital + Reserves and Surplus. A company is said to be evenly-geared if the proportion between the two sources of finances is equal which means a capital-gearing ratio of 1. A company with a capital gearing ratio of more than 1 is called high-geared company which is subjected to high degree of financial risk threatening long-term solvency of the company. A low ratio (lesser than 1) depicts lower content of fixed cost bearing securities in the capital structure which is considered less risky by debenture holders and preference shareholders. But a lower ratio may not serve the interests of equity shareholders as it limits their gains which could be achieved by the employment of fixed cost securities atleast in a phase of prosperity. It is very difficult to suggest an ideal capital-gearing ratio because it is governed by numerous factors such as management's desire to retain control, availability of debt capital prevalent business conditions etc.

(iv) Coverage Ratios

Long-term solvency of a firm not only depends upon the adequacy of owners equity but it is also affected to a large extent by the availability of adequate surplus or profit which could be used to pay outsiders claims for interest and instalment of principal on due dates. The long-term creditors are interested in coverage ratios which measure the ability of a firm to service their debts. A firm can survive in the long-term only if it generates sufficient profits to meet its long-term creditors claims, satisfy shareholders expectations for reasonable dividend and also build up reserves for economic stability. Therefore, the solvency may be considered in the light of the quantum of profits.

How many times the annual claims for interest and preference dividend are covered by the profit in a particular financial year is an important consideration in the analysis of long-term solvency of a firm?

We may calculate total Coverage Ratio to determine the extent to which the fixed interest and preference dividends are covered by operating profits as under:

$$\text{Total Coverage Ratio} = \frac{\text{Profit Before Interest and Taxes}}{\text{Total Fixed Charges}}$$

Illustration—12

Calculate Coverage Ratio from the information given below:

10,00,000 Equity shares of 10 each,	10000000
12% debentures	6000000
8% preference share capital	5000000
Operating profit before interest and taxes	Rs. 60,00,000

Corporate Tax rate = 50%

Solution

$$\text{Total Coverage Ratio} = \frac{\text{Profit before Interest and Taxes}}{\text{Total Fixed Charges}}$$

Total fixed charges = Interest and debenturs = 7,20,000

Preference Share dividend = 4,00,000

11,20,000

$$\text{Total Coverage Ratio} = \frac{60{,}00{,}000}{11{,}20{,}000} = 5.35 \text{ times}$$

Interpretation of coverage ratio. Like any other ratios, the interpretation of coverage ratio requires a lot of industry experience. There is no standard coverage ratio for comparison with the actual ratio. However, a ratio of 5.35 signifies that the fixed-income-bearing securities holders need not worry even if the operating profit declines to 1/5.35 level. An analyst for debt-holders may fix a reasonable standard coverage ratio. A ratio higher than the standard one would be interpreted positively to indicate solvency and a lower ratio will a sign of danger signal or lack of solvency.

Higher coverage ratio favours the long-term creditors but it may not be the interest of the company. If the profits are abnormally low, a higher coverage ratio is certainly due to low debt content in the capitalization of the company. It may mean that the company has not used a proper coverage to enhance the worth of its shareholders. A low coverage ratio is a sign of worry both to management and lender of money and preference shareholders. If it is desired to know the extent of cushion provided separately to lenders of money and preference equity holders, he may calculate (a) Interest Coverage Ratio and (b) Dividend Coverage by using the following formula:

$$\text{Interest Coverage Ratio} = \frac{\text{Profit before interest \& Taxes}}{\text{Interest Charges}}$$

$$\text{Dividend Coverage Ratio} = \frac{\text{Profit after Interest and Taxes}}{\text{Preference Dividend}}$$

Using the figures of the previous illustration, these ratios are computed below:

$$\text{Interest Coverage Ratio} = \frac{60{,}00{,}000}{7{,}20{,}000} = 8.33$$

Profit after Interest & Taxes:

Total Profit =		60,00,000
Less:		
Interest	7,20,000	
Taxes	26,40,000	33,60,000
Profit Available for Appropriation =		26,40,000

$$\text{Dividend Coverage Ratio} = \frac{26,40,000}{4,00,000} = 6.6.$$

The interpretation of these ratios will be in the same way as total coverage ratio i.e. a higher ratio will be better from lender of money and preference shareholders point of view and vice versa.

Activity Ratios

Activity ratios are concerned with the judgement of operational efficiency which is governed by the utilization of assets of any enterprise. Proper management of assets pushes up the sale and operating profits. The rapidity with which the assets are converted or turned over into sales reflects the extent of efficiency of utilization of assets. Thus, the Activity Ratios attempt to show the extent of generation of Sales (turnover) as a result of employment of a certain asset like inventory, debtors, other current assets, fixed assets etc. These ratios are also called Turnover Ratios as they attempt to measure the conversion of assets into turnover by establishing a relationship between turnover and different types of assets. Computation and interpretation of the Activity Ratios which are generally used to judge the efficiency of assets utilization are explained below:

(A) Inventory-Turnover Ratio. This ratio measures the rapidity with which the inventory (unsold stock) is replaced during an accounting year. It is calculated by dividing the cost of goods sold by average inventory. Thus,

$$\text{Inventory-Turnover} = \frac{\text{Cost of goods Sold}}{\text{Average Inventory}}$$

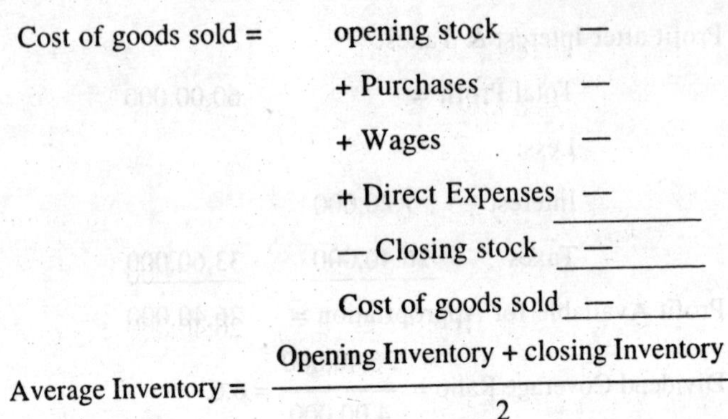

Cost of goods sold = opening stock —

\+ Purchases —

\+ Wages —

\+ Direct Expenses —

— Closing stock —

Cost of goods sold —

$$\text{Average Inventory} = \frac{\text{Opening Inventory} + \text{closing Inventory}}{2}$$

In case the data for cost of manufacture to determine cost of goods sold are not available, the Inventory-turnover ratio may be calculated simply by dividing the sales by closing inventory as shown below:

$$\text{Inventory-turnover} = \frac{\text{Sales / turnover}}{\text{Closing Inventory}}$$

The inventory-turnovers ratio based on cost of goods sold and average inventory is a logical measure as compared to the I-T ratio based on sales and closing inventory for the simple reasons that in the former case both the numerator and denominator are valued at cost as against the later in which numerator is valued at market value whereas the denominator is cost-based. Secondly, the concept of average inventory is better as its application helps in smoothening out the wide fluctuations in inventory holding at different time periods. Thirdly, the closing inventory may be valued or shown at a lower figure in an effort to show better position to trade creditors and others through window dressing technique.

Despite there merits of the first method, it may not be possible to use it for want of necessary data by an outsider. Therefore, the second method gains importance and favours with outside financial analyst.

Interpretation

A higher inventory turnover ratio indicates that a lower amount of money is tied up in inventory, which means better inventory management. Against it, a lower I-T Ratio means huge inventory level involving higher cost of holding inventories to the economic disadvantage of the firm. The financial analyst should not draw conclusion on the basis of a single figure of inventory-turnover ratio but he should consider few ratios in the past and also pay attention to the qualitative aspects of the inventory. A low ratio may be due to the inclusion of obsolete items of inventory which are not saleable. If the excessive inventories are deliberately kept for gains in near future, then this fact may be noted while interpreting the ratio. Similarly, a high I-T Ratio may be the result of buying inventory items in small lots due to assured regular supplies by sellers.

(B) Debtors-turnover Ratio. This ratio is used to test the rapidity with which the debtors are converted into cash. It is calculated by dividing the credited sales by average debtors.

$$\text{Debtors-turnover} = \frac{\text{Credit Sales}}{\text{Average debtors}}$$

Supposing the annual credit sales in an organisation amounted to Rs. 36,00,000 and the amount of average debtors (opening debtors plus closing debtors divided by 2) for the same period was Rs. 6,00,000 the Debtors-turnover ratio will be,

$$\text{Debtors-turnover} = \frac{36{,}00{,}000}{6{,}00{,}000} = 6 \text{ times.}$$

Generally, a higher Debtors-turnover ratio indicates successful credit policy and a low ratio is an indication of a rigid credit policy.

In case the informations with regard to Credit Sales and opening and closing debtors are not available, then the Debtors-turnover may be computed by dividing the Total Sales by closing debtors. However, the comparison should be made consistently on an uniform basis.

Average Debt Collection Period

A clear idea of a firm's credit policy may be had by computing average debt-collection period which is defined as a period of time for which a firm has to wait before collection of cash from debtors. It is computed as follows:

$$\text{Average Collection Period (debt collection period)} = \frac{\text{Debtors}}{\text{Credit sales per day}}$$

(Average credit sales is arrived at by dividing total credit sales by 360 on the assumption that the sales are effected uniformly throughout the year)

Using previous figures the Average collection period is calculated as under:

$$\text{Average Collection-period} = \frac{6,00,000}{\frac{36,00,000}{360}}$$

$$= 6,00,000 \times \frac{360}{36,00,000}$$

$$= 60 \text{ days}$$

A shorter collection period is always preferable to a longer debt collection period as the former clearly indicates that the debtors are more frequently converted into cash values whereas the later implies requirements of more working capital to finance trade debtors. The analyst should not only take into account the firm's terms of credit but also take into consideration the industry norm for debt collection period while commenting upon the credit policy of the firms under his consideration. If the average collection period is more than the credit period allowed to customers and also the industry norm, then it is presumed that the firm's credit and collection performance is poor. A too low debt-collection period may also not be in the interest of a firm as it restrict credit sales and thus forgoe expected gains out of credit sales.

It may be pointed out that the Debtors-turnover ratio and the Average Collection period are closely related to each other. The debtors turnover ratio can be obtained by dividing days in a year by average collection period. In the same manner, the days is a year may be divided by debtors-turnover to arrive at the average collection period as show below. (same data are used)

$$\text{Debtors-turnover} = \frac{\text{Days in a year}}{\text{Average collection period}}$$

$$= \frac{360}{60} = 6 \text{ days.}$$

$$\text{Average collection period} = \frac{\text{Days in a year}}{\text{Debtors-turnover}}$$

$$= \frac{360}{6} = 60 \text{ days.}$$

Ageing Schedule

All the debtors are not the same quality-wise. There may be some debtors who are prompt in making payments where as some others make payments not before the expiry of period of credit. Few debtors remain outstanding even after the expiry of period of credit. Average collection period does not serve the purpose of an analyst who is interested in the study of quality of debtors. Ageing Schedule gives a better picture and a firm may develop a proper strategy of debt collection or review its credit policy in the light of information which an Ageing schedule provides. Ageing schedule shows outstanding amount against debtors period-wise as shown in an hypothetical schedule as follows:

Outstanding Days	*Outstanding Amount*	*Percentage to total Debtors*
upto 30	66,000	11.00
31 - 35	1,20,000	20.00
36 - 40	1,50,000	25.00
41 - 45	1,80,000	30.00
46 - 50	30,000	5.00
51 - 55	24,000	4.00
56 - 60	18,000	3.00
61 and above	12,000	2.00
Total	6,00,000	100.00

An analysis of the above table reveals particular percentage of debtors which remain unpaid for particular days and amount. If the period of credit allowed to debtors is 45 days, 14% of the debtors are over-due. On the basis of such a study slow-paying debtors can be spotted and the firm can deal with such debtors suitabley.

Assets-Turnover Ratio

Investments in the form of different assets help produce and sell goods which generate surplus for achievement of business objectives. The performance activity can also be judged by the calculation of Assets - turnover ratio which expresses relationship between sales and total assets employed as shown below:

$$\text{Assets-turnover ratio} = \frac{\text{Sales}}{\text{Total Assets}}$$

The correctness of this ratio depends upon the right meaning attached to the meaning of "Total Assets." Total assets simply means all fixed assets at their depreciated values plus the net current assets only. Capitalised expenditure, if any, shown in the Balance Sheet as an asset is not considered as asset for the purpose of ratio computation. Thus total assets represent capital employed which includes owners equity plus borrowed funds minus capitalised expenditure.

Illustration—13

From the following Balance Sheet, calculate total assets or capital employed for the purpose of computing assets-turnover ratio :

BALANCE SHEET AS ON (Rs. crores)

Share capital	100	Fixed Assets less depreciation	150
Reserve & Surplus	8		
15% debentures	50	Current Assets	40
Loans	20	Pre-operative expenses	3
Creditors	10		
Bills payable	5		
	193		193

Solution

Table Assets:	Fixed Assets		150
	Current Assets	40	
	Less current liabilities	15	
			25
	Total		175
Alternately :	Owners Equity		
	Share Capital		100
	Reserve and Surplus		8
			108
	Borrowed funds:		
	15% debentures	50	
	Loans	20	
			70
			178
	Less Pre-operative Exp.		3
	Total		175

Suppose the sales amount to Rs. 525 crores, then the assets-turnover ratio will be,.

$$\text{Assets-turnover ratio} = \frac{525}{175} = 3 \text{ times.}$$

The assets-turnover ratio of 3 shows that every rupee invested in assets generates a sale of Rs. 3. A higher ratio is indicative of better utilization of assets and a low ratio depicts under-utilization of assets. For a better understanding the ratio may be compared with similar ratio in the past and the industry ratio. If inter-firm comparison is to be made, then the age of the assets employed in the firms should also he considered as the ratio with old depreciated assets is likely to be more as compared with new assets with more cost and less depreciation.

Illustration—14

Balance sheet of Preet and Co. Ltd. for the year ended on 31st March, 1994 stood as under:

Liabilities	*Amount*	*Assets*	*Amount*
Capital: 10,00,000 shares		*Fixed Assets:*	
of 10 each fully paid	1,00,00,000	Net Block (cost less	1,20,00,000
12% preference		depreciation)	
Share Capital	20,00,000	Capital work in progress	55,00,000
Reserve and Surplus:		*Investment:*	
General Reserve	25,00,000	Govt. Bonds	10,00,000
Capital Reserve	5,00,000	Investment in Subsidiary	15,00,000
Share Premium A/c	20,00,000	Investment in	
Surplus in P&L A/c	30,00,000	Share	10,00,000
		Current Assets,	
Loan Funds:		*Loans & Advances:*	
14% Debentures	25,00,000	Inventories	25,00,000
Public Deposits	5,00,000	Debtors	10,00,000
Secured loans	10,00,000	Bill Receivable	5,00,000
Unsecured loans	5,00,000	Marketable Securities	5,00,000
		Loans to subsidiary Co.	2,00,000
Current Liabilities		Miscellaneous expen-	
and Provisions:		diture not written off	11,00,000
Creditors	12,00,000		
Bills payable	5,00,000		
Outstanding expenditure	1,00,000		
Tax Payable	5,00,000		
	2,68,00,000		2,68,00,000

Other Informations

(i) During the year the company earned a profit before interest and taxes and preference dividend, Rs. 50,00,000.

(ii) All debtors are realizable at short notice.

(iii) Loans to subsidiaries can be withdrawn by a short notice

(iv) Management desires a return of 24% on total assets.

You are required to calculate the following accounting ratios:

A. Return on Investment Ratio (ROI)
B. Liquidity /Quick/Acid Test Ratio
C. Debt - Equity Ratio
D. Current Ratio.
E. Capital-gearing ratios.

Also comment on the profitability, liquidity and solvency of the company.

Solution

$$\text{(A) Return on Investment (ROI)} = \frac{\text{Profit before Interest \& Taxes}}{\text{Capital employed}}$$

$$\text{ROI} = \frac{\text{Profit before Int. and Taxes}}{\text{Total Assets} - \text{Misc. Expenses}}$$

$$= \frac{50{,}00{,}000}{2{,}68{,}00{,}000 - 11{,}00{,}000} = \frac{50{,}00{,}000}{2{,}57{,}00{,}000}$$

$$= 0.1945 \text{ or } 19.45\%.$$

The Return of 19.45% is on the gross investment or capital employed. For better understanding of profitability, it may be further calculated on net capital and proprietors capital as under :

$$\text{Return on Net Capital} = \frac{\text{Profit before Interest \& Taxes}}{\text{Gross Capital} - \text{Current liabilities}}$$

$$= \frac{50{,}00{,}000}{2{,}57{,}00{,}000 - 23{,}00{,}000}$$

$$= \frac{50{,}00{,}000}{2{,}34{,}00{,}000} = 0.2136$$

$$\text{or } 21.36\%$$

$$\text{Return on Proprietors capital} = \frac{\text{Profit before Interest and Taxes}}{\text{Gross Capital} - (\text{Current Liabilities} + \text{Loan Funds})}$$

$$= \frac{50,00,000}{2,57,00,000 - (23,00,000 + 45,00,000)}$$

$$= \frac{50,00,000}{2,57,00,000 - 68,00,000}$$

$$= \frac{50,00,000}{1,89,00,000} = 0.2645$$

or 26.45%.

The return of 19.45% does not fulfil the desires of management. Therefore, the company's profitabilitv is poor.

(B) Liquid/Quick/Acid Test Ratio $= \frac{\text{Liquid Assets}}{\text{Current Liabilities}}$

$$= \frac{22,00,000}{23,00,000}$$

= C.9565 or 95.65%.

Compared with the customery ratio of 1:1, the Acid Test is almost satisfied. Hence, the company enjoys liquidity.

(C) Debt - Equity Ratio $= \frac{\text{Long-term debts}}{\text{Shareholders Equity}}$

$$= \frac{40,00,000}{2,00,00,000} = 0.2$$

or 20%.

The debt-content of 20% as compared to shareholders equity is much below the usual norm of 100%. Thus, the company's degree of financial risk is very low and it enjoys long-term solvency. Such a low proportion of debts cannot be said to be in the interest of shareholders, especially when the company is passing through a phase of prosperity.

(D) Current Ratio $= \frac{\text{Current Assets}}{\text{Current Liabilities}}$

$$= \frac{47,00,000}{23,00,000}$$

$= 2.043$ or 204.3%.

Compared with the customery current ratio of 2:1, the ratio of 204.3% very well satisfies the short-term solvency of the company.

$$\text{(E) Capital-gearing Ratio} = \frac{\text{Preference Capital + Debentures}}{\text{Equity Capital + Reserve and Surplus}}$$

$$= \frac{20,00,000 + 25,00,000}{1,00,00,000 + 80,00,000}$$

$$= \frac{45,00,000}{1,80,00,000} = 0.25 \text{ or } 25\%.$$

Capital-gearing Ratio of 0.25 or 25% is too low which means the company has not used proper leverage to lift shareholders earnings. It enjoys long-term solvency from long-term creditors point of view.

Illustration —15

The Jolly Plastics Ltd. published its annual accounts for the year ended on 31st March, 1995 as under:-

BALANCE SHEET AS AT 31ST MARCH 1995

Rs. (000)

Share capital:		Land & buildings	60,00
10,00,000 shares of		Plant & machinery	80,00
10 each fully paid	10,000	Furniture and fixtures	5,00
12% preference capital of	20,00	capital work in progress	60,00
10 each			
General reserve	25,00	Investments in	10,00
Share premium A/C	20,00	Govt. securities	
Dividend equalisation fund	10,00	Investment in subsidiary Co	15,00
Workmen compensation and welfare fund	5,00	Investments in debentures	1500

Debenture redemption fund	10,00	Unsold stock	30,00
		Work in progress	5,00
Profit and loss A/C	30,00	Bills receivable	5,00
14% debentures	60,00	Shares of Blue-Chip	12,00
Public deposit	10,00	Companies	
Secured loans	10,00	Sundry debtors	25,00
Unsecured loans	5,00	Cash balances	5,00
		Pre-operative exp.	10,00
Trade creditors	15,00		
Bills payable	5,00		
Secured interest	7,00		
Tax payable	5,00		
	3,37,00		3,37,00
Contingent liability 5,00			

PROFIT AND LOSS ACCOUNT FOR THE YEAR ENDED AT 31ST MARCH 1995

(Rs 000)

To Opening Stock	30,00	By Sales	3,00,00
" Purchases	1,70,00	By Closing Stock	50,00
" Wages	50,00		
" Manufacturing Expenses	5,00		
" Gross Profit c/d	95,00		
	3,50,00		3,50,00
To Salaries	540	By Gross Profit b/d	95,00
" Printing & Stationery	20	By Other Incomes	5,00
" Postage and Telegrams	10		
" Rent	3,00		
" Insurance	40		
" Depreciation	30,00		
" Advertising and Other Selling Expenses	2,50		
" Interest on Debentures and Loans	11,25		

" Profit	47,15		
Total	1,00,00		1,00,00
" General Reserve	10,00	By Profit	47,15
" Dividend Equalization Fund	4,00		
" Debenture Redemption	5,00		
" Labour Welfare Fund	3,50		
" Provision for Tax	20,00		
" Profit and Loss A/c	4,65		
	47,15		47,15

You are required to comment on the profitability, liquidity and solvency of the above company in the light of the industry norms as given below:

	Industry Norms:
Gross Margin	28%
Net Margin	16%
Return on Total Resources	15%
Earning per share	5.0
Liquidity Ratio	1.0
Current Ratio	2.0
Proprietary Ratio	50%

Profitability

$$\text{Gross Profit Ratio} = \frac{\text{Gross Profit}}{\text{Sales}} = \frac{9{,}500}{30{,}000}$$

$$= 0.3166$$

or 31.66%

$$\text{Net Profit Ratio} = \frac{\text{Net Profit}}{\text{Sales}} = \frac{4715}{3{,}00{,}00} = 0.1572$$

or 15.72%

Return on Total Resources = $\dfrac{4715}{32,700}$ = 0 1442

or 14.42%

Earning Per Share= $\dfrac{\text{Earning Before Interest \& Taxes}}{\text{Number of Shares Outstanding}}$

$= \dfrac{4715 + 1125}{1000 + 200} = \dfrac{5840}{1200} = 4.87$

Liquidity Ratio : $\dfrac{\text{Liquid Assets}}{\text{Current Liabilities}} = \dfrac{4700}{32,00} = 1.46$

or 146%

Current Ratio = $\dfrac{\text{Current Assets}}{\text{Current Liabilities}} = \dfrac{\text{Liquid Assets+Non-liquid Assets}}{\text{Current Liabilities}}$

$= \dfrac{4700 + 3500}{3200}$

$= \dfrac{8200}{3200} = 2.56$

or 256%.

Proprietory Ratio = $\dfrac{\text{Shareholders Funds}}{\text{Total Assets}}$

Shareholders Funds =	Share Capital	12000
	General Reserve	2500
	Share Premium	2000
	Dividend Equalisation Fund	1000
	Workmen Compensation Fund	500
	Debenture Redemption Fund	1000

P & L A/C	3000
	22,000
Less Pre-operative Expenses	1000
Total	21,000

$$\text{Proprietory Ratio} = \frac{21,000}{33,700} = .623$$

Or 62.3%

Type of Ratio	*Company Ratio*	*Industry Ratio*
G/P Ratio	31.66	28%
N/P Ratio	15.72	16%
R O I (Gross)	14.42	15%
E.P.S.	4.87	5.0
Liquidity Ratio	1.46	1.0
Current Ratio	2.56	2.0
Proprietary Ratio	62.3	50%

Comments

Gross margin of .3166 or 31.66% is more than the industry gross margin of 28%. Hence, the gross profitability is fairly good. But the Net profit margin and Return an investments of 15.72% and 14.42% are a little less than the industry norms for the same. The EPS of 4.87 is also lesser than the industry EPS of 5.00. In this manner, though the gross profitability is higher than the industry norm yet the net profit margins, ROI and EPS are below industry norms. The causes for below standard performance need to be investigated to pinpoint the factors for less than standard performance. However, the company enjoys sufficient liquidity and short-period solvency as reflected by liquidity and current ratios. The proprietory ratio of .623 or 62.5% as compared to 50% for industry shows that the company is more reliant an shareholders funds for financing its assets. This ratio suggest long-term solvency of the company.

Illustration—16

Using the data of annual accounts as given in illustration No. 15, Calculate coverage ratios such as (a) Total Coverage Ratio, (b) Interest Coverage Ratio and Dividend Coverage Ratio. Do you think the profitability is sufficient to satisfy fixed-charges bearing security holders?

(a) Total Coverage Ratio = $\dfrac{\text{Profit before Interest and Taxes}}{\text{Total Fixed Charges}}$

$$= \frac{4715 + 1125}{1080} = \frac{5840}{1080}$$

$= 5.41$ times

(b) Interest Coverage Ratio = (for Debentures) $\dfrac{\text{Profit before Interest \& Taxes}}{\text{Deb. Interest Charges}}$

$$= \frac{4715 + \text{Interest on deb.}}{840}$$

$$= \frac{4715 + 840}{840} = \frac{5555}{840}$$

$= 6.61$ times

(c) Dividend Coverage Ratio = (Preference Dividend) $\dfrac{\text{Profit after Interest and Taxes}}{\text{Preference Dividend}}$

$$= \frac{4715}{240} = 19.64 \text{ times}$$

Comments: Fixed-cost bearing securities i.e. debentures and preference share capital are covered by profit to the extent of 6.61 and 19.46 times respectively. In our opinion, the profitability is sufficient to satisfy them, as they will not loose the interest and preference dividend even if the profit is declined to 1/6th and 1/19th of the present level respectively.

Illustration—17

Calculate the relevant Activity Ratios from the data contained in Income Statement and Balance Sheet of Illustration No. 15.

Main Activity Ratio to judge the utilization of various types of assets are (i) Inventory-turnover ratio, (ii) Debtors-turnover ratio (iii) Debt collection period, (iv) Total resources turnover ratio. 25% of the sales is credit sales.

Solution:

(1) Inventory-turnover $= \dfrac{\text{Cost of gross sold}}{\text{Average Inventory}}$

Cost of good sold =	Opening stock	3000
	Purchases	17000
	Wages	5000
	Mfg. Expenses	500
		25500
	Less closing stock	5000
	Cost of goods sold =	20500

Average Inventory $= \dfrac{\text{Opening Inventory + Closing Inventory}}{2}$

$= \dfrac{3000 + 500}{2} = \dfrac{8000}{2} = 4000.$

Inventory-turnover ratio $= \dfrac{20500}{4000} = 5.15$ times

(2) Debtors-turnover ratio $= \dfrac{\text{Credit Sales}}{\text{Average Debtors}}$

Since the information with regard to opening and closing debtors is not supplied, the debtors-turnover ratio may be calculated by dividing the annual credit sales by closing account of debtors including Bills Receivable.

Debtors-turnover ratio $= \dfrac{\text{Credit Sales}}{\text{Debtors + B/R}} = \dfrac{7500}{3000} = 2.5$ times

(3) Debt - Collection Period = $\frac{\text{Debtors}}{\text{Credit Sales per day}}$

$$= \frac{30,00,000}{\frac{75,00,000}{360}}$$

$$= 30,00,000 \times \frac{360}{75,00,000}$$

= 144 days 4.8 months.

(4) Total Resource-turnover = $\frac{\text{Sales}}{\text{Total Assets}}$

$$= \frac{3,00,00,000}{3,27,00,000} = 0.917$$

or 91.7%

	Name of Activity Ratio	*Ratio*	*Comment*
(1)	Inventory-Turnover	5.125	Activity can be interpreted only after considering few ratios in the past years or industry Ratio.
(2)	Debtors-turnover	2.5	Same as (1)
(3)	Debt Collection Period	144 days or 4.8 months	If the credit to customer is granted for any period lesser than 144 days, the Debt collection period of 144 days signifies a poor credit and collection performance.
(4)	Total Resource-turnover	.917 or 91.7%	It means a rupee invested in assets generates a sales of Rs. 0.917. If the standard set for sales is higher, than this ratio is certainly poor and the company is suggested to increase its efforts for more production and sales.

Illustration —18

A public limited company proposes to use the following accounting ratio to project its Balance Sheet for the next year. You are required to prepare the projected Balance Sheet.

Estimated Sales for next year	450000
Sales to net worth	2.5 times
Total Debt to net worth	0.65 : 1 or 65%
Current liabilities to net worth	0.25 : 1 or 25%
Current Ratio	3.6 : 1
Sales to inventory	5 times.
Average Collection Period =	36 days (year of 360 days)
Fixed Assets to net worth =	75%.

Solution:

$$\text{Sales to net worth} = \frac{\text{Sales}}{\text{Net worth}} = \frac{2.5}{1}$$

or Sales : Net worth

2.5 : 1

$$450000 : ? \quad \frac{1 \times 450000}{2.5} = 180000 \text{ (Net worth)}$$

Total Debt to net worth = 0.65 :1

? : 180000

$$= \frac{0.65 \times 180000}{1} = 117000 \text{ (Total Debt)}$$

Current liabilities = 0.25 : 1

to Net Worth ? : 180000

$$= \frac{.25 \times 18000}{1} = 45000 \text{ (current liabilities)}$$

Current Ratio = CA : CL

3.6 : 1

? : 45000

$$= \frac{3.6 \times 45000}{1} = 162000 \text{ (Current Assets)}$$

Sales to inventory = 5 : 1

450000 : ?

$$\frac{1 \times 450000}{5} = 90000 \text{ (Inventory)}$$

Average collection = 36 days

Period

$$\text{Debtors} = \frac{450000 \times 36}{360} = 45000 \text{ (Debtors)}$$

Fixed Assets to Net Worth = 0.75 : 1

= ? : 180000

$$= \frac{0.75 \times 180000}{1} = 135000 \text{ (Fixed Assets)}$$

PROJECTED BALANCE SHEET

Share Capital		Fixed Assets	1,35,000
(Net worth)	1,80,000	Stock	90,000
Debentures and loans	72,000	Debtors	45,000
Current liabilities	45,000	Cash (Balancing figure)	27,000
	2,97,000		2,97,000

Illustration —19

Prudential Financial Services Ltd. has received loan applications for two companies A and B which were operating with the following financial ratio:

	A Co.	B Co.
Acid Test Ratio	1.25:1	0.95:1
Current Ratio	2.15:1	1.80:1
Debt - Equity Ratio	1.50:1	1.65:1
Interest Coverage Ratio	8 times	6 times.

Loan is repayable after 2 years. After the grant of loan, the debt-equity ratio in A and B Ltd. will change to 1.85:1 and 2:1 respectively.

You are required to give your opinion whether the loans can be granted to both the companies?

Solution

Granting of loans is governed by the following:

(a) Availability of loanable fund.
(b) Degree of financial risk.
(c) Profitability and Repaying capacity of borrower.

So for as granting loans to company A is concerned, all the necessary fundamental, are favourable. It enjoys short-term as well as long-term solvency as the Acid Test Ratio, Current Ratio and Debt-Equity Ratio are favourable as compared to customary norms for the same. Interest-coverage ratio is quite high and the borrower is expected to repay the interest on loan on times. If loanable funds is not a constraint the loan to B can also be granted as it is also more or less equally good company as shown by its solvency ratios and the interest coverage ratios. Debt-Equity Ratio of 2:1, after the grant of loans, remains within the accepted norm.

QUESTIONS

1. What do you mean by Financial Statements? What purpose the construction of such statements serve in an enterprise?
2. What are different forms in which the financial statements of a public limited company can be presented? Do you have any suggestion to offer in this connection?
3. Name the parties which are interested in financial statement analysis and clearly show their respective interests.
4. What are different accounting concepts and conventions on which the book-keeping and accountancy is based? How is the sound knowledge

of conventions and concepts of accounting is helpful to a management accountant?

5. Do you think the concept of 'cost' and convention of 'conservatism' have outlived their utility in accounting analysis for management purposes? If so, give argument in support of your answer.
6. Give a brief account of the techniques of Financial Statement analysis.
7. What is an Accounting Ratio? Explain the significance of Accounting Ratio technique in financial analysis of a company.
8. How do you classify accounting ratios? Which basis of classification do you consider more appropriate?
9. The success of accounting ratio technique depends upon many things. What precaution will you take in the analysis and interpretation of financial statements?
10. How do you apply the accounting ratio technique in the measurement of profitability of a business concern? Do you think that an increase in Gross Profit Ratio is always an enhancement of profitability?
11. Explain the concepts of 'capital employed' and 'profit' as they are used in the measurement of Return on Investment (ROI).
12. How do the E.P.S. and P/E ratios help an investors in making investment decisions?
13. Explain the following Accounting Ratio:
    a. Acid Test Ratio
    b. Current Ratio
    c. Debt - Equity Ratio
14. "Current Ratio should always be 2:1 to represent adequate short-period Solvency." Comment on this statement

    OR

    "Current Ratio is a quantitative test and not a qualitative test of the adequacy of working capital." Critically examine this statement.
16. Distinguish between liquid and other current assets and the purpose with which the liquidity ratio and current ratio are computed.
17. What are proprietary and capital gearing ratios? Explain the uses of these ratios.
18. What is an Activity Ratio ? What purpose an activity ratio serve? Explain with examples the calculation of few popular Activity Ratios.
19. How will you analyse the financial statements from the view point of—
    (a) An investor
    (b) Lender of money
    (c) Management.
20. The Balance Sheet and Income Statement of New Life Limited stood as under:

	31st December 1994 (Rs.)	31st Dec. 1995 (Rs.)
Land and Buildings	14,00,000	11,20,000
Plant and Machinery	25,75,000	20,60,000
Furniture and fixtures	1,50,000	4,20,000
Government securities	75,000	4,25,000
Inventories	4,50,000	8,50,000
Work in progress	2,50,000	4,50,000
Bills Receivable	50,000	30,000
Debtors	2,50,000	4,00,000
Cash and Bank Balance	75,000	69,000
Miscellaneous Expenditure	1,50,000	1,20,000
	4,25,000	59,35,000
Share capital : 2,50,000 shares of Rs. 10/-	25,00,000	25,00,000
Reserves and Surplus	6,00,000	8,50,000
Profit and Loss A/C	4,00,000	5,10,000
15% Debentures	10,00,000	10,00,000
Loans	5,00,000	6,00,000
Creditors	3,50,000	4,00,000
Tax Payable	50,000	50,000
Outstanding rent	25,000	25,000
	54,25,000	59,35,000

INCOME STATEMENT

FOR THE YEAR ENDED AT 31ST DEC. 1995

Sales	95,00,000	
Other incomes	6,50,000	1,01,50,000
Less Cost of goods sold		83,50,000
		18,00,000
Less Administration	6,90,000	
Expenses		
Selling & distribution		

Expenses	32,00,000	
Financial charges	4,00,000	
Miscellaneous Exp.	30,000	
		14,40,000
Profit for the year		3,60,000

Using the relevant accounting ratios, you are required to examine the (a) Profitability, (b) Liquidity and (c) Solvency of the Company. Also compute the Activity Ratios and comment upon them.

21. Comment on the liquidity and short-term and long-term solvency of the following company with the help of relevant accounting ratios i.e. Acid Test ratio, Current Ratio and Debt-Equity/Capital-gearing ratio.

BALANCE SHEET OF X LTD AS AT 30TH JUNE 1994

Share Capital		Land and Building	1,50,00,000
1000000 shares of Rs. 10 each	1,00,00,000	Plant and Machinery	3,50,00,000
2,00,000 cumulative Pref. Shares	20,00,000	Furniture and Fixtures	5,00,000
		Stock	55,00,000
General Reserve	1,00,00,000	Debtors	50,00,000
Capital Reserve	50,00,000	Investments	10,00,000
Profit and Loss	80,00,000	Cash at Bank	5,00,000
12% debentures	2,00,00,000	Cash in hand	1,00,000
Secured loans	50,00,000	Preliminary Expenses not written off	34,00,000
Sundry creditors	50,00,000		
Tax liability	10,00,000		
	6,60,00,000		6,60,00,000

(M. Com. Bus. Mgt. J.M.I. 1995)

22. From the following particulars, prepare the Balance Sheet of A Limited:

Current ratio	1.5
Current assets/Fixed assets	1:2
Fixed assets to turnover	1:1
Gross profit	25%

Debtors velocity	2 months
Creditors velocity	2 months
Stock velocity	3 months
Debt-equity ratio	2:5
Working capital	Rs. 2,00,000

Working should form part of answer

(C.A. Final)

23. From the following particulars relating to a firm which sells its goods both for cash as well as on credit, calculate Debt-Collection Period:

Sundry debtors as on 1st Jan.	1994	75,000
Sundry debtors as on 31st Dec.	1994	1,10,000
Bills Recoverable as on 1st Jan.	1994	25,000
Bills Recoverable as on 31st Dec.	1994	20,000
Total Sales for the year	1994	5,50,000
Cash sales included in total sales		75,000
Provision for doubtful debts as on	31.12.94	5,000

3

Statement of Changes in Financial Position

(Funds Flow and Cash Flow Analysis)

The primary objective of the traditional Income Statement and Balance Sheet is to report to the interested parties the operational performance and economic position of an enterprise. An intelligent reader can gather sufficient idea about costs, revenues, profit/loss assets, liabilities and owners equity from these statements. Under the Companies Act, a company is required to include the figures of previous year in the financial accounts so that the interested parties may compare individual figures for better understanding of the corporate performance and economic position. The schedules attached to published account explain important items for the knowledge of the concerning parties. The format of published accounts has been revised from time to time with a view to providing more and more informations to the shareholders, creditors and others. No body can deny the usefulness of the traditional form of annual accounts which form an important basis for making financial decisions.

No doubt the annual accounts in their traditional forms are very important but they suffer from certain limitations. The serious limitation of a Balance Sheet is that it is a static document as it shows the economic position at a point of time and fails to show fully the movements or changes in the assets, liabilities and owners equity. From the financial accounts in their usual form, it is not clear as to how the funds were generated and how they were utilised between the closing dates of two Balance Sheets. In order to provide such informations, another document known as Statement of Changes in Financial Position is prepared. This document shows the changes in financial position between the closing dates of the Balance Sheets.

In this connection it is important to understand clearly the meaning of the word 'Fund' which is used in three different senses. In a narrow sense, fund means cash and the statement based on this concept is known as Cash Flow Statement. In a broader sense, fund means all financial resources which flows through working capital accounts and fixed capital accounts and a fund flow statement based on this concept is almost a new form of Balance Sheet. The APB (Accounting Principles Board, U.S.A.) has recommended the preparation and presentation of statement of changes in financial position according to the broadest sense of the term 'Fund.' However, the meaning of the 'Fund' in both the narrow as well as broader senses do not find favour with many academicians and practitioners who prefer to consider Fund in the sense of Working Capital i.e. Current assets minus Current liabilities. In this chapter, we shall illustrate the preparation of statement of changes in financial position based on all the three concepts of Fund.

A Funds Flow Statement is known by different names such as: (i) Where Got Where Gone Statement, (ii) Statement of sources and application of funds, (iii) Statement of changes in working capital, (iv) Statement showing summary of financial operations, (v) Statement of sources and application of working capital, (vi) Statement of changes in financial position, (vii) Funds Flow statement, etc. It may be noted that there is no official name of the statement as its preparation is still obligatory. Only few enlightened firms in India publish this statement for the guidance of their members and creditors. However, it is advisable that the title of the statement reflects the concept of fund on which it is based.

Use of Funds Flow Statement

The Funds Flow Statement is increasingly being used as a tool of financial analysis by the management, bankers, financial institutions, investors and other parties interested in understanding the changes in financial position of an undertaking. The use and significance of a Funds Flow Statement to different parties can be understood from the following:

Management

A Funds Flow Statement is an important tool in the hands of management which is interested to know the changes in financial position with a view to evaluating their financial policies and take decisions for future. The historical funds flow statement tells the management the different sources from which the funds became available and the manner in which they were utilised. The knowledge of the sources and application of funds can threw light on many problems such as: (i) why did the organisation experience shortage of working capital despite handsome profits in the past year, (ii) how the company was able to declare dividend despite meagre profits, (iii) why were additional funds raised to finance expansion programme despite sufficient internal accruals, (iv) how the company was able to redeem its debentures and repay loans, (v) how the company possesses more than adequate funds despite poor operational performance of the enterprises, (vi) how the additional demand for working capital was met?

The historical Funds Flow Statement also helps the management in understanding and evaluating the firm's financing policies. It will tell the management whether the budgeted financing decisions were adhered to and if not what were the reasons for it. In case of unwarranted imbalances in the sources and application of Funds, the management can take remedial measures to correct the situation in future. Thus a funds flow statement can be used as a control device to make the financial planning more effective.

The Funds Flow Statement can also be prepared for future. A projected Fund Flow Statement shows the expected sources of funds and their application in a defined future period of time. The future developmental plans, payments to lenders of money, dividend decisions, working capital needs etc. depends upon the availability of funds. In case the expected funds inflow is lesser than the expected fund outflow, the management can revise its future financial plans and follow a more realistic approach towards its financial decisions.

Financial Institutions

The financial requirements of industry for term loans are met by the specialised financial institutions and working capital needs are generally satisfied by commercial banks which ask for a copy of Funds Flow statement from the borrowing party. The historical funds flow statement provides sufficient guidance about the financial policies of the borrower and the projected funds flow statement gives an insight into the funds generating capacity and the manner of its utilization. No doubt the loans provided by financial institutions are generally fully secured against the assets of the borrowing company but it is the repaying capacity of the borrower which is more significant in decision-making by the lender of money. The financial institutions can provide funds to their best advantage if the projected funds flow statement show adequate funds from business operations and further issue of equity capital to provide them better protection.

Debentureholders

Debentureholders are the long-term creditors whose loan money is repayable after 5 to 7 years. They also interpret the Funds Flow statements in the same manner as the specialised financial institutions and take decisions to continue or not as the debentureholders of the borrowing company.

Trade Creditors

These include the firms which supply on credit the raw materials and other components for a short-period of time. The creditors are interested in the liquid position of the debtor company which depends largely on the funds from business operations. A study of funds flow statement clearly tells about the liquid position and the supplier of raw materials can review its own credit policy in the light of the liquidity position indicated by the funds flow statement.

Shareholders

A prudent shareholder keeps watch on financial policies being followed by the company in which he has financial stake as a equity shareholder. A study of funds flow statement for the past few years throw sufficient light on the manner in which the funds are being generated and the way they are utilized. It also contains the data for operational inflow which greatly affect the liquidity of the enterprise. A shareholder may retain its shareholdings if it finds that the company has persued right financial policies and it also has adequate potential for generating funds, specially from business operations to meet his expectations for dividend and appreciation in the capital value of investment. The potential shareholder can also form an idea about the financial health of an organisation from the study of its funds flow statement and take decision about his investment plan.

Limitations

The funds flow statement serves a useful purpose as is evident from the foregoing explanation. However, it suffers from certain limitations. Firstly, a funds flow statement cannot replace the traditional financial statements. Infact, a funds flow statement is prepared from the balance sheets and other important informations pertaining to sources and uses of funds. Secondly, a funds flow statement is not as much revealing as a balance sheet. It simply fills the gaps where a balance sheet fails to reflect the changes in financial position. Thirdly, it is based on the informations contained in the traditional final accounts. Therefore, it also suffers from the same limitations with which the usual published accounts suffer. Fourthly, it is argued that the component of cash is more important than the working capital because it is the cash and not the other components i.e. stock and receivables, which is required to pay off the liabilities of a concern. Fifthly, it is also argued that a balance sheet is itself in the nature of a fund flow statement as the liability side depicts the sources from which the funds generates and the assets side show the application of those funds and as such a funds flow statement is not significant.

Some of the arguments do not carry much weight. The fact remains that a funds flow statement serve a peculiar purpose of showing changes in the financial position through sources and application of funds between the dates of two balance sheets.

Preparation of Funds Flow Statement (Based on Working Capital Concept)

The preparation of a Funds Flow Statement is not difficult if we could identify the various sources of funds and the items for which these sources are used. The main sources of funds are: (i) Issue of equity capital and debentures; (ii) Sale of any assets for cash; (iii) Sale of investments; (iv) Raising of additional loans; (v) Non-trading receipts; (vi) Business operations. Let us briefly explain each of these sources as under:

1. Issue of Share Capital

The issue of additional shares for cash is a source of fund as it makes a positive change in the amount of fund which existed just before the happening of this transaction. The introduction of fresh capital as a source of fund increases immediately the working capital by the amount of cash receipts on capital account. If the shares are issued for consideration other than for cash, say for the acquisition of an asset, the fund will remain unaffected as the transaction will not bring any change in working capital. In such a case the transaction brings a change in non-current items only. The Asset Account and Capital Account are both non-current accounts.

2. Issue of Debentures

The debenture issue involves cash account and debenture account. The former is a current account and the latter is a non-current account. Therefore, it will form a source of funds. The working capital will be increased by the amount of cash received against debenture Account. If the debentures are issued not for cash or for the acquisition of any other current asset, the issue will not generate fund.

3. Sale of Fixed Assets

If a fixed asset is sold during the year for cash, it brings a positive change in the Fund and as such becomes a source of fund. In case, it is sold on credit, then also the fund inflow will take place as the credit sale of a fixed asset increases the debtors and decreases the fixed asset account.

4. Sale of Long-term Investment

Like sale of any other fixed assets, the sale of long-term investment also causes a positive change in the fund and thus becomes its source. The transaction of sale involves cash inflow and investment outgo. The former is a current account while the later is a non-current account.

5. Raising of Additional Loans

On raising additional loans, Cash Account (a current account) and Loan's Account (a non-current account) are affected. Therefore, the flow of fund takes place. The change increases the fund; therefore, it is a source of fund.

6. Non-trading Receipts

Non-trading receipts are the receipts which do not occur in the usual course of business. Compensation received, income tax refund, profit on sale of asset or investment, dividend received, etc., are the examples of non-trading receipts. The receipts on these accounts cause the fund to change positively. Therefore, they should be shown as a source of fund and the funds from business operations has to be adjusted accordingly.

7. Fund from Business Operations

The business operations results in profit or loss. In case of profit the fund is changed positively. Therefore, the profit becomes a source of fund. To find the real fund from business operations, the Trading and Profit and Loss Account has to be recast (we shall see a little later as to how is it done).

The Funds so generated may be utilised for the following purposes: (i) Repayment of preference share capital, (ii) Redemption of debentures, (iii) Purchase of fixed assets, (iv) Purchase of long-term investments, (vi) Non-trading payments, (vii) Operational losses, etc. In order to understand as to how these transactions cause the changes in Fund, a brief explanation is provided below:

1. Redemption of Preference Share Capital

On redemption of redeemable preference share capital, the cash outflow takes place. Cash is an important component of working capital which declines on repayment. On the other hand, the Capital Account is reduced by the amount of cash outflow. Thus the transaction affects one current account (cash account) and other non-current account (Capital Account).

2. Redemption of Debentures

The redemption of debentures uses the fund the same manner as the redemption of preference share capital. It also involves one non-current account and the other current account; therefore, the changes in flow of funds takes place.

3. Purchase of Fixed Assets

The purchase of a fixed assets affects cash, a current account and asset, a non-current account. Therefore, the transaction causes the fund to change negatively or the use of fund.

4. Purchase of Long-term Investment

Like purchase of an asset, the purchase of investment also uses fund.

5. Non-trading Payments

There are non-trading or unusual payments such as taxes and dividend which are shown as uses of funds and the fund from business operations is adjusted by adding back these items to the net profit as shown by the traditional profit and loss account.

Thus all the transactions which bring a change in the working capital cause the change in the flow of funds between the closing dates of two Balance Sheets. Only the transactions which change one current account alongwith a non-current account are either a source or an a application of Fund.

Proforma of a Funds Flow Statement

The Income Statement and Balance Sheet are prepared in accordance with the proforma as prescribed under the Indian Companies Act but there is no prescribed proforma for a Funds Flow Statement because the law does not require its preparation and publication. Therefore, a firm can prepare a Funds Flow Statement in any manner it deem fit. A specimen proforma of the statement in an account form is given below:

Funds Flow Statement
For the Year Ended on 31st March, 1989

Sources		*Application*	
1. Funds from business operations	—	1. Loss of funds due to operations	—
2. Issue of additional capital	—	2. Redemption of preference shares	—
3. Issue of debentures	—	3. Redemption of debentures	—
4. Sales of investment	—	4. Purchase of investments	—
5. Sales of Assets	—	5. Purchase of assets	—
6. Loans raised	—	6. Payment of Loans	—
7. Non-trading receipts	—	7. Tax paid	—
		8. Dividend paid	—
		9. Non-trading payments	—
		10. Increase in Working Capital	—
Total		Total	

A funds Flow Statement can also be prepared in a horizental form as under:

Funds Flow Statement as on 31st March, 1989

Source of Funds

1.	Funds from Business Operations	—
2.	Issues of shares	—
3.	Issues of debentures	—
4.	Sale of investment	—
5.	Sale of asset	—
6.	Loan raised	—
7.	Non-trading receipts	—
	Total Funds Generated	—

Application of Funds

1.	Loss of funds due to business operations	—
2.	Redemption of preference capital	—
3.	Redemption of debentures	—
4.	Purchase of Investments	—
5.	Purchase of asset	—
6.	Payment of loan	—
7.	Non-trading payments	—
	Total Funds Used	

Increase/Decrease in Working Capital

It may be noted that the positive funds from operations (profit)is the source of fund whereas negative operational funds (loss) represents use of funds. There will be either positive or negative operational flow of funds and accordingly it will figure only on one side of Funds Flow Statement. In case the total funds from all sources exceed the total application or use of funds, the balancing figure will be shown as Increase in Working Capital. Conversely, the decrease in Working Capital will be shown as the source of fund.

Steps in Preparation of Funds Flow Statement (Working Capital Basis)

For the preparation of a Funds Flow Statement, we need Balance Sheets and Income Statements for the last two years and other informations which are not revealed by the annual accounts but which have otherwise affected the movements of fund during the financial year. In case only the Balance Sheets are available, then other information affecting the funds from business operations and the financial position should be collected. The other informations needed for the preparation of a Funds Flow Statement are the depreciation charged on assets, provision made for taxation and dividend, capital expenditure written off, asset discarded without any recovery, loss on sale of assets, profit on sale of any capital asset, transfer from one account to another account, taxes and dividend paid during the year, interim dividend paid, non-trading incomes and expenditure or losses debited to Profit and Loss Account, etc. With such an information in hand, we can proceed to prepare the Funds Flow Statement in the following manner:

Step -I. Calculation of Funds from Business Operations

Funds from business operations result due to usual business operations of the firm. In order to know the profit earned or less suffered during a financial year, the Income Statement is prepared for that year. The profit or net operational inflow causes the Fund to change. Similarly, the loss or net operational outflow brings a change in the Fund. To calculate the net operational flow of Fund, the profit as shown by the traditional Income Statement need to be recast as it contains certain items of non-fund and non-operating nature. For example, depreciation is a non-fund item which does not result in the outflow of cash or it does not require any current expenditure to be incurred during the financial year. Therefore, the amount of depreciation charge should be added back to the profit in the calculation of Funds from Business Operations. Similarly writing-off of goodwill, patents, trade marks, preliminary expenses, discount on issue of shares and debentures, etc. are the items which figure on the debit side of Income Statement but they are also in the nature of depreciation not affecting the flow of funds. Such items, therefore, should be added back to profit. All appropriations of profits such as transfers to different reserves, provisions for taxation, proposed dividend, etc. not being operating costs should be added back to the profit figures. From the total so arrived at, the non-operating incomes like dividend received, income tax refund, compensation received, profit on sale of asset, etc. should be deducted to arrive at the figure of total operational inflow. The funds from business operations for the financial year can be calculated by deducting the profit at the beginning of the year from the total operational inflow for the year. The usual items added and subtracted from the profit as per income statement in search for Funds from Business Operations are as shown below:

Profit / Loss as Per Income Statement (at the end of the Year)

Add:	— Depreciation	...
	— Preliminary expenses	
	— Discount on issue of shares and debentures written off	...
	— Goodwill, trade mark, patents written off	...
	— Loss on sale of machine	...
	— Loss on investment sold	...
	— Interim dividend paid	...
	— Provision for taxation	...
	— Proposed dividend	...
	— Machine lost	...
	— Transfer to Reserves	... ...
Less	— Profit on sale of machine, investment or any other fixed asset	...

— Dividend received ...
— Tax Refund ... ...

Less Profit / loss at the beginning of the year ...

Funds from Business Operations ...

Step-II. Determination of Other Sources and Application of Fund

After having calculated the funds from business operations, the next step should be to find out the other sources and application of fund. For this purpose the Balance Sheet items should be carefully compared. How is a source or application identified is briefly explained below:

1. Share Capital

If the amount of current year's share capital is more than that of the previous amount, then it implies that the increase had been due to additional share issue and hence source of fund. Conversely, if the current year's capital has gone down, then it means repayment of capital and an application of fund. If the capital has increased due to issue of Bonus shares or issue of capital for consideration other than for cash, then such an issue will not affect the working capital and will not form a source of fund.

2. Debentures

An increase in the amount of current year's debentures amount ordinarily means a source of fund and a decrease an application of fund.

3. Loans

If a loan has been raised during the year for the first time, the current year's Balance Sheet will show it and it will form a source of fund. In case loan also stood in the previous year's Balance Sheet, then the comparison will reveal whether additional loan has been raised or a part of already existing loan repaid. An increase in current year's figure definitely means raising of additional loans and thus source of fund. The decrease in current years figure is obviously repayment and hence an application of fund.

4. Reserves and Surplus

Under this head, we find different types of reserves and credit balance of profit and loss account. The management accountant preparing the Funds Flow Statement should clearly understand that (i) the reserves which have been created during the year out of profit and which have already been considered in the computation of Funds from operations need not be considered again, (ii) if the profit on sale of asset or investment is directly transferred to Balance Sheet without its appearance in Income Statement, then such a Capital Reserve will not constitute a source of Fund as the total amount from such sale including capital profit will be treated as a source of fund, (iii) the amount received as premium on issue of additional shares is a source of funds, (iv) payment of dividend out of Dividend Equalization Fund constitute an application of Fund, (v) the Profit and Loss Account at the end of the year form the basis for the calculation of Funds from business operations.

5. Provision for Dividend and Taxation

These appear as a current liability in a Balance Sheet. If these are also treated as current liability, then no adjustment in Profit and Loss Account is needed and these can conveniently be treated alongwith other current liabilities in a separate schedule known as Schedule of Changes in Working Capital. We will learn about this schedule a little later in this chapter. In fact, the provisions out of profit do not constitute source of fund as they do not effect working capital.

6. Fictitious Assets

The fictitious assets such as goodwill, patents, trade mark, etc. when purchased originally constitute an application of fund. But, when we write them off in future years, they do not form a source of fund. However, they are added back in the profit to arrive at total funds from business operations.

7. Fixed Assets

If the value of an asset in the current year is more than the value in the previous year, it simply means the asset has been acquired during the year and hence an application of fund. On the other hand, a decrease in the current year's figure indicate sale and hence a source of fund. In this connection it may be clearly noted that the additional informations relating to depreciation, loss of assets, etc., should be taken into account and a separate fixed asset account prepared to know the net source or net application of fund. Total value realized from the sale of asset after allowing for profit or loss is always shown as source.

8. Investments

An investment as a source or an application of fund is treated in the same manner as fixed assets. Increase in the value of current years investment implies application and decrease means a source of fund. If additional informations regarding purchase or sale of investment are provided, then a separate Investment Account may be prepared to find out the actual purchase or sale forming application or source of fund.

9. Transfers

Transfers from one account to another do not affect a Fund Flow. For example, the transfer of 'Advances for Machinery' to Machinery Account does not cause any change in Fund. Such a transfer therefore, has to be ignored.

10. Miscellaneous Expenditures

Under this head, we find all those expenses which are yet to be written off by a company. The writing off of such an expenditure decreases the current year's figure but it cannot be treated as a source of fund. It is rightly written back to profit while calculating the funds from business operations. Any fresh expenditure of this nature will increase the current years figure and the additional expenditure should be treated as an application of fund because it effects the working capital.

11. Interim Dividend

It is the dividend which is paid during the financial year in expectation of better performance by a company. This appears as an expenditure on the debit side of a Profit and Loss Account. Since it is an usual or non-operating expenditure, it should be added back to the net profit to arrive at funds from business operations and then shown as an application of fund.

Step-III

After bringing in all the items of sources and application of fund, the Funds Flow Statement should be balanced. In case the 'Sources' exceed the 'Application,' there is an increase of working capital which means an use of Fund. On the other hand, if the Applications are more than the Sources, the difference will represents the Decrease in working capital or source of Fund ,

Schedule of Changes in Working Capital

The Schedule of changes in Working Capital is not considered as a part of Funds Flow Statement but it is generally accompanied with the Funds Flow Statement. All current assets and current liabilities are brought into the Schedule of Changes in Working Capital. The increase or decrease in individual items of current assets and current liabilities affecting the net change in working capital are depicted in the Schedule. The net increase or decrease in working capital is the same as shown in the Funds Flow Statement. If there is any variation between the two figures of increase/decrease of working capital as per Fund Flow Statement and schedule of changes in working capital, then it is an indication that some mistake has been committed somewhere in the calculation of funds from business operations in the determination of other sources and application of funds. The change in the individual items of current assets and current liabilities effect the working capital in the following way:

— Increase in current asset : Increase in working capital

— Decrease in current asset : Decrease in working capital

— Increase in current liability : Decrease in working capital

— Decrease in current liability : Increase in working capital

The Schedule of changes in Working Capital may be prepared as per the proforma given below:

Schedule of Changes in Working Capital

Current Assets/ liabilities	*Previous year*	*Current year*	*Increase in W.C.*	*Decrease in W.C.*
A. Current Assets:				
Stock				
Debtors				

Prepaid Expenses

Cash at Bank

Cash in hand

Other current Asset

TOTAL (A)

B. Current Liabilities:

Trade creditors

Bills Payable

Outstanding Exp.

Bank draft

Unclaimed dividend

Other current liability

TOTAL (B)

Increase/Decrease in

Working Capital

(A - B)

After having understood the basic concepts and other issues in the preparation of a Funds Flow Statement and Schedule of Changes in Working Capital, we are now in a position to prepare these statements.

It may be understood that the first Balance Sheet of an organisation is in the nature of a Fund Flow Statement. This is explained with the help of an illustration as shown below:

Illustration—1

ABC Ltd. was incorporated on Ist January, 1995. It started commercial production in March, 1995. The Balance Sheet of the Company for the year ended on 31st March, 1996 stood as under :

Balance Sheet As on 31st March, 1996

Capital & Liabilities	*Amount*	*Properties & Assets*	*Amount*
Equity Capital:		Land and Buildings	6,50,000
50,000 shares of 10/- each	5,00,000	Plant and Machinery	3,50,000
General Reserve	25,000	Stock	1,00,000

Profit & Loss Account	95,000	Debtors	40,000
Loans from IFCI	4,00,000	Cash at Bank	20,000
Sundry creditors	1,30,000	Cash in hand	5,000
Bills Payable	10,000	Preliminary Expenses	35,000
Outstanding Expenses	5,000		
Provision for Tax	35,000		
	12,00,000		12,00,000

You are required to represent the above Balance Sheet in the form of Funds Flow Statement and also prepare a Schedule of Changes in Working Capital.

Solution

Funds from Business Operations:		
Profit and Loss Account		95,000
Add : Transfer to general Reserves	25,000	
Provision for Tax	35,000	60,000
		1,55,000
Less Profit at beginning		
Funds from Business Operations		1,55,000

Funds Flow Statement
As on 31st March, 1996

Source of Funds		*Application of Funds*	
Funds from business operation	1,55,000	Purchase of Land & Buildings	6,50,000
		Purchase of Plant & Machinery	3,50,000
Issue of share capital	5,00,000	Preliminary expenses paid	35,000
Loans raised	4,00,000	Increase in Working Capital	20,000
	10,55,000		10,55,000

Schedule of Changes in Working Capital for the Year Ended on 31st March, 1990

	Previous Year	*Current Year*	*Increase in W.C.*	*Decrease in W.C*
A. Current Assets:				
Stock	—	1,00,000	1,00,000	—
Debtors	—	40,000	40,000	—
Cash at bank	—	20,000	20,000	—
Cash in hand	—	5,000	5,000	—
Total	—	1,65,000		
B. Current Liabilities				
Creditors	—	1,30,000	—	1,30,000
Bills Payable	—	10,000	—	10,000
Outstanding Expenses	—	5,000	—	5,000
Total	—	1,45,000	1,65,000	1,45,000
Net Increase in Working Capital			—	20,000
			1,65,000	1,65,000

Illustration—2

The same ABC Ltd. has prepared its Balance Sheet for the year ended on 31st March, 1997 as under.

Liabilities	*1996*	*1997*	*Assets*	*1996*	*1997*
Share capital	5,00,000	5,00,000	Land and buildings	6,50,000	5,85,000
Reserve	25,000	70,000	Plant and machinery	3,50,000	6,00,000
Profit and Loss A/C	95,000	1,10,000	Furniture and fixtures	—	1,15,000
Loans	4,00,000	5,50,000			
Sundry creditors	1,30,000	1,50,000	Stock	1,00,000	1,10,000
Bills Payable	10,000	25,000	Debtors	40,000	50,000
Outstanding Expenses	[illegible],000	4,000	Bills Receivable	—	10,000
Provision for Tax	[illegible],000	60,000	Cash at bank	20,000	15,000
Provision for dividend	—	50,000	Cash in hand	5,000	6,000
			Preliminary Expense	35,000	28,000
	12,00,000	15,19,000		12,00,000	15,19,000

Additional informations:

1. During the year no land and buildings was purchased.
2. Depreciation on plant and machinery charged, Rs. 60,000.
3. Tax paid Rs. 35,000.

Prepare the statement of sources and application of Fund for the year ended on 31st March, 1997.

Solution

Funds from Business Operations:		
Profit and Loss A/C		1,10,000
Add: Depreciation on		
Land and Buildings	65,000	
Plant and Machinery	60,000	
Preliminery Expenses written off	7,000	
Transfer to Reserves	45,000	
Provision for Tax	60,000	
Provision for Dividend	50,000	
		2,87,000
		3,97,000
Less : Profit at the beginning of the year		95,000
Funds from Business Operations		3,02,000

Land and Buildings Account

To balance b/d	6,50,000	By Profit and Loss A/c	65,000
		By balance c/d	5,85,000
	6,50,000		6,50,000

Plant and Machinery Account

To balance b/d	3,50,000	By Profit and Loss A/C	60,000
To Bank (purchases)		(Depreciation)	
(balancing figure)	3,10,000	By Balance c/d	6,00,000
	6,60,000		6,60,000

Provision for Tax Account

To Bank (Tax paid)	35,000	By Balance b/d	35,000
To Balance c/d	60,000	By Profit and Loss A/C	60,000
		(new provision)	
	95,000		95,000

Funds Flow Statement
for the Year Ended on 31st March, 1997

Sources		*Applications*	
Loans raised	150,000	Purchase of Plant and Machinery	3,10,000
Funds from Business Operations	302,000	Purchase of Furniture and Fixtures	1,15,000
Decrease in Working Capital	8,000	Tax Paid	35,000
	4,60,000		4,60,000

Schedule of Changes in Working Capital
for the Year Ended on 31 March 1990

Current Assets/Liabilities	*1996*	*1997*	*Increase in W.C.*	*Decrease in W.C.*
Stock	1,00,000	1,10,000	10,000	—
Debtors	40,000	50,000	10,000	—
Bills Receivables	—	10,000	10,000	—

Cash at bank	20,000	15,000	—	5,000
Cash in hand	5,000	6,000	1,000	—
Total Current Assets	1,65,000	1,91,000		
Creditors	1,30,000	1,50,000	—	20,000
Bills Payable	10,000	25,000	—	15,000
Outstanding Expenses	5,000	4,000	1,000	—
Total current liabilities	1,45,000	1,79,000		
Total Increase/Decrease In Working Capital			32,000	40,000
Net Decrease in Working Capital			8,000	—
		Total	40,000	40,000

Illustration—3

The Profit and Loss Account and Balance Sheet of Modern Auto Ltd. for the year ended on 31st March, 1990 are given below:

Profit and Loss Account
for the year Ended on 31st March, 1990

To Materials	60,00,000	By Sales	1,25,00,000
To Wages	30,00,000	By Stock	50,00,000
To Manufacturing expenses	5,00,000		
To Gross Profit c/d	80,00,000		
	1,75,00,000		1,75,00,000
To Salaries	3,50,000	By Gross Profit b/d	80,00,000
To Rent	1,50,000	By Commission	50,000
To Postage and telegrams	5,000	By Rent received	10,000
To Printing and Stationery	10,000	By Dividend	10,000
To Advertising	50,000	By Profit on sale of machine	1,00,000
To Commission paid	1,00,000		
To Loss on sale of investment	20,000		

To Depreciation on land and building	9,50,000		
To Depreciation on Plant and Machinery	9,00,000		
To General expenses	35,000		
To Net Profit c/d	56,00,000		
	81,70,000		81,70,000
To General Reserve	18,00,000	By Profit for 1989	20,00,000
To Proposed dividend	10,00,000	By Profit for 1990	56,00,000
To Provision for taxation	22,00,000		
To Profit carried forward	26,00,000		
	76,00,000		76,00,000

Balance Sheet as on 31st March, 1990

1989	*Liabilities*	*Amount (1990)*	*1989*	*Assets*	*Amount (1990)*
75,00,000	Share capital	1,00,00,000			
10,00,000	General Reserve	28,00,000	54,00,000	Goodwill	54,00,000
			85,50,000	Land and Buildings	95,00,000
10,00,000	Contingency Reserve	10,00,000	1,00,00,000	Plant and Mach.	90,00,000
20,00,000	Profit and Loss A/C	26,00,000	10,00,000	Furn. and Fitting	15,00,000
1,00,00,000	14% Debentures	75,00,000	80,000	Spare tools	1,00,000
75,00,000	Loans	50,00,000	20,60,000	Investments	15,60,000
20,00,000	Creditors	30,00,000	30,00,000	Stock	25,00,000
1,25,000	Bills Payable	1,00,000	10,00,000	Debtors	15,00,000
—	Outstanding Rent	10,000	4,00,000	Bills Receivable	5,00,000
1,00,000	Unclaimed dividend	50,000	3,00,000	Cash at bank	10,00,000
			1,00,000	Cash in hand	5,00,000
70,000	Tax Payable	50,000	2,05,000	Discount on share issue	1,50,000
8,00,000	Proposed dividend	11,00,000			
3,20,95,000		3,32,10,000	3,20,95,000		3,32,10,000

Prepare a Statement showing Sources and Application of Fund.

Solution

Funds from Business Operations

Profit as on 31.3.1990		26,00,000
Add: Depreciation on Land and Buildings	9,50,000	
Depreciation on Plant and Machinery	9,00,000	
Loss on Sale of Investment	20,000	
General Reserve	18,00,000	
Proposed Dividend	10,00,000	
Provision for Tax	22,00,000	
Preliminary Expenses written off (Discount on share issue)	55,000	69,25,000
		95,25,000
Less: Dividend Received	10,000	
Profit on Sale of Machine	1,00,000	1,10,000
		94,15,000
Less Profit (1989)		20,00,000
Funds from business operations		74,15,000

Land and Buildings Account

To Balance b/d	85,50,000	By Profit and Loss A/c (Depreciation)	9,50,000
To Bank (Purchases Balancing figure)	19,00,000	By Balance c/d	95,00,000
	1,04,50,000		1,04,50,000

Plant and Machinery Account

To Balance b/d	1,00,00,000	By Profit and Loss A/c (Depreciation)	9,00,000
		By Bank (sale)	2,00,000
To Profit and Loss a/c Profit	1,00,000	By Balance c/d	90,00,000
	1,01,00,000		1,01,00,000

Investment Account

To Balance b/d	20,60,000	By Profit and Loss a/c (Loss)	20,000
		By Bank (sales) Balancing figures)	4,80,000
		By Balance c/d	15,60,000
	20,60,000		20,60,000

Provision for Tax Account

To Bank (Tax paid)	22,00,000	By Balance b/d	70,000
To Balance c/d	50,000	By Profit and Loss (Appropriation)	22,00,000
	22,70,000		22,70,000

Proposed Dividend Account

To Bank (paid)	7,00,000	By Balance b/d	8,00,000
To Balance c/d	11,00,000	By Profit & Loss Appropriation	10,00,000
	18,00,000		18,00,000

STATEMENT OF SOURCES AND APPLICATION OF FUND AS ON 31ST MARCH, 1990

Sources		*Application*	
1. Issue of capital	25,00,000	Redemption of debentures	25,00,000
2. Sale of Investments	4,80,000	Repayment of Loans	25,00,000
3. Sales of Machinery	2,00,000	Purchase of land and Buildings	19,00,000
4. Funds from Business operations	74,15,000	Purchase of Furniture	5,00,000
5. Non-trading Income:		Purchase of spare tools	20,000
		Tax Paid	22,20,000

Dividend	10,000		
		Dividend Paid	7,00,000
		Increase in Working Capital	2,65,000
	1,06,05,000		1,06,05,000

Schedule of Changes in Working Capital
For the Year Ended on 31st March, 1990

	1989	*1990*	*1989 Increase*	*1990 Decrease*
Stock	30,00,000	25,00,000	—	5,00,000
Debtors	10,00,000	15,00,000	5,00,000	—
Bills Receivables	4,00,000	5,00,000	1,00,000	—
Cash at bank	3,00,000	10,00,000	7,00,000	—
Cash in hand	1,00,00,000	5,00,000	4,00,000	—
Creditors	20,00,000	30,000,000	—	10,00,000
Bills Payable	1,25,000	1,00,000	25,000	—
Outstanding Rent	—	10,000	—	10,000
Unclaimed dividend	1,00,000	50,000	50,000	—
		Total Increase/Decrease	17,75,000	15,10,000
Net Increase in Working Capital				2,65,000
			17,75,000	17,75,000

Illustration—4

From the following Balance Sheets and adjoining informations, prepare (i) A Schedule of Changes in Working Capital, and (ii) Funds Flow Statement:

	1989	*1990*
PROPERTIES AND ASSETS		
Land and Buildings	12,00,000	19,90,000
Plant and Machinery	20,00,000	18,00,000
Furniture and Fixtures	1,50,000	2,00,000
Loose Tools	50,000	50,000
Investment in shares RPC Ltd.	1,00,000	50,000
Stock	1,50,000	2,50,000
Sundry debtors	50,000	1,60,000
Bills Receivable	20,000	56,000
Prepaid Expenses	5,000	4,000
Cash at Bank	15,000	29,000
Cash in hand	5,000	10,000
Total	37,45,000	45,99,000
Capital and Liabilities		
Share Capital	20,00,000	30,00,000
General Reserve	2,50,000	2,60,000
Share Premium Account	2,00,000	2,00,000
Profit and Loss Account Appropriation A/c	1,50,000	1,75,000
Loan	10,00,000	8,00,0000
Creditors	75,000	90,000
Bills Payable	25,000	20,000
Outstanding Expenses	5,000	4,000
Tax Payable	40,000	50,000
Total	37,45,000	45,99,000

Additional Informations

1. Depreciation charged on Land and Buildings Rs. 1,20,000.
2. Depreciation on Plant and Machinery Rs. 2,00,000.
3. Furniture damaged and written off during the year Rs. 10,000.
4. Investment costing Rs. 25,000 was sold for Rs. 35,000 and some shares costing Rs. 25,000 were disposed off at cost value.
5. Tax paid during the year Rs. 60,000.

Solution

Adjusted Profit and Loss Account

To Depreciation on Land and Buildings	1,20,000	By Opening Balance	1,50,000
		By Profit on Sale of Investment	10,000
To Depreciation on Plant and Machinery	2,00,000	By Funds from Business Operations (Balancing figure)	4,25,000
To Loss on Furniture	10,000		
To Provision for taxation	70,000		
To Transfer to General Reserve	10,000		
To Closing Balance	1,75,000		
	5,85,000		5,85,000

Land and Building Account

To Balance b/d (Depreciation)	12,00,000	By Profit and Loss a/c	1,20,000
To Bank (Purchases)	9,10,000	By Balance c/d	19,90,000
	21,10,000		21,10,000

Plant and Machinery Account

To Balance b/d	20,00,000	By Profit and Loss a/c (Depreciation)	2,00,000
		By Balance c/d	18,00,000
	20,00,000		20,00,000

Investment Account

To Balance b/d	1,00,000	By Bank (sale)	35,000
To Profit and Loss a/c	10,000	By Bank (sale)	25,000
(Profit on sale)		By Balance c/d	50,000
	1,10,000		1,10,000

Furniture Account

To Balance b/d	1,50,000	By Profit and Loss a/c (damaged furniture)	10,000
To Bank (Purchases)	60,000	By Balance c/d	2,00,000
	2,10,000		2,10,000

Taxation Account

To Bank (Tax paid)	1,50,000	By Balance b/d	40,000
To Balance c/d	50,000	By Profit and Loss a/c	70,000
	1,10,000		1,10,000

FUNDS FLOW STATEMENT

AS ON 31.12.1990

Sources of Fund

1. Issue of Share Capital	10,00,000
2. Sale of Investments	35,000
3. Sale of Investments	25,000
4. Funds from Business Operations	4,25,000
Total Sources	14,85,000

Application of Funds

1. Purchase of Land and Building	9,10,000
2. Purchase of Furniture	60,000

3. Tax Paid	60,000
4. Repayment of Loan	2,00,000
	12,30,000
5. Increase in working capital	2,55,000
Total Application of Fund	14,85,000

Schedule of Changes in Working Capital for the Year Ended on 31st December 1990

Components of working capital	*1989*	*1990*	*Increase*	*Decrease*
Stock	1,50,000	2,50,000	1,00,000	—
Debtors	50,000	1,60,000	1,10,000	—
Bills Receivable	20,000	56,000	36,000	—
Prepaid Expenses	5,000	4,000	—	1,000
Cash at Bank	15,000	29,000	14,000	—
Cash in hand	5,000	10,000	5,000	—
Creditors	75,000	90,000	—	15,000
Bills Payable	25,000	20,000	5,000	—
Outstanding Expenses	5,000	4,000	1,000	—
		Total Increase/Decrease	2,71,000	16,000
	Net Increase of Working Capital		—	2,55,000
		Total	2,71,000	2,71,000

Illustration — 5

The Flora Chemical Ltd. furnishes the following Balance Sheet for the year ended on 31st March, 1989 and 31st March 1990.

	31.3.1989	31.3.1990
PROPERTIES AND ASSETS:		
Fixed Assets	27,00,000	30,00,000
Less Accumulated depreciation	5,00,000	6,00,000

	22,00,000	24,00,000
Investment in RPL Ltd.	2,50,000	3,00,000
Stock	4,25,000	5,50,000
Debtors (less bad Debt Reserve, Rs. 50,000 and Rs. 60,000 respectively)	7,00,000	1,50,000
Bills Receivable	1,10,000	1,60,000
Unexpired Premium	25,000	30,000
Discount on Issue of Shares	35,000	25,000
Total	31,45,000	36,15,000
CAPITAL AND LIABILITIES:		
Share Capital	15,00,000	16,50,000
General Reserve	5,50,000	6,00,000
Capital Reserve	—	15,000
Profit and Loss Appropriation A/c	3,70,000	5,00,000
Creditors	5,00,000	5,80,000
Proposed Dividend	75,000	1,00,000
Provision for Taxation	1,50,000	1,70,000
Total	31,45,000	36,15,000

Other Informations

1. During the year fixed assets having written down value of Rs. 25,000 (depreciation written off Rs.1,00,000) were sold for Rs. 45,000.
2. Tax equal to last year's provision was paid during the current year.
3. Proposed dividend of last year was paid in the current year.
4. The investment in the current year was revalued and profit on revaluation Rs. 15,000 was transferred to Capital Reserve.
5. During the current year Bad debts of Rs. 10,000 were written off by debiting the same to Bad debt Reserve Account.

You are required to prepare a Fund Flow Statement and also the Schedule of Changes in Working Capital.

Solution

Calculation of Funds from Business Operations:

	Profit and Loss a/c (31.3.1990)		5,00,000
Add:	Depreciation	2,00,000	
	Discount of issue of shares written off	10,000	
	Transfer to General Reserve	50,000	
	Provision for dividend	1,00,000	
	Provision for taxation	1,70,000	
			5,30,000
			10,30,000
Less:	Profit on scrapped Asset		20,000
			10,00,000
Less :	Profit and Loss A/c (31.03.1989)		3,70,000
	Funds from Business Operations		6,40,000

Working Accounts

Fixed Assets Account

To Balance b/d	27,00,000	By Scrapped Asset A/C	1,25,000
To Bank (Purchase) (Balance figure)	4,25,000	By balance C/D	30,00,000
	31,25,000		31,25,000

Accumulated Depreciation Account

To Scrapped Asset (Accumulated Dep.)	1,00,000	By Balance b/d	5,00,000
To Balance C/d	6,00,000	By Profit and Loss A/c (Dep. for current year)	2,00,000
	7,00,000		7,00,000

Scrapped Asset Account

To Fixed Asset	1,25,000	By Accumulated Depreciation	1,00,000
To Profit and Loss A/c (Profit on sale)	20,000	By Bank (Sale)	45,000
	1,45,000		1,45,000

Investment Account

To Balance b/d	2,50,000		
To Capital Reserve	15,000	By Balance C/d	3,00,000
To Bank (Purchases)	35,000		
	3,00,000		3,00,000

Funds Flow Statement as on 31st March, 1990

Sources		*Applications*	*Amount*
Issue of Capital	1,50,000	Purchase of Fixed Assets	4,25,000
Sale of scrapped asset	45,000	Payment of divide	75,000
Funds from Business Operations	6,40,000	Payment of Taxes	1,50,000
		Purchase of Investments	35,000
		Increase in working capital	1,55,000
	8,35,000		8,35,000

Schedule of Changes in Working Capital

	1989	*1990*	*Increase*	*Decrease*
Stoc'.	4,25,000	5,50,000	1,25,000	—
Debtors (net)	1,00,000	1,50,000	50,000	—
Bills Receivable	1,10,000	1,60,000	50,000	—
Unexpired Premium	25,000	30,000	5,000	—
Creditors	5,00,000	5,80,000	—	80,000
Total Increase/Decrease			2,30,000	80,000
Net Increase in Working Capital				1,50,000
Total			2,30,000	2,30,000

Illustration — 6

The Balance Sheet of a firm for the years ended on 31st December, 1989 and 31st December, 1990 stood as under:—

Liabilities	*1989*	*1990*	*Assets*	*1989*	*1990*
Trade Creditors	90,000	1,00,000	Cash in hand	15,000	13,000
Bills Payable	15,000	20,000	Cash at Bank	35,000	45,000
Bank Loan	80,000	75,000	Sundry debtors	1,05,000	1,25,000
Loan from X	—	50,000	Stock	75,000	60,000
Capital Accounts	8,55,000	9,60,000	Bills Receivable	10,000	12,000
			Plant and Mach.	8,00,000	8,50,000
	10,40,000	12,05,000		10,40,000	12,05,000

Other Informations

1. During the year the partners withdrew Rs. 80,000 for personal use.
2. Accumulated Depreciation on Plant and Machinery as on 1st January 1990 was Rs. 80,000 and on 31st December, 1990 Rs. 1,05,000.
3. The Land was revalued during the year. The appreciation in its value Rs. 1,00,000 was directly included in the Partners Capital Accounts.

You are required to prepare the Schedule of Changes in working capital and Fund Flow Statement.

Schedule of Changes in Working Capital for the Year Ended on 31st December, 1990

	1989	*1990*	*Increase*	*Decrease*
Cash in hand	15,000	13,000	—	2,000
Cash at Bank	35,000	45,000	10,000	—
Sundry debtors	1,05,000	1,25,000	20,000	—
Stock	75,000	60,000	—	15,000
Bills Receivable	10,000	12,000	2,000	—

Trade Creditors	90,000	1,00,000	—	10,000
Bills Payable	15,000	20,000	—	5,000
			32,000	32,000
Increase/decrease in working capital			NIL	

Fund Flow Statement
as on 31st December 1990

Sources:		*Application*	
Loan from X	50,000	Purchase of Plant and Machinery	75,000
Operational Inflow	1,10,000	Payment of Bank Loan	5,000
		Drawings	80,000
	1,60,000		1,60,000

Working Notes:

Capital Account

To, Cash (money withdrawn)	80,000	By Balance b/d	8,55,000
To Balance C/d	9,60,000	By Land and Building (Appreciation)	1,00,000
		By Net Profit (Balancing figure)	85,000
	10,40,000		10,40,000

Accumulated Depreciations Account

By Balance C/d	1,05,000	To Balance b/d	80,000
		By Profit and Loss A/c (Depreciation)	25,000
	1,05,000		1,05,000

Plant and Machinery Account

To Balance b/d (Cost - 8,00,000 + 80,000	8,80,000		
To Bank (purchase (Balancing figure)	75,000	By Balance C/d (8,50,000 + 1,05,000)	9,55,000
	9,55,000		9,55,000

Funds From Business Operations

Net Profit for 1990	85,000
Add Depreciation	25,000
Operational Inflow	1,10,000

Illustration —7

The Balance Sheets of Modern Pipes and Fittings Ltd. for the years ending on 31st December, 1989 and 31st December, 1990 are available in the following forms:

	31.12.1989	*31.12.1990*
Capital and Liabilities:		
Equity Capital	1,50,00,000	2,40,00,000
Reserve and Surplus	3,50,00,000	2,60,00,000
Profit and Loss a/c	40,00,000	60,00,000
Capital Reserve	—	10,00,000
Debentures	—	70,00,000
Loans	70,00,000	40,00,000
Creditors	40,00,000	50,00,000
Bills Payable	20,00,000	10,00,000
Provision for Taxation	20,00,000	30,00,000
Provision for Dividend	10,00,000	20,00,000
	7,00,00,000	7,90,00,000
Property and Assets		
Goodwill	20,00,000	20,00,000
Land and Buildings	2,80,00,000	2,50,00,000

Plant and Machinery	2,50,00,000	2,20,00,000
Furniture	20,00,000	30,00,000
Investments	50,00,000	50,00,000
Stock	20,00,000	1,50,00,000
Debtors	20,00,000	30,00,000
Cash Balances	20,00,000	30,00,000
Preliminery Expenses	20,00,000	10,00,000
	7,00,00,000	7,90,00,000

Other Informations

1. The increase in capital has been due to issue of Bonus Shares in proportion to 3 for every 5 shares held.
2. An interim dividend of Rs. 10,00,000 was paid during the year.
3. Final dividend on account of last year paid, Rs. 10,00,000.
4. Investment costing Rs, 30,00,000 was sold for Rs, 40,00,000 and the profit of Rs. 10,00,000 was directly transferred to Capital Reserve Account, and the investments of the same cost were purchased in the last month of the current year.
5. A machine having a written down value of Rs. 10,00,000 was discarded as it had lost its value.
6. Depreciation charged on—
   (i) Land and Buildings Rs. 30,00,000.
   (ii) Plant and Machinery Rs. 30,00,000.
   (iii) Furniture Rs. 5,00,000.

You are required to prepare a Statement of Changes in Financial Position based on working capital concept and also the Schedule of Changes Working Capital.

Solution

Schedule of Changes in Working Capital for the Year Ended on 31st December, 1990

Components of working capital	*1989*	*1990*	*Increase*	*Decrease*
Stock	20,00,000	1,50,00,000	1,30,00,000	—
Debtors	20,20,000	30,00,000	10,00,000	—

Cash Balance	20,00,000	30,00,000	10,00,000	—
Creditors	40,00,000	50,00,000	—	10,00,000
Bills Payable	20,00,000	10,00,000	10,00,000	—
	Total Increase/Decrease		1,60,00,000	1,10,00,000
	Net Increase in Working Capital			1,50,00,000
	Total		1,60,00,000	1,60,00,000

Working Notes:

Funds From Business Operations:

	Profit and Loss A/C (31.12.1990)		60,00,000
Add:	Interim dividend	10,00,000	
	Machine discarded	10,00,000	
	Depreciation:		
	Plant and Machinery	30,00,000	
	Land & Buildings	30,00,000	
	Furniture	5,00,000	
	Provision for tax	20,00,000	
	Provision for dividend	20,00,000	
	Preliminary Expenses written off	10,00,000	
			1,35,00,000
			1,95,00,000
	Less Profit and Loss A/C (31.12.1989		40,00,000
	Funds from Business Operations		1,55,00,000

Land and Buildings Account

To Balance b/d	2,80,00,000	By Profit and Loss a/c (Depreciation)	30,00,000
		By Balance C/d	2,50,00,000
	2,80,00,000		2,80,00,000

Plant and Machinery Account

To Balance b/d	2,50,00,000	By Profit and Loss A/c (depreciation)	30,00,000
To Bank (Purchases)	10,00,000	By Profit and Loss A/c (Machinery discarded)	10,00,000
		By Balance C/d	2,20,00,000
	2,60,00,000		2,60,00,000

Furniture Account

To Balance b/d	20,00,000	By Profit and Loss A/c (Depreciation)	5,00,000
To Bank (Purchases)	15,00,000	By Balance c/d	30,00,000
	35,00,000		35,00,000

Investment Account

To Balance b/d	50,00,000	By Bank (Sales)	40,00,000
To Capital Reserve	10,00,000	By Balance c/d	50,00,000
To Bank (Purchases)	30,00,000		
	90,00,000		90,00,000

Provision for Taxation Account

To Bank (Tax paid)	10,00,000	By Balance b/d	20,00,000
To Balance C/d	30,00,000	By Profit and Loss a/c (current provision)	20,00,000
	40,00,000		40,00,000

Provision for Dividend

To Bank (Dividend paid)	10,00,000	By Balance b/d	10,00,000
To Balance C/d	20,00,000	By Profit and Loss (Current provision)	20,00,000
	30,00,000		30,00,000

Funds Flow Statement
as on 31st December, 1990

Sources		*Applications*	
Sales of Investments	40,00,000	Purchase of Plant and Machinery	10,00,000
Issue of Debentures	70,00,000	Purchase of Investments	30,00,000
Funds from Business Operations	1,55,00,000	Purchase of Furniture	15,00,000
		Tax paid	10,00,000
		Interim dividend	10,00,000
		Final dividend	10,00,000
		Loan repaid	30,00,000
		Increase in Working Capital	1,50,00,000
	2,65,00,000		2,65,00,000

Illustration —8

The management of Rana Synthetics Ltd. provides you the following Balance Sheet data and other informations and asks you to prepare a Funds Flow Statement and Schedule of Changes in Working Capital.

	1989	*1990*
Capital and Liabilities:		
Share Capital in share of 10/-	50,00,000	75,00,000
12.5% Debentures	50,00,000	25,00,000
General Reserve	10,00,000	15,00,000
Investment Fluctuation Fund	1,15,000	1,00,000
Share Premium Account	—	3,00,000
Profit and Loss Account	5,00,000	8,00,000
Trade Creditors	2,60,000	1,47,000
Bills Outstanding	10,000	5,000
Provision for Taxation	1,50,000	2,00,000
	1,20,35,000	1,30,52,000
Property and Assets:		
Land and Buildings	60,00,000	65,00,000

Plant and Machinery	50,00,000	53,00,000
Furniture	1,00,000	90,000
Trade Investments	5,00,000	4,75,000
Debtors	2,50,000	2,20,000
Stock	1,50,000	4,59,000
Cash balances	30,000	5,000
Share Issue Expenses	5,000	3,000
	1,20,35,000	1,30,52,000

Other Informations

1. During the year Debentures of the face value of Rs. 25,00,000 were redeemed at a premium of 5%.
2. Dividend on Investment Rs. 40,000 was received. This included Rs. 10,000 as pre-acquisition profit which was credited to Investment Account.
3. During the year, a further capital of the face value of Rs. 15,00,000 was issued at a premium of Rs. 2 per share.
4. Share worth Rs. 10,00,000 were issued to the supplier of a machine for Rs. 8,00,000 and raw material Rs. 2,00,000.
5. Investment costing Rs. 15,000 were written off against Investment Fluctuation Fund.
6. Appreciation in the value of Land Rs. 5,00,000 was credited to General Reserve Account.
7. Depreciation charge: Plant and Machinery Rs. 5,00,000; Furniture Rs. 10,000

Solution

Funds Flow Statement
as on 31st December, 1990

Sources of Funds:	
Funds from Business Operations	9,07,000
Issue of shares including Premium	18,00,000
Dividend Received	40,000
Total	27,47,000

Application of Funds:

Redemption Debentures	26,25,000
Increase in Working Capital	1,22,000
	27,47,000

Schedule of Changes in Working Capital for the Year Ended on 31st December 1990.

	1989	*1990*	*Increase*	*Decrease*
Debtors	2,50,000	2,20,000	—	30,000
Stock	1,50,000	4,59,000	3,09,000	—
Cash Balances	30,000	5,000	—	25,000
Trade Creditors	2,60,000	1,47,000	13,000	—
Bills Outstanding	10,000	5,000	5,000	—
Provision for taxation	1,50,000	2,00,000	—	50,000
			3,27,000	1,05,000
Increase in Working Capital			—	1,22,000
Total			3,27,00,	3,27,000

Working Notes:

Funds from Business Operations:

Profit and Loss A/c (1990)		8,00,000
Add: Non-operating/non-current items:		
Depreciation on		
Plant and Machinery	5,00,000	
Furniture	10,000	
	5,10,000	
Premium on Redemption of debentures	1,25,000	
Share Issue Expenses	2,000	
		6,37,000
		14,37,000
Less dividend		30,000

		14,07,000
Less Profit and Less A/C (1989)		5,00,000
Funds from Business Operations		9,07,000

Share Capital Account

To Balance C/d	75,00,000	By Balance b/d	50,00,000
		By Bank (new issue)	15,00,000
		By Machine	8,00,000
		By Raw materials	2,00,000
	75,00,000		75,00,000

Debenture Account

To Bank (Paid with Premium)	26,25,000	By Balance b/d	50,00,000
		By P. and L. A/c	1,25,000
To Balance C/d	25,00,000	(Premium debited)	
	51,25,000		51,25,000

General Reserve Account

To Balance C/d	15,00,000	By Balance b/d	10,00,000
		By Land and Buildings (appreciation)	5,00,000
	15,00,000		15,00,000

Investment Fluctuation Fund

To Investment A/c (written off)	15,000	By Balance b/d	1,15,000
To Balance b/d	1,00,000		
	1,15,000		1,15,000

Land and Buildings Account

To Balance b/d	60,00,000	By Balance C/d	65,00,000
To General Reserve (Appreciation)	5,00,000		
	65,00,000		65,00,000

Plant and Machinery Account

To Balance b/d	50,00,000	By Profit and Loss (Depreciation)	5,00,000
To Share Capital	8,00,000	Bay Balance c/d	53,00,000
	58,00,000		58,00,000

Furniture Account

To Balance b/d	1,00,000	By Profit and Loss (Depreciation)	10,000
		By Balance C/d	90,000
	1,00,000		1,00,000

Investment Account

To Balance b/d	5,00,000	By Investment Fluctuation Fund	15,000
		By Dividend	10,000
		By Balance C/d	4,75,000
	5,00,000		5,00,000

Cash Flow Statement

We have seen the preparation of Funds Flow Statement which treated 'Fund' in the sense of working capital. The statement of changes in financial position can also be prepared on the basis of the cash concept of the word 'Fund.' It is knows as Cash Flow Statement if Fund is considered in the sense of cash. The preparation of Cash Flow Statement is important to understand the paradoxical situation in which a firm finds difficulty in honouring its short-period business commitments despite the existence of sufficient working capital as indicated by the Fund Flow Statement (working capital basis). This happens when a large proportion of working capital is tied up in the form of inventories and other working assets. The Fund Flow Statement based on working capital concept does not take into account the qualitative structure of working capital. Cash is a peculiar component of working capital. It should be distinguished from other components in any scheme of short-period financial planning. The Cash Flow Statement enables a firm to know the availability of cash from different sources and the manner of its utilizaion. A projected Cash Flow Statement tells the management about the cash position at different timings. The management can arrange for additional necessary cash in case cash outflow exceeds the cash inflow in any particular period of time. Similarly surplus cash, if any, can be invested for effective utilizationof cash balances.

Construction of Cash Flow Statement

A Cash Flow Statement is prepared to show the movements of cash between the closing dates of two Balance Sheets. It starts from the opening cash and ends with the closing balance of cash showing different sources from where cash was received and the manner in which it was utilised during the period for which Cash Flow Statement is prepared. The usual transactions resulting in cash inflows are, (i) Issue of shares; (ii) Issue of debentures; (iii) Sale of investments; (iv) Sale of assets; (v) Cash from business operations. Cash outflows due to its application for various purposes such as—(a) Redemption of preference shares, (b) Redemption of debentures, (c) Repayment of loans, (d) Payment of taxes, (e) Payment of dividend, (f) Cash losses due to operations.

The preparation of Cash Flow Statement is not difficult if a complete set of informations in the form of Profit and Loss Account and Balance

Sheet is given. An increase of share capital, debentures and loans clearly means that cash inflow took place due to additional issue of shares and debentures and obtaining further loans during the year. A decrease in current years figures of the liabilities will mean liquidation of liabilities and hence an application of cash. A comparison of non-current assets like Land and Buidlings, plant and machinery, furniture, trade investment, etc. will tell whether there had been increase or decrease in cash or an item resulted in cash inflow or cash outflow. For instance, an increase in curent year's amount of furniture clearly means cash outflow due to purchase of additional furniture. Conversely, a decrease in curent years amount of furniture means sale and hence anapplication of cash. We have already seen how variations in non-current assets and liabilities generate or use funds (cash). Again the general rules can be laid down as under:

Increase in Non-current liability = Cash Inflow

Decrease in Non-current liability = Cash Outflow

Increase in Non-current asset = Cash Outflow

Decrease in Non-current asset = Cash Inflow

Note: The net cash inflow or outflow can be arrived at only after preparing the relevant account by allowing for appropriate adjustments, if any.

Cash From Business Operations

The business activities of production and sales increase cash to the extent of profit calculated on cash basis. The traditional Profit and Loss Account is based on certain accounting concepts and conventions such as accrual and matching principles according to which non-operating and non-cash items are also brought into it. Therefore, the net profit as shown by a traditional Profit and Loss Account cannot be equivalent to cash and as such it needs certain adjustments to arrive at net cash inflow or cash losses due to business operations. The adjustments are required in respect of the non-operating and non-cash items which do not affect the cash flows. In other words, the traditional Profit and Loss Account based on accrual principle should be converted on cash basis by excluding from it all non-cash items. The items which do not result in cash flows are credit purchases and sales, outstanding and accured expenses and incomes, depreciation, capital losses, etc. The calculation of cash from business operations is explained with the help of the following Profit and Loss Account of an imaginery firm.

Profit and Loss Account for the Year Ended on 31st December, 19

To opening stock		25,000	By Sales:		
To Purchases:			Cash	4,50,000	
Cash	1,50,000		Credit	1,50,000	6,00,000
Credit	30,000	1,80,000			
			By closing stock		25,000
To Manufacturing Expenses		60,000			
To Gross Profit c/d		3,60,000			
		6,25,000			6,25,000
To Salaries	50,000		By Gross Profit b/d		3,60,000
Add outstanding	30,000		By Commission		1,000
		80,000	By Interest	2,500	
			Accrued interest	1,500	4,000
To Selling and distribution expenses	30,000				
Add outstanding rent of werehouse	1,500				
		31,500			
To Insurance Premium	2,500				
Less unexpired	500	2,000			
To Depreciation		15,000			
To Patents written off		10,000			
To Net profit carried to Balance Sheet		2,51,500			
		3,65,000			3,65,000

You are required to calculate Cash from Business Operations.

Solutions

Cash In Flows From Business Operations:

Cash sales	4,50,000	
Commission	1,000	
Interest	2,500	4,53,500

Cash Outflows Due to Business Operations:

Cash Purchases	1,50,000	
Manufacturing Expenses paid	60,000	
Salaries paid	50,000	
Selling and disribution Expenses	30,000	
Insurance Premium	2,500	2,92,500
Net Cash from Business Operations		1,61,000

The cash from business operations can also be calculated by adding back to and subtracting from the net profit the non-cash debits and non-cash credits respectively as shown below:-

Profit and Loss Account (31-12-19-)			2,51,500
Add:	Credit Purchases	30,000	
	Salaries outstanding	5,000	
	Rent Payable	1,500	
	Depreciation	15,000	
	Patents written off	10,000	61,500
			3,13,000
Loss:	Credit sales	15,000	
	Accrued Interest	1,500	
	Unexpired Premium	500	1,52,000
	Cash from business operations		1,61,000

Adjustments for Changes in Current Assets and Current Liabilities

In addition to the adjustments for changes in non-cash and non-operating items, the adjustments are also required in respect of the changes in current assets and current liabilities in the computation of cash from business operations. A constant change takes place in the structure of current assets and current liabilities due to business operations. For example, the debtors, stock, cash balances, creditors, all undergo change and there is generally difference between their opening and closing balances. The variations in working capital also affects the cash flows. A decrease in debtors between the closing dates of two Balance Sheet is a clear indication of cash inflow to the extent the debtors amount is reduced. Similarly, a decrease in creditors means cash outflow due to payment of a part of creditors during the year. The changes in current assets and current liabilities affecting changes in cash position should, therefore, be taken into account in the calculation of cash from business operations.

There are two methods to deal with the current assets and current liabilities in the preparation of cash from business operations. The variations in working capital components may either be shown in the Cash Flow Statement itself or they may be considered separately in the calculation of cash from business operations. The former course is adopted when notional concept of cash is followed and later method is applied when actual cash concept is implemented.

According to 'Notional Cash' concept a decrease in current assets and an increase in current liability is taken as a source of cash. Similarly an increase in current assets and decrease in current liability is considered as an application of cash. The 'Notional Cash Concept' can be understood with the help of an example. Suppose a firm has purchased raw material worth Rs. 5,000 on credit and it has not paid the amount by the end of accounting year. In this case Rs. 5,000 will appear as creditors on the liability side of the Balance Sheet of the firm, and this will be taken as a source of cash. How is this when there is no actual receipt of cash. The 'Notional Cash Concept' assumes that the firm will borrow Rs. 5,000 and make payment to the supplier of raw materials. Thus borrowing Rs, 5,000 means a source of cash.

Generally, it is the actual cash concept which is followed in the preparation of Cash Flow Statement. It means actual cash received and actual cash paid are brought into the C.F. Statement and the variations in current assets and current liabilities are separately treated in the statement of cash from business operations. The C.F. Statement is not followed by a Schedule of changes in working capital as the working capital items figure in the Cash Flow Statement either directely or through the Cash from Business Operations.

It has been pointed out earlier that an increase in current assets (except cash) and decrease in curent liabilities is taken as application of cash and decrease in a current asset and increase in current liability is treated as a source of cash. The increase/decrease current assets and current laibilities should be adjusted in net profit to arrive at cash from business operations in the following manner:

1. Increase/decrease in debtors. Increase in debtors means the excess of current year's debtors (closing) over the previous year's debtors (opening) and decrease in debtors is just oposite of it. The debtors arise due to credit sales which are recorded at the credit side of Profit and Loss Account and the debtors are shown on the asset side of a Balance Sheet. The credit sales increase the profit without an equal increase in cash; therefore, the closing balance of debtors should be deducted from net profit. The debtors at the beginning, if any can be assumed to have been collected during the year and as such they should be added to net profit. Thus

Cash from Business Operation = Net Profit + (Opening debtors — closing debtors)

" " " OR = Net Profit – Increase in closing debtors

" " " OR = Net Profit + Decrease in closing debtors.

2. Increase or decrease in Stock. In a Trading Account, the opening stock appears on debit side and closing stock on the credit side. The net profit is reduced by the amount of opening stock whereas the closing stock increases the net profit without decrease or increase in cash. Therefore, the opening stock should be added back and closing stock subtracted from the net profit to arrive at cash from business operations. In other words, the increase in closing stock should be subtracted and decrease add to net profit to arrive at cash from business operations as is clear from the following equations :

Cash from Business Operations = Net Profit (Opening stock - closing stock)

" " " OR = Net Profit - Increase in closing stock

" " " OR = Net Profit + Decrease in closing stock.

3. Change in prepaid expenses. The payment of pre-paid expenses decreases cash but it is not charged to the Profitt and Loss Account of the current year since it belongs to the next accounting year. Consequently, the profit for curent year is more by the amount of prepaid expenses. In order to calculate cash from operations, the pre-paid expenses at the end should, therefore, be deducted. The prepaid expenses at the beginning of the curent year are charged to the curent year's Profit and Loss Account due to which the profit is reduced without decrease in cash. Therefore, the opening balance of prepaid expenses should be added back to net profit for arriving at cash from business operations. Thus

Cash from Business Operations = Net Profit + (opening prepaid expenses minus closing prepaid expenses)

" " " OR = Net Profit - Increase in closing prepaid expense

" " " OR = Net Profit + Decrease in closing prepaid expense

4. Changes in accrued incomes. Accrued incomes are the incomes earned but not actually received during the year for which they belong. According to accrual principle, accrued incomes are credited to Profit and Loss Account due to which the net profit is increased without increase in cash to that extent. Therefore, the accrued incomes at the end should be deducted from profit to arrive at cash from business operations. Any amount of accrued incomes at the beginning of the accounting year should be added to net profit because this is received during the current year.

Cash from Business Operations = Net Profit ± (accrued incomes at the beginning minus accrued incomes at the end)

Or = Net Profit — Increase in accrued incomes

Or = Net Profit + Decrease in accrued incomes

5. Change in creditors. The trade creditors including bills payable arise due to credit purchases which are transferred to Trading Account and the creditors are shown on the liability side of the Balance Sheet. We know that the operating profit is reduced by the amount of credit purchases without corresponding decrease in cash balances. Therefore, trade creditors at the close representing credit purchases should be added back to profit to arrive at cash from business operations. If there is any balance of creditors at the beginning of the current year, they should be deducted from profit becasue creditors being short-term liability, are generally paid within the year's time. Thus

Cash from Business operations = Net Profit + (Creditors at close minus creditors at the beginning)

OR = Net Profit + Increase in creditors

OR = Net Profit — Decrease in creditors.

6. Change in outstanding expenses. The profit as shown by a traditional Profit and Loss Account is reduced by the amount of the outstanding expenses for the current year without decreasing cash; therefore, it should be increased by adding back to it the amount of outstanding expenses to arrive at cash from business operations. The previous year's outstanding, if any is paid during the current year; therefore, it should be deducted from profit. Thus Cash from Business Operations =

Net Profti as per P.&L. A/c ± (Closing balance of outstanding expenses minus opening balance of Outstanding expenses)

OR Net Profit + Increase in outstanding expenses

OR Net Profit - Decrease in outstanding expenses

7. Incomes received in advance. The incomes received in advance is treated as a curent liability. Such an income is not taken into account in the calculation of profit as it pertain to next accounting year but the cash balance is increased by the amount of such a receipt. Therefore, it should be added to net profit to arrive at the cash from business operations. Any income of this nature standing at the beginning should be deducted as last year's advance receipts are adjusted in the current year. Thus,

Cash from Business Operations = Net Profit + (closing balance of advance incomes minus opening balance of advance incomes)

OR " " = Net Profit + Increase in incomes received in advance

OR " " = Net Profit – Decrease in incomes received in advance.

Thus Cash from Business Operations can be calculated by collecting and summarising the relevant informations in the following form:

Statement of Cash from Business Operations

Net Profit as per Profit and Loss A/C			—
1.	*Add:*	*Decrease in Current Assets:*	
		Decrease in debtors	—
		Decrease in stock	—
		Decrease in Pre-paid expanses	—
		Decreases in Accrued Incomes	—
	Add:	*Increase in Current Liabilities:*	
		Increase in creditors	—
		Increase in bills payable	—
		Increase in outstanding expenses	—
		Increase in incomes received in advance	—
2.	Less:	*Increase in Current Assets:*	
		Increase in debts	—
		Increase in stock	—
		Increase in pre-paid expenses	—
		Increase in accrued incomes	—
	Less:	*Decrease in current liabilities:*	
		Decrease in creditors	—
		Decrease in Bills Payable	—

		Decrease in outstanding expenses	—
		Decrease in advance incomes	—
3.	Add:	*Non-current expenses:*	
		Depreciation	—
		Assets discarded	—
		Preliminery expenses written off	—
		Provision for losses, etc.	—
4.	Less	*Non-operating incomes:*	
		Profit on sale of asset	—
		Tax refund	—
		Unusual incomes	—
	Cash From Business Operation or Cash Losses		—

Illustration

Calculate cash from business operations and also prepare Cash Flow Statement from the following Balance Sheet of X Ltd.:

Balance Sheet of X Ltd.

	1989	*1990*		*1989*	*1990*
Capital	50,000	50,000	Land & Buildings	35,000	35,000
Profit and Loss A/C	10,000	12,000	Machines	25,000	22,500*
Creditors	15,000	18,000	Investments	5,000	7,000
Bills Payable	5,000	3,000	Debtors	15,000	18,500
Outstanding Expenses	1,000	500	Bills Receivable	5,000	6,000
Advance from Customers	8,000	9,000	Accrued Incomes	2,000	1,000
			Prepaid Insurance	1,000	500
			Cash Balances	1,000	2,000
	89,000	92,500		89,000	92,500

* Depreciation charged on machines = 2,500.

Solution

Statement of Cash from Business Operations

Net Profit (1990) (12,000 – 10,000)			2,000
Add:	Decrease in accrued incomes	1,000	
	Decrease in pre-paid expenses	500	
	Increase in creditors	3,000	
	Increase in advance from customers	1,000	5,500
			7,500
Less:	Increase in debtors	3,500	
	Increasein bills receivable	1,000	
	Decrease in Bills Payable	2,000	
	Decrease in outstanding Exp.	5,00	7,000
			500
Add:	Depreciation		2,500
			3,000
Cash from Business Operations			

Cash Flow Statement

Opening Cash Balance	1,000	Purchase of Investments	2,000
Cash from Business Operations	3,000	Closing Cash Balanee	2,000
	4,000		4,000

Alteratively

Cash Flow Statement

Opening Cash Balance	1,000	*Cash Outflows:*	
Add: Cash Inflows		Purchase of Investments	2,000
		Increase in debtors	3,500
Decrease in debtors	1,000	Increase in bills receivable	1,000

Decrease in pre-paid expenses		500	Decrease in bills payable	2,000
			Decrease in outstanding expenses	500
Increase in creditors		3,000	Closing Cash balance	2,000
Increase in advance from customers		1,000		
Operating Profit	2,000			
Add Depreciation	2,500			
		4,500		
		11,000		11,000

QUESTIONS

1. What do you mean by a funds flow statement? What puropose does a Funds Flow Statement serve? Explain clearly.
2. Describe the method of preparation of a Funds Flow Statement.
3. How are the funds from operations calculated? Explain with an example.
4. What are the different ways in which working capital may be increased or decreased?
5. Give a list of 'non-fund' items and 'fund' items?
6. Bharat Industries Ltd. Commenced its business operations on 1st Jan. 1994. The Balance of the company for the year ended on 31st Dec. 1994 stood as under:

Share Capital	3,50,000	Building	2,50,000
General Reserve	50,000	Machinery	2,00,000
Profit and Loss A/c	10,000	Furniture	50,000
Loans	150,000	Investments	60,000
		Debtors	75,000
Sundry creditors	80,000	Unsold stock	20,000
Outstanding Interest	20,000	Miscellaneous Expenditure	5,000
	6,60,000		6,60,000

Set out the above Balance Sheet in the form of a Funds Flow Statement. Also show the schedule of changes in working capital.

7. From the following Balance sheets of Agro-chemical Ltd. and additional informations prepare (a) a statement of charges in working capital and (2) Funds Flow Statement:

Liabilities	*1994*	*1995*	*Assets*	*1994*	*1995*
Share Capital	3,50,000	3,50,000	Building	250,000	4,00,000
General Reserve	50,000	60,000	Machinery	200000	2,50,000
Profit and Loss	10,000	50,000			
15% debenture	—	1,50,000	Furniture	50,000	75,000
Loans	1,50,00	2,00,000	Investments	60,000	40,000
Sundry creditors	80,000	1,00,000	Debtors	75,000	1,25,000
Outstanding interest	20,000	44,000	Unsold stock	20,000	70,000
Provision for Tax	—	10,000	Miscellaneous Expenditure	5,000	4,000
	6,60,000	9,64,000		6,60,000	9,64,000

Additional Informations

(i) During the current year depreciation charge on machinery and furniture amounted to Rs. 30,000 and 10,000 respectively.

(ii) No depreciation was charged an Building.

(iii) Income tax paid during the year, Rs. 15000.

(iv) Miscellaneous expenditure written off Rs. 1000.

8. Nav Jeevan Ltd. has published Balance Sheets for 1994 and 1995 as under:

Assets/Liabilities	*1994 (Dec 31)*	*1995 (Dec 31)*
Liabilities:		
Equity share capital	30,00,000	35,00,000
12% preference capital	15,00,000	12,00,000
General reserve	8,00,000	10,00,000
Profit and Loss A/C	5,00,000	8,00,000
Debentures	10,00,000	15,00,000
Current liabilities	5,50,000	8,50,000
Total	73,50,000	78,50,000

PROPERTY AND ASSETS:		
Fixed assets	55,00,000	60,00,000
Investments	5,50,000	6,50,000
Current Assets	10,00,000	11,00,000
Expenditure not written off	3,00,000	1,00,000
Total	73,50,000	78,50,000

Additional Informations

1. A machine costing Rs. 8,50,000 was sold for Rs. 6,25,000.
2. Depreciation on fixed assets charged, Rs. 8,25,000.
3. Dividend Paid an Equity Shares for 1994, Rs. 4,50,000.
4. 20% of the Preference Shares at a premium of 10% were redeemed at the end of current year.

You are required to prepare a Funds Flow Statement on 31/12/1959.

9. The Summarised Balance Sheets of x y z Ltd. as at 31st Dec. 1993 and 1994 are given below:

	1993	*1994*		*1993*	*1994*
Share Capital	4,50,000	4,50,000	Fixed Assets	4,00,000	3,20,000
General Reserve	3,00,000	3,10,000	Investment	50,000	60,000
Profit & Loss	56,000	68,000	Stock	240,000	2,10,000
Creditors	1,68,000	1,34,000	Debtors	210,000	4,55,000
Provision for Tax	75,000	10,000	Bank	144,000	1,97,000
Mortgage Loan	—	2,70,000			
	10,49,000	12,42,000		10,49,000	12,42,000

Additional Informations

(i) Investment Costing Rs. 8,000 were sold during the year 1994 for Rs. 8,500.

(ii) Provision for tax made during the year was Rs. 9,000.

(iii) During the year, part of the fixed assets costing Rs. 10,000 was sold for Rs. 12,000 and the profit was included in the Profit and Loss Account.

(iv) Dividend paid during the year amounted to Rs. 40,000.

You are required to prepare a statement of Sources and Application of Funds.

M. Com. Business Management 1995 (J.M.J.)

10. From the following Summarised Balance Sheets of Joyati Structural Ltd. as on 31st December 1994 and 31st Dec. 1995, Prepare .

(I) A statement of Sources and Application of Funds.

(II) A statement of Changes in Working Capital.

	Amount (Rs)	*Amount (Rs)*		*Amount (Rs)*	*Amount (Rs)*
Liabilities	31.12.94	31.12.95	Assets	31.12.94	31.12.95
Share Capital	3,00,000	4,50,000	Fixed Assets	3,50,000	5,50,000
Reserve and surplus	1,50,000	3,50,000	Investments	50,000	30,000
Long-terms liabilities	1,25,000	—	Stock	15,000	2,75,000
			Debtors	1,75,000	1,50,000
Sundry creditors	2,25,000	2,75,000	Cash Balances	80,000	75,000
			Prepared expenses	20,000	45,000
Provision for tax	50,000	95,000	Miscellaneous Expenditure	25,000	45,000
	8,50,000	11,70,000		8,50,000	11,70,000

Additional Information

1. Depreciation written off during 1995, Rs. 80,000.
2. On 31st Dec. 1995 accumulated depreciation on fixed assets amounted to Rs. 1,75,000 and on 31st Dec. 1994, Rs. 1,25,000.
3. Machinery Costing Rs. 50,000, accumulated depreciation thereon being Rs. 30,000 was discarded and written off during 1995.
4. During the current year, investment costing Rs. 10,000 were sold for Rs. 12,500.
5. Dividend paid during the year amounted to Rs. 32,500.

11. From the following condensed Balance Sheets of Premium Industries Ltd., Compute the funds from business operations and cash from operations.

	1993	1994
Equity share capital	65,000	6,50,000
Reserve & Surplus	2,50,000	3,80,000
Accumulated depreciation	50,000	60,000
Secured Loans	1,50,000	2,00,000
Trade creditors	2,25,000	1,80,000
Outstanding Expenses	15,000	10,000
	13,40,000	14,80,000
Fixed Assets at Cost	5,00,000	7,40,000
Investments	3,00,000	2,75,000
Inventories	1,50,000	1,25,000
Debtors	3,50,000	2,75,0000
Cash Balances	40,000	65,000
	13,40,000	14,80,000

12. Prepare a Cash Flow Statement from the Summarised Balance Sheets of Rama Vision India Ltd. as given below:—

	1994	1995
Liabilities:	(Rs.)	(Rs.)
Share capital	4,50,000	5,60,000
Reserves	1,12,000	1,30,000
Profit and Loss A/c	65,000	70,000
Loans	1,50,000	—
Creditors	3,35,000	3,35,000
Provision for Tax	60,000	95,000
	11,72,000	11,90,000
Assets:		
Land & Buildings	4,50,000	4,25,000
Plant & Machinery	3,35,000	3,75,000
Stock	2,02,000	1,80,000
Debtors	1,70,000	1,50,000

Cash	15,000	25,000
Bank Balance	—	15,000
Goodwill	—	20,000
	11,72000	11,90,000

Other Informations Relating to Current Year

1. An asset for Rs. 1,10,000 was purchased by issuing company company's shares at per value.
2. Machinery purchased for cash, Rs. 15,000.
3. A loss of Rs. 1500 on the disposal of a particular machine was transferred to Reserve A/c.
4. Income Tax Provision made during the year Rs. 70,000.

4

Capital Budgeting

The expenditure incurred in an enterprise may be classified into two categories viz., Revenue expenditure and Capital expenditure. Revenue expenditure is that expenditure, which is incurred to meet day to day expenses on items such as purchase of raw materials, payment of wages and other expenditure of running the business in an usual manner. All the items of revenue expenditure find their place in the Income Statement which is prepared at the end of a financial year which is usually a period of one calender year. The service or benefit of the revenue expenditure is realized by a firm in the short period of one year. Most of the business firms prepare operating budgets which are concerned with operating incomes and expenses for a financial year. For example, every firm running its enterprise fairly on large scale, prepare a Case Budget which deals with expected receipts and likely payments of cash during a given period not exceeding one year. The preparation of an operating budget is relatively an easy task as it is not very difficult to forecast for future when the period is short. Cost and demand conditions relating to a firm in a short period are fairly unchanged and as such it is easier to take dependable decision in such a period.

On the other hand, Capital budgeting is concerned with the capital expenditure decisions. A capital expenditure is defined as an expenditure which is incurred for the acquisition of an asset which gives service for long period of time. For the purpose of capital budgeting, a long-period is a period of more than one year. The expenditure on land, plant and machinery, fixtures and furniture, etc. is called capital expenditure as the service life of these assets is more than one year. In a capital-intensive industry, the proportion of capital expenditure to total investment is quite large. An industrial enterprise spends large sum of money on fixed assets with the main idea, that it will yield sufficient returns in future. These capital budgeting decisions are concerned with making investments in capital projects in expectation of future net gains to the enterprise. Since the amount involved in capital profits is quite heavy, the business firms should very carefully determine their requirements for capital expenditure and evaluate beforehand the profitability of the capital projects in which it intends to make investments. The firms should prepare capital budget which is a formal plan or list of the investment project which a firm proposes to carry out. Capital budgeting may be defined as a long-range formal planning process for making and financing proposed capital outlays. John J. Hampton has defined capital budgeting as "the decision-making process by which firms evaluate the purchase of major fixed assets including building, machinery and equipment." The decision to invest in other companies by purchasing their whole or majority of equity shares is also covered under capital budgeting. Hampton has rightly observed, "It (capital budgeting) also covers decisions to acquire other firms, either through the purchase of their common stock or groups of assets that can be used to conduct an ongoing business."

Importance of Capital Budgeting

Capital budgeting decisions are unusual decisions in the life of an undertaking. They are large, permanent commitment, which influence the long-term flexibility and profitability of a concern. Infact, the ultimate success of a project implementation depends upon the right decisions with regard to capital expenditure. The management must exercise great care and caution in capital budgeting for the following reasons:

1. Capital budgeting decisions are irreversible, in the sense, that they cannot be withdrawn without substantial loss of money and time for example, if a capital project for the construction of a warehouse had been implemented and at some stage of construction it is contemplated to withdraw the investment for certain reason, then it cannot be done without great loss of money which has already been spent on the construction of the project.

2. They are subject to greater degree of risk and uncertainty due to the time factor. The capital expenditure is recoverable over a period of many years in future and the success of a capital project depends largely on the correct forecasting for the demand of the product/service which the

capital expenditure on the project will produce. It is very difficult to forecast with high degree of certainty for distant future, as compared to short period. Therefore, there is a always risk of loss or uncertainty of profit out of a capital project.

3. Capital budgeting decisions involve huge investments in permanent assets, specially in capital intensive industries and as such they are very significant and require a lot of exercise in terms of cost-benefits.

Classification of Investment Proposals

The management has to solve many problems at one time or the other, involving huge investments in long-term assets to help run the enterprise on most economic lines. It has to take decision on issues such as , (a) whether to continue with an existing plant or replace it by the new one, (b) whether to create new production capacity by the addition of similar assets to the existing ones, (c) whether to diversify products and purchase entirely new machinery for the purpose, (d) should the enterprise conduct research on production and marketing problems and purchase necessary research equipment? (e) Should the additional requirements for building be met by new construction or purchasing an old structure or hiring on lease? (f) Are the cost-saving and cost reduction machines desirable?

According to the types of problems involved, the investment proposals may be grouped under the following six categories:

1. Replacement of existing assets.
2. Additions to existing plants.
3. Purchase of entirely new plant for diversifying existing product line.
4. Re-arrangement of an existing plant involving additional funds.
5. Acquisition of equipment for conduct of research for development.
6. Introduction of Cost-saving and cost reduction plant and machinery.
7. Installation of equipments to meet statutory requirements such as safety measures and pollution control devices, etc.

Nature of Capital Projects

In order to properly ascertain the requirements for capital expenditure, the management should understand the nature of capital project which has originated in the enterprise. A Capital project can be either (a) mutually exclusive project or (b) a complementary project or (c) an independent project. A mutually exclusive project is one, the acceptance of which necessarily involves the rejection of all other projects. For example, the tube-well and the pumping set for irrigation are the two mutually exclusive projects for a cooperative farming society. If the society selects the system of tube-well for irrigation, it has to reject the pumping-set project. complementary investment proposals are those which have to be considered jointly. The investment in one project necessarily suggests the investment in other project. For example, the construction of factory building and provision of residential quarters for labour, adjacent to factory are complimentary projects if the provision of the latter is essential under law. An independent project is one which has no allternatives and it has either to be accepted or rejected.

The management has to select one project out of the other competing proposals. Where the investments are complimentary, they have to be combined and treated as a single project. Thus, complimentary investments are paired and mutually exclusive investment eliminated before each one is considered as an alternative to other independent investment. The final selection of a project depends upon the relative profitability of each case and the availability of finances with the enterprises.

STEPS IN CAPITAL BUDGETING DECISIONS

A Capital investment proposal may involve following steps:

1. Identification of Investment Opportunities

The first step in capital budgeting process is the identification of investment opportunities. The management should understand the exact nature of the problem which gives rise to a capital project. A capital budgeting problem arises when management considers the replacement, expansion, diversification and other changes which necessitate capital expenditure.

2. Preparation of Capital Budget and Approval of Proposal

Capital expenditure proposals may originate in any department of firm. The production department, marketing division and research and development wing are the important constituents, which submit proposals for investment in long-term assets. It is the duty of the management to critically analyse the proposals and give final approval to the same. However, the Board of Management may decentralize the powers and authorise the departmental heads to approve the purchases of fixed assets, if the amount involved is not large. The approval of projects involving substantial amount is the responsibility of the top management which may involve concerned officers and other technical staff in discussions before giving final approval to the proposals. The proposals are given definite shape in the form of a capital budget which includes items of expenditure and the amount needed to buy them.

3. Calculation of Cash Flows

The process of capital budgeting is largely influenced by the right calculation of cash flows, which will accrue to the firm over the estimated life of the project. Cash flow is a technical concept which includes both cash outflow and cash inflows. It is not the same as net income as shown by a Income statement at the end of a financial year. The net income as calculated under conventional accounting method needs some adjustment to arrive at cash inflows. There are few items which are debited to conventional Income statement but they do not result in the outflow of cash. Adjustments for all such items has to be made to arrive at the right value of cash flows. Depreciation is an item which is added back to net income as it does not result in the outflow of cash.

Cash outflow refers to the amount which will be paid for the acquisition of fixed assets. In some cases the installation of new plant increases the requirement for working capital. If the new plant is capable of producing goods at faster rate, it will increase the demand for more cash to be tied up in the form of more raw materials, receivables and inventories of finished goods. Such an increase in working capital should be treated as cash outflows and added with the initial cash outflow on project similarly, the expenditure on massive advertising campaign to dispose off additional production should be included in the total outflow of cash. The cash outflow resulting at the beginning of the first year known as zero period and it is indicated by a minus sign in the analysis table prepared for the economic evaluation of capital project.

Cash inflow means, net increase in cash balances due to the implementation of project. The management accountant is required to calculate the cash inflows over the expected life of the project. For the sake of simplicity, the net cash inflows are calculated on yearly basis i.e. at the end of accounting year of the firm. The calculation of cash inflow is a difficult task, as it requires forecasting of demand and operating cost during the life of the project. The accountant has to compile past sales and cost figures, and take stock of existing economic conditions and likely changes in future in his effort to forecast net incomes and cash inflows. In this connection it is important to remember that standard and uniform procedures are followed so that different investment proposals are evaluated on uniform and objective basis.

Incremental After-Tax Cash Flow Streams

The incremental after-tax cash inflow stream over the life of a project is the only relevant information for economic evaluation of the budgetary proposals. Therefore the cash inflow should be calculated on an incremental basis. The incremental cash inflow can be known by substracting the cash flow which would have resulted with the old equipments from the inflow after the implementation of the project. Corporate taxes have to be deducted from the cash inflows, because it is the after-tax income, which is relevant for financial decision-making.

Illustration—1

A firm has expected some cash inflows with its existing plant which has a life of 10 years. After the lapse of 4 years, it proposes to introduce a new product for the manufacture of which, a new machine costing Rs. 180000 will be needed. The life of the new machine is estimated at 6 years. The value of existing plant at present is estimated at Rs. 1,00,000 with no salvage value. New machine will be scrapped after six years. Depreciation is charged according to straight-line method. Following table shows the cash flow streams with and without the proposal and the net incremental cash inflows.

TABLE SHOWING CASH INFLOWS WITH PROPOSAL

Year	Annual Sales	Cost of operation	Sales Revenue	Depre-ciation	Income before-Tax	Tax 50%	Income After-tax	After-tax cash-inflow
(1)	(2)	(3)	(4)	(5)	(6)	(7)	(8)	(9)
1.	4,50,000	3,00,000	1,50,000	50,000	1,00,000	50,000	50,000	1,00,000
2.	5,25,000	3,50,000	1,75,000	50,000	1,25,000	62,500	62,500	1,12,500
3.	5,75,000	3,83,000	1,92,000	50,000	1,42,000	71,000	1,21,000	1,71,000
4.	7,00,000	4,70,000	2,30,000	50,000	1,80,000	90,000	90,000	1,40,000
5.	10,00,000	6,70,000	3,30,000	50,000	2,80,000	1,40,000	1,40,000	1,90,000
6.	11,25,000	7,50,000	3,75,000	50,000	3,25,000	1,26,500	1,62,500	2,12,000

TABLE SHOWING CASH-INFLOW WITHOUT PROPOSAL

((1)	(2)	(3)	(4)	(5)	(6)	(7)	(8)	(9)
1.	3,00,000	2,00,000	1,00,000	20,000	80,000	40,000	40,000	60,000
2.	3,50,000	2,30,000	1,20,000	20,000	1,00,000	50,000	50,000	70,000
3.	3,80,000	2,50,000	1,30,000	20,000	1,10,000	55,000	55,000	75,000
4.	4,50,000	3,00,000	1,50,000	20,000	1,30,000	65,000	65,000	85,000
5.	6,00,000	4,00,000	2,00,000	20,000	1,80,000	90,000	90,000	1,10,000
6.	7,00,000	4,60,000	2,40,000	20,000	2,20,000	1,10,000	1,10,000	1,30,000

TABLE SHOWING INCREMENTAL AFTER-TAX CASH FLOWS

Year	Cash flow with proposal	Cash flow without proposal	After - tax incremental cash flow
0	–1,80,000	0	–1,80,000
1	1,00,000	60,000	40,000
2	1,12,500	70,000	42,500
3	1,21,000	75,000	46,000
4	1,40,000	85,000	55,000
5	1,90,000	1,10,000	80,000
6	2,12,000	1,30,000	82,000

(Note: Imaginary Sales and cost figures have been used).

The case under illustration-1 is a simple one. On the introduction of a new capital project, many problems such as the need for additional working capital, tax incentives for new investment, salvage value of plant, etc. arise and they have to be dealt properly in the calculation of cash inflows.

Need for Additional Working Capital

With the introduction of a new machine which is intended to produce more, the working capital requirements go up. The initial outlay has to be increased with the additional amount of working capital which becomes inflow on the completion of the project. It is also possible that the working capital is freed with the introduction of new machine. In that case, the initial outlay should be reduced by the amount freed. In the final year, the capital which was freed is treated as inflow of cash.

Tax Concessions for New Investment

The law of the land may permit the concession in taxes on new investments with a view to help create employment in the country. Investment tax credit is a saving in taxes and the initial investment has to be reduced by such savings.

Salvation Values

The salvage values means the value of the asset scrapped. It is also known as residual value. This is treated as inflow in the final year . The treatment of salvage value creates some problem when it is more or less than its expected value. If it cash salvage value of an existing asset is less than its book value, it suffers a loss which will produce tax-savings. in the reverse case, additional tax will have to be paid. To calculate cash inflow in the final year, the tax savings will be added to and additional taxes on gains substracted from the cash salvage value.

4. Computation of Cost of Capital

Capital is a scarce commodity. Therefore, it should be used economically. The capital, whether it is equity or debt has a cost. Cost of equity capital is the rate of dividend which the shareholders, in general, expect from the company. Thus, it is the minimum rate which should be yielded by a project in order to maintain the capital in its present use. Generally speaking, the before-tax cost of loan capital is the interest rate it is carrying. Cost of capital involved in financing a project guides management in choosing or rejecting a budgetory proposal. A budgetory proposal is considered if it is able to earn atleast equal to its cost of capital. Any project which is not expected to yield income equal to cost of capital is outrightly rejected. The cost of financing varies with the pattern and nature of financing. During prosperity phase, the Debt - financing is cheaper as compared to equity capital.

5. Evaluation of Budgetary Proposals

The cash flows over the life of the project form the basis for economic evaluation of the capital expenditure proposal Therefore, the correctness of cash flow streams is a pre-requisite for the success of capital budgeting decisions. Once The cash flow stream is rightly determined , one can proceed to ascertain the economic variability of the projects by the application of tools of analysis. The techniques of evaluating budgetory proposals may be divided into two broad categories as under:

6. Traditional or Non-Discounting Methods

There are two imptant methods which are considered traditional or Non-discounting techniques of project evaluation . These are (a) Pay Back Period (PBP) method and (B) Accoúnting Rate of Return (ARR) method. Modern or discounting methods include (I) Internal Rate of Return (IRR) method and (II) Net Present Value (NPV) method. A detailed explanation of all these methods is provided hereunder:

Traditional or Non-Discounting Methods

(A) Pay Back Period Method (PBP)

This method has been very popular among the industrial firms in the past. Since the discovery of more sophisticated techniques of evaluating investment proposals, the pay back period method is gradually loosing its utility as a supplemental tool is still recognised. According to this method, The period within which the original investment will be paid back is ascertained and compared with the period within which the firm desires. The recovery of the same. Pay Back period has been defined as a period or length of time (years) within which the original investment is fully recovered. If an initial outlay of Rs. 12,000 is recoverable in a period of four years, then 4 years period is known as pay back period.

Selection of Project

If the desirability of an independent project is being considered an the basis of Pay Back Period (PBP) method, then the project will be selected only if the Pay Back period is equal to or less than the Pay Back period already decided by the management. It means the project will be rejected if the expected Pay Back period is more than the minimum period set up by the management. In case of two or more competing projects, the project with the short Pay Back period is preferable but its Pay Back period should not exceed the standard Pay Back period, if any.

Calculation of Pay Back Period

The calculation of pay back period is quite simple. In case the yearly cash inflows are inform, then the pay pack period can be found out simply by dividing the original investment by the amount of yearly cash inflow. If an investment of Rs. 12,000 generates Rs. 3000 every year as net cash inflow for 6 years, the pay back period of investment is 4 years (initial investment of Rs. 12,000 divided by 3,000). Symbolically it can be expressed as under:

$P = \frac{O}{I}$ where P stands for pay back period.

O indicates original investment
I represents yearly cash inflows.

Illustration —2

The capital expenditure of Rs. 1,000 as massive advertising compaign is likely to produce an incremental cash inflow of Rs. 3000 every year for 5 years. Calculate the pay back period and comment on the desirability of expenditure if the management desires the recovery in 3 years time.

Solution

$$P = \frac{O}{I}$$

$$P = \frac{10,000}{3,000}$$ 3-1/3 years i.e. 3 years and 4 months

Comment

The capital expenditure is not worthwhile as its pay back period is more than the desired pay back period.

Uneven Cash Inflow

The assumption of uniform cash inflow may not hold good in actual practice and varying cash inflows may be produced in different years. In case the cash inflows are uneven, the PBP can be calculated by cumulating the cash inflows as shown in the illustration 3.

Illustration—3

The introduction of a new capital asset costing Rs. 25000 in an enterprise increases the productive capacity due to which it produces the following net incremental cash inflows over the 8 years life of the asset.

Year	*Cash Inflow*
0	–25,000
1	9,000
2	8,000
3	7,000
4	6,000
5	5,000
6	4,000
7	3,000
8	2,000

Calculate the Pay Back period.

Solution

Years	*Cash flows*	*Cumulative Cash flows*
0	– 25,000	- 25,000
1	9,000	- 16,000
2	8,000	- 8,000

3	7,000	- 10 00
4	6,000	+ 5,000
5	5,000	+ 10,000
6	4,000	+ 14,000
7	3,000	+ 17,000
8	2,000	+ 19,000

From the above it is clear that at the end of 3rd year, an amount of Rs. 1,000 remains to be recovered, which is covered in 4th year. The total cash inflow of 4th year is 6,000; assuming that it accrues evenly throughout the year, Rs. 1,000 can be paid back in 2 months time $\frac{(12 \times 1000)}{6,000}$. Thus the total Pay Back period is 3 years and 2 months.

Illustration —4

Two mutually exclusive projects are under the consideration of the management of an enterprise. Assuming the Selling price and cost of production as constant, The following information has been compiled :

	Project - A	***Project - B***
Initial Investment	**15,000**	**18,000**
Annual Sales	**15,000**	**18,000**
Operating Costs (excluding depreciation)	**11,250**	**12,000**
Annual Cash Inflow	**3750**	**6,000**

Calculate Pay Back period and comment on the desirability of a project.

Solution

Pay Back Period, Project A = $\frac{1500}{3750}$ **= 4 years.**

Project B = $\frac{18,000}{6,000}$ **= 3 years**

Since the Pay Back Period of project B is 3 years which is shorter than A,s 4 years, project B is desirable.

Merits and Uses of Pay Back Period Method

Pay Back Period as a Tool of decision-making is still used as a supplemental tool. Main merits of this technique are as follows:

1. It is simple to understand and easy to calculate,
2. Those firms which lay emphases on liquidity than profitability prefer this method to evaluate economic viability of projects. A firm will give more weightage to liquidity than profitability if it is experiencing shortage of funds and intends to finance Some other move profitable project.
3. Even those firms which apply other more scientific methods to evaluate capital projects use Pay Back Period as a supplemental tool.
4. Firms prefer this method when they fear conditions of uncertainty under which they are more interested to recoup original investment as early as possible.
5. This method is an appropriate method to evaluate small projects with short Pay Back period and for which cash inflows cannot be calculated with high degree of accuracy.

Defects of Pay Back Period Method

The popularity of Pay Back period as a tool of evaluating investment proposals has considerably gone down due to the following defects in the method:

1. It does not take into account the time value of money. The value of similar cash inflows accruing at the end of 1st, 2nd, 3rd, and subsequent years cannot be the same whereas the Pay Back period method treats all of then at par. The value of Rs. 100 to be received at the end of first year and second year is not the same due to interest factor or profitability of capital. The PBP of two projects involving similar cash outflows may be the same and an analyst depending for his judgement on This method may conclude that both the projects are equally desirable this type of conclusion will be erroneous if the cash inflow of the two projects widely differ Consider the following two projects:

	Project A	*Project B*
Initial Cash Outflow	26,000	26,000
Cash Inflow:		
1st year	8,000	5,000
2nd year	7,000	6,000
3rd year	6,000	7,000
4th year	5,000	8,000
5th year	4,000	5,000
6th year	3,000	3,000
7th year	2,000	2,000
8th year	2,000	1,000

It will be seen that the PBP in each case is 4 years within which the original investment is fully recovered. The equally of PBP does not mean that both the projects are equally good. Project A Produces larger cash inflows in the first two years as compared to cash inflows of project B in the same years. The excess cash inflows of project A can be re-invested and its total value can be increased. In this way, project A is definitely better than B. This type of problem is not properly handled by the Pay Back period method.

2. The Pay Back period method does not take into account the cash flow stream over the whole life of the projects. If the life of a project is 8 years and the original investment is paid back only in the first four years, the cash inflows of the remaining four years will be ignored by the analyst using this method of project evaluation. Any method which does not take into account the cash inflows of all the years cannot be said to be scientifically correct. It is possible that the position is altered in some cases if the cash flow stream over the whole life of the projects is subjected to statistical analysis. Consider the information of the following two projects.

	Project A	*Project B*
Initial Investment	16,000	21,000
Annual cash inflow during pay back period	4,000	7,000

Life of project	8 years	8 years
Total cash inflow during whole life	28,000	23,000
Pay Back period	4 years	3 years

The Pay Back period in the above case suggests that Project B is desirable as its Pay Back period is shorter than that of A but the consideration of the total cash-inflows of the two projects clearly shows that Project A is better as it generates an excess of Rs. 12,000 which is greater than the excess inflows of B. Infact, the cash inflows from project B taper off suddenly after the recovery of original investment.

3. The Pay Back period method lay too much emphasis on the recovery of initial investment. It means, it is concerned more with liquidity than profitability of the capital projects We know that an enterpreneur not only wants to recover his capital outlay but also seeks to earn a reasonable rate of return on it. The major defect of Pay Back period method is its neglect of profitability.

4. The comparison of two or more projects with different life span is not possible with this method. If two projects involve similar cash outlays and generate uniform cash inflows but have different economic lives, then the project with longer life will be desirable despute the fact that they have similar Pay Back periods.

(B) Accounting Rate of Return Method

Accounting Rate of Return (ARR) is another traditional method which had gained popularity among the entrepreneurs for evaluating investment proposals. According to this method, a rate of return based on accounting informations is calculated and compared with the minimum rate of return desired by the management. The project is accepted if it is likely to yield atleast equal to the minimum desired rate of return. In case the average expected rate of return in less than the standard rate specified, then the project is not considered worthwhile and finally rejected. Since the rate of return in based on the financial statements, i.e. the Income statement and Balance Sheet, the method is also known as Financial statement method. Other popular names given to this method are the Book Value Method and unadjusted Rate of Return method.

Calculation of Accounting Rate of Return (ARR)

Accounting Rate of REturn (ARR) is simply the function of the annual income and the investment required to produce that Income. It can be arrived at by dividing the after-tax annual average income by the investment required. In this connection the concepts of annual net income' and 'investment' should be carefully understood. In this case the net income is not the same as annual cash inflow. The cash inflow includes depreciation but the net income excludes the same because the depreciation under the conventional accounting method is treated as an expense against income To calculate the average annual income, the income for different years over the life of the project is calculated by preparing the projected Profit and Loss Account. The average annual income should be calculated on an incremental basis as is done in case of cash inflows. About investment, there is much difference among the accounting experts. Some use original investment while others prefer to use average investment i.e. half of the original investment as denominator for finding out the average rate of return. There is one more thinking that the additional investment tied up in working capital due to the acceptance of the project should also be added with the average investment while using it as denominator. The use of different investment figures will give markedly different rates of return but the final decision will not be affected if the same amount is applied in case of all competing projects The formula to calculate APR may be expressed as under:

$$\% \text{ APR} = \frac{\text{After - tax incremental annual net Income}}{\text{Original Investment or Average Investment}} \times 100$$

Illustration—5

The management accounting office of a private company has compiled the following informations relating to two capital projects:

	Project A	*Project B*
Life of project	8 years	8 years
Original Investment	16,000	20,000
Annual average incremental sales	20,000	25,000
Operating Incremental Expenses (excluding depreciation)	15,000	18,000

Excess annual Income	5000	7000
Depreciation	2000	2,500
Annual excess income (before tax)	3,000	4,500
Tax 50%	1,500	2,250
After - tax net annual income	1,500	2,250

You are required to comment on the desirability of the project if the specified standard rate of return is 20%.

Solution

$$\text{Average rate of Return from project A (ARR)} = \frac{\text{Excess Annual net income}}{\text{Average Investment}} \times 100$$

$$= \frac{1500}{8,000} \times 100 = 18.75\%$$

$$\text{ARR firm Project B} = \frac{2,250}{10,000} \times 100 = 22.50\%$$

Comment: Project A has necessarily to be rejected as it yields an ARR of 18.75 which is less than the specified rate of interest (20%) Project B is expected to yield more than the minimum rate specified and as Such it is desirable.

The introduction of new capital investment if necessiates additional working capital, then it is added with the average initial investment to find out the average rate of return. If additional working capital of Rs. 1000 is required for each investment, the rate of return would be reduced as shown below:

$$\text{APR for A} = \frac{1,500}{8,000 + 1,000} \times 100 = 16.6\%$$

$$\text{APR for B} = \frac{2250}{10000 + 1000} \times 100 = 20.4\%$$

Merits of ARR Method

The chief merits of accounting rate of return method are as under:

1. Like Pay Back period, the ARR is simple to understand and easy to calculate.
2. It attempts to measure the expected profitability with which business firms are mainly concerned.
3. It takes into account the entire cash inflows minus depreciation in the computation of average rate of return.

Defects of ARR Method

Since the ARR method takes into account entire cash flow stream and measures profitability it is an improvement over the Pay Back method which ignores both of these important aspects. However, it suffers from the following defects:

1. It ignores the times value of money. All income accruing in different years of the projects are given equal weightage in the computation of the average annual income. An income produced in the final year cannot be equal to the same amount of income earned at the end of first year of the project. It does not adjust the inçome according to time value and as such this is a great defect of this method.
2. It avoids the use of cash inflows in measures profitability by accounting profits. The net income is not suitable for making investment decisions.
3. It does not consider the length of life of projects According to this method, a project with higher accounting rate of profit but short life span is considered desirable project as compared to any other project which yields relatively a little less rate of profit but for a longer period of time. In actual practice many firms may wish to implement other project with lesser yield but for a long time.
4. Under this method, the concept of investment is flexible. Average rate of return defends much on the meaning we assign to investment. Therefore, the method does not provide precise answer to the problem.

2. Modern or Discounted Cash Flow Techniques

One of the serious defects with which the traditional methods suffer is that they ignore the time value of money in their calculations. Modern or Discounted cash flow techniques duly recognise the differences in the value of cash flows accruing at different times over the life of a project.

It is the human nature to discount future gains in view of the fact that future is full of risks and uncertainties. People in general believe in the maxim, "A bird in the hand is worth two in the bush." Similar principle is applicable to the management of money. Business firms allow cash discount for making prompt payments; investors are prepared to fact with their surplus funds only when they are offered attractive interest rates; bankers rates of interest differ for varying periods investment (higher rate for longer periods and lower rates for short period investment), etc. are the few examples of business practices which are based on the principle that the present is more valuable than future. Therefore, the future gains have to the discounted to compare with the present gains on an uniform basis.

Process of Discounting

By discounting we mean that the cash inflows arising at different points of time are reduced to the present value. The present value is affected by the rate of discounting which is either the cost of capital or any other rate specified for the purpose The process of compounding and discounting may be explained by an example. Suppose an investment of Rs. 100 at the rate of 10% p.a. is made at the beginning of 1990. In this case Rs. 100 invested at the beginning of 1990 will become Rs. 110 at the end of 1st year (1990), Rs. 121 at the end of the second year (1991) and Rs. 133.10 at the end of third year (1992). This is calculated by using the compound interest formula which is as under

$$A = P\left(1+\frac{r}{100}\right)^n$$

where A stands for amount
P represents principal
r denotes invest rate
n stands for the number of years.

In compounding we move from the present to the future. The amount realizable or payable in future is more than its present value. The discounting process is just opposite of compounding. In discounting, we move from the future to the present and the discounted or present value is lesser than the future receipts a payments. Taking the above example, It can be said that the present or discounted value of Rs. 110, Rs. 121 and Rs. 131.1 to be received @ 10% interest per annum at the end of first, second and third year respectively is Rs. 100. The cash flow of a particular can be discounted by using the following formula:

$$\text{Discount value or present value} = \frac{Fn}{(1+v)^n}$$

where Fn stands for the cash flow of nth year; r stands for percentage rate of interest or discount rate and n for number of years.

Illustration—6

A project involving an initial investment of Rs. 20,000 generates the cash flows over its life of 4 years as under.

Years	*Cash flows*
0	–20,000
1	8,000
2	10,000
3	12,000
4	9,000

Calculate the present value discounting cash flows at 10% rate.

Solution

Years	*Cash flows*	*Present Value*	
0	-20,000	$\frac{20,000}{\left(1+\frac{10}{100}\right)^0}$	20,000
1	8,000	$\frac{8,000}{\left(1+\frac{10}{100}\right)^1}=8,000\times\frac{10}{11}$	727.7
2	10,000	$\frac{10,000}{\left(1+\frac{10}{100}\right)^2}=10,000\times\frac{10}{11}\times\frac{10}{11}$	8,264.4
3	12,000	$\frac{12,000}{\left(1+\frac{10}{100}\right)^3}=12,000\times\frac{10}{11}\times\frac{10}{11}\times\frac{10}{11}$	9,015.8
4	9,000	$\frac{9,000}{\left(1+\frac{10}{100}\right)^4}=9,000\times\frac{10}{11}\times\frac{10}{11}\times\frac{10}{11}\times\frac{10}{11}$	6,147.1

From the above method of calculating the present value, it would be felt that the method is quite cumbersome. The use of matter mathematical tables has relieved the analysts of this difficulty. The tables provide discount factor for rupee are accruing after different years at varying rates of discounting. The analyst has simply to locate the discount factor and multiply it with the cash flow to arrive at the present value. Use of discount factor may be appreciated from the following:

Year	*Cash flows*	*Present value factor at 10%*	*Present value*		
0	–20,000	1.0000	20,000 × 1	=	20,000
1	8,000	0.9091	8,000 × .9091	=	7272.8
2	10,000	0.8264	10,000 × .8264	=	8284.0
3	12,000	0.7513	12,000 × 7513	=	9015.6
4	9,000	0.6830	9,000 × .6830	=	6147.0
	39,000				30,719.4

Since the cash flows are discounted to find out the present value for comparison with the actual investment, the methods dealing with discounting the cash flows are known as Discounted Cash Flow methods. There are two methods which deal with discounting of cash flows they are,

(A) Internal Rate of Return Method (IRR)

This method is different from the Accounting Rate of Return (ARR) method which is concerned with the unadjusted rate of return based on net income and investment. According to IRR method, a rate of return known as Internal Rate which the project is likely to yield over its life is computed on the basis of the annual cash flows. Internal Rate of return may be defined as a rate which, if employed to discount the cash flows will equate the aggregate discounted or present value of cash flows with the original investment. An entrepreneur cannot afford to pay more than the internal rate as interest on the loans borrowed for financing the project. Therefore, the internal rate is also defined as the maximum rate which can be paid on the borrowed funds without any loss on the project. In the following equation, the value of and will be the internal rate of return.

$$OI = \frac{F_1}{(1+r)} + \frac{F_2}{(1+r)^2} + \frac{F_3}{(1+r)^3} + \frac{F_n}{(1+r)^n}$$

where OI stands for original investment

$F_1, F_2, F_3, \ldots F_n$, represent the cash inflows of years 1 to n

r represents the internal rate of return.

Illustration—7

The introduction of a new machine with a life of 3 years and involving a cash outlay of Rs. 3000 is likely to produce cash flows as under:

Years	*Cash Inflows*
1	1,100
2	1,210
3	1,331

Calculate the Interval Rate of Return assuming that the machine does not possess any salvage value at the end of its life.

Solution

Years	*Cash Inflows*
0	– 3,000
1	1,100
2	1,210
3	1,331

Substituting the values in the equation, we get,

$$OI = \frac{F_1}{(1+r)} + \frac{F_2}{(1+r)^2} + \frac{F_3}{(1+r)^3}$$

$$-3000 = \frac{1100}{(1=r)} + \frac{1210}{(1=r)^2} + \frac{1331}{(1=r)^3}$$

To find out the value of r, we until have to assume the value of r felt the value of r be 5%, then

$$-3000 = \frac{1100}{\left(+\frac{5}{100}\right)} + \frac{1210}{\left(+\frac{5}{100}\right)^2} + \frac{1331}{\left(+\frac{5}{100}\right)^3}$$

$$\text{or } -3000 = \frac{1100}{\left(\frac{21}{20}\right)} + \frac{1210}{\left(\frac{21}{20}\right)^2} + \frac{1331}{\left(\frac{21}{20}\right)^3}$$

$$\text{or } -3000 = \frac{1100}{(1.05)} + \frac{1210}{(1.05)^2} + \frac{1331}{(1.05)^3}$$

or – 3000 = 1047.6 + 1097.5 + 1150.1

or - 3000 = 3295

From the result, it is clear that the present value of 3295 is not equal to original investment of Rs. 3000. In order to equate the two sides, we will have to assume other value of r. A higher value of r can further reduce the present value of cash inflows. Let the new rate be 10%.

$$-3000 = \frac{1100}{\left(1+\frac{10}{100}\right)} + \frac{1210}{\left(1+\frac{10}{100}\right)^2} + \frac{1331}{\left(1+\frac{10}{100}\right)^3}$$

$$\text{or } -3000 = \frac{1100}{(1.1)} + \frac{1210}{(1.1)^2} + \frac{1331}{(1.1)^3}$$

or - 3000 - 3000

This the two sides of the equation are equal which means the discounted value of cash inflows is equal to the original investment with a discount rate of 10%. Therefore, the Internal Rate of Return is 10%.

From there expression, it will be experienced that the calculation of internal rate is a tedious job as it can be calculated only by a trial and error approach. The difficulty in calculation is lessened to a great extent by the use of present value factor. The problem as given above may be solved by using present value factor as shown below:

Year	*Cash Flow*	*Present value at 5%*	*Present value*	*Present value at 10%*	*Present value*
0	–3000	1	- 3000	1	–3000
1	+ 1100	0.9524	1048	0.9091	1000
2	1210	0.9070	1097	0.8264	1000
3	1331	0.8638	1150	0.7513	1000
			3295		3000

Selection of Project

The internal rate of return is compared with the rate specified by the management. In case the IRR of a project is at least equal to or more than the specified rate, the project is considered worthwhile and approved for implementation. Conversely, if the IRR is less than the specified rate, the project is regarded as economically unsound and as much rejected. The specified rate is the rate of return which must be yielded by the capital investment. This rate is either the cost of capital or any other rate which the management considers as reasonable under the given circumstances. Thus the specified rate is the minimum rate or cut off rate. Any project yielding an internal rate lesser than the cut off rate is rejected. If the management has not pre-determined any rate and one project out of two or more competing projects has to be selected, then the project with the highest internal rate of return will be preferred and others rejected.

Selection of Rate for Discounting Cash Flows

There is no formula which can be used to select a rate of discounting which will equate the aggregate present values with the original investment. As already pointed out the internal rate is computed by trial and error approach according to which, in the first instance a rate is choosen for discounting the cash inflows. It will rarely happen that the present value by an arbitrary rate of discounting is equal to initial investment the present values of cash inflows will be either more or less than the investment. The first trial will suggest the next probable rate. For example, if the discounted values of cash-inflows with a discount rate of 10% is more than the original investment, the rate of discounting should be enhanced inorder to further reduce the discounted values so that they become equal to investment. If the two rates have been tried, one with which the aggregate discounted values of cash inflows is more than the original investment and the other which has reduced the cast inflows below the original investment, then the internal rate can be found out by the interpolation as under:

$$IRR = MR + \left(\frac{PV_1 - OI}{PV_1 - OI + OI - PV_2} \times Rd \right)$$

where IRR = Internal Rate of return

MR = Minimum rate of discounting

Pv_1 = Present value with minimum rate

Pv_2 = Present value with maximum rate

OI = Original investment

Rd = Difference in two discounting rates.

Illustration — 8

From the following, calculate the IRR using interpolation formula. The IRR lies in between 5% and 12%.

Years	*Cash flows*
0	– 3000
1	1100
2	1210
3	1331

Solution

Years	*Cash flows*	*Discount factor at 5%*	*Present value*	*Discount factor at 12%*	*Present value*
0	–3000	1.0000	– 3000	1.0000	–3000
1	1100	0.9524	1048	0.8929	982
2	1210	0.9070	1097	0.7972	965
3	1331	0.8036	1150	0.7118	947
			3295		2849

$$IRR = MR + \left(\frac{PV_1 - OI}{PV_1 - OI + OI - PV_2} \times Rd \right)$$

$$= 5\% + \left[\frac{3295 - 3000}{3295 - 3000 + 3000 - 2894} \times 7\% \right]$$

$$= 5\% + \left[\frac{295}{295 + 106} \times 7\% \right]$$

$$= 5\% + \left[\frac{295}{401} \times 7\% \right]$$

$$= 5\% + \frac{2065}{401} \times 5\% + 5.1 = 10.1\% \text{ or } 10\% \text{ approx.}$$

Illustration—9

Two projects A and B requiring an original investment of Rs. 11600 and Rs. 13750 are under the consideration of the management. The life of each project is 4 years after which they are fully scrapped. Expected cash flows over the life of the projects are given below:

Years	*Project A Cash Inflows*	*Project B Cash Inflows*
1	6,000	7,000
2	5,000	6,000
3	5,000	6,000
4	4,000	6,000

You are required to calculate the Internal Rate of Return and comment on the desirability of the project.

Solution

Original Investment = 11600

Years	*Cash Inflow*	*Discount factor (25%)*	*Present value*	*Discount factor 28%*	*Present value*
1	6,000	.8000	4800	.7813	4687
2	5,000	.6400	3200	.6104	3052
3	5,000	.5120	2560	.4768	2384
4	4000	.4096	1638	.3725	1490
			12198		11613

Original Investment = Rs. 13750

Years	*Cash Inflow*	*Discount factor (20%)*	*Present value*	*Discount factor 30%*	*Present value*
1	7,000	.7813	5469	.7692	5384
2	6,000	.6104	3662	.5917	3550
3	6,000	.4768	2860	.4552	2731
4	6,000	.3725	2235	.3501	2100
		14226			13765

Comments: The IRR for project A is 28% as the present value with this rate of discounting is approximately equal to original investment of Rs. 11600. Project B possesses an internal rate of 30%. Thus project B is better than project A. If the standard rate of return is, say 25%, then both the projects may be undertaken provided finance is not a limiting factor.

Merits of IRR

The IRR as a tool of project evaluation possesses the following merits:

1. Theoretically it is a sound technique as it duly recognises the time value of money.
2. It suggests the maximum rate which can be paid on borrowings for financing a project.
3. It is based on the concept of cash flow stream which is superior to income for making capital expenditure decisions.

4. It takes into account the entire cash flow stream for the computation of projectability rates.

Demerits

Though the IRR technique is conceptually quite sound. Yet it suffers from the following defects:

1. The IRR is found out by empirical method i.e. trial and error method which takes a lot of time to arrive at the internal rate.
2. The technique is difficult to understand by less educated entrepreneurs.
3. It may not guide properly if the life of the competing projects significantly differ. For example, if project A involves Rs. 10,000 and produces cash inflow of Rs. 12,000 at the end of one year, the IRR is 20% Another project B involves similar cash outlay but produces cash inflow of Rs. 3,000 for 5 years, the IRR in this case is 15%. A comparison of Internal rates of return suggests that project A is better but it assumes a steady return of 20% from the investment in the remaining 4 years also which is a wrong assumption and it may mislead the management in decision-making.
4. The existence of multiple rates for non-conventional budgetory expenditure might confuse the management in decision-making. Non-Conventional projects are those projects which involves cash-outlays not only in the beginning but also in the middle of the projects.

(B) Net Present Values Method (NPV Method)

This is another discounted cash flow technique which fully recognises the time value of money and takes into account the entire cash flow stream of a project. According to this method, the cash flows of a project are discounted by a pre-determined rate which is either the cost of capital or any other rate which the management deem acceptable or reasonable. The discounting of cash flow stream with a pre-discounting of cash flow stream with a pre-determined or fixed rate will rarely equate the aggregate present value of cash inflows with the original investment. It will be observed that the present value of cast inflows in either move or less than the original investment. The difference between the present value of cash inflows and the original investment is known as net present value which may be positive or negative. In case the present value is more than the original investment, the NPV is positive. If the original investment exceed the present value of cash inflows, the NPV is negative. The NPV is zero if the PV of cash flows and original investment are equal. The equation of the present value is as under:

$$PV = \frac{cf_1}{(1+r)} + \frac{cf_2}{(1+r)^2} + \frac{cf_3}{(1+r)^3} + \dots \frac{cf_n}{(1+r)^n}$$

where Pv = Present value of cash flows

cf_1, cf_2, cf_3,... cf_n, stands for cash inflows of various years

r stands for pre-determined rate of discounting

Selection of Project

A project is considered economically feasible if the NPV is positive. Any investment proposal with negative NPV is not accepted or rejected. The existence of positive NPV means that the project will yield the desired rate of return and still leave some income. Negative NPV shows the project is inability to yield the desired rate of return. A project whose NPV is zero is also acceptable as it will just recover the expected rate of return. Thus, only those projects which generate positive NPV are profitable. As regards the selection of a particular project out of many competing projects, the project with the highest positive NPV, being more projectable will be accepted.

Illustration—10

Project A, B and C are the three mutually exclusive projects which cost Rs. 11600, 13750 and 1500 respectively. The cash inflows over their lives have been estimated as shown below. You are required to select one project assuming that the standard rate of return is fixed at 28%

	Project A	*Project B*	*Project C*
Cash Outflow	–11,600	–13,750	–15,000
Cash Inflows:			
1st year	6,000	7,000	8,000
2nd year	5,000	6,000	7,000
3rd year	5,000	6,000	5,000
4th year	4,000	6,000	5,000

Solution

	Project A			*Project B*		*Project C*	
	Cash flows	*Discount factor (28%)*	*Present value*	*Cash flows*	*Present value*	*Cash flows*	*Present value*
Cash Outflow:	11,600	1.0000	11,600	- 13,750	13,750	—15,000	15,000
Cash Inflows:							
Ist year	6,000	0.7813	4,687	7,000	5,469	8,000	6,250
2nd year	5,000	0.6104	3,052	6,000	3,662	7,000	4,273
3nd year	5,000	0.4768	2,384	6,000	2,860	5,000	2,384
4th year	4,000	0.3725	1,490	6,000	2,235	5,000	1,862
Present Value			11,613		14,226		14,769
Net Present Value			+ 13		+ 476		—231

Thus project A and B have shown positive NPV which means both the projects can yield a return of 28% per annum. Project C with negative NPV means that it cannot yield the standard rate of return and as such be rejected. Since, we have to select one project, the choice will go in favour of Project B which is likely to produce more NPV.

Merits of NPV Method

The merits of NPV method may be enumerated as under:

1. Theoretically, it is a sound method as it duly recognises the time value of money.
2. It considers the full cash flow stream in the computation of NPV.
3. As compared to IRR method, it is easier to rank the budgetary proposals with this method.

Demerits of NPV Method

The method suffers from the following limitations:

1. It involves discounting of cash flows which is relatively a difficult process.
2. The method is not commonly understood.

3. It is based on pre-determined rate of discounting which is a generally cost of capital. The whole success of capital budgeting depends upon the correctness with which the cost of capital is estimated. The method pre-supposes that the enterprise shall be able to borrow funds at the pre-determined rate and employ them profitably. The NPV will lead properly so long as these assumptions hold good.

4. The NPV method might not lead to logical conclusion if the projects involve considerably varying investments and the difference between their net present values is not significant. Suppose project A and project B require an original cash outlay of Rs. 10,000 and Rs. 25,000 respectively. Project A produces a NPV of Rs. 85 while the NPV from B is 100. In this care, project A may be more desirable as it involves lesser capital outlay and its NPV is not significantly different from that of B. The NPV method does not correlate the NPV of a project with its investment.

5. The NPV method does not give any consideration to the lives of the competing projects. The NPV of two projects will not guide properly in the selection of a single project if the lives of the two are uneven. In case the two projects involve equal initial capital and also produce similar net present values, these should not be valued equally. The project with short life is certainly a better project.

Profitability Index or Benefit-Cost Approach

The profitability Index (PI) or Benefit-Cost technique is applied to determine the relative profitability of alternative projects involving different initial cash outflows. Profitability Index or Benefit-Cost Ratio is arrived at simply by dividing the Present value of Cash Inflows by the present value of cash outflow as shown below:

$$\text{PI or B/C Ratio} = \frac{\text{Present value of cash Inflows}}{\text{Present value of cash Outflows}}$$

It will be noticed that the Net Present value method of projects appraisal is an absolute technique whereas the PI or B/C ratio technique is a relative measure. The net present value in case of the projects with different cash outlays may be the same but such projects cannot be said to be equally good in view of the fact that the initial capital expenditure is different. Profitability Index is, undoubtedly, a better technique when the projects are required to be ranked according to their relective worth to the enterprise.

The selection of project on the basis of PI or B/C Ratio is very simple. If an independent project is being considered then it will be accepted only if the profitability Index is greater than one otherwise it will get rejection. In the case of mutually exclusion projects, the project having index greater than one with highest PI or B/C Ratio will be accepted and all others rejected. If only one project is to be selected under capital-rationing, the selection of projects depends on the availability of funds and the profitability of projects. The projects are arranged in descending order and the projects in that order are selected according to availability of capital.

Illustration—11

Using the relevant figures of Illustration-10, calculate the profitability Index/Benefit-Cost Ratio and comment on the same.

Solution

$$\text{Profitability Index} = \frac{\text{Present Volume of Cash Inflows}}{\text{Present Value of cash outflow}}$$

$$\text{PI for Project A} = \frac{11613}{11600} = 1.001$$

$$\text{PI for Project B} = \frac{14226}{13750} = 1.034$$

$$\text{PI for Project C} = \frac{14769}{15000} = 0.985.$$

The PI or B/C Ratios of Project A and B are greater than one, hence these projects are capable of Yielding desired rate of return; if availability of funds is not a limiting factor, then these may be accepted for implementation. However project C which has shown Index lesser than one can not meet profitability expectations and as such is liable to be rejected

Similar conclusion was drawn when we used NPV method for project selection. Since the PI or B/C Ratio method is based on NPV, it is not entirely a new method. The basic difference lies in the fact that the NPV method is a measure of absolute profitability in terms of initial cash outflow, whereas the PI is a relative measure.

Handling of Risk and Uncertainty in Capital Budgeting

Modern business is full of risks and uncertainties which arise due to dynamic changes of varied nature constantly taking place in a complex economic system under which a business enterprise has to operate. It is not possible to anticipate with certainty the full course of events which will influence the enterprise in a particular direction in the long-period of time. Therefore, it is unrealistic to evaluate a capital expenditure proposal under the assumption of certainty under which events affecting decisions are known and determinate due to which the risk attached to a capital project remains constant. We have already examined the capital projects with an assumption of certain cash flows over the live of projects. In the paragraphs that follow, we will study the techniques which may be used to handle risk and uncertainty involved in capital projects.

It may be pointed out that risks and uncertainty involved in long-term capital projects cannot be eliminated. However, it can be minimised through scientific calculations and control techniques. Risk may be defined as the expected loss of profit due to inexact forecast of future events which adversely affect the decision of an entrepreneur. In other words, the risk is a situation in which future state of the economy and industry are known and it is possible for the decision-maker to objectively assign probabilities to the outcome of events which are of repetitive nature. Uncertainty refers to a situation in which it is not possible to visualise all the events which will effect the decision and assign probabilities to their occurances on any objective basis. The decision-makers working under conditions of uncertainties can only guess the future course of events, due to their non-repetitive or specific nature. It may be pointed out that even in cases where an event is of repetitive nature, many decision-makers use their best guesses based on subjective considerations instead of objective method to assign probability to the outcome of the event. In such cases the distinction between risk and uncertainty disappears. The difference between risk and uncertainty is considered by many financial experts as hypothetical and they prefer to use the two terms interchangeably. We would also prefer not to make any distinction between the two terms.

Risk and uncertainty involved in a capital project is handled by using different method of analysing the same. The methods used for the purpose may be classified into two broad categories: (I) Traditional or Conservative methods and (2) Quantitative or modern methods.

Traditional or Conservative Methods

The method included under the group are: (1) shorter Pay-Back Period method, (ii) Risk adjusted discount rate, (iii) certainty equivalent approach.

Shorter Pay-Back Period

This method is based on the belief that the projects with shorter Pay-Back period involve lesser risk as compared with the projects with longer Pay-Back period. Accordingly, the risk can be minimised by selecting that project which ensures the recovery of capital investment in a shorter period of time. The management may fix a minimum period within which the original investment may be paid back. Such a minimum period is termed as cut off period. The estimated Pay-Back period of any proposed project should not exceed the cut off period which signifies the risk tolerance level of the firm. The cut-off period of a risky projects is lesser than what it would be under risk-free consideration, as the effort of the management is to recover the capital investment as early as possible. Suppose, there are two projects with equal expected life of 7 years and initial capital investment Rs. 10 lakh in each case and the management forecast a Pay-Back period of 4 years and 5 years for project I and II respectively. In such a case, it is obvious that the firm will select project I and reject project II. If the cut-off Pay-Back period is 3-1/2 years, both the project will be rejected. This is a very simple method of handling risk, and suffers from all the merits and limitations of the Pay-Back period method discussed earlier in case of projects evaluation under condition of certainty.

Risk Adjusted Discount Rate

Discount rate is the minimum desired rate of return which is generally the cost of capital for a firm. This is the rate which is used for discounting the cash flows of risk free projects. In case the project is exposed to risk and uncertainty, the risk-free discount rate is adjusted to provide for risk involved in the project. The discount rate is raised by adding what is called the 'risk premium' to it. The risk-premium to be added to the discount rate defends upon the degree of risk. It varies directly with variations in the risk which means a higher premium is added to a more risky project. Supper, the management desires a rate of return of 15% an capital employed under risk-free economic conditions. If it is required to implement a project under risk and uncertainty conditions, then a risk premium; of say 4% may be added to 15% to provide for risk. In such a case the cash flows will be discounted by 15 + 4 = 19% discount rate which will obviously give lesser present value of the cash flows. It is likely that the project, when discount by 19% may be rejected. The risk adjusted discount rate may also be compared with the internal rate of return. All the projects with IRR lesser than 19% will have to be rejected.

The risk adjusted discount rate technique to provide for risk in capital budgeting rightly lakes care of the risk averse attitude of the entrepreneurs. It is also simple to understand and easy to apply. But the rate of allowance of risk (risk-premium rate) makes it a controversial technique. How much weight should be assigned to risk premium is an issue on which different views may be expressed.

Certainty Equivalent Approach

There are financial and accounting experts who think that it is not proper to use the adjusted Discount Rate to provide for risk in capital projects became in their opinion it is not the discount rate but the cash flows which are subject to risk and as such adjustment or necessary changes may be made in cash flow forecasts. According to certainty equivalent approach, the cash flows are conservatively estimated to arrive at the definite cash flows for various years during the life of the project. The cash flows estimated under assumptions of normal risk are further reduced to a figure which is considered to be definite by the use of the correction factor or certainty equivelant coefficient. For example if the cash flow for any year under normal risk is Rs. 50,000 but the management thinks that 80 per cent of it will be definite, then 0.8 is the certainty equivalent coefficient corrective factor, which should be used to reduce 50,000 to a definite figure of 40,000 (50,000 × .8). The C.E. coefficient can also be determined objectively by dividing the risky cash flow by risk-free cash flow as under:

$$\text{C.E. Coefficient} = \frac{\text{Risk-free cash flow}}{\text{Risky cash flow}}$$

The Risk free cash flow is always lesser than the risky cash flow. Therefore, the C.E. coefficient will be lesser than 1. Thus the risky cash flows are first reduced by multiplying them by the respective C.E. Coefficient and then calculated the present values by the Discount Rate (cost of capital).

Illustration—12

Two projects involving an initial capital outlay of Rs. 50,000 in each but with varying degrees of risk are under the consideration of the management of a company. The estimated cash inflows over the life with certainty-equivocals are given below. You are required to give your opinion as to which of the two projects should he selected if the risk-free cut-off rate is 15%.

Years	*Project A*		*Project B*	
	Cash inflow	*Certainty Coefficient*	*Cash inflows*	*Certainty Coefficient*
1	20,000	.6	25,000	.7
2.	30,000	.7	40,000	.8
3.	35,000	.8	30,000	.9
4.	25,000	.7	20,000	.8
5.	20,000	.5	10,000	.6

Year	Project A			Project B		
	Certain cash flows	*Discount factor @ 15%*	*Present values*	*Certain cash flows*	*Discount factor @ 15%*	*Present value*
0	-50,000	1	-50,000	-50,000	1	-50,000
1	12,000	0.8695	10,434	17,500	0.8695	15,216
2	21,000	0.7561	15,876	32,000	0.7561	24,195
3	28,000	.6575	18,410	27,000	0.6575	17,752
4	17,500	.5717	10,005	16,000	.5717	9,147
5	10,000	0.4972	4,972	6,000	.4972	2,983
Aggregate Present Value		59697		Aggregate Present Value		69,293
Net Present value		9697				19,293

The analysis of data shows that the NPV of projects A and B is 9697 and 19,293 respectively. It is obvious that Project B yields higher NPV and as such it should be selected.

Quantitative or Modern Method

The quantitative or modern methods to handle risk in capital Budgeting include the following:

1. Standard Deviation Method
2. Coefficient of Variation Method
3. Sensitivity Analysis
4. Probability Assignment
5. Decision-tree Analysis.

1. Standard Deviation Method

It is a statistical technique which may be used to measure risks involved in alternative capital projects. Project with lower degree of risk may be preferred to any other project carrying higher degree of risk. Standard deviation is the square root of the arithmetic average of the squares of the deviations measured from the mean. It can be profitably used to understand the risk complexion of the two projects which have identical cost and net present values. Following formula is used to measure standard deviation:

Example - 13 $\sigma = \sqrt{\frac{fdx}{n}}$

A company has projected the following cash inflows alongwith their probabilities for the two mutually exclusive projects having the same cash outflow:

Year	*Project A*		*Project B*	
	Cash inflows (000)	*Probability*	*Cash flows (000)*	*Probability*
1	10,000	.1	8,000	.1
2.	15,000	.2	10,000	.1
3.	25,000	.1	20,000	.2
4.	15,000	.4	12,000	.4
5.	10,000	.2	10,000	.2

Measure risk using standard deviation method and give your opinion about the desirability of a project.

Solution

Calculate of S.D. for Project A

Cash Inflow	*Deviation from Mean (1500)*	*Square of Deviations*	*Probability*	*Weighted Square Deviations* Σd^2
(1)	*(2)*	*(3)*	*(4)*	*(3×4)*
10,000	–5,000	2,50,00,00	.1	25,00,000
15,000	0	0	.2	9
25,000	+ 10,000	10,00,00,000	.1	1,00,00,000
15,000	0	0	.4	0
10,000	–5,000	2,50,00,000	.2	50,00,000
			Ef = 1	1,75,00,000

$$\sigma = \sqrt{\frac{1,75,00,000}{1}} = 4,183.3$$

STANDARD DEVIATION FOR PROJECT B

Cash Inflow	*Deviation for Area*	*Square of Deviation*	*Probabilities*	*Weighted Square deviation*
1	*2*	*3*	*4*	*(3 × 4)*
8,000	-4,000	1,60,00,000	.1	16,00,000
10,000	-20,000	40,00,000	.1	40,00,000
20,000	+ 8,000	6,40,00,000	.2	1,28,00,000
12,000	0	0	.4	0
10,000	-2,000	40,00,000	.2	8,00,000
			Ef = 1	1,56,00,000

$$\sigma = \sqrt{\frac{15600000}{1}} = 3949.6$$

The S. D. of 4183.3 of Project A and 3949.6 in cash of B shows that the degree of variability of expected return for Project A is higher than that of project B. It means project A is more risky and preference be given for project B.

2. Co-efficient of Variation Method

We learned that the standard deviation provides an absolute measure of risk which may mislead the management without the consideration of the average expected return for alternative projects. Therefore, it is advisable to compute the relative measure of dispersion. Coefficient of variation correlates the standard deviation and mean value of frequency distribution. It is calculated as under:

$$\text{Coefficient of Variation} = \frac{\sigma s}{n}$$

$$\text{or Per cent C. V.} = \frac{\sigma s}{n} \times 100$$

Using the date of the example 13, compute the coefficient of variation of the two projects and give your final recommendation about the selection of the project.

% Coefficient of Variation for project A

$$= \frac{\sigma s}{a} \times 100$$

$$= \frac{4183.3}{15{,}000} \times 100 = 27.8\%$$

% of Coefficient of variation for Project B

$$= \frac{\sigma s}{a} \times 100$$

$$= \frac{3949.6}{12{,}000} \times 100 = 32.9\%.$$

Comment: Higher Coefficient of variation of 32.9% for Project B as compared to C.V. of 27.8% for project A suggests a different action. As per these calculations project B is more risky and management may, obviously prefer project A.

3. Sensitivity Analysis

Sensitivity analysis is concerned with determining the likely change in the rate of return or net present value of a project as a result of changes in Key factors. A key factor is a factor which considerably effect the cash flows and net present value of a project. Few important key factors in the analysis of any capital project are the cost, price, competition, economic life of project, rate of inflation etc. The management would like to know the behaviour of the NPV with a change in a key factor. The sensitivity analysis may also be done by estimating the cash inflows on the assumption of (a) Pessimistic, (b) Most likely and (c) Optimistic future condition and calculating the NPV by a cut off rate. The project showing wide variation in Pessimistic and optimistic calculation will imply a higher degree of risk. The selection of the project depends upon the amount of favourable positive effect on the Net present value of the project.

Sensitivity analysis provides a better insight into the risk complexion of the projects. But the application of this technique in real life situations poses many problems such as the identification of the key factors and change in their values for the purpose of analysis. Actually a firm operates under a complex economic environment and there are a number of inter-related factors which simultaneously effect the performance in various directions and degrees. Hence, it is not justified to do a single key factor sensitivity analysis which may sometimes lead to wrong decision. A simultaneous multi-factor sensitivity analyses is really a very difficult task. These limitations reduced the practical utility of this tool to a great extent.

Illustration - 14

Two projects known as x and y are under the consideration of the management of ABC Ltd. Each project involve an initial Capital outlay of Rs. 180000. The management consider 15% as the desirable rate of return. The experts have forecasted following cash inflow over the life of the project.

Year	Project X	Project Y
	50,000	40,000
	70,000	90,000
	80,000	80,000
	50,000	70,000
	20,000	15,000

Assuming an increase in cost variable of 5% and other variables remaining the same, calculate the profitability of the projects and comment in the results.

Solution

Since all other factors are assumed as remaining constant when the cost of project goes up by 5% we will not change the estimated cash flows.

CAPITATION OF NPV OF THE PROJECTS

Year	Discount factor @ 15%	Project X Cash Inflows	Project X Present value	Project Y Cash Inflows	Project Y Present value
0	1	-1,80,000	1,80,000	-1,80,000	1,80,000
1	.8695	50,000	43,475	40,000	34,780
2	.7561	70,000	52,927	90,000	68,049
3	.6575	80,000	52,600	80,000	52,600
4	.5717	50,000	28,585	70,000	40,019
5	.4972	20,000	9,944	15,000	7,458
			1,87,531		2,02,906
		Less	1,80,000		1,80,000
		NPV	7,531		22,906

The above analysis shows the NPV of 7531 and 22906 for project X and Y Thus, the Project Y is more profitable. In case the sensitivity lest is conducted, the NPV of the two projects would get reduced as the cost factor has shown an increase of 5% in both the cases. NPV after taking into account the change in the cost factor will be as under:

Project X's NPV = 1,87,531 –(1,80,000 +5% of 1,80,000)
= 1,87,531 –1,89,000 = –1,469

Project X's NPV = 202906 –(1,80,000 +5% of 1,80,000)
= 2,02,906 –1,89,000 = 13,906.

Thus the sentitivity test has shown that the project X yields negation NPV of—1469 and , therefore it should be outrightly rejected. Project Y is still profitable.

4. Probability Assignment

The assumption that the cash flows for different years are equally likely is not always valid. In most of the cases, the probability of occurring cash flows in different years is different. Therefore the cashflows are to be assigned probability according to expectation of their realization. Probability measures the likelihood of happening or not happening of a certain event. The risk inherent in a capital project is taken care of by assigning probability (weights) to the cash flows of all the years. However, the assignment of probability to estimated cash flows is a delicate job. Generally, the probabilities are assigned on subjective basis due to non-repetitive nature of capital projects.

Example - 15

Preet and Co. propose to install a machine out of two available models in the market. Each machine costing Rs. 12000 has an equal expected life of 5 years but the cash inflows are likely to differ due to technical differences. The company estimates the cash flows and their associated probabilities as follows:

	Machine A		*Machine B*	
Years	*Expected cash Inflows*	*Probability*	*Expected Cash inflows*	*Probability*
1	10,000	.10	20,000	.20
2	14,000	.20	25,000	.15
3	20,000	.30	28,000	.20
4	25,000	.30	30,000	.25
5	10,000	.10	20,000	.20

What will be your recommendation as regards the selection of the machine if the company desires a profit of 12%.

Solution

Calculation of Expected Net Present Value for each machine

Year	Discount Factor @ 12%	Machine A Cash inflows	Probability	Expected value	Present value	Machine B Cash inflow	Probability	Expected value	Present value
1	.8928	10000	.10	1000	893	20000	.20	4000	3379
2	.7972	14000	.20	2800	2332	25000	.15	3750	2990
3	.7118	29000	.30	6000	4271	28000	.20	56000	3986
4	.6355	25000	.30	7500	4766	30,000	.25	7500	4766
5	.5674	10000	.10	1000	567	20000	.20	4000	2270
			PV		12,729	Less cost			12,000
			Less Cost		12,000	Less Cost			12,000
			NPV		729	NPV			5583

Recommendation

The company should purchase Machine B as it will generate a greater NPV of 5583 as cup and to NPV of 729 for Machine A.

5. Decision-Tree Analysis

This is an important analysitical technique to handle risk involved in a Capital project. According to it, the decision alternations are identified and each alternative is studied in the light of the future probable conditions followed by future decision. A graphic display of the relationship between a present decision and possible future events, future decisions and their consequences provides a picture which resembles that of a tree and as such it is called a decision tree analysis. The decision tree depicts an investment decision which involve a sequence of decision over tree. In other words a decision tree is a pictorial representation in tree from which shows the projected cash flows under each alternative for various chance events, probability of accruing each event. Net present rulers, expected rules etc.

Illustration—14

A firm is considering to purchase a machine which requires a cash outlay of Rs. 1000. The useful life of the machine is expected to be 2 years with no savage value. The firm forecast the cash flows and the related probabilities for the two years as follows:

I Year	*Cash flow*	*Probability*
(i)	5000	0.3
(ii)	6000	0.4
(iii)	8000	0.3

II Year	*Cash flow*	*Probability*	*Cash flow*	*Probablity*	*Cash flow*	*Probability*
(i)	4000	0.2	7000	0.3	8000	0.2
(ii)	5000	0.5	8000	0.4	10000	0.6
(iii)	7000	0.3	9000	0.3	12000	0.2

The desired rate of return is 10% Plate the above data is the form of a decision tree and comment on the profitability of the machine.

Solution

DECISION TREE

Year-0	*Year-1 Prob.*	*Year-1 Cash flow*	*Year-2 Prob. flows*	*Year-2 Cash flow value*	*Net present Value of cash*	*Joint Prob.*	*Expected Net Present*
			.3	4000	–2151	.06	–129
	.3	5000	.5	5000	–1325	0.15	–199
Cash			.3	7000	331	0.09	29
Out			.3	7000	1240	0.12	148
flow	.4	6000	.4	8000	2962	0.16	320
Rs.			.3	9000	2888	0.12	346
10000							
			.2	8000	3880	0.06	232
	.3	8000	.6	10000	5532	0.18	995
			.2	12000	7184	0.06	431
						1.00	2173

Expected Present value = NPV x Jt. Probability

Comment

Since the Expected Not present value at 10% cut off rate is positive i.e. Rs. 2173 the machine may be bought by the firm.

CALCULATION OF NET PRESENT VALUE

Alter-nations		I-year	II-year	Present Value of 10% I-year	II-year	Total	Net Profit value
(a)	(i)	5000	4000	4545*	3304*	7849	−2151
	(ii)	5000	5000	4545	4130	8675	−1325
	(iii)	5000	7000	4545	5786	10331	331
(b)	(i)	6000	7000	5454	5786	11240	1240
	(ii)	6000	8000	5454	6608	12062	2062
	(iii)	6000	9000	5454	7434	12888	2888
(c)	(i)	8000	8000	7272	6608	13880	3880
	(ii)	8000	10000	7272	8260	15532	5532
	(iii)	8000	12000	7272	9912	17184	7184

*5000 × 0909 = 4545 and so on

* 4000 × 826 = 3304 and so on

NPV = Total Present Value—Initial Investment

QUESTIONS

1. What do you mean by Capital Budgeting? Explain the steps involved in a capital budgeting process.
2. How are the Cash Inflows for the purpose of Capital Budgeting are computed? Explain with example.
3. Capital Budgeting decisions assume special significance in an organisation." What is that significance? Explain clearly.
4. What are traditional or non-discounting and Discounted Cash Flow techniques of evaluating Capital expenditure proposals? Explain any one of the technique fully.
5. What is a Pay-Back Period? Calculate the Pay-Back Period in the following case.

Years	*Net Incremental Cash Flows*
0	−50000
1	13500
2	12000
3	10500
4	9000
5	8000
6	6000
7	4000

What is your recommendation? Is the desired Pay-Back period 4 years?

6. What are the merits and limitation of Pay-Back Period as a project evaluation method?
7. What is an Accounting Rate of Return (ARR) method? Is it a superior technique as compound the Pay-Back method?
8. What do you mean by a 'Discounted Cash Flow'? Explain the process of discounting by an example.
9. Discuss the salient features of the Discounted Cash Flow Techniques of evaluating the capital investment projects.
10. "Profitability Index or Benefit-cost Ratio technique is superior to Net Present Value method." Do you agree with the statement? Give reasons in support of your answer
11. How will you provide for risk and uncertainty in capital-Budgeting discussions? Explain clearly.
12. Give a brief account of the Traditional or Conventional method which are commonly used for handling risks in capital budgeting.
13. State the Quantitative or modern methods which are used to handle risk in capital budgeting and explain any them in detail.
14. Two mutually exclusion project A and B requiring an initial investment of Rs. 50000 each and under the consideration of management. The desired rate of return is 10%. Projects are likely to generate net cash-inflows over their life as under:

Year	*Project A*	*Project B*
0	–50000	–50000
1	10000	15000
2	15000	25000
3	25000	30000
4	12000	20000
5	5000	10000

You are required to calculate:

(i) Pay-Back period of each project.
(ii) Average rate of Return for each project which one of the projects be selected if availability of firms is a limiting factor.

15. Two proposals relating to installation of two different types of machines for the manufacture of product A and B respectively are under the consideration of an enterpreneur who would like to instal a single machine for want of adequate funds. The relevant data are given below:

	Machine A	*Machine B*
Cost of Machine	25000	35000
Economic life	4 years	4 years
Scrap Value	1500	1500
Installation Cost	1000	1500
Additional Working Capital	5000	6500
Yearly Income before Depreciation and Taxes	15000	20000
Annual Depreciation	5875	7000

The enterprises experts an annual return of 15% and the corporate tax is 50% you are required to give you recommendation based on Net Present Value method.

16. Using discounted Cash Flow technique evaluate the following capital expenditure proposals:

		Proposal A	*Proposal B*
Investment cost		180000	225000
Economic life		'5'years	5 years
Earnings before Interest and Taxes...	*Year*		
	1	60000	80000
	2	80000	80000
	3	50000	60000
	4	40000	50000
	5	30000	40000

Assume a tax rate of 40% and cost of capital 12%.

17. X Ltd. is considering to expand by the installation of an additional machine costing Rs. 250000. The machine is likely to generate cash income after-tax though its life of 5 years as under.

Year	*Cash Inflows*
0	–25,000
1	75,000
2	90,000
3	1,00,000
4	80,000
5	60,000

The company desires a return of 18% on capital investment. Since it is operating under uncertain condition, it has few a risk premium of 2%. Using NPV method, comment on the profitability of the project.

18. A capital expenditure proposal is expected to generate the following Cash-inflows. The certainty equivalents for the cash flows are given against each year's cash-inflow.

Year	*Cash inflows*	*Certainty equivalents*
0	– 250000	1
1	75000	0.9
2	90000	0.6
3	100000	0.5
4	80000	0.8
5	60000	0.7

Should the project be accepted if the risk-free discount rate is 12%.

19. The cash flows with their probabilities are given below:

	Project A		*Project B*	
Year	*Cash Inflows*	*Probability*	*Cash-Inflows*	*Probability*
1	25000	.1	20000	.1
2	35500	.2	25000	.1
3	65000	.1	50000	.2
4	38000	.4	30000	.4
5	25000	.2	20000	.2

Calculate standard deviation and coefficient of variation for projects A and B to show the extent of risk. Which project would for recommend for acceptance.

20. Write short notes on
   (i) Sensitivity Analysis
   (ii) Decision-tree analysis
   (iii) Management attitude towards risk.

5

Budgets and Budgetary Control

The management of business activities on scientific basis is essential for optimising the use of resources with a view to achieving ultimate objectives of running an enterprise. The principles of scientific management suggest the systematised approach to the problems of production, marketing, personnel, finance, etc. According to it, every activity affecting the overall business objectives should be pre-planned and nothing should be left to chances. The management should be clear about the approach to be followed to accomplish a particular task and there must exist a system for taking corrective action wherever things go wrong or beyond the expectations of the management. Managerial control becomes essential in case of public limited companies and government undertakings which are run by hired managerial personnel with little interest in the results of such enterprises. The proprietors have, therefore, to think of a device which may encourage the management to work with greater care and caution to serve the interests of all by optimising the use of investments in the form of man, money and materials. Budgeting is one such device which helps the management to understand the business programmes in their right perspective and take steps to achieve business objectives.

Meaning of Budget, Budgeting and Budgetary Control

We know about central and state governments budgets which are presented in the parliament and state assemblies every year. These deals with the expected revenues and expenditure for a years time. In the field of commerce, business firms prepare different types of budgets such as sales budget, production budget, cash budget, etc. A budget is a formal business plan for some future period. According to J.J. Hampton "A budget is a formal plan expressed in dollars.'' Charles T. Horngren states, "A budget is a formal quantitative expression of management plan." Brown Howard are of the view that "a budget is a pre-determined statement of management policy during a given period which provides a standard for comparison with the results actually achieved.'' According to the Institute of Cost and Works Accountant, England a budget is "a financial or quantitative statement prior to a defined period of time, of a policy to be persued for that period to attain a given objective.'' From these definitions, the salient features of a budget may be noted as under:

1. A budget is a document in writing.
2. It pertains to a policy which is to be executed during budget period.
3. It relate to a defined period in future.
4. A budget is expressed in terms of physical quantities, money values or both.
5. Some specific objectives are to be achieved through the establishment of budgets.
6. Budgets provide a basis or standard for comparison with actual performance for control purposes.

Budgeting means planning for future. It involves the preparation of departmental budgets, budgetory control and related issues. The budgetory control is concerned with the management of business activities with the help of budgets. In this way, budgets serve as a control device. The Institute of Cost and Works Accountants, England, has defined budgetory control as "the establishment of departmental budgets relating to the responsibilities of executives to the requirements of a policy, and the continuous comparison of actual with budgeted results, either to secure by individual action the objectives of that policy or to provide a firm basis for its revision." J. Batty defines budgetory control as "a system which uses budgets as a means of planning and controlling all aspects of producing and/or selling commodities and services." In the opinion of Brown and Howard, "Budgetory control is a system of controlling costs which includes the preparation of budgets, coordinating the departments and establishing responsibilities, comparing actual performance with the budgeted and acting upon results to achieve maximum efficiency."

A close study of the above definitions of budgetary control clearly brings out the important features of the system as under:

1. Budgetary control involves the establishment and preparation of departmental budgets i.e., budgets for different types of

activities like sales, purchases, production, capital equipment, cash, etc.

2. It specifies the responsibilities of the departmental heads who are required to achieve the targets set out in the budgets for the realisation of business objectives.
3. It calls for continuous comparison of actual results with the budgeted specifications for the purpose of controlling activities concerning production and sales.
4. Budgetory control is aimed at enhancing over-all efficiency and profitability of an organisation through proper planning, coordination and control of activities for which budgets are prepared.
5. Budgets may be revised, if found necessary.

From the above it will be realized that budgets and budgetory control are not the two separate subjects to be studied separately. In fact, they are inter-linked as the budgetary control is not possible without budgets and budgets are meant for controlling business activities.

Objects of Budgetary Control

The management of an organisation is primarily concerned with the realization of organisational objectives. In its efforts to achieve these objectives, it has to manage the enterprise efficiently by optimising the use of resources and eliminating or minimising the wastes, if any. Budgetory control is one of the important techniques which help the management in controlling business activities in a desired direction.

It serves the following objectives in an enterprise:

1. Formalise Business Objectives

The business objectives are formalised in the form of different types of budgets which sets targets in physical and/or monetary values.

2. Coordination and Balanced Efforts

Budgeting seeks to achieve coordination between departments. Budgets for different departments are prepared only after taking into account their inter-dependence. For example, production budget is influenced by the sales budget and the available production facilities. The coordination which is an essential element in management becomes effective when budgets are rightly drawn and implemented.

3. Communication

Budgeting fills the communication gap between management and employees through departmental budgets which are used as a vehicle to communicate the targets in explicit terms to various levels of management. Since budgeting accomplish the task of communicating goals and targets, the top management is not required to tell and guide the departmental heads about their areas of responsibilities.

4. Control

Controlling of various types of activities is the prime objective of budgeting. Budgets serve as an index of effeciency expected of the employees. The comparison of actual performance with the budget specifications sharply tells the difference. Management action is needed in case the actual performance is less than the desired performance. Thus budgeting fulfills the objective of control which is always desirable for smooth functioning of an enterprise.

5. Delegation of Authority

Budgeting aims at effective delegation of authority and decentralization of responsibility. This objective is achieved by communicating the functional budgets to different levels of management.

Advantages of Budgetary control

Budgetary control has assumed a special significance in almost every organisation. There is hardly any enterprise and government department in which budgeting is not done. The budgetary control system enables the management to enhance over-all efficiency for the achievements of organisational objectives. It contributes in the development of an undertaking in the following manner:

1. Budgetary control provides an action plan which is prepared after a great deal of exercise on various issues which might affect the execution of the plan. With the adoption of formal budgets, everybody in the organisation knows and understands his responsibilities which prevents all sorts of confusions as regards authority and responsibility.

2. With a prior knowledge of work to be done the management can develop an appropriate strategy for the achievements of the targets set out in the budgets.

3. Budgeting develops a sense of responsibility among the employees who are required to do a particular work in a given period of time. The powers can be delegated without much fear of its being misused.

4. Budgetary control provides for the preparation of variance report which contains a comparatives study of actual and budgeted figures with variances. An adverse variance, i.e. actual performance falling short of budgeted performance, is brought to the knowledge of top management which finally takes corrective action to avoid such a situation in the next budget period. In this manner control becomes more effective.

5. Budgeting helps in the coordination of business activities without which an enterprise cannot run in perfect harmony. For example, production budget is drawn in accordance with the expected sales as set out in Sales budget. Similarly, purchase budget is prepared according to quantity production as shown in production budget.

6. Budget serves as a medium of written communication. It ensures better understanding and harmoneous relation between top management, managers and workers.

7. Delays in the implementation of the business programmes is avoided by the preparation and implementation of budgets well in time.

8. Overheads budget sets limit to expenditure on various items. Any expenditure beyond the limit specified can be incurred only with the prior sanction of the competent authority. Thus there is opportunity to scrutinize the expenditure before it is actually incurred. Thus over-spending of overheads can be checked and scarce financial resources put to proper use.

9. Budgets, if properly drawn economise the use of resources. For example, if the budget for inventories is rightly drawn up, it will reduce the requirements of the money to be tied up in inventories.

10. Budgets suggest the arrangement the facilities well in advance for maintaining the operational efficiency of any enterprise. For instance, Cash budget clearly indicates the deficit/surplus cash position at different timings and accordingly additional working capital may be procured or

surplus cash invested for effective working of the organisation.

11. Budgetary control provides a basis for rewarding the employees who perform better. It is generally not used as a punitive measure.

12. A sound budgetary control system can contribute in the set up the standard costing which can act a complementary to budgeting.

Limitations of Budgetary Control System

Budgets and budgetary control system is, undoubtedly, very important for running an enterprise on scientific basis for optimising the use of available resources and achieving organisational objectives. However, the system suffers from certain limitations and the management should keep them in view while adopting and implementing the system. The main limitations are as under:

1. Budgets are Estimates

The figures contained in a budget . are simply an estimate about future. Budgets are prepared on the basis of certain assumptions about future. It is likely that the assumptions might not hold good. In that case, the whole budget will have to be recast. The revision of budgets in accordance with the changes in business conditions is a must for the success of budgeting.

2. Wrong Budgets may be Prepared

The success of budgetary control system largely depends upon the accuracy with which the budgets are prepared. If the forecasting is done on the basis of inadequate informations or subjective considerations of management, then the wrong budgets will be formulated. Wrong budgeting leads to wrong strategies which leads to wastage of resources and thus the very purpose of budgeting is forfeited.

3. Mismanagement

Budgetary control becomes effective only when the managers who are responsible for implementing the budgets are efficient and duty-conscious. Budgeting itself is no guarantee for success in business if the management is inefficient or indifferent to the budgetary control system. There can be no substitute for better management.

4. Employees Resistance

Sometimes, the employees who are charged with the responsibility of operating the budgets and achieve the desired results oppose budgeting due to their inefficient character which is exposed when they fail to achieve the targets. Many a times, the resistance to budgeting is just psychological. The top management can lessen the workers' resistance to budgeting by the preparation of realistic budgets with the consent and cooperation of all those who are concerned with the implementation of budgeting in the organisation.

5. Rigidity

Generally, the management prepares the budgets for next year by making some changes here and there in the existing budgets. This method of budget preparation introduces an element of rigidity in budgeting which can be eliminated by introducing the system of zero base budgeting in which a fresh thought is given to the whole issue of budgeting.

6. Costly Affair

The system involves cost in terms of money, time and energy. Efforts should be made to reduce the cost by developing an appropriate and simple method of budgeting and control system.

Every system has its limitations, so is the case with budgets and budgetary control system. Most of the limitations can be avoided by intelligent management of the budgetary control system. Following points deserve special attention of top for being successful in budgeting:

1. Defining business objectives. The management should define business objectives both short-term and long-term in unambiguous terms so that everyone in the organisation understand them and budgets are prepared realistically.

2. Defining duties and responsibilities. The authority, duties and responsibilities of each level of executives should also be clearly defined. For this purpose, an organisation chart should be laid down.

3. Fixation of budget period. Budget period is a period of time for which a budget is prepared. It should be clearly fixed.

4. Identification of key factors. Key factors means the basic or fundamental factors which powerfully hinder the budgets operations. The availability of skilled labour, raw materials or machine capacity may be a limiting factory. The management should prepare budget keeping in view the availability of basic facilities.

5. Cooperation of employees. Budgeting cannot be successful without the cooperation and involvement of all these who are directly or indirectly concerned with the preparation and implementation of budgets. The management should involve all departmental heads in the preparation of budgets and seek their valuable opinion, support and cooperation which are vital for the success in budgeting.

6. Support of top management. Budgeting cannot succeed if the top management is indifferent and lack enthusiasm for successful implementation of budgetory control system. The whole-hearted support of management is essential for the achievement of business objectives through the device of budgets and budgetary control.

7. Realistic budgets. Realistic budgets based on objective assessment of things are necessary for success in budgeting. Budgets prepared on the assumptions of idealistic conditions will set the targets on higher side which will cause frustration among the executives.

8. Revision of budgets. The management should revise the budgets if the circumstances so warrants. Budget revision becomes necessary if the factors influencing budgeting have drastically changed. It is also needed when some errors with the existing budgets are found at later date.

9. Efficient accounting system. There must exist an efficient accounting system to provide necessary data to the system of budgetary control. The accounting department should be actively involved in the process of budgeting.

10. Proper communication system. The management should develop effective means of communication between different levels of management. The system of communication should enable the flow of information from top to bottom and from bottom to top without any hinderence. Any communication gap will retard the smooth functioning of the budgetary control system.

11. Appointment of budget committee and budgetary controller. The task of preparation of budgets may be entrusted to a Budget Committee consisting of various departmental heads and a budgetary controller may be appointed to act as a coordinator or convener of Budget Committee.

12. Introduction of incentive plan. Since the budgeting tends to be mechanical over a period of time, the management should keep alive the interest of executives in budgeting by educating them about the need and importance of budgeting for the enterprise with which their fate is associated. The management may introduce an incentive plan to reward all those who are able to achieve the performance expected of them.

Organisation for Budgetary Control System

An efficient organisation for budgetory control is highly important for achieving the objectives of budgeting. It provides the framework within which the managerial functions of preparation, execution and control of budgets take place for the successful performance of business programmes. The organisation for an effective budgetory control consist of a Budget Committee and appointment of a Budgetory Controller.

Budget Committee

Budgeting is a continuous process. It requires full attention of the management so that timely action is taken on issues concerning the preparation, maintenance and administration of budgets. Generally, the top management appoints a committee known as Budget Committee which works under the supervision of a budget officer. The Budget Committee consists of the executive heads of different departments in the undertaking. Following functions are usually performed by a Budget committee:

1. Defines management policies relating to budgeting.
2. Prescribes general guidelines for the preparation of budgets.
3. Collects and provides necessary informations to divisional managers for the preparation of budgets.
4. Scrutinizes, revises and approves the budgets as prepared by different divisional managers. In this process it reconciles the divergent views of the the departmental heads.
5. Coordinates departmental activities through budgets.
6. Receives budget performance reports to fix responsibilities and suggest corrective actions in case of less than expected performance of any department.

7. Suggests revision of budgets, if necessary.
8. Prepares Master Budget which integrates the departmental budgets and also includes the estimated Profit and Loss Account and Balance Sheet.

The Budget Committee works in an advisory capacity but its recommendations are generally accepted by the top management. Thus, the Budget Committee is a powerful committee which performs a very useful role for the success of budgetary control system in an enterprise.

Budgetary Controller

The top management appoints an officer to supervise and guide the Budget Committee in the discharge of its functions. This officer is variously designated as Budget Officer, Budget Director, Budget Coordinator or Budgetary Controller in different organisations. He is generally a controller or chief accountant well versed in accounting and budgeting matters. The Budgetary controller is attached to the chief executive to whom he is accountable in matters of budgeting. He is expected to perform the following functions:

1. To call meetings of the departmental heads and educate them in the mechanism of budgeting.
2. To repare budget programme and budget schedules.
3. To develop necessary forms for the preparation of budgets and other reports.
4. To review and maintain budget manual.
5. To coordinate the efforts of departmental heads who are involved in budget preparation.
6. To act as the secretary or coordinator of Budget Committee and guide its functioning.
7. To prepare summary budgets for the consideration of the Budget Committee.
8. To get the budgets approved by the Board of Management before they are passed on to the departmental heads for execution.
9. To consider in the Budget Committee the proposals of the departments.
10. To conduct special studies needed for the preparation and finalization of budgets.

It should be noted that the functions of the Budget Committee and that of Budgetary Controller are not different. In fact, the functions of Budget Committee form part of the duties of Budgetary Controller who performs most of his functions through the Budget Committee. However, the budgetary controller is responsible and accountable to management for the smooth functioning of the budgetary control system. He seeks the opinion of the Board of Management on the critical issues and acts according to the instructions of the Board which formulates budget policies and set business objectives. A simple organisation chart for budgetary control system is presented below:

Board of Directors Budget Committee—Budgetary Controller

Marketing Manager	*Production Manager*	*Purchase Manager*	*Financial Manager*
1. Sales Budget 2. Selling & Distribution Budget	1. Production Budget 2. Plant utilization Budget 3. Maintenance budget	1. Material Purchase Budget	1. Capital Expenditure Budget 2. Overheads cost Budget. 3. Cash Budget. 4. Master Budget.

Personal Manager
1. Labour Cost Budget.

Types of Budgets

Budgeting in an undertaking may be done for a particular segment or it may cover all the activities depending upon the need and resources of the enterprise. The large scale business enterprises prepare different types of budgets covering almost all activities where control is desired. In order to understand the nature of budgets, it is desirable to know their classification which is usually done on time, functions and flexibility basis.

According to time, budgets can be of three types viz., (i) Long-term budgets, (ii) Short-term budgets, and (iii) Current budgets. Long-term budgets are concerned with planning activities for a long-period—a period of 5 to 10 or more years whereas short-period budgets cover a period of 1 to 2 years. Current budgets relate to the current period within a short-period of 1 year. An yearly budget is generally broken on monthly, quarterly or half-yearly basis for effective implementation of the same.

According to functional classification, a budget relates to a particular activity which can be a selling, production, purchasing or any other activity. The budgets prepared according to functions are known as functional budgets. The popular functional budgets prepared in a large scale enterprise are,

1. Sales budget
2. Production budget
3. Purchase budget
4. Capital expenditure budget
5. Overhead cost budgets
6. Cash budget
7. Research and development budget.

On the basis of flexibility, budgets are grouped into two categories, namely—(i) Fixed budgets—and(ii) Flexible or Variable budgets. A fixed budget is one which rigidly specifies the targets for a particular level of activity. The targets are not revised during the budget period irrespective of the fact that the actual level of activity attained in much different from the budgeted figure. Consequently the variances are violent and it becomes difficult to isolate the reasons for variances due to change in the level of activity. Fixed or static budgets can serve the purpose only if the budgets can be prepared with high degree of accuracy and budget period is short because the forecast for short period can be made with reasonable degree of accuracy. On the other hand, a flexible budget is one which permits the change in accordance with the changes in the level of activity. According to flexible budgeting, budgets for different levels of activity are prepared and the management enjoys the benefit of adopting any one of them according to changes in the attainment of the level of activity. Thus, the flexible budget has a series of fixed budgets for different levels of activity. It is always preferable to prepare flexible budget particularly when the economic conditions frequently change and it is difficult to forecast with any fair degree of accuracy.

Preparation of Budgets

The preparation of realistic budgets is essential for success in budgeting. Budgets are prepared after having set the objectives, goals and strategies for the achievement of over-all business objectives. In this section, we will study as to how different types of functional budgets are prepared.

Sales Budget

A sales budget is a statement expressed in physical quantities or/and values of anticipated sales during a specified period of time. Sales forecasting is the basic step in the preparation of a sales budget. It is done by sales department under the charge of a sales manager in consultation and cooperation with the Budget Controller. The forecasting of sales is not an easy job. It requires a lot of skill and knowledge in the techniques of sales forecasting, collection of relevant facts and figure and an understanding of business environment in which the firm is placed. The techniques of sales forecasting for new products are different from those used for established products.

In case of established products, historical data relating to sales quantities and expenditure on selling compaign are available within the firm. The sales department also possesses good knowledge about its market share, nature of competition, availability of substitutes, consumers preferences etc. The sales data for the last few years are compiled in a form what is known as 'Time Series' which is statistically dealt to fit a trend line and extrapolate the sales figures for future. This technique is quite simple and widely used by business firms for the purpose of sales forecasting. However, it can be profitably used only if the Time Series do not show violent fluctuations and corrections are rightly made for seasonal and stochastic variations.

The amount of sales in any given period is much affected by the amount spent on advertisement and other sales promotion techniques. A study of correlation between expenditure on advertisement and amount of sales in different time periods will reveal the degree of impace of advertising cost on amount of sales. Thus sales should be predicted only after due consideration to the advertisement budget for the period for which sales budget is being prepared.

The sales force i.e. salesmen, selling agents and sales managers, being in actual field of selling activity, can contribute a lot in correct forecasting of sales by sending their assessment of sales to head office for the budget period. The management should accept the estimated figures as reported by sales personnel only after due allowance for subjectivity of field staff.

In case of new product, the question of availability of any data within the firm does not arise. Therefore, sales forecasting is done by conducting market research which consists of conducting market surveys for the collection of relevant data needed for sales budget. The market research tries to find out the consumers demand for company's products. It is carried out through a well-designed questionaire which is either sent to potential buyers for being filled and returned by them or get filled in through the personal investigation method. The data so collected are compiled and adjusted in the light of other factors which might affect consumers demand.

The consideration of prevailing and expected economic environment within and outside the industry is essential before any decision on budgeted sales is taken. The management should give proper valuation in their estimation for sales for factors such as the structure of national income, government fiscal and monetary policies, industrial policy, import-export policy, demographic structure, etc., insofar as they influence the demand for firm's products.

In a modern age of competition, sales is generally a limiting factor. In case of certain products, sales may not be a constraint and the estimated sales might be much higher than the production facilities available within the firm. Under such a situation, the possibilities of increasing production should be fount out and the production budget be prepared first.

The data of budgeted sales can be arranged in a number of ways. They can be grouped according to commodity, territory or salesmen-wise. Consider the following form of a sales budget according to commodity-wise:

Sales Budget
for the 6-Months Ending on 30th June, 1987

Months	Product A		Product B		Total	
	Quantity	Value	Quantity	Value	Quantity	Value

Illustration—1

Priyadarshani Cement Ltd. manufactures two types of cement known as 'Black' and 'White'. The cement is sold in the three states of U.P. Haryana and Punjab through stock dealers. From the following data relating to budget period ended on 30th June, 1987 and the adjoining information, you are required to prepare a Sales Budget for 6-months period beginning from 1st July and ending on 31st Dec., 1987.

Commodity	Territories					
	Uttar Pradesh		*Punjab*		*Haryana*	
	Budgeted	*Actual*	*Budgeted*	*Actual*	*Budgeted*	*Actual*
Black Cement	25,000	24,000	20,000	18,000	10,000	10,000
White Cement	15,000	12,000	10,000	10,000	5,000	4,500
Total	40,000	36,000	30,000	28,000	15,000	14,500

Other Informations

1. The construction activity is expected to go up by 10% and accordingly the demand in all states except in Punjab, is likely to increase in the budget period. The Sales Department visualises a decrease in sales by 5% in Punjab.

2. The company has decided to appoint few more dealers in U.P. and it forecasts an additional sales of 5,000 bags of black cement through the new dealers.

3. With a vigorous advertisement campaign, the demand in Haryana for both black and white cement is likely to increase by 20% in addition to the 10% as pointed out above.

4. The company expects to make direct supplies to local bodies in the states of U.P. and Haryana. It hopes to sell 2,000 bags of black cement in each of these states.

5. Adequate production facilities exist and there is no limiting factor.

6. The selling price per bag is estimated at Rs.60 and 100 for black and white cement respectively.

PRIYADARSHNI CEMENT LTD.

Sales Budget
For 6-Months (1st July to 31st December, 1987)

Territories	*For 1st Jan. to 30th June, '87*				*July-Dec., 1987*			
	Black Cement (Bags)		*White Cement (bags)*		*Budget for 6-Months*			
	Budgeted	*Actuals*	*Budgeted*	*Actuals*	*Black (Bags)*	*White (Bags)*	*Black (Rs.)*	*White (%)*
U.P.	25,000	24,000	15,000	12,000	33,400	13,200	20,04,000	13,20,000
Punjab	20,000	18,000	10,000	10,000	17,100	9,500	10,26,000	9,50,000
Haryana	10,000	10,000	5,000	4,500	15,000	5,850	9,00,000	5,85,000
Total	55,000	52,000	30,000	26,500	65,500	28,550	39,30,000	28,55,000

Statement of Sales Forecast (Bags)

	U.P.		*Punjab*		*Haryana*	
	Black	*White*	*Black*	*White*	*Black*	*White*
Present Sale	24,000	12,000	18,000	10,000	10,000	4,500
Increase due to construction activity (10% of existing)	+ 2,400	+ 1,200	—	—	+ 1,000	+ 450
Estimated decrease for Punjab (5%)	—	—	- 900	- 500	—	—
Additional sales by new dealers	+ 5,000	—	—	—	—	—
Increase due to massive advertising compaign (20% of existing)	—	—	—	—	+ 2,000	+ 900
Direct Supplies	+ 2,000	—	—	—	+ 2,000	
Total	33,400	13,200	17,100	9,50	15,000	5,850

Selling and Distribution Cost Budget

The selling budget is followed by a selling and distribution cost budget which provides an estimated expenditure on selling and distribution of the goods as shown in the sales budget. The sales overhead costs consist of expenditure on items such as salaries to salesmen and their commission, advertising, warehouse charges, delivery van's fuel and repairs charges, sales office expenditure, etc. All such and similar other expenditure of sales are classified commodity-wise or territory-wise and shown in the selling cost budget in an orderly manner. The principles involved in the classification and presentation of selling and distribution cost in the budget are similar to that of sales budget.

Illustration—2

New Hosiery Products Ltd. operates in North and West regions of India. From the following selling and distribution cost budget with actual expenditure for the 6-months period which expired on 30th June, 1987 and the adjoining information, you are required to prepare a Selling and Distribution Cost Budget of the company for the next budget period which will end on 31st December, 1987.

Selling and Distribution Cost Budget for the Half Year Ended on 30th June, 1987

Elements of selling cost	*North*		*West*	
	Budgeted	*Actuals*	*Budgeted*	*Actuals*
1. Fixed selling overheads:				
Salesmen's salaries	9,500	9,500	6,000	6,000
Sales office salaries	6,000	6,000	2,500	2,500
Travelling allowances	2,000	2,500	1,000	1,250
Sales office rent	1,000	1,000	500	500
Show room charges	500	500	400	400
Advertising	2,000	2,500	1,500	2,000
Total (A)	22,000	23,000	12,500	13,250
2. Variable selling overheads:				
Salesmen's commission	10,000	8,000	6,000	5,000
Packing charges	2,500	2,000	1,500	1,250
Carriage outward	5,000	4,000	3,000	2,500
Delivery Van's fuel and maintenance	4,000	3,200	2,000	1,600
Total (B)	21,500	17,200	12,500	10,350
Total (A) + (B)	43,500	40,200	25,000	23,600

Other Informations

The management has decided to incorporate the following decisions in the selling and distribution cost budget for the next budget period:

1. Existing salesmen's salary is to be increased by 15% and salaries of office personnel be enhanced by 10%.
2. One additional salesman in each region be appointed at a consolidated salary of Rs.1,000 p.m.
3. Travelling allowances be increased by 10% of the actual incurred in current period.
4. Advertisement budget be enhanced by 50%.
5. The salesmen are entitled to a commission of 2%. Sales in next six months are expected to go up by 30% in each region.
6. Fuel consumption will increase in proportion to increase in sales.

Production Budget

The production budget deals with the amount of goods to be produced during the budget period. Sales budget is the forerunner of production budget. It suggests the quantities which should be produced in order to maintain sales and delivery schedules. Other considerations in the preparation of a production budget are:

1. The opening and desired closing inventories
2. Installed plant capacity and existing utilization.
3. Availability of necessary production inputs.
4. Production cycle.
5. Production policy of management.

An analysis of the above factors will suggest the amount of goods that can be produced within the factory. If the calculated production is less than the budgeted sales, then the firm will not be in a position to maintain the sales budget and earn sufficient profits for which potential exists. In such a situation, the firm should explore the following possibilities before taking a final decision on production budget:

1. Can the inventory level be reduced?
2. Can the plant utilization capacity be increased or additional plant installed to fill the gap?

New Hosiery Products Ltd.
Selling and Distribution Cost Budget
for Six Months (1st July to 31st December, 1987)

(Rs.)

Cost Constituents	*Budget for current period*			*Actuals for current period*			*Budget for Next Period*		
	North	*West*	*Total*	*North*	*West*	*Total*	*North*	*West*	*Total*
Fixed/Semi-variable cost									
Salesmen's salary	19,500	16,000	35,000	19,500	16,000	35,500	28,425	24,400	52,825
Sales office-salary	6,000	2,500	8,500	6,000	2,500	8,500	6,600	2,750	9,350
Travelling Allowances	2,000	1,000	3,000	2,5000	1,250	3,750	2,750	1,375	4,125
Sales office rent	1,000	500	1,500	1,000	500	1,500	1,000	500	1,500
Show room rent	500	400	900	500	400	900	500	400	900
Warehouse Rent	1,000	600	1,600	1,000	600	1,600	1,000	600	1,600
Advertising	2,000	1,500	3,500	2,500	2,000	4,500	3,000	2,250	5,250
Total	32,000	22,500	54,500	33,000	23,250	43,275	32,275	75,750	
Variable cost:									
Salesmen's commission	10,000	6,000	16,000	8,000	5,000	13,000	10,400	6,500	16,900

Packing charges	2,500	1,500	4,000	2,00	1,250	3,250	2,600	1,625	4,225
Carriage outward	5,000	3,000	8,000	4,000	2,500	6,500	5,200	3,250	8,450
Delivery Van's-fuel and maintenance	4,000	2,000	6,000	3,200	1,600	4,800	4,160	2,080	6,240
Total	21,500	12,500	34,000	17,200	10,350	27,550	22,360	13,455	35,815
Total Overheads	43,500	25,000	68,500	40,200	23,600	63,800	75,635	45,730	1,11365

Checked by ________ Prepared by ________

3. Is there any possibility of additional work to be done outside through the system of sub-contracting.
4. Is it possible and desirable to introduce over-time or additional shift working to increase production?

Statement of Changes

	North	*West*
Existing Salesmen's salary	19,500	16,000
Add 15%	2,925	2,400
	22,425	18,400
Additional Salesman's salary	6,000	6,000
Sales office salary	6,600	2,750
Travelling allowances	2,500	1,250
Add 10% increase	250	125
Sales office rent	1,000	500
Show room rent	500	400
Warehouse rent	1,000	600
Advertising	2,000	1,500
Add increase	1,000	750
	43,275	32,275
Salesmen's commission	8,000	5,000
Add 30% increase	2,400	1,500
Packing	2,000	1,250
Add 30% increase	600	375
Carriage outward	4,000	2,500
Add 30%	1,200	750
Delivery Van's—fuel and maintenance	3,200	1,600
Add 30%	960	480
Total	22,360	13,455

In case sales is a limiting factor and adequate production facilities exist, the final shape to the production budget should be given only after the consideration of the issues such as,

1. Possibility of increasing sale through massive advertising campaign.
2. Creation of additional demand by price reduction and other sales promotion techniques.
3. Utilization of surplus plant capacity for production of other goods or sub-letting the same to other producers.

A detailed enquiry into the above issues will lead the production manager to set up a realistic production budget which can be presented commodity-wise, department-wise or period-wise.

Illustration—3

Piryadarshani Cement Ltd. has budgeted sales as under:

Months	*Black Cement*	*White Cement*
July 1987	5,000	2,000
August	10,000	4,000
September	12,000	5,000
October	15,000	6,000
November	13,500	5,000
December	10,000	6,550
January 1988	12,000	5,000
	77,500	33,500

The company maintains inventory equal to half of the sales for next month and there is no work-in-progress at the end of any month.

Prepare the Production Budget for the half year ending on 31st December, 1987.

PIRYADARSHANI CEMENT LTD.

Production Budget for Half-Year Ending on 31st Dec., 1978

Product Y	*Months*					
	July	*August*	*Sep.*	*October*	*November*	*Dec.*
Black Cement						
Budgeted Sales	5,000	10,000	12,000	15,000	13,500	10,000
Add closing inventories (50% of next month)	5,000	6,000	7,500	6,750	5,000	6,000
	10,000	16,000	19,500	21,750	18,500	16,000
Less opening inventories	2,500	5,000	6,000	7,500	6,750	5,000
Budgeted Production	7,500	11,000	13,500	14,250	11,750	11,000
White Cement						
Budgeted Sales	2,000	4,000	5,000	6,000	5,000	6,550
Add closing inventory	1,000	2,500	3,000	2,500	3,275	2,500
	3,000	6,500	8,000	8,500	8,275	9,050
Less opening inventory	1,000	1,000	2,500	3,000	2,500	3,275
Budgeted production	2,000	5,500	5,500	5,000	5,775	5,775

Production Cost Budget

The production cost budget is prepared to know the estimated expenditure on the budgeted production as set out in production budget. The production cost consists of the cost of raw materials, labour and production overhead costs. Therefore, the Production Cost Budget includes the cost of each of these components on the budgeted production. Separate budgets for raw materials, labour and overheads can also be prepared for better understanding and control of each of the element of cost.

Raw Materials Budget

The raw material budget deals with the quantities of raw materials and components required to produce the budgeted production. The production department determines the quantity of raw materials and the Purchase Department furnishes the rates at which the raw materials can be purchased. Total cost of each type of raw material required is arrived at by multiplying the quantity and rate of raw material.

Illustration—4

Priyadarshani Cement Ltd., has budgeted the production of Black and White Cement as 69,900 bags and 24,550 bags respectively for the 6-months period which will end on 31st December, 1987. The production engineer has reported the consumption of different types of raw materials in the production of one bag of 50 kgs. as under :

Material No.	*Black Cement*	*Material*	*White Cement*
MO 1	20 kgs.	MO 5	25 kgs.
MO 2	15 "	MO 6	10 "
MO 3	10 "	MO 7	10 "
MO 1	5 "	MO 8	5 "

The purchase department estimates the cost of raw materials as under:

Raw Materials	*Rate per bag (Rs.)*
MO 1	30.00
MO 2	35.00
MO 3	20.00
MO 4	40.00
MO 5	50.00
MO 6	70.00
MO 7	80.00
MO 8	60.00

You are required to prepare the Materials Budget for the half-year ended on 31st December, 1987. There is no wastage in production.

Material Budget for the Half Year ended on 31st December, 1987

Code Number of raw materials	*Quantity*	*Rate per Bag*	*Value (Rs.)*
MO 1	13,80,000 kgs. (27,600 Bags)	30/-	8,28,000
MO 2	10,35,000 (20,700 Bags)	35/-	7,24,500
MO 3	6,90,000 (13,800 Bags)	20/-	2,76,000
MO 4	3,45,000 (6,900 Bags)	40/-	2,76,000
	69,000 Bags		21,04,500
MO 5	6,13,750 kgs. (12,275 Bags)	50/-	6,13,750
MO 6	2,45,500 (4,910 Bags)	70/-	3,43,700
MO 7	2,45,500 (4,910 Bags)	80/-	3,92,800
MO 8	1,22,750 (2,455 Bags)	60/-	1,47,300
	24,550 Bags		14,97,550
Total	93,550 Bags		36,02,050

Raw Materials Purchase Budget

The raw materials purchase budget represents the physical quantities of different types of raw materials and other components which must be purchased during a given time period for the maintenance of production schedules. It also shows the money values required to purchase the budgeted raw materials. The quantities which must be purchased are arrived at only after the consideration of the opening and closing inventories of raw materials. The purchases to be made are also governed by the storage capacity and availability of necessary finances.

Illustration—5

Priyadarshani Cement Ltd. furnishes the following details regarding consumption and inventory levels of raw materials:

Materials	*Budgeted consumption for 6 months*	*Opening Stock 1-7-1987*	*Closing stock 31-12-1987*	*Rate of purchase*
MO 1	27,600	3,000	5,000	30
MO 2	20,700	2,500	3,500	35
MO 3	13,800	2,000	4,000	20
MO 4	6,900	1,000	1,000	40

You are required to prepare the Raw Materials Purchase Budget.

PRIYADARSHANI CEMENT LTD.

Materials Purchase Budget for Half Year (July to December)

(Bags)

Particulars	*MO 1*	*MO 2*	*MO 3*	*MO 4*
Budgeted consumption	27,600	20,700	13,800	6,900
Add desired closing stock	5,000	3,500	4,000	1,000
	32,600	24,200	17,800	7,900
Less opening stock	3,000	2,500	2,000	1,000
Quantity to be purchased	29,600	21,700	15,800	6,900
Rate of purchase	30/-	35/-	20/-	40/-
Value of Purchases (Rs.)	8,88,000	7,59,500	3,16,000	2,76,000

Labour Cost Budget

Labour cost budget represents the total amount of money which will be needed for payment to workers, direct as well as indirect, during the production budget period. It can be prepared only if the total number of labour hours to produce the budgeted quantity and the rate per hour are known. The nature of production suggests the kind of labour required and the work study tells the total labour hours required to achieve budgeted production. Labour rates can be collected from the personnel department. That should, however, be modified in the light of the likely changes in wage-rates. Total labour cost is arrived at by multiplying together the labour hours and the wage rate. A comparison of the existing labour force in terms of hours and the budgeted labour hours will disclose whether additional labour will be required or some existing labour will be rendered surplus.

Illustration—6

M/s. Ram Nath & Sons produces a chemical— 'ST' which requires the employment of skilled and semi-skilled workers. From the following details prepare labour cost budget:

	July	*August*	*September*
Budgeted production (Tons)	1,500	2,000	2,500
Number of workers required :			
Skilled	5	5	6
Semi-skilled	3	3	4
Hourly wage-rate: Skilled	15.00	15.50	16.00
Unskilled	8.00	8.50	8.50

The production unit works on the basis of a single shift of 8 hours daily and there are only 25 effective working days in a month.

Solution

Labour Cost Budget
(July to September, 1987)

Y	*July*	*August*	*September*
Budgeted production (Tons)	1,500	2,000	2,500
Number of hours required:			
Skilled	1,000	1,000	1,200
Semi-skilled	600	600	800
Hourly wage-rate:			
Skilled	15.00	15.50	16.00
Semi-skilled	80/-	8.50	8.50

Total Labour Cost :			
Skilled	15,000.00	15,500.00	19,200.00
Semi-skilled	4,800.00	5,100.00	6,800.0.00
Total Labour Cost	19,800.00	20,600.00	26,000.00

Production Overheads Budget

This budget presents a forecast of indirect expenses which are linked with production. All expenses of production office such as salaries of office personnel including works manager's salary, factory rent, depreciation, insurance, light and fuel, stationery, etc., are included in this budget. The total production expenses are classified into fixed and variable components. They can further be grouped into controllable and un-controllable categories with a view to exercise better control over them. The budget officer finalises the budget in consultation with the production manager. Following Production Overheads Budget prepared with imaginary figures gives sufficient idea about its format and presentation:

Production Overheads Budget
(for Three Months- July to September 1987)

Elements of cost	*July*	*August*	*September*
Production office salaries	9,600	9,600	9,600
Provision for A.D.A.	-	900	900
Works manager's salary	3,200	3,500	3,500
Stationery	500	500	500
Rent	1,800	1,800	1,800
Depreciation	1,250	1,250	1,250
Light and Fuel	600	600	600
Labour welfare charges	1,000	1,000	1,500
Proportionate Power House charges	800	800	800
Total	18,950	20,150	20,650

The production cost budget can be prepared by bring in it all the elements of cost of production, i.e. raw materials, labour and overheads. For a better understanding of cost structure, it is preferable to represent the cost of production data in the form of a cost sheet which shows the prime cost and other costs separately. The management can be better served if the budget for the preceeding period alongwith the actuals is also presented with the production cost budget for future.

Illustration—7

M/s. New Era manufacturers furnishes the following information relating to their production cost budget which ended on 30th June, 1987:

	Budgeted units (950 units)		*Actual production 1,050 units)*
Materials consumed (1,000 units)	15,000	1,100 units	18,150
Labour	12,000		13,200
Variable overheads:			
Power	1,900		2,100
Excise duty	3,800		4,200
Fixed overheads:	5,000		5,000

The firm asks you to build up the production cost budget for the 6-months period commencing from 1st January 1988 on the basis of the following further informations:

1. The firm expects to produce 1,200 units during the next budget period.
2. The raw material units required will increase proportionately but the price per unit will remain unchanged.
3. Labour efficiency will be maintained but the wage rate will increase by 20% over the previous level.
4. Variable overhead rate will be maintained but fixed overheads will increase by 15%.

Solution

NEW ERA MANUFACTURING COMPANY

Production Cost Budget
(for 6-Months—1st Jan. to 30th June, 1988)

Particulars	*Budget*			*Actuals*			*Budget*		
	Jan. to June '87 (950 units)			*Jan. to June '87 (1,050 units)*			*1st Jan. to 30th June 1988 (1,200 units)*		
	Units	*Amount*		*Units*	*Amount*		*Units*	*Amount*	
Variable cost:									
Raw material	1,000	15,000	15.79	1100	18,150	17.29	1,263	20,839	17.37
Labour		12,000	12.03		13,200	12.57		18,100	15.08
Power		1,900	2.00		2,100	2.00		2,400	2.00
Excise duty		3,800	4.00		4,200	4.00		4,800	4.00
Total Variable Cost		32,700	34.42		37,650	35.86		46,139	38.45
Fixed Cost		5,000	5.26		5,000	4.76		5,750	4.79
Cost of Production		37,700	39.68		42,650	40.62		51,889	43.24

Dated......................

Prepared By...................... ....
Management Accountant

Explanatory Notes:

1. Units of raw materials required for the proposed production:

$$\frac{1,000 \times 1,200}{950} = 1,263 \text{ units}$$

2. Price of raw materials per unit = 18,150 divided by 1,100 = 16.50
3. Cost of 1,263 units = 1,263 × 16.50 = 20,839
4. Labour cost per unit = 12.57
   Increase 20% = 2.514
   15.084

Total labour cost = 1,200 × 15.084 = 18,100.

Research and Development Budget

Generally, large scale business enterprises set up research and development wing within their organisations to carry on research for developing new products and/or improving upon the existing ones with a view to minimising cost and earn maximum profits. Such enterprises prepare Research and Development Budget which depends upon the existing projects in hands and the new projects to be undertaken within the budget period. This budget has no direct linkage with sales, production or other operating budgets. The management decides the nature of research to be carried within the firm and also the expenditure to be incurred thereon. It also decides about the treatment to be given to the research and development expenditure i.e. what part of expenditure to be capitalised and what portion be treated as an ordinary business expenditure. The Research and Development Budget helps the management to carry on the research activities on a continuous basis for the benefit of the organisation.

Cash Budget

A cash budget deals with the expected cash inflows and cash outflows during a specified period of time for which the budget is prepared. The possible sources of cash inflows are: (a) cash sales, (b) realisation from debtors, (c) issue of shares and debentures, (d) raising loans, (e) sales of investments: (f) sale of any fixed asset. The cash-outflow results due to—(i) purchase of raw materials, (ii) payment of wages, (iii) disbursement of overheads, (iv) purchases of fixed assets and investments, (v) redemption of debentures and loans, (vi) payment of dividend, (vii) discharge of tax obligations, etc. The budget officer forecasts the cash flows and cash requirements during budget period which must syncronize with the periods of other functional budgets as most of the informations for cash budget are derived from other budgets.

For a better cash planning and control, it is important that the budget period is divided into smaller periods. For example, a 6-monthly cash budget may be prepared on monthly basis with a view to knowing cash position at the end of every month. The cash budget enables the management to arrange the deficit cash balance well in time for maintaining operational efficiency of the enterprise. Similarly, surplus cash balance as shown in the budget at the end of any period can be invested in temporary investments. Thus cash planning in an enterprise is effective only when cash budget is in operation.

Preparation of Cash Budget

A cash budget may be prepared by using any one of the following methods:

1. Receipt and Payment method
2. Adjusted Profit and Loss method
3. Balance Sheet method.

1. Receipt and Payment Method

According to this method, Cash Budget includes all the cash receipts whether they are on revenue account or capital account. Similarly all expected capital and revenue expenditures are brought in a cash budget. The accruals i.e. income earned but not received and expenditure due but not paid are excluded from the cash budget. Thus a cash budget is a sort of cash account which records cash receipts and cash payments and shows expected cash balance at the end of the budget period. The informations for cash budget are derived from other budgets. For example, the sales budget will provide the amount of sales and the receipts from sales and realization from debtors can be estimated by taking into account the terms of sales. The raw materials purchase budget, labour budget and overheads budget will provide information relating to payments for raw materials, wages and overhead charges. The management can forecast payments on account of capital expenditure, tax, dividend, etc. The difference of cash receipts and cash payments for a period is either positive or negative, which is carried to next period.

Illustration—8

From the following budget data prepare Cash Budget for 3-months July to September, 1989:

Months	*Sales*	*Purchases*	*Wages*	*Overheads*
June	85,000	48,000	10,000	12,500
July	90,000	52,000	11,000	13,500
August	1,20,000	60,000	14,000	15,000
September	1,30,000	62,000	14,000	16,000

Other Informations

1. 20% sales is for cash and the remaining amount is realised in the month following that of sales.
2. Suppliers supply raw materials at one months credit.
3. Wage-bill is paid in the first week of next month.
4. Overheads are paid in cash.
5. Monthly rent payment is Rs.1,000.
6. Advance Income Tax of Rs.15,000 is payable in September.
7. Bonus of Rs.10,000 is payable to workers in July.
8. Plant costing Rs.80,000 is due to be installed in July. The bill will be paid in August.
9. Interest on 12% 50,000 debentures is realised in July and January every year.
10. Cash balance on Ist July is Rs.5,000.

Solutions

Cash Budget for the 3 Months Period
(July to September, 1989)

	July	*August*	*September*
Receipts:			
Opening balance	5,000	11,500	-51,500
Cash sales	18,000	24,000	26,000
Collection from debtors (80% of 85,000)	68,000	72,000	96,000
Debenture Interest (6 months)	3,000	—	—
Total	94,000	1,07,500	70,500
Payments:			
Purchases	48,000	52,000	60,000
Wages	10,000	11,000	14,000

Overheads	13,500	15,000	16,000
Rent	1,000	1,000	1,000
Bonus	10,000	—	—
Income Tax	—	—	15,000
Plant	—	80,000	—
Total	82,500	1,59,000	1,06,000
Closing Balance	11,500	(-51,500)	(-35,500)

Adjusted Profit and Loss Method

Under this method the profit as shown in the Profit and Loss Account prepared in the conventional manner forms the basis for cash forecast. The profit is adjusted by adding back to it the non-cash items such as depreciation, outstanding expenses, other provisions etc. The other items which increase the total cash inflows are the increase in share capital, debenture and loans, current liabilities (creditors) and decrease in fixed assets, debtors and stock etc. Out of the total cash-inflows calculated as above, the items which results in cash outflow are substracted to arrive at the cash position at the end of the period. The items which reduce the cash position are accrued incomes, advance payments, dividend payment, redemption of debentures and loans, decrease in creditors, payment for fixed assets, increase in debtors and stock etc. This method of cash forecast may also be called as the Cash Flow Statement method as the net income as per the conventional income Statement is converted into a cash flow forecast. The main sources of information for cash forecast as per this method are the profit and loss account and balance sheet. This method suitable to prepare a long-period cash budget.

Illustration—9

From the following Balance Sheet and Projected Profit and Loss Account, prepare the Cash Budget according to adjusted Profit and Loss Account method:

Balance Sheet
For the Year Ended on 31st Dec., 1986

Share Capital	1,50,000	Land and Buildings	1,25,000
General Reserve	50,000	Plant and Machinery	80,000
Profit and Loss A/c	25,000	Furniture and fixtures	15,000
Debentures	80,000	Sundry debtors	75,000
Creditors	1,00,000	Stock	50,000
Bills Payable	20,000	Bills Receivable	10,000
Outstanding Salaries	3,000	Prepaid Rent	3,000
		Cash at bank and hand	70,000
	4,28,000		4,28,000

Projected Profit and Loss Account
for the Year Ended on 31st Dec., 1987

To Opening Stock		50,000	By Sales	3,00,000
To Purchases		2,25,000	By Closing Stock	45,000
To Gross Profit C/d		70,000		
		3,45,000		3,45,000
To Salaries	10,000		By Gross profit b/d	70,000
Less last years outstanding	3,000			
	7,000			
Add outstanding	1,000	8,000		
To commission		1,500		
To Rent	9,000			
Add last years prepared	3,000			
		12,000		
To Interest		8,000		
To Establishment charges		2,500		
To Advertising expenses		2,000		

To Depreciation :				
Plant & Machinery	8,000			
Land & Building	6,000			
Furniture	1,500			
		15,500		
To Net Profit		20,500		
		70,000		70,000
To Dividend		30,000	By Net Profit (31-12-86)	25,000
To General Reserve		10,000	By Profit for 1987	20,500
To Balance carried		5,500		
		45,500		45,500

On 31st Dec. 1986, the position of some of the items was as under:

Share capital	2,00,000
Debentures	1,00,000
Creditors	80,000
Debtors	90,000
Bills Payable	25,000
Bills Receivable	8,000

Purchase of Plant and Machinery during 1987 28,000

Purchase of Furniture and Fixtures 21,500

Solution

Cash Budget (Adjusted Profit & Loss Method) for the year ended on 31st December, 1987

Cash Balance (31.12.1986)			70,000
Add:			
Net Profit for 1987		20,500	
Depreciation :			
Plant and Machinery	8,000		
Land and Building	6,000		
Furniture	1,500		
		15,500	
Decrease in prepaid rent		3,000	
Decrease in stock		5,000	

Decrease in bills receivable	2,000	
Increase in bills payable	5,000	
Issue of share capital	50,000	
Issue of debentures	20,000	1,21,000
Less:		
Purchase of plant & machinery	28,000	
Purchase of furniture & fixtures	21,500	
Dividend	30,000	
Decrease in outstanding salaries	2,000	
Increase in debtors	15,000	
Decrease in creditors	20,000	1,16,500
Cash Balance as on 31st December, 1987		74,500

Balance Sheet Method

Under this method a projected Balance Sheet is prepared in which cash balance is not an estimated item but a difference between total projected assets and total estimated liabilities. In other words, the excess of projected assets over projected liabilities represents cash balance. If the liabilities are more than the assets, the balance shows the overdraft.

Illustration—10

Using the informations of illustration No. 9 prepare a projected Balance Sheet as on 31st December, 1987 to show the Cash position as on that date :

Solution

Projected Balance Sheet
as on 31st December, 1987

Share capital	2,00,000	Land & Buildings	1,25,000	
Debentures	1,00,000	Less Depreciation	6,000	
				1,19,000
General Reserve	60,000	Plant & Machinery	80,000	
Profit & Loss A/c	5,500	Less depreciation	8,000	
Creditors	80,000		72,000	

		Add Purchases	28,000	
Bills Payable	25,000			1,00,000
Outstanding salaries	1,000	Furnitures & Fixtures	15,000	
		Less depreciation	1,500	
			13,500	
		Add Purchases	21,500	
				35,500
		Debtors		90,000
		Bill Receivable		8,000
		Stock		45,000
		Cash and Bank Balance (Balancing figure)		74,500
	4,71,500			4,71,500

Flexible Budgets

We have so far dealt with fixed budgets which are prepared for a specific level of activity. Such budgets are based on the assumption that the future can be forecast with certainty and there is no significant difference between actual performance and budgeted data. In actual practice, the assumption of accurate forecasting does not hold good, particularly when the future is distant and economic environment full of uncertainties. Consequently the actual level of activity attained is different from the budgeted one and the comparison between budgeted and actual data will be unrealistic as it will throw no light on the variations arising due to the change in the actual level of activity. In order to remove rigidity and introduce flexibility in budgeting flexible budgets are prepared. A flexible budget also known as variable or sliding scale budget is one which permits adaptability in accordance with the changes in the level of production. It is prepared for varying levels of production activity and thus provides a realistic basis for comparing performance of different departments/products.

The preparation of a flexible budget is not difficult. Actually there is no difference between the preparation of a fixed budget and flexible budget except that in the later case costs and other data are estimated for varying levels of activity. In other words, a flexible budget consists of a series of fixed budgets. The element of fixed cost in the total cost make a lot of difference whenever the level of production is changed. The total fixed cost for all levels of production remains the same but the cost per unit of output decreases with an increase in the output and vice versa. Therefore, fixed cost should be segregated from the total cost and shown separately in a flexible budget.

Illustration—11

Modern Manufacturing Company Ltd. has budgeted the following expenses for the production of 1,000 Super-washing machines:

	Per unit (Rs.)
Direct Materials	700
Direct labour	500
Direct chargeable expenses	100
Variable overheads	50
Administration expenses (Rs.1,00,000 fixed for all levels of production)	100
Selling and distribution Expenses (60% fixed)	25
Total cost per unit	1,475

You are required to prepare flexible budget for 8,000, 9,000 and 12,000 machines.

Solution

Flexible Budget

	1000 units		*8000 units*		*9000 units*		*12000 units*	
Particulars	*Per unit*	*Total*	*Per unit*	*Total*	*Per unit*	*Total*	*Per unit*	*Total*
Materials	700	7,00,000	700	56,00,000	700	63,00,000	700	84,00,000
Labour	500	5,00,000	500	40,00,000	500	45,00,000	500	60,00,000
Direct exp.	100	1,00,000	100	8,00,000	100	9,00,000	100	12,00,000
Prime cost	1,300	13,00,000	1,300	1,04,00,000	1,300	1,17,00,000	1,300	1,56,00,000
Variable overheads	50	50,000	50	4,00,000	50	4,50,000	50	6,00,000

Variable selling and distribution expenses	10	10,000	10	80,000	10	90,000	10	1,20,000
administration expenses	100	1,00,000	125	1,00,000	11.11	1,00,000	8,33	1,00,000
selling and distribution fixed cost	15	15,000	1.87	15,000	1.67	15,000	1.25	15,000
Total	1,475	14,75,000	1374.37	1,09,95,000	1372.78	1,23,55,000	1369.58	1,64,35,000

Performance Budgeting

We have seen different types of functional budgets which are prepared by a manufacturing organisation. These budgets highlights the targets in physical quantities alongwith their money values. A manufacturing concern is said to have adopted performance budgeting if its concentration is on physical targets and evaluation of the actuals with the budgeted figures with a view to exercise proper control over its activities for better performance. The budgeting adopted by private entrepreneurs is generally performance-oriented but if is not always true in case of government departments which set their targets in money values instead of physical quantities. Performance budgeting assumes special significance when government expenditure on developmental activities is desired to be evaluated in terms of physical targets. A government department may be satisfied if it is able to exhaust the funds allocated to it for a budget period without any regard to the amount of benefits derived from expenditure. It is so when the budgeted expenditure is not linked with the physical targets to be achieved for the achievement of some broader objective by the government. The modern governments have realized the disadvantages of the traditional budgeting and the performance budgeting is gaining popularity with them. The concept of performance budgeting developed when the Hoover Commission recommended in 1949 that the performance budgeting should be adopted for budgeting the Federal Government expenditure. The Estimate Committee and Administrative Reform Commission have also recommended the use of performance budgeting in government departments in India.

According to performance budgeting, the expenditure is presented programme and activity-wise and actual performance is recorded alongwith the targets for the consideration of decision-makers. In case of a manufacturing concern the target may be to achieve a certain rate of profit on capital employed (ROI) but the targets for non-profit making government organisations will depend upon the nature of work they carry out. For example, the over-all objective of expenditure on literacy programme may be fixed as increasing the literacy rate from 50 per cent to 60 per cent during the budget period. Similarly, the objective of expenditure may be set as an increase in the rate of employment, bringing additional land under cultivation of a particular crop, extension of areas under forests, etc. But the targets have to be interpreted in physical terms so that the effectiveness of expenditure is judged from the comparison of actuals with the budgeted figures. Effective performance budgeting needs careful consideration of the following:

1. Fixation of objective for which expenditure is to be incurred.
2. Establishment of responsibility centres.
3. Identification of programmes to be carried out by each responsibility centre.
4. Interpretation of programme in physical quantities or targets for each activity relating to a programme.
5. Forecasting the resources needed to implement the programme and also the expected income resulting therefrom.
6. Developing information and reporting system both in physical and monetary values for the purpose of control.
7. Evaluation of performance periodically and take corrective actions, wherever needed.

Zero-Base Budgeting

Traditional method of budgeting known as incremented based budgeting is based on past year's programmes and performance which is generally regarded as satisfactory for developing future budgets. In this type of budgeting, the targets set in the past year are not questioned and some additions are made in the last year's budget itself to incorporate the necessary additional expenditure on on-going and new business activities to be carried out in the budget period. This is a very simple method which calls for few alterations and additions without going into the details of the whole budgeting process in the light of changed circumstances. The traditional method of budgeting is not workable where management is conscious of innovative changes in the present business and administrative policies for achieving maximum over-all efficiency of the organisation.

Zero-base Budgeting pre-supposes the non-existence of any budget in the past and evaluates the budget activities in terms of benefits and costs in the light of prevailing business environment and likely changes in future. It is synonymous with budgeting from scratch—from zero, requiring justification of everything irrespective of trends or past levels of expenditure. In other words, Zero-base budgeting implies constructing a budget without any reference to what has gone before. It is essentially an exercise of reappraisal of purposes, methods and resources. The budget so prepared is likely to be more realistic to serve the best interests of an organisation. Zero-base budgeting has been defined by Peter A. Phyrr as under:

> "A planning and budgeting process which requires each manager to justify his entire budget request in detail right-from the scratch (hence the term zero-base) and shifts the burden of proof to each manager to justify why he should spend any money at all. The approach in turm requires an indepth analysis of all the 'decision packages' to be evaluated on systematic and rational lines and also ranked in order of importance."

Zero-Base Budgeting (ZBB) as a system of budgeting was used by the U.S. Department of Agriculture for a year in 1964. It was developed in its present form by Peter A. Phyrr at the Taxes Instrument, U.S.A. It was given a boost subsequently by Jimmy Carter who as the governor implemented the system in the state of Georgia and later as the President in the Federal Government. Government of India proposed the adoption of Zero-base concept in the budget preparation for the year 1987-88 onward. The zero-base budgeting concept has been successfully implemented in a large number of U.S. Organisation including such giants as Taxas Instruments, Southern California, Edison, Xerox and New York Telephone Company.

Integral Parts of Zero-base Budgeting

Zero-base budgeting involves the following:

1. Identification of Decision Units

The decision units will be based on the level of responsibility. Different departments are generally, identified as Decision Units which are capable of carrying out different programmes or activities to achieve a single objective. The Decision Units are the responsibility based budget centres under the charge of different senior officers of the organisation. For example, the Education Department could be a Decision Unit with the objective of increasing literacy and providing quality education. However, Adult Education, Child Education, Technical Education could be sub-functions or sub-units for which separate budgets will be prepared. Top management should specify the Decision Units in terms of resources required, capital projects, special projects or major expansion schemes.

2. Preparation of Decision-Packages

The Decision Package is the building block of the zero-base budgeting process. A number of decision packages make up one Decision Unit. A decision package is a document that identifies and describes a specific activity in such a manner that management can evaluate it and rank it against other activities competing for limited resources and decide whether to approve or disapprove it. If, for example, Adult Education is the decision Unit, the objective of improving literacy among adults can be achieved through starting adult education centres in each district or through TV programme on adult education, etc. There activities are the Decision Packages or independent activities, each capable of being measured in terms of cost, targets and objectives achieved.

It is important that Decision Packages be developed in an effective manner. It involves examining alternative methods or activities of achieving the objectives and different levels of efforts of performing the operations. The Decision Packages will contain the following informations:

- Goals of the Decision Unit
- Discription of the programme and activity
- Specific measure of performance
- Benefits expected from the performance
- Consequences of not approving the package
- Projected or expected costs.
- Costs and benefits for all alternatives studied including the recommended one.

It may, however, be pointed out that the preparation of decision packages is a gigantic task which requires technical knowledge, experience and resources. In order to economise resources and avoid, unnecessary controversy, sóme organisations may use less formal ways of presenting alternative ways of performing an activity, i.e. compromise solutions but this approach will be inconsistent with the very idea of zero-base budgeting.

3. Ranking of Decision Packages

The ranking process is concerned with deciding about how met" and "where" the limited resources are to be allocated. A Decision Unit with highest Benefit-cost Ratio is preferred and ranked as Number one. If the costs are incurred and the benefits obtained in the same year, the calculation of the Benefit-cost Rates is more straightforward. However, if the benefits are obtained over a long period, the BCR should be based on the Present Values of benefits and costs discounted at appropriate rates. In case of government expenditure, the more appropriate measure is social values, and the social benefit-cost Ratio will guide the ranking of Decision, Packages. It may, however, understood that the funds will be provided on the basis of financial cost. Thus the Decision packages of individual Decision Units will be brought together and ranked in the order of importance on the basis of Benefit-Cost Ratios. The list will show the Decision Packages of various Decision Units in discending order of Benefit-Cost Ratios. Decision Packages will be choosen from the top one after another to make up the available quantum of funds.

There may be few persons in the government who may not like the test of evaluation and ranking in case of very high priority or committed or policy programme. The zero-base budgeting process in the above manner will suggest the policy-makers the likely cost or loss of carrying on or undertaking a new programme, and as such it will be in their own interest to adopt this new method of budgeting.

4. Preparation of Detailed Operating Budget

The ranking process provides a number of approved Decision Packages which constitute the budget for the organisation as a whole and for the individual budget centres. The decision packages incorporate in themselves the discription of the activities and the performance level appropriate to the expenditure level contained in the decision package. This will provide the basis for reporting of actuals against budgets and review of performance.

The Difference

A budget analyst cannot loose sight of a traditional budgets which contain a lots of informations about the programmes and activities which have been undertaken in the past. Budgeting from the scratch does not mean that there is always a search for new data and old data as contained in a traditional budget cannot be used. Basic difference between the traditional or incremental budgeting and the zero-base budgeting may be realized from the following:

1. A traditional budget is function-oriented but a zero-base budget is a programme or project-oriented.
2. In case of traditional budgeting, the existing programmes or projects are self-perpetuating for which no rejustification is required. Justification is needed only for new programmes or projects. Zero-base budgeting presenting that all programmes or projects whether on-going or new, must be justified on the ground that they all compete for the same scarce resources.
3. Traditional budgeting views critically only the cost increases whereas the zero-base budgeting critically examines existing levels of expenditure, as the level of expenditure approved for the last budget is not necessarily acceptable for the current budget.
4. Traditional budgeting is input-oriented i.e., resources required; zero-base budgeting is output-oriented i.e., results achieved.

Benefits from ZBB

Following benefits accrue to an organisation which implement Zero-Base Budgeting on the right basis:

1. Continuous reviewing of on-going schemes ensures effective utilization of limited funds in the best possible projects and manner.
2. The programmes or activities which have outlived their utility are pruned and thus the organisation can be saved from unproductive expenditure.
3. Ranking of projects and programmes on cost-benefit analysis basis secures an efficient allocation of funds.
4. It facilitates the accommodation of high priority projects by reducing existing activities.

5. ZBB helps in the management of projects, programmes and activities according to availability of funds. If the cuts in budgets become imperative due to shortage of funds, the BCR for different programmes will be a correct guide in such a decision-making. Instead of introducing ad hoc cuts in budgets, the activities making upto the quantum of funds available will be choosen.
6. It provides an in-built system for reviewing actual costs and performance against budget.
7. It improves communication all round, particularly top management's awareness of what is contained in each budget centre's proposal.
8. It promotes innovative ideas in terms of alternative ways of performing an activity and alternative levels of efforts.

Problems with ZBB

Like any other technique of planning, the Zero-base budgeting is not an unmixed blessing. Following problems may be encountered in the implementation of ZBB in any organisation or government department.

1. Zero-base budgeting is a costly affair as it involves too much energy, time and money in the collection and analysis of data regarding alternative projects, programmes and activities. It can freeze an organisation in a paper work blizzard for several months in a year.

2. The evaluation of legal necessity or technical feasibility of Decision Packages is itself a highly difficult and technical job which might not be done rightly in the absence technically qualified personnel for the purpose. It cannot be said that a Zero-base budget is always realistic and in the best interest of the organisation.

3. ZBB requires measurements on performance levels and cost effectiveness that might not be readily available.

4. There is every possibility that "Pet" projects might be ranked arbitrarily as there is no way of avoiding 'pet projects' being given a high ranking.

5. It may complicate communication and administration of data as more and more people are involved in this exercise.

6. Zero-base budgeting provides more scope for manipulation as the officers incharge of different budget activities are, generally, in the habit of exaggerating the importance of activities of their respective departments.

7. Benefits of many programmes or decision units are not measurable in terms of physical quantities or money values. The success of ZBB depends upon the evaluation of benefits and ranking the decision units on that basis. ZBB fails to work as an effective tool of planning due to problem of measurement or inaccurate measurement of benefits.

8. Divergent activities are impossible to be compared with one another and ranked. Education, health and policy activities cannot be compared with each other. Therefore, ZBB cannot be taken to its logical end. There have to be adjustments and compromises.

Pre-requisites for Success

From the study of the problems associated with the Zero-base budgeting, it will be wrong to conclude that ZZB is an unreal concept and it cannot be translated to achieve maximum benefits out of the budget activities. ZBB can be made an effective tool of planning and control provided management properly appreciate the problems and provides a framework suitable for formulation of realistic and objective budgetary proposals with the cooperation of all concerned in the organisation. Pre-requisites for the success of ZBB may be stated as under:

1. Top management's strong involvement is a must for the success of ZBB. Other officers associated with the formulation and implementation of the ZBB should also cooperate in the joint exercise to make the system a success.
2. Imaginative approach and a genuine commitment to change on the part of managers at all levels in the organisation are highly important for the success of ZBB.
3. In order to discourage 'pet projects, the decision packages may be discussed in groups and prejudices should not be allowed to affect budgeting processes and the evaluation and ranking should be done as objectively as possible.
4. The area wherein ZBB could be applied should be choosen carefully and ZBB applied deliquently.

QUESTIONS

1. Clearly bring out the meaning of Budget, Budgeting and Budgetoary control.
2. Discuss the objects, advantages and limitations of Budgetary control system.
3. What do you mean by Budgetory Control? Suggest a suitable organisation for efficient Budgetory Control System.
4. What are different types of functional budgets which are prepared by a large scale manufacturing concern? Explain the method of preparation of a Sales Budget or a Cash Budget.
5. What do you understand by a Flexible Budget? How does fixed cost per unit vary in case of a budget for varying levels of activity?
6. What is Performance Budgeting? How is different from traditional budgeting?
7. Define Zero-base Budgeting and explain the steps involved in the implementation of Zero-base budgeting.
8. Examine the benefits and limitation of Zero-base Budgeting. How ZBB can be made an efficient tool of management planning and control?
9. A company manufactures two products known as x and y and sells the same into two different sales territories called High Zone and Low Zone territories. You are required to prepared Company's Sales Budget from the following informations. Current year's budgeted and actual sales are tabulated below :

Products	*High Zone*		*Low Zone*	
	Budgeted	*Actuals*	*Budgeted*	*Actuals*
X	10,000	9,000	8,000	11,000
Y	8,000	10,000	10,000	9,000

Informations

1. Market studies have revealed that the sales of X will not be affected if its price is increased from Rs.5 to 6 per unit and the sales of Y will increase by 10 per cent if the price is reduced from the present level of 9 to 8. This change in price structure has to be brought in the new budget.
2. The company has launched an aggressive advertisement compaign which is likely to increase sales in both the territories by 10% .
3. An increase in sales equal to 5% of the previous year's sales of both the products in their respective markets is expected due to direct supplies to government.

10. A company expects to sell one of its standard product in the first half year of 1996 as shown below:

January	500 units	@ Rs.15 per unit
February	550 "	"
March	700 "	"
April	600 "	"
May	650 "	"
June	500 "	"

The company desires to hold inventory equal to budgeted sales for the following two months.

You are required to prepare the Purchase Budget to be interpreted both in terms of physical units and money values.

11. Prepare a 6-monthly Cash Budget (April-Sept. 1994) from the following informations:

Months	*Estimated Sales (Rs.)*	*Estimated Purchases (Rs.)*	*Wages*
March	65,000	35,000	12,000
April	80,000	45,000	15,000
May	60,000	50,000	10,000
June	80,000	60,000	10,000
July	90,000	40,000	11,000
August	1,00,000	50,000	10,000
September	60,000	40,000	12,000

Other Informations

1. Period of credit allowed to customer is one month.
2. Suppliers allow one month as period of credit.
3. Monthly overheads payments amount to Rs.4000.
4. Half of the estimated Sales are for cash.
5. A machine costing Rs.80,000 is to be purchased in June. The payment for the machine is to be made in three equal instalments, the first instalment being paid in June.
6. Cash Balance on 1st April 1994 is estimated at Rs.8000.
7. The deficiency of cash in any month is to be met by overdrafts.

12. A company is presently operating at 50% capacity and producing 800 units. The cost structure is as follows:

Cost per unit (Rs.)

Materials	160
Labour	80
Direct expenses	15
Administrative expenses (60%) fixed),	80,000
Selling and distribution overheads (40% fixed)	60,000

You are required to prepare a flexible budget for 75% and 100% capacity utilization.

13. R & Co. produces a standard product for which costs per unit are as under:

Raw Materials	Rs. 15
Labour cost	Rs. 10
Direct expenses	Rs. 3
Variable overheads	Rs. 2

Semi-variable over-heads at 100% capacity utilisation (1000 units) are expected to be Rs. 10,000 and these overheads vary in steps of Rs.1000 for each change in output of 100 units. Fixed overheads are estimated at Rs.15,000. Products are expected to be sold at Rs. 80 per unit.

You are required to prepare Flexible Budget for 100%, 90%, 70% and 50% level of activity.

6

Standard Costing and Variance Analysis

Cost control and cost reduction have assumed special significance in all spheres of productive activity of modern industrial setup. A manufacturing firm facing perfect competition can survive only if it is able to keep its cost of production within limits and every other firm can enhance its profits without raising price to the extent it is able to reduce its cost of production by the elimination of wastages in production process. The total cost involved in production is broadly classified into three categories, viz. raw material cost, labour cost and overhead charges and the management has to economise the use of each element of cost in order to achieve the ultimate objective of optimum profit for the enterprise. Standard costing helps the management in their endeavour to achieve the maximum production efficiency which leads to optimum profits. Under standard costing system standards for each element of cost are pre-determined and efforts are made to achieve them and any shortfall is reported to management for critical review and appropriate action in the next production period.

Standard cost is defined as pre-determined cost based on normal conditions of production and standard costing as a system of costing which involves specification of standard cost for each element of cost comparison of actual costs with the standards, determination of variances i.e., the deviation of actual costs from the standard costs, identification of causes for adverse variances and presentation of relevant cost information to management for corrective action in case of adverse variances. The standard costing is based on the principle—'What the cost ought to be?' From this standpoint the standard cost is different from the estimated cost which provides an idea as to what the cost will be. The standard cost is pre-determined after careful studies of production methods and techniques and the most likely cost of inputs whereas the estimated cost is simply based on personal estimation which generally is the average of the cost incurred in the past. The very purpose of standard cost and estimated cost differ as the former is set with the main purpose of cost control and cost reduction whereas the later is estimated just for rough estimation of profit margins. It may be noted that the standard costing is not a separate method of cost accounting but it is a technique which is used to achieve certain objectives. The main objectives of standard costing technique are as stated below:

1. Cost Control

Standard costing technique is basically used for controlling cost of production. The comparison of actual performance with the standard is done with a view to know the extent of variation between the actual performance and the standard performance specified. The management is satisfied if the actual performance is equal to or more than the standard specified. If the actual performance is more than the standard, the variance (difference between actual and standard) is said to be favourable and represented by the capital letter (F) while preparing performance reports. The management becomes conscious in case the actual performance has deviated from the standard negatively. The variance in such a case is known as adverse (A). Causes for adverse variances are located and corrective action taken. In this manner the cost control becomes effective.

2. Cost Estimation for Price Quotation

The management has to estimate the cost when price has to be quoted well in advance of actual production. Standard costing technique provides realistic basis for price fixation. One way of deciding the cost price is the rough estimates based on management's intuition but such an estimation may not generally be found nearer to actual costs. The subjective estimation has no scientific basis and as such fails to explain the reasons for gaps in actual and estimated costs. Under standard costing technique cost data are collected and cost is determined in the light of past performance and the expected changes in variables affecting cost of production.

3. Comparison of Efficiency

Sometimes the management wants to compare the performance of different products, processes and operations for taking various decisions. The comparison is valid only when standard cost of one product or process is compared with the other as the standard costs exclude all abnormal wastes and effectives and they are more in tune with the current conditions of production.

Standard costing has become inevitable due to the fact that the traditional cost accounting system fails to achieve the above objective which are highly important for the success of an enterprise. Traditional cost accounting suffers from the following limitations:

1. Traditional costing deals with the past costs known as historical costs which are not suitable for price-quotation as they are influenced by abnormal factors such as excessive use of raw materials, wastage of labour abnormal overhead charges, etc. Price quotation is bound to become abnormally high due to inclusion of abnormal costs in cost structure and it may not be acceptable to many customers. The idea of average cost will also not work as the average is largely affected by the extreme performance in some periods of production.

2. Under traditional costing a complete set of informations is available only after the completion of production cycle or accounting year; therefore, they cannot be used in formulating pricing and production policies for future.

3. Historical costs cannot be used for cost control purposes as they might be either too high or too low. Any comparison of current costs with the abnormal costs in the past will be misleading.

Advantages of Standard Costing

The importance of standard costing has been realized by modern enterprises, particularly by those which are engaged in the production of standardised products. Standard costing technique eliminates the limitations of historical costing and helps an enterprise in the following manner:

1. Facilitates Cost Control and Cost Reduction

Cost control becomes effective when standards are predetermined and efforts are made to achieve them. The adverse variances necessiate either the revision of standards itself or rigrous control over the business operations. In this way the standard costing facilitates cost control and cost reduction in an organisation. An early action to cure adverse variance surely contributes in cost reduction.

2. Helps in Fixing Reasonable Price Quotation

The cost data are readily available under standard costing system and the price can be quoted on the basis of standard costs without fear of under or over pricing. Standard cost is the pre-determined normal cost of normal output and as such forms proper basis for price fixation.

3. Generates Cost Consciousness

Standard costing generates cost consciousness among all those who are concerned with productive activity. The workers become conscious of their work because they know that they will be judged by amount of work they do. Every department works with greater seriousness to achieve the standards fixed for them. There is greater cooperation and coordination among the various operations of the whole activity. All this enables the enterprise to eliminate wastages and reduce the cost to the minimum.

4. Makes Delegation of Authority Effective

Everyone in the organisation is required to accomplish a particular job for which standards already stand fixed. Therefore, the management can delegate authority with greater degree of safety. It is possible to fix responsibility of departments and individuals when standard costing system is implemented in an enterprise.

5. Optimise Use of Resources

There is optimum use of resources in the undertakings following standard costing which emphasises on the reasonable degree of efficiency. To achieve the desired degree of efficiency as reflected by the standards, resources are put to their best use. Efforts are made to optimise the use of existing plant, working capital and other resources.

6. Simplify Performance Reports

The performance reports presented in the form of variance analysis are simple to understand as they clearly distinguish between favourable and adverse variances. The busy top management can concentrate on adverse variances and take appropriate action in the matter.

Disadvantages and Limitations

The standard costing technique suffers from certain limitations. It also harms the interests of the enterprise if not rightly implemented. Main disadvantages and limitation of the technique are as under:

1. Difficult Standard Specification

The success of standard costing depends upon the accuracy with which standards for different elements of costs are fixed. In practice, it has been found difficult to fix standards for every type of activity. For example, it is difficult, though not impossible to fix standards for non-standardised products and repair jobs which frequently change with changes in customs, tastes and preferences of the buyers.

2. Rigidity of Standards

A standard is fixed under certain assumptions and it holds good only under the assumed conditions of work. Any change in the environment of production renders the standards rigid and un-suitable for comparison with the actuals. The frequent revision of standards is a difficult task which limits the use of the technique.

3. High Standards Cause Frustration

Management in their endeavour to achieve maximum efficiency may fix high standards which might not be attainable by the employees of normal capabilities and under the given operating facilities. Non-achievement of standards cause frustration among the workers who begin to feel that standard costing is implemented to extract more and more work out of them. Such a feeling on the part of workmen forfeit the very purpose of standard costing.

4. Wrong Standards are Harmful

A wrong standard is one which is either too high or too low. Such standards cannot form proper basis for comparison. A too high a standard causes adverse psychological effect on the workers whereas a too low standard does not encourage them to utilise their full capabilities in the accomplishment of the business goals. It is rightly said that it is better not to have standard costing at all than to have wrong standards.

5. Difficult Identification of Causes for Adverse Variances

Sometimes it is very difficult to identify the real causes for adverse variances. It may also be not possible to distinguish between controllable and non-controllable factors which have caused an adverse variance.

6. Lack of Managerial Enthusiasm and Competence

The apathy of management towards standard costing makes the technique quite ineffective. If the system is not well-planned due to incompetence of management, than the standard costing would fail to achieve the object of cost control.

From the above it will be appreciated that the standard costing technique is highly important for an enterprise as it facilitates cost control, helps in formulating production and price policies, generates cost consciousness and through effective managerial control optimise the use of resources. But the objectives of standard costing can be achieved only if standards are rightly fixed and reviewed from time to time so that they form suitable basis for comparison under the changing conditions. The standard costing is most suitable to industries which produce standardised products but its use is limited in case of small concerns engaged in non-standardised products and repair jobs.

Types of Standards

Different firms may fix different standards and the same firm may adopt different standards at different points of time. This difference in standards arises due to the variation in circumstances or conditions under which standards are fixed. On the basis of circumstances the standards may be classified as under:

1. Ideal Standard

A standard is said to be an ideal if it is based on ideal conditions of work. An ideal standard assumes maximum efficiency on the part of man, machines, material and management. It pre-supposes most favourable conditions of work and rules out any possibility of loss arising out of abnormal conditions such as break-down of machines, failure of power, labour strikes, change in government policy, defective raw materials, etc. In actual practice ideal conditions do not prevail and an ideal standard may be found unsuitable as a control device. A firm which has adopted ideal standards will experience perpetual adverse variances because the ideals are hardly achieved. The existence of adverse variances causes frustration among the employees and they tend to ignore the ideal standards. In this way they become more theoritical than of any practical use.

2. Attainable Standard

It is one which can be attained under the conditions and circumstances prevailing within the organisation. In the fixation of attainable standard the management takes into account the expected conditions of production and distribution. Thus an attainable standard is based not on ideal conditions but on actual expected conditions. The attainable standard will have to be revised according to changes in the conditions affecting the operational efficiency of the organisation. Thus an attainable standard is more realistic and can be used as an effective tool of cost control and cost reduction.

3. Basic Standard

The basic standard is a fixed standard which is used for comparison for fairly long period of time. It may be based either on ideal conditions or expected conditions of work performance in the year for which it relates. Since a basic standard remains unaltered, it does not suggests 'what the cost for the current year ought to be?' Therefore, it cannot be used for valid comparisons as the distant past is not proper to compare the present, specially when the innovations in the current year have changed technicalities of production. However, it can be used to show the trends in income and price level changes.

4. Normal Standard

Normal standard can also be termed as historical standard as it is based on the average performance in the past years. It can be fairly a satisfactory standard if the performance in the past has been fairly stable. In case of constantly improving efficiency or erratic performance the normal standard will fail to serve the purpose. It suffers from all the defects of an arithmetic average based on a series of items which include few extreme items.

Fixation of Standards

In a manufacturing concern, standards are fixed for raw materials, labour and overhead charges. Standards have to be specified both for physical quantities and monetary values. The success in standard costing is largely depended upon the accuracy of standards. An accurate standard is a standard which specifies highest degree of efficiency under the given and expected condition of work. It is neither based on ideal conditions nor pessimistic assumptions of facts.

Standards for Raw Materials

Following standards are fixed in respect of raw materials:

1. Material Usage Rate Standard, 2. Material Price Standard, 3. Material Cost Standard and 4. Material Yield Standard.

1. Material Usage Rate Standard

It is concerned with the standard quantity of raw material which is needed to manufacture an unit of output. How much quantity of raw material may be consumed in the production of a single commodity should be determined very carefully. The product study involving raw material and plant conditions help in this connection. Past experience, if any should also be used in the determination of quantity standard. The quantity of raw material required for the manufacture of a single product is generally governed by the quality of product, nature of plant and the quality of raw materials itself. All these and similar other variables affecting the quantity requirements should be studied carefully to set standard for quantity consumption. Where more than one type of raw material is used, the usage rate for each type of raw material may be fixed and recorded separately.

2. Material Price Standard

The material price standard is influenced by the sources from which the raw materials are drawn for consumption. If the raw material is used out of opening stock, the account books will tell the price of such raw material. Current purchase price adjusted to likely changes may be taken standard if raw material is consumed out of current purchases. In case the firm manufactures raw material internally, the standard cost of manufacture will form the standard price. The average price may be fixed as standard if the firm is depending for its supplies on all the three sources of raw materials. Under the conditions of erratic fluctuations in prices the fixation of price standard possess a great difficulty which can be solved to a great extent by taking the average price of the past few years. The price standard is also influenced by the purchase policy of the organisation. If the raw material is purchased in bulk, the buyer is in a position to induce the seller to offer better terms of trade. The bulk purchases are generally economical.

3. Historical Cost Standard

It is expressed in terms of value which is arrived at by the multiplication of the standard quantity of material and the standard price per unit of output. For example, if the standard quantity of wood required to manufacture a chair of a specified size is 3 cft. and the price of wood is Rs. 40 per cft., the Material Cost Standard for a single chair will be 3 x 40 = Rs. 120.

4. Yield Standard

The yield or net output depends upon the rate of loss or wastage arising out of material processing. Where a raw material is transformed into a final product or the production involves certain processes of manufacture, some quantity of raw material is lost during the course of production. The rate of normal loss of material is known by past experiences of production. It should be determined carefully as a high rate will conceal inefficiencies and a low rate will lead to wrong yield variances.

Standards for Labour

Following standards are fixed in respect of labour:

1. Standard Labour Rate

Piece-rate or Time wages may be paid by a firm. If the piece rate system is adopted, the prevalent rate adjusted to likely changes may be adopted as standard wage rate. In case of time wages, hourly wage rate has to be calculated after taking into account the expected wages to be paid during the budget period. The wages for each grade of labour is to be determined separately. The minimum wages form the standard if it has to be paid to a certain category of labour under the Minimum Wage Act. The agreements with trade unions regarding wages, bonus, over-time payments, etc., should be duly accounted for in the fixation of wage rate.

2. Standard Labour Time

Time taken to produce similar goods in the past by workers of normal efficiency may be taken as standard time. The time may be expressed either in terms of number of days or number of hours. Time and motion studies and job evaluation techniques help in the fixation of standard time. In such studies, it has to be ensured that workers of normal efficiency are employed to work under normal conditions of work.

3. Standard Labour Cost

It is expressed in monetary values and calculated by multiplying the labour hours by hourly rate of wages.

Standards for Overhead Costs

Overheads are defined as the costs of factory, office or selling department which are not directly identifiable with production. Therefore, they are separately estimated for each operating department or cost centre for a specified level of activity. The fixation of standard rate for overhead costs necessitate the division of total overhead costs into its fixed and variable portions and estimation of production units or production hours. Overhead recovery rate is calculated by dividing the estimated overhead costs by the production units or production hours.

Since the fixed overheads remain the same for all levels of production within certain production range, the rate of fixed overhead cost decline with every increase in production and vice versa. But the variable overhead costs vary with production and the rate per unit of output remains the same.

Standard cost is determined for each product or service. The details of standards for each element of cost may be provided in the form of a standard cost statement as shown below:

STANDARD COST STATEMENT FOR PRODUCT NO. DE

(Estimated Production - 315 units in six-months ending on 30th June, 1990)

Elements of cost		*Quantity/ hours*	*Rate*	*Total cost*	*Cost per unit*
1. Direct Materials:					
Grade A		200 kgs.	50.00	10,000	50.00
Grade B		150 "	40.00	6,000	40,00
Total		350 "	45.71	16,000	45.71
Less Normal Loss (10%)		35 "	—	—	—
	(M)	315 "	—	16,000	50.79
2. Direct Labour:					
X-grade labour		2,000 hours	4.00	8,000	25.40
Y-grade labour		2,000 "	2.00	4,000	12.70
	(L)	4,000 "	3.00	12,000	38.10
3. Overhead charges					
Variable overheads		—	4.50	1,417.50	4.50
Fixed overheads		—	—	3,000.00	9.52
	(O)			4,417.50	14.03
Standard Cost (M+L+O)				32.417.50	102.91

Variance Analysis

The ultimate objective of standard costing is to regular the business operations in the most efficient manner so that the cost of production does not exceed the pre-determined level. To achieve this objective, the mere fixation of a standard is useless so long as it is not compared with actual performance and causes for poor performance, if any, are found out to pinpoint the responsibility of executives/departments and remedy the situation in the next production period. The variance analysis is concerned with the calculation of variances and preparation of variance reports which include the favourable and unfavourable variances. Since the management is pre-occupied with many activities, it is not possible for them to go into details of everything. Therefore, the attention of the management is drawn to adverse variances which need corrective action. This is quite in true with the principle of Management By Exception

(MBE). A deeper probe into the causes for adverse variances will reveal that some of the variances have resulted due to the factors beyond the control of operative managers. Such variances are termed as non-controllable variances for which individuals cannot be held responsible. However, the controllable adverse variances are well within the control of the concerning individuals if proper care and caution is exercised. Therefore, management fix the responsibility for controllable variances. Generally the zero variance and favourable variances do not attract the attention of the management; it does not mean that everything is well with such variances. It is quite possible that a favourable variance occurs because of low standard which needs revision.

Calculation of Variances

The calculation of variances is not difficult if the data of actuals are available to the management accountant. The difference between the standard and the actual is termed as Variance. In other words, the variance is the extent of deviation of actual cost from the standard cost. It shows either the over-spending or saving in costs. If the actual cost is more than the standard cost the variance shows over-spending which means an adverse or unfavourable situation and vice versa. An adverse variance is indicated by the letter 'A' and a favourable variance is shown by 'F'. The variances are calculated for total costs and for each element of costs for which standards are fixed. Generally, the total costs involved in a product is divided into material cost, labour cost and overhead cost and variances are calculated for each one of them.

Material Variance

In case of material following variances are computed:

1. Material Cost Variance (MCV)

It is the difference between the standard cost of material specified and the actual cost of material consumed. The cost variance arises either due to difference in price or quantities or both. Therefore, it is further analysed into Material Price Variance and Material Usage or Quantity Variance.

(a) *Material Price Variance (MPV).* It arises due to the difference between the standard price specified and actual price paid and is calculated by multiplying the difference of prices by the actual quantity of raw material used. The formula is as under:

Material Price Variance = Actual Quantity (Standard Price – Actual price)

Or MPV = AQ (SP - AP)

(b) *Material Usage Variance (MUV).* It is due to the difference between the standard quantity of material specified and the actual quantity of material consumed. The variance is calculated by taking the difference of the standard and actual quantities of raw materials and multiplying the same by the standard price. The formula is as under:

Material Usage Variance (MUV) = Standard Price (Standard quantity-actual quantity)

Or MUV = SP (SQ - AQ)

Illustration—1

From the following informations, calculate (a) Material Cost Variance (b) Material Price Variance and (c) Material Usage Variance and check the calculations.

	Standard	*Actual*
Quantity of raw material	50 kgs.	48 kgs.
Price per kg.	Rs. 4.00	Rs. 3.75
Value	Rs. 200.00	Rs. 180.00

Solution

(a) Material Cost Variance = Standard Cost – Actual Cost

Or SC – AC

MCV = 200 – 180 – 20 (F)

(b) Material Price Variance = Actual quantity (St. Price - Actual Price)

Or AQ (SP = AP)

MCV = 48 (4.00 – 3.75) = 48 × 0.25 = 12 (F)

(c) Material Usage Variance = St. Price (St. Quantity - Actual Quantity)

$$MUV = SR(SQ - AQ)$$

$$= 4\,(50 - 48) = 4 \times 2 = 8\ (F)$$

Check, Material Cost Variance - Material Price Variance + Material Usage Variance

$$20\ (F) = 12\ (F) + 8\ (F)$$

Where more than one grade of raw material is used in manufacturing, the Material Mixture Variance and Material Yield Variance are calculated in place of Material Usage Variance because the usage or quantity variance is caused by the differences in the composition of mixture and yield rates.

Material Mixture Variance

In actual practice the composition of actual mixture might differ from the standard specified for various reasons such as limited supply of one type of raw material, change in the desired quality of product, etc. The change in the actual mixture causes difference in Usage Variance. Therefore, Material Mix Variance is to be separated from the total usage variance in order to know the effect of change in the composition of mixture. The Material Mixture Variance (MMV) is that portion of Material Usage Variance which is due to the difference between the standard and the actual composition of mixture. It is calculated with the help of the following formula:

Material Mix Variance = (Standard cost of Actual Production– Actual cost of actual mix)

Material Yield Variance (MYV) : The yield variance arises due to the difference in the standard yield specified and the actual yield obtained. In case the total standard weight of mixture and the total weight of actual mixture do not change, the Material Yield Variance (MYV) can be calculated with the help of the following formula:

Material Yield Variance (MYV) = (Standard Yield - Actual Yield)

The difference in yields in such a case is due to the difference in standard or normal loss and the actual loss. Therefore, the Material Yield

Variance can also be calculated by using the formula,

Material Yield Variance (MYV) - St. Rate (Standard Loss - Actual Loss).

Illustration—2

From the following informations, calculate—(a) Material Cost Variance, (b) Material Price Variance, (c) Material Mix Variance, (d) Material Yield Variance and check the calculations

	Standard			*Actual*		
	Quantity	*Rate*	*Value*	*Quantity*	*Rate*	*Value*
Material X	120	12	1,440	110	13,	1,430
Material Y	80	15	1,200	90	16	1,440
Total	200		2,640	200		2,870
Less Loss	20			26		
Net Output	180		2,640	174		2,870

Solution

(a) Material Cost Variance (MCV) – St. Cost of Actual Production — Actual cost

$$MCV = \frac{2,640 \times 174}{180} - (2,870)$$

$= 2,552 - 2870 - 318$ (A).

(b) Material Price Variance (MPV) = AQ (SP – AP)

MPV for X $= 110 (12 - 13) = 110 \times 1 = 110$ (A)
MPV for Y $= 90 (15 - 16) = 90 \times 1 = 90$ (A)

Total 200 (A)

(c) Material Mix Variance (MMV) = Standard cost of standard mix) — (Standard cost of actual mix)

MMV $= 2,640 - (110 \times 12)$ — (90×15)
$= 2,640 - (1,320 + 1,350)$
$= 2,640 - 2,670 = 30$ (A)

(d) Material Yield Variance (MYV) = St. Rate (St. Loss - Actual Loss)

$$\text{Standard Rate} \quad \frac{\text{St. Cost}}{\text{St. Output}} = \frac{2{,}640}{180} = 14\frac{2}{3}$$

$$\text{MYV} = 14\frac{2}{3}\ (20 - 26) = 14\frac{2}{3}\ (6) = 88\ (A)$$

Check, MCV = MPV + MMV + MYV

318 (A) = 200 (A) + 30 (A) = 88 (A).

Calculation of Revised Standard Proportions

If the standard and actual material inputs are not the same, the revised standard proportions in terms of actual inputs have to be calculated to compute the Material Mixture Variance. The formula to calculate revised standard Mix in terms of actual input is as follows:

$$\textbf{Revised standard Proportion of actual input} = \frac{\text{St. Proportion of a material}}{\text{Total St. Quantity}} \times \text{Actual Input}$$

The revised standard for each grade of raw material is used in place of original standard fixed in the calculation of Material Mix Variance as under:

MMV - St. Rate (Revised standard Quantity - Actual Quantity)
= SR (RS – AQ)

Illustration —3

The production cost data of a company which uses standard costing are derived as under:

	Standard			*Actual*		
	Quantity	*Rate*	*Value*	*Quantity*	*Rate*	*Value*
Material X	120	12	1,440	125	13	1,625
Material Y	80	15	1,200	90	14	1,260
Total	200		2,640	215		2,885
Less Loss	20		—	29		—
Net Output	180		2640	186		2,885

Calculate (a) MCV, (b) MPV, (c) MMV, (d) MYV

Solution

(a) MCV = St. cost of actual production - Actual cost

$$= \left(\frac{2,640}{180}\right) - 2,885 = 2,728 - 2,885 = 157 \text{ (A)}.$$

(b) MPV = AQ (SP — AP)

MPV for X = 125 (12 — 13) = 125 (A)

MPV for Y = 90 (15 — 14) = 90 (F)

Total 35 (A).

(c) MMV : For calculating MMV the revised standards in terms of actual input will be calculated as follows:

$$\text{Revised St. for X} = \frac{120}{200} \times 215 = 129$$

$$\text{Revised St. for Y} = \frac{80}{200} \times 215 = 86$$

MMV = SP (RS - AQ)

MMV for X = 12 (129 — 125) = 48 (F)

MMV for Y = 15 (86 — 90) = 60 (A)

Total Mix Variance = 48 (F) + 60 (A) = 12 (A).

(d) *Material Yield Variance (MYV).* When there is difference between the standard input and actual input, the standard loss in terms of actual input is to be calculated and then Material Yield Variance calculated as per the following formula:

MYV – SR (Revised St. Loss – Actual Loss)

In the above case, standard loss in terms of actual input or Revised standard loss is,

$$\text{RSL} = \frac{20}{200} \times 215 = 21.5$$

$$MYV = \frac{2,640}{180}(21.5 - 29) = 14\frac{2}{3}(75) = 110 \text{ (A)}$$

Check, MCV = MPV + MMV + MYV

157 (A) = 35(A) + 12 (A) + 110 (A).

Labour Cost Variance (LCV)

Labour cost variance is the difference between the standard labour cost specified and the actual labour cost incurred. The standard labour cost is calculated by the multiplication of labour hours and the hourly wage-rates. Similarly, actual labour cost is arrived at by multiplying the actual hours by the actual rates of wage-payment. The formula for the calculation of labour cost variance is as under:

Labour Cost Variance (LCV) = Standard Labour Cost — Actual Labour Cost

Or LCV = (St. hours × St. Hourly rate) – (Actual Hours × Actual Hourly rate)

The Labour Cost Variance arises either due to differences in wage-rates or labour efficiency or both. Therefore, it is further analysed into Labour Rate Variance (LRV) and Labour Efficiency Variance (LEV).

Labour Rate Variance (LRV)

Like material price variance, the Labour Rate Variance arises due to the difference between the standard labour rate prescribed and the actual wage rate paid. The variance is favourable if the wage rate paid is less than the standard wage rate and it is adverse when the actual wage rate is higher than the standard wage rate. It is calculated by using the following formula:

Labour Rate Variance (LRV) = Actual Hours (St. wage rate – Actual wage rate)

Or LRV = AH (SWR - AWR).

Labour Efficiency Variance (LEV) or Labour Time Variance (LTV)

Labour efficiency is judged by the number of hours the workers take to complete the standard work. The Labour Efficiency Variance (LEV) is that portion of labour cost variance which is due to the difference between the standard hours for a job specified and the actual number of hours worked. The LEV is favourable if the actual number of hours taken is less than the standard hours prescribed to complete the work and vice versa.

To calculate the LEV the difference in hours is valued at standard wage rate. Thus:

Labour Efficiency Variance (LEV) = St. Rate (Standard Hours – Actual Hours)

Illustration —4

The labour cost data pertaining to the manufacture of a product by a factory are given below:

	Standard	*Actual*
Number of units	40	40
Number of units per hour	13	15
Wage rate per hour	Rs. 5	Rs. 5.50

You are required to calculate—(a) Labour Cost Variance (LCV) (b) Labour Rate Variance (LRV) and (c) Labour Efficiency Variance (LEV).

Solution:

(a) Labour Cost Variance (LCV) = St. Cost – Actual Cost.

Standard Labour Cost = No. of units × No. of hours per unit x wage rate

= 40 × 13 × 5 = 2,600

Actual Labour Cost = 40 × 15 × 5.5 = 3,300

Labour Cost Variance = SLC – ALC

= 2,600 — 3,300 = 700 (A)

(b) Labour Rate Variance (LRV) = Actual Hrs. (St. Labour Rate – Actual Rate)

= 600 (5.00 – 5.50)

= 300 (A).

(c) Labour Efficiency Variance (LEV) = St. Rate (St. Hours – Actual Hours)

= 5 (520 – 600)
= 400 (A)

Check, LCV = LRV + LEV
700 (A) = 300 (A) + 400 (A).

Illustration—5

From the cost data as set out in the following table, calculate—(a) Labour Cost Variance, (b) Labour Rate Variance, and (c) Total Efficiency Variance.

Type of Labour	*Standard*			*Actual*		
	Production = 150 units			*Production = 150 units*		
	Hours	*Rate*	*Cost*	*Hours*	*Rate*	*Cost*
Men	520	5	2,600	600	5.50	3,300
Women	400	4	1,600	320	4.50	1,440
	920	—	4,200	920	—	4,740

Solution

(a) Labour Cost Variance (LCV) = Standard Cost – Actual Cost
= 4,200 – 4,740 = 540 (A)

(b) Labour Rate Variance (LRV) = Actual Hrs. (St. Rate–Actual Rate)
LRV for Men = 600 (5.00—5.50) = 300 (A)
LRV for Women = 320 (4.00—450) = 160 (A)
Total 460 (A)

(c) Total Labour Efficiency Variance = St . Rate (St. Hours — Actual Hours)

LEV for Men = 5 (520 — 600) = 400 (A)
LEV for Women = 4 (400 – 320) = 320 (F)

Total 80 (A)

Check, LCV = LRV + LEV

540 (A) = 460 (A) + 80 (A).

Idle Time Variance

If it is desired to separate the effect of idle time on efficiency of labour, the Idle Time Variance (ITV) is caluclated. Idle Time is the time for which the workers remain idle or without work due to some abnormal factors such as breakdown of power or machine. Idle Time Variance (ITV) is that portion of total labour efficiency variance which is due to the idle time of workmen. It is calculated simply by multiplying the idle time by the standard wage rate for a grade of labour. Thus, Idle Time Variance (ITV) - Idle Time X Standard Wage Rate.

Illustration—6

Taking the cost data of illustration—5 and assuming that the workers both men and women were idle for 25 hours, calculate Labour Idle Time Variance (LTV) and revised labour efficiency variance (RLEV).

Solution

Idle Time Variance = No. of hours workers remained idle x St. Wage rate

Idle Time Variance (ITV) for Men = 25 × 5 = 125 (A)

Idle Time Variance (ITV) For Women = 25 × 4 = 100 (A)

Total 225 (A)

Revised Labour Efficiency Variance (RLEV) To calculate RLEV, the idle time is deducted from the actual time taken. The formula of total efficiency variance is modified slightly to compute the revised labour efficiency variance as under:-

RLEV = ST. Rate {(St. Hours – (Actual Hours - Idle Time)}

RLEV for Men = 5 [(520 – (600 — 25)]

= 5 (520 – 575) = 275 (A)

RLEV for Women = 4 [400 – (320 — 25)]

= 4 (400 – 295) = 420 (F)

Total = 145 (F)

Total Efficiency Variance = Revised Labour Efficiency Variance + Idle Time Variance

80 (A) = 145 (F) + 225 (A)

Where more than one grade or type of labour is used and the actual composition of labour differs from the standard composition, the total efficiency variance is classified into Labour Mix Variance or Gang Composition Variance and Revised Efficiency Variance or Yield Variance. For the calculation of Labour-Mix Variance, the revised standard hours in terms of actual hours worked are determined by the use of the following formula:

$$\text{Revised Standard Hours} = \frac{\text{Standard Hours}}{\text{Total Standard Hours}} \times \text{Total Actual Hours.}$$

The revised standard hours are used in place of standard hours in the computation of Labour Mix Variance. Following formula is used for the purpose:

Labour Mix Variance = St. Rate (Revised St. Hours – Actual Hours).

or LMV = SR (RSH – AH)

The formula for revised or rest of efficiency variance and Yield variance is as under:

Revised Efficiency Variance = St. Rate (St. Hours – Revised St. Hours)

Or REV = SR (AH – RSH)

Yield Variance – Average St. Rate (Standard Hours – Actual Hours)

Illustration—7

A manufacturing firm produces a standardised product known as 'KT.' For the production of a unit of product it had set the following standards for labour:

Type of Labour	*Hours required to produce a single commodity*	*Hourly rate of wages*	*Total*
Skilled worker	8	5.00	40.00
Semi-skilled worker	9	3.00	27.00

Un-skilled worker	3	2.50	7.50
	20		74.50

The firm produced 500 units. Actual hours worked and the wage rate paid were as under:

	Actual Hours	Wage Rate	Total Cost
Skilled worker	3,750	5.50	20,625,00
Semi-skilled worker	5,000	3.00	15,000,00
Unskilled worker	2,750	2.75	7,562.50
	11,500		43,187.50

You are required to calculate: (a) Labour Cost Variance, (b) Labour Rate Variance, (c) Labour Mix Variance, (d) Labour Revised Efficiency Variance and (e) Labour Yield Variance.

Solution

(a) *Labour Cost Variance (LCV)* = Standard Cost — Actual Cost

Standard Cost of skilled workers = 40 × 500	=	20,000
Standard cost of semi-skilled workers = 27 × 500	=	13,500
Standard cost of unskilled workers = 7.5 × 500	=	3,750
Total		37,250

Labour Cost Variance (LCV) = 37,250 – 43,187.50 = 5,937.5 (A)

(b) Labour Rate Variance (LRV) = Actual Hours (St. wage rate – Actual wage rate)

LRV for skilled workers = 3,750 (5.00 – 5.50)	=	1,875 (A)
LRV for semi-skilled workers = 5,000 (3.00—3.00)	=	0
LRV for un-skilled workers = 2,750 (2.50 – 2.75)	=	687.50 (A)
Total		2,562.50 (A)

(c) Labour Mix Variance (LMV). Since the actual hours worked (11,500 and standard hours (20 × 500 = 10,000) are not the same, the labour mix variance can be calculated by computing revised standard hours in terms of actual hours worked as under:

Revised standard hours for skilled workers= $\frac{4,0000 \times 11,500}{10,000}$ = 4,600

Revised standard hours for semi-skilled workers = $\frac{1,500 \times 11,500}{10,000}$ = 5,175

Revised standard hours for un-skilled workers = $\frac{1,500 \times 11,500}{10,000}$ = 1,725

Labour Mix Variance (LMV) = St. Rate (Revised St. Hours – Actual Hours)

LMV for skilled workers	= 5 (4,600 — 3,750) =	4,250 (F)
LMV for semi-skilled workers	= 3 (5,175 — 5,000) =	525 (F)
LMV for unskilled workers	= 2.5 (1,725 — 2,750) =	2,562.5 (A)
	Total	2,212.5 (F)

(d) Revised Labour Efficiency Variance (RLEV) = St. Rate St. Hrs. Revised St. hours)

RLEV for skilled workers	= 5(4,000–4,600) =	3,000 (A)
RLEV for semi-skilled workers	= 3(4,500 – 5, 175) =	2,025 (A)
RLEV for un-skilled workers	= 2.5 (1,500 – 1,725) =	562.5 (A)
	Total	5,587.5 (A)

(e) Labour Yield Variance = Average St. Rate (St. Hours – Actual Hours)

Or LYV = ASR (SH)–AH

$$= \frac{37,250}{10,000} (10,000 - 11,500)$$

= 3.725 (1,500) = 5,587.5(A) which is equal to RLEV

Check, LCV – LRV + LMV + LEV or LYV

5,937.50 = 2,562.5 (A) + 2,212.5 (F) + 5,587.5 (A).

Illustration — 8

A gang of workers normally consists of 30 men, 15 women and 10 boys. They are paid at standard hourly rates as under:

Men Rs. 0.80

Women Rs. 0.60

Boys Rs. 0.40

In a normal working week of 40 hours, the gang is expected to produce 2,000 units of output. During the week ended 31st December, 1977, the gang consisted of 40 men, 10 women and 5 boys. The actual wages paid were @ Rs. 0.70, Re 0.65 and Re 0.30 respectively. 4 hours were lost due to abnormal idle time and 1,600 units were produced.

Calculate: (1) Wage Variance, (ii) Wage Rate Variance, (iii) Labour Efficiency Variance, (iv) Gang Composition Variance labour mix variance, and (v) Labour Idle Time Variance.

Solution

The cost data as given in the question may be converted and tabulated as under:

Type of labour	*Standard (2,000 units)*			*Actuals (1,600 units)*		
	Hours	*Rate*	*Cost*	*Hours*	*Rate*	*Value*
Men	30x40 = 1,200	0.80	960	40x40 = 1,600	0.70	1,120
Women	14x40 = 600	0.60	360	10x40 = 400	0.65	260
Boys	10x40 = 400	0.40	160	5x40 = 200	0.30	60
Total	2,200	—	1,480	2,200	—	1,440

(i) Wage Cost Variance (WCV) = St. Cost of Actual Production — Actual Cost

$$WCV=\left(\frac{1,480\times1600}{2,000}-1,440\right)= 1,184 - 1,440 = 256\ (A)$$

(ii) Wage rate Variance (WRV) – Actual Hours (St. Rate x Actual Rate)

WRV for Men = 1,600 (0.80 — 0.70)	=	160(F)
WRV for Women= 400 (0.60 — 0.65)	=	20(A)
WRV for Boys = 200 (0.40 — 0.30)	=	20(F)
Total		160(F)

(iii) Abour Efficiency Variance (LEV) = St. Wage Rate per hour (St. hours for actual production - Actual hours paid)

$$\frac{1,480}{2,200}\left(\frac{2,200\times1,600}{2,000}-2,200\right)$$

$$= 0.6727\ (1,760 - 2,200) = 0.6727 \times 440 = 296\ (A)$$

Since there is a difference between actual hours paid (AHP and Actual Hours Worked (AHW), the total efficiency variance will be classified into Revised Labour Efficiency, Variance and Idle Time Variance.

Revised Labour Efficiency Variance (RLEV) = St. hourly rate (St. hours for actual production - Actual hours worked)

$$RLEV\ \frac{1,480}{2,200}\left(\frac{2,200\times1,600}{2,000}-1,980\right)$$

$$= 0.627\ (1,760 - 1,980) = 0.6727 \times 220 = 148\ (A).$$

Note : Actual hours worked is equal to actual hours paid minus idle time.

The Idle time is calculated as under:

Men	40×4	= 160 hours
Women	10×4	= 40 hours
Boys	5×4	= 20 hours
Total Idle Time		220 Hours

Thus Actual Hours Worked (AHW) = Actual Hours Paid – Idle Time

= 2,200 – 220 = 1,980

(v) Ideal Time Variance (ITV) = No: of Hours lost × St. Hourly Rate

= 220 × 0.6727 = 148 (A).

(vi) Labour Mix Variance (LMV) = Standard cost of standard mix— standard cost of actual mix)

Or LMV = SCSM – SCAM

SCSM = Rs. 1,480.

SCAM is the aggregate cost of actual hours for different grades of labour valued at their corresponding standard rates as calculated below:

Standard cost of actual mix :

Grade of labour	*Actual Hours*	*Standard Rate*	*Cost*
Men	1,600	0.80	1,280
Women	400	0.60	240
Boys	200	0.40	80
	2,200		1,600

LMV = SCSM – SCAM

= 1,480–1,600 = 120(A)

Check, WCV = WRV + LMV + RLEV + ITV

256(A) = 160(F) + 120(A) + 148(A) + 148(A)

256(A) = 416(A) + 160(F).

Overheads Variances

Overhead cost is the aggregate cost of indirect materials, indirect labour and indirect expenses which are incurred in factory, office and for selling and distribution of products or services. For the purpose of variance analysis overheads are classified in two bread categories viz. Variable Overheads and Fixed Overheads. Thus, the total cost variance will comprise the variable overhead variance and fixed overhead variance.

Overhead Cost Variance

It measures the difference between the standard or budgeted overhead costs and the actual overheads incurred. If the actual production is different from the standard production, than the standard overheads for actual production is compared with the actual overheads to calculate the variance. The variance is favourable in case the actual overhead cost is lesser than the standard overhead cost and it is adverse if the actual overhead cost is more than the standard cost for actual production. The Overhead cost variance may be expressed in the form an equation as under:

Overhead Cost Variance (OHCV) = St. Overhead Cost for actual production- Actual Overhead Cost

St. Overhead Cost for actual production = Actual Production x—St. Overhead Rate per unit of output

Overhead rates may be calculated as follows:

$$\text{Standard overhead rate per unit} = \frac{\text{Standard/Budgeted overheads}}{\text{Standard/Budgeted Output}}$$

$$\text{Standard overhead rate per hours} = \frac{\text{Standard/Budgeted overheads}}{\text{Standard/Budgeted Hours.}}$$

Illustration—9

From the following data obtained from the records of a manufacturing concer, calculate the overhead cost variance:

Budgeted Output		450 units	
Budgeted overheads:			
	Fixed	900	
	Variable	450	
		——	Rs. 1,350
Actual Output			225 units
Actual Overheads:			
	Fixed	900	
	Variable	900	
		——	Rs. 1,800.

Solution

Overhead Cost Variance = Standard Overhead Cost for Actual Production — Actual Overhead Cost

Or OCV = SOC for Actual Production – AOC

$$\text{Standard Overhead Cost Rate} = \frac{\text{Budgeted Overheads}}{\text{Budgeted Output}}$$

$$= \frac{1,350}{450} = 3.00$$

SOC for actual Production = Actual Production × Standard Output Rate

= 225 × 3 = 675

OCV = 675 – 1,800 = 1,125(A).

Illustration—10

Taking the data of illustration—9 calculate separately the variable overhead cost variance and Fixed Overhead Cost Variance.

Solution

Variable Overhead Cost Variance (VOCV) = Recovered/Absorbed Variable Overhead Cost – Actual Variable Overhead Cost

$$\text{Rate of Variable Overhead Cost per unit} = \frac{\text{Budgeted Variable Overheads}}{\text{Budgeted Output}}$$

$$\text{Rate of Variable Overhead Cost per unit} = \frac{450}{450} = 1.00$$

Recovered/Absorbed Variable Overhead cost = Actual Production x Rate of VOC

= 225 × 1 = 225

Variable Overhead Cost Variance = 225 – 900 = 675 (A)

Fixed Overheád Cost Variance = Fixed Overhead Cost for actual production — Actual Fixed Cost

$$\text{Rate of Fixed Overhead Cost per unit} = \frac{\text{Budgeted Fixed Cost}}{\text{Budgeted Output}}$$

$$= \frac{900}{450} = 2.00$$

Recovered/Absorbed Fixed Overhead Cost = 225 × 2 = 450

Fixed Overhead Cost Variance = 450 – 900 = 450 (A)

Check, Overhead Cost Variance = Variable Overhead Cost Variance + Fixed Overhead Cost Variance

1,125 (A) = 675 (A) + 450 (A).

Components of Variable Overhead Cost Variance

The variable overhead cost variance is caused by the difference in expenditure and efficiency. Therefore, Variable Overhead Expenditure Variance and Variable Overhead Efficiency Variance are to be calculated.

Variable Overhead Expenditure Variance (VOH Expenditure Variance)

It is the difference between the standard variable e\overheads for actual hours worked and the actual variable overheads incurred. Thus VOH Expenditure Variance = Standard VOH far actual heurs – Actual VOH for actual Hours.

Variable Overhead Efficiency Variance(VOH Efficiency Variance)

It arises when the actual production differs from the standard production for actual hours worked. Therefore, the VOH Efficiency Variance is equal to the difference between the standard variable overheads for actual production and the standard variable overheads for actual hours worked. Thus,

VOH Efficiency Variance = (SVOH for actual Production)—(St. VOH for Actual Hours)

Illustration—10

From the following, calculate: (a) Total Variable Overhead Variance, (b) Variable Overhead Expenditure Variance, and (c) Variable Overhead Efficiency Variance.

	Standard	*Actual*
Variable Overheads	1,800	1,690
Production	75	67
Labour Hours	36	30

Solution

Standard Variable Overhead per unit = $\frac{1,800}{75}$ = 24

Standard Variable Overhead per hour = $\frac{1,800}{36}$ = 50

Standard Variable Overheads for Actual Production = Standard Variable Overhead rate per unit x Actual Production

= 24 × 65 = 1,560

Standard Variable Overheads for Actual Time = St. Variable overheads rate per hour × Actual Hours

= 50 × 30 = 1,500

Expenditure Variance = St. Variable Overheads for actual time—Actual Variable Overheads

= 1,500 – 1,690 = 190(A)

Efficiency Variance = Standard Variable Overheads for Actual Time—Standard Variable Overheads for Actual Time

= 1,560 – 1,500 = 60(F)

Variable Overhead Cost Variance = St. Variable Overheadsfor actual production—Actual Variable overheads.

= 1,560 – 1,690 = 130(A)

Thus Total Variable Overhead Variance = Expenditure Variance + Efficiency Variance

130(A) = 190(A) + 60(F).

Fixed Overhead Variances

The fixed overheads do not change with variation in the volume of production. The total fixed overhead variance is simply the difference between the Standard Fixed Overheads for actual production and the actual overheads incurred for the same output. Thus,

Fixed Overhead cost Variance = Standard Overheads for Actual output — Actual overheads incurred

The total fixed overheads cost variance is further analysed into Expenditure Variance and Volume Variance.

Expenditure Variance arises if the actual overhead cost for the same level of production during the specified period of time is different from the standard overhead cost. It is expressed as under:

Expenditure Variance = Standard or Budgeted overheads — Actual Overheads.

Volume Variance occures in case there is difference between standard hours for budgeted or normal production and the standard hours for actual production. In terms of quantity production, the X Volume Variance arises due to difference in the standard volume of production and the Budgeted or Normal Production valued at standard fixed overhead rate. The formula for the computation of this variance may be expressed as under:

Volume Variance = Recovered Overheads — Budgeted Overheads

Or Volume Variance = Standard Fixed overhead rate (St. hours for actual production — Standard Hours.)

Illustration—11

The data relating to fixed overhead costs of a manufacturing firm are available as under:

	Standard	*Actual*
Labour Hours	4,800	5,200
Output (Units)	2,400	2,000
Fixed Overheads	1,600	1,300

Calculate Fixed Overhead Cost Variance and its components of Expenditure Variance and Volume Variance.

Solution

Standard overhead rate per hour $= \dfrac{1,600}{4,800} = 0.33$

Standard Overhead rate per unit $= \dfrac{1,600}{2,400} = 0.66$

Actual overhead rate per hour $= \dfrac{1,300}{5,200} = 0.25$

Actual overhead rate per unit $= \dfrac{1,300}{2,000} = 0.65$

Labour Hours for Actual Production (Normal Labour Hours) $= \dfrac{4,800 \times 2,000}{2,400}$

= 4.000 hours.

Total Fixed Overhead Cost Variance = Total standard fixed overh eadcost for actual produ- ction – Actual cost

Or Recovered Overhead Cost — Actual Overhead Cost

= (Standard Rate × Actual Output) — (Actual Rate × Actual Production)

(0.66 × 2,000) – (0.65 × 2,000)

1,333 produ 1,300 = 33(F).

Expenditure Variance = Standard Overheads – Actual Overheads =

1,600 – 1,300 = 300 (F).

Volume Variance = St. Fixed overhead hourly rate (St. Normal Hours produ St. labour Hours)

= 0.33 (4,000 – 4,800) = 267(A)

Thus Total Fixed Overhead Cost Variance = Expenditure Variance + Volume Variance

33(F) = 300(F) + 267(A)

Illustration—12

Following data relating to fixed overheads pertain to a manufacturing concern:

Budgeted production for Jan. 1990	450	units
Actual production for Jan. 1990	400	units
Standard fixed overhead rate	Rs. 20	per unit
Actual Fixed overheads	Rs. 5,000	

Calculate: (a) Fixed Overhead Cost Variance

(b) Expenditure/Budgeted Variance

(c) Volume Variance and check your calculations.

Solutions

(a) Fixed Overhead Cost Variance (FOCV) =
Recovered Overheads – Actual Overheads

Or (Actual Units × Standard Rate) – Actual Overheads.
(400 × 20) – 5,000
8,000 – 5,000 = 3,000(F).

(b) Expenditure/Budgeted Overhead Variance =
Budgeted Overheads - Actual Overheads.
(450 × 20) – 5,000
9,000 – 5,000 = 4,000(F).

(c) Volume Variance = Recovered Overheads – Budgeted Overheads.

= (400 × 20) – 450 20)
8,000 – 9,000 = 1,000 (A)

Check, Total FOCV = EV = VV
3,000(F) = 4,000(F) + 1,000(A).

Components of Fixed Overhead Volume Variance

The Volume Variance can further be analysed into the following variances:

(i) Efficiency Variance. It is that portion of the Fixed Overhead Volume Variance which arises due to the difference in the actual time taken to complete a work and the standard hours allowed for the completion of the same work. If the actual time taken is lesser than the standard time allowed than the Efficiency Variance is considered favourable and vice versa. The formula for its calculation is as under:

Efficiency Variance = St. Fixed overhead rate (St. Hours allowed Actual Hours)

(ii) Capacity Variance. There may be difference between actual capacity and planned capacity of the machine or plant due to Idle Time which occures for various reasons. The Capacity Variance measures this difference by valuing it at standard fixed overhead rate. It is measured by the following formula:

Capacity Variance = St. fixed overhead rate (Actual Hours–Standard Hours.

Illustration—13

	Standard	*Actual*
Labour Hours	25,000	25,500
Units of Output	5,000	5,200
Fixed Overheads	10,000	11,000

Calculate: (i) Total Fixed Overhead Variance,

(ii) Expenditure Variance,

(iii) Volume Variance with its components of—(a) Efficiency Variance, (b) Capacity Variance,

Solution

$$\text{Standard Rate per unit} = \frac{10{,}000}{5{,}000} = 2.00$$

$$\text{Standard Rate per Hour } \frac{10{,}000}{25{,}000} = 0.40$$

(i) Total Fixed Overhead Cost Variance = Recovered Overheads— Actual Overheads

= (Actual units × St. Rate) – Actual Overheads

(5,200 × 2) – 11,000
10,400 – 11,000 = 600(A)

(ii) Expenditure Variance = Budgeted Overheads – Actual Overheads

10,000 – 11,000 = 1,000(A)

Total FOCV = EV + VV

600(A) = 1,000(A) + 400(F)

(a) Efficiency Variance = St. Fixed overhead rate (St. Hours allowed – Actual hours)

= 0.40 (26,000 – 25,500)
0.40 × 500 = 200(F)

(b) Capacity Variance = St. fixed overhead rate (Actual hours— Standard Hours)

= 0.40 (25,500 – 25,000)
0.40 × 500 = 200(F)

Thus Volume Variance = Efficiency Variance + Capacity Variance

400(F) = 200(F) + 200(F)

Thus Total Fixed Overhead Cost Variance 600(A) consists of Expenditure Variance 1,000 (A), Efficiency Variance 200(F) and Capacity Variance 200(F).

Calender Variance. It is that part of Capacity Variance which arises due to the difference between the budgeted number of hours/days and the actual number of hours/days in the same budget period. The difference in budgeted hours and effective working hours is caused by unexpected holidays during the budget period. Following formula can be used for the computation of Calender Compender Variance:

Calender Variance = Possible Overheads – Budgeted Overheads

Or = (Possible hours × St. hourly rate) – Budgeted overheads

The Calender Variance will be unfavourable if the possible overheads are less than the budgeted overheads and vice versa.

Illustration—14

Budgeted Hours for the year	2,400
Budgeted overheads for the year	7,200
Actual possible hours in the year	2,250

Calculate Calender Variance for the year

Solution

Calender Variance = Possible Overheads – Budgeted Overheads

= (Possible hours × St. hourly rate) – Budgeted Overheads

$$= \left(2,250 \times \frac{7,200}{2,400}\right) - 7,200$$

$$= 6,750 - 7,200 = 450(A).$$

Note: If it is desired that the Calender Variance is calculated separately, then the Capacity Variance is to be revised and calculated by using the following formula:-

Revised Capacity Variance = Standard Overheads × Possible Overheads

Illustration—14

Calculate the Fixed Overhead Variances from the data given below:

	Budgeted for Jan. 1990	*Actual for Jan. 1990*
Number of working days	26	24
Number of production units	26,000	25,000
Fixed Overheads	39,000	38,000

Budgeted Fixed Overheads Rate = Re 1 per hour

Actual Hours worked during Jan. 1990 = 40,000.

Solution

The information required to calculate variances is firstly obtained as under:

Standard Labour Hours (SLH) = 39,000 hours

Labour Hours Allowed for actual production or

$$\text{Normal Labour Hours (NLH)} = \frac{39{,}000 \times 25{,}000}{26{,}000} = 37{,}500 \text{ hours.}$$

$$\text{Possible Labour Hours (PLH)} = \frac{39{,}000 \times 24}{26} = 36{,}000$$

Standard Rate Per Hour (SRH) = Re 1 (given)

$$\text{Standard Rate per unit} = \frac{39{,}000}{26{,}000} = 1.50$$

$$\text{Actual Rate per unit} = \frac{38{,}000}{25{,}000} = 1.52$$

(A) Total Fixed Overhead Cost Variance = Recovered/Absorbed Fixed Overhead Cost — Actual Overhead Cost

Or (Actual units × St. Rate) – (Actual Units × Actual Rate)

Or Actual Units (Standard Rate – Actual Rate)

25,000 (1.50 – 1.52) = 25,000 × 0.02 = 500(A)

A (i) Expenditure Variance = Standard/Budgeted Fixed Overhead Cost – Actual Fixed cost

= 39,000 – 38,000 = 1,000(F)

A(ii) Volume Variance = Recovered/Absorbed Overheads – Budgeted Overheads

Or St. Fixed overhead Rate(St. Hours for actual production – St. Hours)

Or SRH (NLH – SLH)

1 (37.500 – 39.000) = 1 × 1,500 = 1,500(A)

ii(a) Efficiency Variance = St. Fixed Overhead Rate (Normal Labour Hours — Actual Hours)

OR = SRH (NLH – ALH)

= 1 (40,000 – 36,000) = 4,000(F)

ii(b) Capacity Variance = SRH (Actual Labour Hours — Possible Labour Hours)

= 1 (40,000 – 36,000) = 4,000(F)

ii(c) Calender Variance = SRH (Possible Labour Hours — St. Labour Hours)

= 1 (36,000 – 39,000) = 3,000(A).

Thus, Total Fixed Overheads Cost Variance = Expenditure Variance + Efficiency Variance + Capacity Variance + Calender Variance

500(A) = 1,000(F) + 2,500(A) + 4,000(F) + 3,000(A).

Two Variance and three Variance Methods of Analysis of Overhead Variances

We have seen above that the overheads are classified into two categories viz. Variable Overheads and Fixed Overheads and possible variances for each category are calculated with a view to understand their causes for the purpose of cost control. It would be observed that the Variable Overheads Variance is classified into Expenditure Variance and Efficiency Variance and the Fixed Overhead Cost Variance is broadly split into Expenditure Variance and Volume Variance. This type of analysis based on Two main reasons namely—(a) difference in allowable overheads and standard overheads, and (b) difference in actual production and standard production for actual hours worked, is known as Two Variance Method of Analysis of Overhead Variances. In case the analysis is based on three variables such as difference in expenditure, efficiency and capacity, the analysis is termed as 'Three Variance Method' of analysis of overheads.

Sales Variances

Cost control is necessary for enhancing profitability. A manufacturing firm gains to the extent it is able to reduce cost through cost control technique. The variances relating to raw materials, labour and overheads indicate their effects on over-all profit of the organisation which attempt to raise profitability by adopting standard costing techniques. It may be noted that the profits can also be raised by raising selling price, increasing the volume of sales and making suitable changes in sales-mix, etc. Therefore, the variance analysis technique should also be extended to cover the sales variances which includes Sales Price Variance and Sales Volume Variance. The sales variances can be studied with reference to turnover and sales margin or profit.

Turnover Variances. The money value of actual turnover is rarely equal to its budgeted value. This difference give rise to what is called 'Sales Revenue Variance.' If the actual value of turnover for a definite budget period is more than the budgeted value, than the Sales Revenue Variance is favourable; otherwise it will be adverse. The sales value variance is caused by the differences in budgeted and actual selling prices and volumes of sales. Therefore, it is split into sales Price Variance and Sales Volume Variance.

Sales Price Variance. The Sales Price Variance is favourable if the actual selling price is more than the standard price and vice versa. Following formula is used for its calculation:

Sales Price Variance = Standard value for actual quantity sole — Actual sales value

Or Price Variance = (Actual Quantity × St. Rate) — (Actual Quantity x Actual rate)

Or Sales Price Variance = Actual Quantity (Standard rate — Actual Rate

Sales Volume Variance. The difference in budgeted quantities and actual quantities sold causes this variance. A favourable variance arises in case the actual volume is more than the budgeted volume of sales; otherwise the variance would be adverse. The Sales Volume Variance can be computed by using the following formula:

Sales Volume Variance = Standard Rate (Standard Quantity – Actual Quantity)

The Volume Variance can further be sub-divided into Sales Mix Variance and Sales Quantity Variance.

Sales Mix Variance (SMV). It is calculated when two or more types of goods are sold. We know that the sales of different types of goods are specified in a certain ratio and actual sales hardly conform to the sales ratios specified. Therefore, Sales Mix Variance arises. The Sales Mix Variance is that part of the Volume Variance which arises due to difference in the standard composition and actual composition of sales. It is calculated by the following formula:

Sales Mix Variance = Standard Sales Prince (Revised St. sales – Actual sales).

Sales Quantity Variance. It arises due to the difference between the standard quantity budgeted and the revised standard quantity of sales. The formula for the calculation of SQV is as under:

SQV = Standard Sales Price (Standard Quantity—Revised Standard Quantity)

Illustration—15

From the following data, calculate, (A) Sales Variance or Turnover Variance, (B) Sales Price Variance, (C) Sales Volume Variance, (D) Sales Mix Variance, and (E) Sales Quantity Variance.

Product	*Standard*		*Actual*	
	Quantity	*Price*	*Quantity*	*Price*
A	250	4	250	4
B	200	5	300	5.25
C	150	6	200	6.50
	600		750	

Solution

(A) Sales Variance = Standard Sales – Actual Sales

= (Standard Quantity × St. Rali – (Actual Quantity X Actual Rate)

or SV = (SQ × SR)–(AQ–AR)

SV for A = (250 × 4) – (250 × 4) = 1000 – 1000 = 0

SV for B =(200 × 5) — (300 × 5.25) = 100 — 1575 = 575(F)

SV for C = (150 × 6) — (200 × 6.50) = 900 — 1300 = 400(F)

Total 975(F)

(B) Sales Price Variance= Actual Quantity (St. Rate—Actual Rate)
(SBV) = AQ (SE – AQ)

SPV for A = 250 (4 – 4)= 250 × 0 = 0

SPV for B = 300 (5–5.25) = 75(F)

SPV for C = 200 (6–6.50) = 100(F)

Total 175(F)

(C) Sales Volume Variance = Standard Rate (St. Quantity—Actual Quantity)
or SVV = SR (SQ—AQ)

SVV for A = 4(250–250) = 0

SVV for B = 5 (200–300) = 500(F)

SVV for C = 6(150–200) = 300(F)

Total 800(F)

Sales Variance = Sales Price Variance + Sales Volume Variance
975(F) = 175(F) + 800(F)

(D) Sales Mix Variance = St. Rate (Revised St. Quantity – Actual Quantity

SMV = SR (RSQ – AQ)

Calculation of Revised Standard Quality =

RSQ for $A = \frac{250x750}{600} = 312.5$

$B = \frac{200 \times 750}{600} = 250.0$

$C = \frac{150 \times 750}{600} = 185.5$

Total 750.00

SMV for A = (312.5 – 250) = 250(A)

B = 5 (250 – 300) = 250(F)

C = 6 (187.5 – 200) = 75 (F)

Total 75(F)

(E) Sales Quantity Variance = St. Rate (St. Quantity—Revised St. Quantity)

or SQV = SR (SQ – RSQ)

SQV for A = 4 (250 – 312.5) = 250(F)

B = 5 (200 – 250) = 250(F)

C = 6 (150 –187.5) = 225(F)

Total = 725(F)

Sales Volume Variance = Sales Mix Variance + Sales Quantity Variance

800(F) = 75(F) + 725(F).

Sales Margin or Profit Variance

Sales variance may also be studied with reference to sales margin or profit. Sales margin is the difference between total standard or Budgeted profit and total Actual profit. Thus

Sales Margin Variance = Budgeted Profit – Actual Profit or SMV = BP – AP

Sales Margin Variance can be classified further into Sales Margin Price Variance and Sales Margin Volume Variance. If more than one item is sold and there is a change in actual sales mix and the budgeted quantity differ from that of actual sales, then Sales Volume Variance (SVV) is split into Sale Margin Mix Variance (SMMV) and Sales Margin Quantity Variance (SMQV). Following formula are used for the calculation of these variances:

Sales Margin Price/Variance = Actual Quantity (St. Margin — Actual Margin)

or SMPV = (SM – AM)

Sales Margin Volume Variance = Sales Margin (St Quantity – Actual Quantity)

SMVV = SM (SQ – AQ)

SMV = SMPV + SMVV

Sales Margin Mix Variance = Sales Margin (Revised Sales Quantity—Actual Quantity)

or SMMV = SM (RSQ – AQ)

Sales Margin Quantity Variance = Sales Margin (St. Quantity — Revised Sales Quantity)

or SMQV = SM (SQ – RSQ)

Illustration — 16

From the following data, calculate the sales variances to explain the differences in Standard/Budgeted profit and Actual profits:

Product	*Standard*		*Actuals*		*Cost per unit*
	Quantity	*Price*	*Quantity*	*Price*	*(Rs.)*
A	8,000	4	9000	4.5	3.5
B	6,000	8	7000	7.5	7.5
C	11,500	6	10,500	6.25	5.25

Solution

Statement of Cost, Sales and Profit

Budget

Product	*Standard Quantity*	*Selling Price*	*Total Sales*	*Cost Per Unit*	*Total Cost*	*Profit Margin*	*Total Profit*
A	8000	4	32000	3.5	28000	0.5	4000
B	6000	8	48000	7.5	45000	0.5	3000
C	11500	6	69000	5.25	60,375	0.75	8625
	25500		149000		1,33375		15625

Actual

Product	*AQ*	*SP*	*TS*	*Cost per Unit*	*TC*	*Profit/Sales Margin*	*TP*
A	9,000	4.5	40,500	3.5	31,500	1.00	9,000
B	7,000	7.5	52,500	7.5	52,500	0.00	0
C	10,500	6.25	65,625	5.25	55,125	1.00	10,500
	26,500		158,625		139,125		19,500

Sales Margin/Profit Variance= Budgeted Profit – Actual Profit

or SMV = 15625 – 19500 = 3875(F)

Sales Margin Price Variance = Actual Quantity (St. Margin–Actual Margin)

SMPV for A = 900–(.5—1.0) = 4500(F)

B = 7000 (.5 - 00) = 3.500(A)

C = 10500 (.75 - 1.0) = 2625(F)

3625(F)

Sales Margin Volume Variance = St. Margin (St. Quantity –Actual Quantity)

SMPV for A = .5 (8000 – 9000) = 500(F)

B = .5(6000– 7000) = 500(F)

C = .75 (11500 – 10500)= 750(A)

250(F)

SMV = SMPV + SMVV

3875(F) = 3625(F) + 250(F)

Sales Margin Volume Variance (SMVV) of 250(F) may be analysed into,

Sales Margin Mix Variance and Sales Margin Quantity Variance

Sales Margin Mix Variance = St. Margin (Revised St. Quantity – Actual Quantity)

Or SMMV = SM (RSQ – AQ)

SMMV for A = .5 (8313.73 – 9000) = 343.13(F)

B = .5(6235.29 – 7000) = 382.35(F)

C = .75 (11950.98—10500) = 1088.23(A)

362.75(A)

Revised Standard Quantity for

$$A = \frac{8000 \times 26500}{25500} = 8313.73$$

$$B = \frac{6000 \times 26500}{25500} = 6235.29$$

$$C = \frac{11500 \times 26500}{25500} = 11950.98$$

26500.000

Sales Margin Quantity Variance = SM (SQ – RSQ)

SMQV for A = .5 (8000 – 8313.73) = 1568.7(F)

B = .5 (6000 - 6235.29) = 117.65(F)

$$C = .75\ (11500 - 11950.98) = 338.23(F)$$

$$\overline{\underline{612.75(F).}}$$

SMVV = SMMV + SMQV

250(F) = 362.75(A) + 612.75(F)

QUESTIONS

1. Define Standard Costing. Explain the importance of Standard Costing to a manufacturing business concern.
2. What are different types of Standards? How the attainable standards for materials and labour fixed?
3. Explain the advantages and limitations of standard costing.
4. What are different types of variances which are calculated in respect of Material and labour? Mention the possible causes for the adverse material variances.
5. X Ltd. had fixed 125 kgs. of raw materials at Rs. 5 per kg. for the manufacture of a particular product. The actual quantity of raw materials consumed in the production of the same product came to the 120 kgs, but the raw materials was bought at a higher rate of Rs. 6.25 per kg. You are required to calculate material cost variance and its components of Material Price Variance (MPV) and Material Usage Variance (MUV).
6. From the following particulars, calculated (a) MCV (b) MPV, (c) MUV:
   Materials purchased 750 kgs. @ .5 per kg.
   Standard quantity of material fixed for one unit of finished product, 15 kgs. at Rs. 4.50 per kg.
   Opening stock of material, nil.
   Closing stock of material = 100 kgs.
   Actual Production, 40 units.
7. From the following information calculate:
   (a) MCV
   (b) MPV
   (c) MMV
   (d) MYV
   Standard quantity, 100 kgs.
   Standard Price, Rs. 8 per kg.
   Standard wastage, 10%
   Actual rate paid, Rs. 8.75 per kg.
   Actual wastage, 12%.
8. Rajan Private Ltd. uses two types of raw materials, X and Y for the

manufacture of an article. The company had laid down the following material-mix for production.

Material X 450 kgs @ Rs. 4.50
Material Y 650 kgs @ B. 6.25

Normal loss is 10% of the total weight put in.

The company had to change the actual-mix as a matter of protection policy. Actual-mix during the period was as under:

Material X 850 kgs @ Rs. 4.00
Material Y 450 " @ Rs. 6.50
Actual loss; 12% of 1300 kgs.
Net output, 1144 units

Calculate : (a) MCV (b) MPV (c) MMV (d) MYV.

9. For the manufacture of 100 units of a product a company had fixed 1250 labour hours @ Rs. 8/- per hour. The production was achieved in 1300 labour hours and the actual rate paid was Rs. 8/50 per hour. Calculate, (a) LCV (b) LRV (c) LEV.

10. Following labour standard was fixed for the productive of 300 units of a product:

Category of Labour	*Number of Hours*	*Hourly Rate*
Men	2400	5.00
Women	2700	3.00
Children	900	2.50

Actual hours worked and the wage rate paid were as under:

Category of Labour	*Number of Hours*	*Hourly Rate*
Men	2200	5.50
Women	3000	3.50
Children	1200	3.00

Calculate : (a) LCV, (b) LRV, (c) LMV, (d) RLEV, (e) LYV.

11. From the following information, calculate:

(a) Labour Cost Variance
(b) Labour Rate Variance
(c) Labour Efficiency Variance
(d) Labour Mix Variance
(e) Labour Idle Time Variance.

Type of Labour	*Standard Production = 200 Units*		*Actuals (Production = 150 Units)*	
	Hours	*Rate*	*Hours*	*Rate*
Shilled labour	150	15	180	20
Semi-skilled	100	10	80	8
Un-skilled	50	5	40	4
	300		300	

Note: 5 hours were lost due to abnormal time.

12. Calculate the Variable Overheads Cost Variance from the following informations :

Budgeted output	750	Units
Budgeted hours	1500	
Budgeted Variable overheads	300	
Actual Variable overheads	400	
Actual output	600	units
Actual hours	1800	

13. Calculate Fixed Overhead Cost Variance (FOCV) and its components of Fixed Overhead Expenditure Variance (FOEV) and Fixed Overhead Volume Variance (FOVV) from the following data:

Standard Hours	7200	
Standard Output	3600	(units)
Standard Fixed Overheads	2400	
Actual Hours	9000	
Actual Output	3000	(units)
Actual Fixed overheads	2000	

14. Hari Ram & Co. supplies you the following informations:

	Budget for July, 1995	*Actual for July 1995*
Number of working days	25	24
Number of units	2500	3000
Fixed overhead	3750	36000

Standard fixed overhead Rate Re 1 per hour Actual Hours Worked during July 1990 = 4000. You are required to calculate,

(a) Total Fixed Overhead Cost Variance (FOCV)
(b) Fixed Overhead Expenditure Variance
(c) Fixed Overhead Volume Variance
(d) Fixed Overhead Efficiency Variance
(e) Fixed Overhead Capacity Variance
(f) Fixed Overhead Calender Variance

15. A company deals in these products known as X, Y and Z. It had fixed sales targets for Jan. 1995 as under:

Commodity	*Quantity*	*Rate*	*Sale Value*
X	400	6	2400
Y	450	5	2250
Z	800	3	2400
	1650		7,050

Acutal results for the same period were as under:

X	450	6	2700
Y	400	5	2400
Z	750	3.5	2625
	1600		7,725

Calculate (a) Sales Variance
(b) Sales Price Variance
(c) Sales Volume Variance
(d) Sales Mix Variance
(e) Sales Quantity Variance

16. Using the informations of question No. 15, calculate the Sales variances to explain differences in Standard Profit and Actual Profit if the cost per unit for x, y and z projects is Rs. 5.50, 4.60 and 2.75 respectively.

7

Marginal Costing and Break-even Analysis

Introduction

Total cost involved in a production may be divided broadly into two categories namely—Variable cost and fixed cost. Variable cost varies directly with changes in the volume of production whereas fixed cost remains the same for all levels of production. Raw material and labour costs vary according to level of production and as such fall in the category of variable cost. If wood required for the production of one table is 2 cft., then the production of 10 tables will require 20 cfts of wood. Similarly, wage-cost for 10 tables will be Rs. 250 if one table cost Rs. 25 as wages. Thus the tendency of variable cost is to change according to changes in the volume of production. On the other hand, fixed cost remains unchanged whether we produce one table or 10 tables. Every production involves some amount of fixed cost which is not influence by the variations in the level of production. Rent of building, insurance premium, local taxes, etc., are some of the examples of fixed cost. A manufacturing firm will have to pay rent of the building, insurance premium and local taxes irrespective of the level of production. The classification of total cost into variable and fixed components is significant for managerial decision-making.

The traditional technique ascertaining the cost of production is the Absorption Costing Technique according to which total cost involved in a production is aggregated without any regard to its constituents. Since Absorption Costing technique does not make any distinction between variable and fixed costs and takes into account total cost, it is also known by the names of Full Cost or Total Cost technique. This is the very old method which had been used by manufacturing firms for product costing and profit reporting. Modern firms are not only concerned with ascertaining cost per unit for price fixation but they are also conscious of cost control and cost reduction for overcoming the keen competition successfully and enhance over-all profitability of their concerns. The traditional or Absorption Costing sometimes fails to guide the management properly in decision-making. Therefore, marginal costing technique is now increasingly been used in the formulation of production and price policies. Under marginal costing, fixed costs are separated from the total cost in the analysis of cost data for decision-making.

Meaning of Marginal Costing

In order to understand the Marginal Costing technique, it is essential to clearly understand the meaning of marginal cost. Marginal cost means the cost of the marginal or last unit produced. It is also defined as the cost of one more or one less unit produced. In this connection a unit may mean a single commodity, one dozen, a gross or any other packet of goods. For example, if a manufacturing firm produces X unit as a cost of Rs. 300 and the production of X+1 units cost Rs. 320, then the cost of the additional one unit is Rs. 20 which is the marginal cost. Similarly, if the cost of production of X-1 units comes down to Rs. 280, then the cost of the marginal unit which was being produced is Rs. 20 (Rs. 300 – 280). It would be observed that marginal cost varies directly with production and marginal cost per unit remains the same. Marginal cost consists of prime cost i.e., cost of materials, labour and all variable overheads. It does not contain any element of fixed cost which is kept separate under marginal cost technique. Marginal costing may be defined as the technique of presenting cost data wherein variable costs and fixed costs are shown separately for managerial decision-making. It should be clearly understood that marginal costing is not a method of costing or process costing like job costing but it is simply a method or technique of the analysis of costing informations for the guidance of the management which try to find out the effect on profit due to changes in the volume of output.

Marginal Costing is a popular term in Great Britain. In U.S.A., the term Direct Costing is used in place of marginal costing. In fact, Marginal Costing and Direct Costing are the two different names of the same technique. Like marginal cost, the direct cost also consists of prime cost and variable overheads. Since marginal or direct costing is concerned with variable costs, it would be better if these terms are replaced by Variable

Costing which more truly represents the spirit of the technique.

Marginal costing technique has given birth to a very useful concept of *Contribution* which represents the difference between sales and marginal costs. Contribution may be defined as the profit before the recovery of fixed costs. Thus contribution goes towards the recovery of fixed cost and profit and is equal to fixed cost plus profit (C = F + P). In case a firm neither makes profit nor suffers loss, the *Contribution* will the just equal to fixed cost (C = F). The concept of contribution is very useful in marginal costing. It has a fixed relation with sales. The proportion of contribution to sales known as P/V ration remains the same under given conditions of production and sales.

Presentation of Sales and Cost Data

As pointed out earlier, marginal costing is not a method of costing but it is a technique of presentation of sales and cost data with a view to guide the management in decision-making. The traditional technique popularly known as total cost or absorption cost technique does not make any difference between variable and fixed cost in the calculation of profits but marginal cost statement very clearly indicates this difference in arriving at the net results of a firm. The difference in the presentation of data according to absorption and marginal costing techniques is clear from the following presentation of imaginary figures:

Absorption Cost Statement (Production =100 Units)

Direct materials		2,500
Direct wages		1,800
Direct chargeable expenses		400
	Prime Cost	4,700
Add:	Factory overheads	1,100
	Factory Cost	5,800
Add:	Administration, selling and distribution overheads	1,160
	Total Cost	6,960
	Profit	1,740
	Selling Price	8,700

Marginal Cost Statement

(Production = 100 Units Sales = 8,700/-

Particulars		*Variable Cost kg.*	*Fixed Cost Rs.*
Direct Materials		2,500	—
Direct Wages		1,800	—
Direct Chargeable Expenses		400	—
	Prime Cost	4,700	—
Factory overheads (7% Variables)		770	330
	Factory Cost	5,470	330
Administration, selling and distribution on cost (80% variable)		928	232
	Total Cost	6,398	562
	Contribution (S - V)	2,302	
	Less Fixed Cost	562	
	Profit	1,740	

Since the marginal cost varies directly with production, the marginal cost per unit of output remains the same for all levels of output. It means the variations in the levels of output does not effect the variable cost per unit of output. The total marginal cost for a volume of output can be calculated simply by multiplying the volume of output with the marginal cost per unit. On the other hand, the fixed cost per unit undergoes a change as a result of any change in the volume of production. As the volume of production increases, the fixed cost unit decreases and vice versa. This can be understood with the help of the following cost data:

Particulars	*Volume of Production*		
	100 Units	*125 Units*	*150 Units*
	Rs.	*Rs.*	*Rs.*
Materials	2,500	3,125	3,750
Labour	1,800	2,250	2,700

Direct charges	400	500	600
Variable factory overheads	770	962.50	1,155
Variable administration selling and distribution expenses	928	1,160	1,392
Total Variable Cost	6,398	7,997.50	9,597
Variable cost per unit	63.88	63.98	63.98
Fixed cost	562	562	562
Fixed cost per unit	5.62	4.50	3.75
Total Cost (V+F)	6,960	8,559.50	10,159
Cost per unit	69.60	68.48	67.73

The cost data contained in the above table clearly show that the variable cost per unit remains constant i.e., Rs. 63.98, whether the firm produces 100 units, 125 units or 150 units. But the fixed cost per unit decreases with every increase in production. For an initial production of 100 units, the fixed cost per unit is Rs. 5.62 but it has gone down to Rs. 4.50 and Rs. 3.75 for a production of 125 and 150 units respectively. As shown in the above table the total cost per unit also decreases with an increase in production simply because of the existence of fixed cost which gets spread over more number of units on an increase in the volume of output.

Profit Under Absorption and Marginal Costing

The profit is the same under both the absorption and marginal costing if there is no opening and closing inventory because in that case the question of valuation of inventory does not arise and as such total cost under both the methods remains the same. Whatever produced is generally not sole in the same period and some amount of closing stock has to be carried to the next financial period. Therefore, closing stock has to be recognized and valued for the purpose of profit measurement. The profit under the two methods differ due to the existence of unsold stock and the difference in the methods of their valuation. Under absorption costing method, the stocks are valued at total unit cost which consists of variable and fixed costs. According to marginal costing, the inventory is valued at marginal cost which consists of variable costs only. The Absorption cost method recognises total cost and those who believe in this method argue that a unit of output benefits from both variable cost and fixed cost and as such unit cost should consists of both types of costs. It has been experienced that total cost is not always helpful in decision-making and the inventory should also be valued at variable cost. The following illustration explains the distinction between the total costing and marginal costing so far as the profit measurement is concerned.

Illustration—1

A manufacturing company provides the following informations regarding the production of a particular product for the year 1986:

Materials consumed		1,50,000
Labour consumed		1,00,000
Variable factory expenses		50,000
Fixed factory expenses		90,000
Administration expenses		40,000
Selling Expenses:		
Variable	25,000	
Fixed	30,000	
		55,000

During the year 1986, the production amounted to 10,000 units out of which 8,000 units @ Rs. 60 could be sold by the end of the year. There was no opening stock. Show the profit according to Absorption Costing and marginal costing techniques.

Absorption Costing: Profit Statement		*Marginal Costing: Statement*	
Raw materials	1,50,000	Sales	4,80,000
Labour cost	1,00,000	Raw materials	1,50,000
Variable factory expenses	50,000	Labour	1,00,000
Fixed factory expenses	90,000	Variable factory expenses	50,000
Administration expenses	40,000	Marginal cost of 10,000 units	3,00,000

Production cost of 10,000 units)	4,30,000		Less value of 2,000 units unsold (3,00,000 x 2,000) / 10,000	60,000
Less value of closing stock: (4,30,000 x 2,000) / 19,000	86,000			
			Variable cost of 8,000 units	2,40,000
Production cost of 8,000 units		3,44,000		
Add Variable selling expenses	25,000		Gross variable contribution	2,40,000
Add Variable selling expenses			Less Variable selling exp.	25,000
Fixed selling Exp.	30,000		Net Contribution	2,15,000
		55,000		
Total Cost		3,99,000	Less fixed costs:	
Profit		81,000	Factory cost	90,000
			Admin. expenses	40,000
		4,80,000	Fixed selling Exp.	30,000
				1,60,000
			Profit	55,000

From the above statements, it is clear that the Absorption Cost Statement shows a profit of Rs. 81,000 whereas profit as per marginal cost statement is Rs. 55,000. There is a difference of Rs. 26,000 (81,000—55,000—55,000) which is due to the difference in the valuation of unsold stocks of 3,000 units under the two methods. The absorption costing has valued inventory at a total cost of Rs. 43 per unit whereas value place on inventory under marginal costing is Rs. 30 per unit.

FEATURES OF MARGINAL COSTING

We are now in a position to bring out the distinctive features of marginal costing. The main features of marginal costing are as follows:

1.Cost Classification

The marginal costing technique makes a sharp distinction between variable costs and fixed costs. It is the variable cost on the basis of which production and sales policies are designed by the firms following the marginal costing technique.

2. Inventory Valuation

Under marginal costing, inventory for profit-measurement is valued at marginal cost in sharp contrast to total unit cost under absorption costing method.

3. Marginal Contribution

Marginal costing technique makes use of marginal contribution for marking various decisions. Marginal contribution which is the difference between sales and marginal cost forms the basis for judging the profitability of different products or departments.

SEPARATION OF FIXED COSTS ELEMENT FROM SEMI-VARIABLE COSTS

Since marginal costing technique keeps fixed costs separate and it is the marginal cost which is considered relevant for decision-making, it is essential that fixed cost element is separated from the semi-variable costs and merged with the other fixed cost and the variable portion is added to the variable cost. To classify the semi-variable costs into fixed and variable element, any one of the following methods may be used:—

1. High-Low method.
2. Degree of Variability Method.
3. Scatter Graph Chart Method.
4. Least Square Method.

1. Least Square Method

According to this method, the minimum and maximum levels of production during a given period alongwith their corresponding semi-variable expenses are considered and variations in output noted. The rate of variable expenses per unit of output is determined to finally know the total amount of variable expenses contained in the semi-variable expenses. Variable expenses per unit is arrived at by dividing the variations in expenses by the variations in output.

$$\text{Per unit variable expenses} = \frac{\text{Variations in Expenses}}{\text{Variations in Output}}$$

Illustration—2

A company furnishes the following informations with respect to its production for the year 1987:—

Year	*Production*	*Semi-variable Expenses*
I Quarter	100 units	1,500
II Quarter	120	1,750
III Quarter	150	2,150
IV Quarter	200	2,900

Using High-Low Method, calculate the variable cost per unit and total variable cost to show the fixed cost separately.

Solutions

The highest and the lowest production is in the IV quarter and I Quarter respectively. Therefore, the production and semi-variable expenses of these quarters will be analysed as under:

Year	*Production*	*Semi-variable*	*Variable Cost*	*Fixed cost*
I Quarter	100	1,500	1,400	100
IV Quarter	200	2,900	2,800	100

$$\text{Variable cost per unit} = \frac{\text{Variation in expenses}}{\text{Variation in output}}$$

$$= \frac{2{,}900 - 1{,}500}{200 - 100} = \frac{1{,}400}{100} = 14$$

Total variable cost in I quarter $- 100 \times 14 = 1{,}400$

Fixed cost in I quarter $= 1{,}500 - 1{,}400 = 1000$

Total variable cost in IV quarter = 200 × 14 = 2,800

Fixed cost in IV quarter = 2,900 – 2,800 = 100.

The only merit of High-Low method is that it is simple to understand and easy to apply. But it is not a scientific method as it takes into account the extreme levels of activity which is not proper. I might give different variable rate if any other two levels of production are analysed for the purpose. A fair rate of variable cost can be ascertained if the two levels of production within the normal range of activity are considered. Another defect of the method is that it assumes variable rate as constant for all levels of output. This assumption is valid only within a certain range of production and that two in a short period.

2. Degree of Variability Method

Under this method the degree of variability for semi-variable expenses is ascertained by the analysis of the data of production and expenses. The variability is expressed as a percentage of semi-variable expenses. It may be observed that some of the semi-variable expenses have a 60% variability whereas others may have 80% or 90% variability. The ascertainment of variability percentage is a difficult task otherwise the method is easy to apply.

Illustration—3

A company has incurred Rs. 2,900 on semi-variable expenses on the production of 200 units. The variability rate is 90%. Find out the fixed and variable cost elements. Also estimate the cost for the next budget period in which output is estimated to be 250 units.

Solution

Variable cost 90% of 2,900 = 2,610

Fixed cost = 2,900 – 2,610 = 290

$$\text{Variable cost per unit} = \frac{2,610}{200} = 13.05$$

Variable cost of 250 units = 250 × 13.05 = 3,262.50

Semi-variable cost = 3,262.50 + 290 = 3,552.50.

Scatter Graph Method

Graphic charts may be used to separate the fixed and variable components from the semi-variable costs. The main steps involved in the preparation of a scatter graph chart are,

1. Represent the output on horizontal axis and costs on the vertical axis.
2. Determine the points of expenses corresponding to different levels of output.
3. Draw a line known as the 'line of the best fit' by inspection. This line is to be drawn through the various points plotted as above.
4. Extend the line so that it touches the vertical axis at a point from which a line parallel to OX - axis should be drawn. This new line is the line of fixed cost.

With the help of the graph so drawn, the variable cost element for any level of output may be known by the difference between 'line of the best fit' and the fixed cost line.

Illustration—4

A manufacturing firm furnishes the following informations:

Months (1987)	*Production (units)*	*Semi-variable expenses (Rs.)*
July	45	95
August	30	73
September	55	110
October	90	165
November	70	135
December	100	185

You are required to prepare a scatter graph chart to represent the fixed and variable cost portions of the semi-variable cost. Also determine the cost for January 1988 in which production is expected to touch 130 units.

From the graph, it is clear that the total cost line (line of the best fit) touches 0 Y - axis at 25 which is the fixed cost. For an output, say 100 units, the variable cost will be Rs. 160 (185 – 25). In this case, variable cost per unit is Rs. 1.60 (160 ÷ 100). Cost for an output of 130 units will be Rs. 233 (130 x 1.60) + 25.

The whole success of scatter-graph method depends upon the accuracy with which the line of the best fit is drawn. Any bias in drawing the line will give wrong figure of fixed cost. Since the 'line' is drawn by a free hand, it is most likely that the same data give different results if used by two different persons.

4. Least Squares Method

The method of least squares is a statistical method which is used for more accurate separation of fixed and variable cost components. A more exact line of the best fit can be obtained by this method. The equation of a straight line is, Y = a + bx where a and b are constants. To fine out the values of a and b, the following normal equation has to be solved:

(Y) = na + b (x) I

(XY) - a (x) + b $(X)^2$ II

The method of solving these equations to fine out the values of a and b can be understood with the help of the following example which takes into account the data shown under scatter-graph chart method.

Months 1987	*Production (units)* X	*Semi-variable expenses* Y	X^2	*XY*
July	45	95	2025	4275
August	30	73	900	2190
September	55	110	3025	6050
October	90	165	8100	14850
November	70	135	4900	9450
December	100	185	19000	18500
	X = 390	Y = 763	X^2 = 28950	XY = 55315

n = Number of items i.e. 6

Putting the values in the normal equations, we get,

763 = 6a + 390b I

55315 = 390a + 28950b II

Multiplying equation I by 65 we get,

49595 = 390a + 25350b..III

Substracting II from III we get,

–5750 = –3600b

Or b = 1.59

Putting the value of b in I we get,

763 = 6a + 390 (1.59)

Or a = 23.89

Thus Y = 23.89 + 1.59(X)

Where 23.89 is the fixed cost and the rate of variable cost is 1.59 Semi-variable cost for 130 units will be,

23.89 + 1.59 × 130 = 230.59

It will be observed that the fixed costs according to scatter-graph method was estimated at Rs. 25 whereas it is Rs. 23.89 as per the method of Least Squares. The difference is due to the fact that the line of the best fit was drawn simply inspection in the former case whereas it is mathematically calculated in the later case.

Marginal Costing and Decision-Making

The effort of the management in an enterprise is to optimise profits or minimise losses. In their efforts to do so they have to review the existing production, pricing and marketing policies from time to time and make necessary adjustments, if needed. Marginal costing technique provides objective basis and facilitates the task of decision-making in respect of the following:

1. Determining relative profitability of products.

2. Determining profitability of alternative product-mix.
3. Make or Buy decisions.
4. Pricing in home and foreign markets.
5. Production with limiting factor.
6. Profit planning.

Ascertaining Relative Profitability of Products

A manufacturing concern engaged in the production of various products is interested in the study of the relative profitability of its products so that it may suitably change its production and sales policies in case of those products which it considers less profitable or unproductive. The concept of P/V Ratio provided by the marginal costing technique is much helpful in understanding the relative profit/ability of products. It is always profitable to encourage the production of that product which shows a higher P/V ratio. Sometimes, the management is confronted with a problem of loss and it has to decide whether to continue or abandon the production of a particular product which has resulted in a net loss. Marginal costing technique properly guides the management in such a situation. If a product or department shows loss, the Absorption Costing method would hastily conclude that it is of no use of produce and run the department and it should be close down. Sometimes this type of conclusion will mislead the management. The marginal costing technique would suggest that it would be profitable to continue the production of a product if it is able to recover the full marginal cost and a part of the fixed cost.

Illustration—5

A company manufactures three products A, B and C. The company has prepared the following budget for the year 1988:

	Total	*Product A*	*Product B*	*Product C*
Sales	4,20,000	80,000	2,50,000	90,000
Factory Cost				
Variable	2,90,500	40,000	1,74,000	76,500
Fixed	29,500	5,000	16,000	8,000
Production Cost	3,20,000	45,000	1,90,000	85,000
Selling and Administration Cost:				

Variable	35,000	14,000	14,000	7,000
Fixed	8,000	3,500	3,200	1,300
Total Cost	3,63,000	62,500	2,07,200	93,300
Profit	57,000	17,500	42,800	–3,300 (less)

On the basis of the above informations, the company management is thinking to discontinue with the production of Product C which has shown loss. The management seeks your expert opinion on the issue before they take a final decision. You are required to comment on the relative profitability of the products.

Solution

The informations contained in the budget may be re-arranged in the form of a Marginal Cost Statement as shown below:

Marginal Cost Statement

Particulars	*Total*	*Product A*	*Product B*	*Product C*
Sales	4,20,000	80,000	2,50,000	90,000
Variable Cost:				
Factory Cost	2,90,500	40,000	1,74,000	76,500
Selling and Admn. Cost	35,000	14,000	14,000	7,000
Total Marginal Cost	3,25,500	54,000	1,88,000	83,500
Contribution	94,500	26,000	62,000	6,500
Fixed Costs	37,500	8,500	19,200	9,800
Profit	57,000	17,500	42,800	-3,300 (less)
Profit-volume Ratio*	22.5%	32.5%	24.8%	7.2%

* It is the ratio of Contribution to Sales.

Recommendations

As shown in the marginal cost statement, the contribution of Product C is Rs. 6500 which goes towards the recovery of fixed cost of Rs. 9,800. If the production of C is discontinued, the company will loose the marginal contribution of Rs. 6,500 whereas it will have to incur fixed cost of Rs. 9,800. The total profit of Rs. 57,000 will be reduced to Rs. 50,500 (57,000 – 6,500). Thus it is advisable that the production of C should not be discontinued. As regards the relative profitability, Product A is more profitable than B and C as the Profit-Volume Ratio in this case is highest. The production and sales of Product A should, therefore, be encouraged.

Determining Profitability of Alternative Product-Mix

Since the objective of an enterprise to maximise profits, the management would prefer that product-mix which is ideal one in the sense that it yields maximum profits. Products-mix means combination of products which is intended for production and sales. A firm producing more than one product has to ascertain the profitability of alternative combinations of units or values of products and select the one which maximises profits. How marginal cost analysis helps the management in this regard is illustrated with the help of the following example:

Example

A manufacturing firm supplies you the following information:

	Product A *(Rs.)*	*Product B* *(Rs.)*
Direct Material per unit	16	14
Direct wages paid	5	4
Variable Expenses (100% of Wages)	5	4
Fixed Expenses ....Rs. 1,300/-		
Sales price per unit	32	26

Sales-mixtures

1. 400 units of Product A and 400 units of Product B
2. 500 units of Product A and 300 units of Product B
3. 600 units of Product A and 200 units of Product B.

You are required to prepare the marginal cost statement to show contribution per unit and suggest the sales-mix which optimise profits.

Solution

MARGINAL COST STATEMENT

	Product A (Rs.)	*Product B (Rs.)*
Sales per unit	32	26
Direct material per unit	16	14
Direct wages per unit	5	5
Variable Expenses	5	4
Cost per unit		
Marginal	26	22
Contribution Per Unit	6	4

Profit from different sales-mix

1. 400 units of A and 400 units of B

   Total contribution—Fixed cost = Profit

   (400 x 6) + (400 x 4) - 1,300 = 2,700

2. 500 units of A and 300 units of B

   (500 x 4) + (300 x 4) - 1,300 = 2,900

3. 600 units of A and 200 units of B

   (600 x 6) + (200 x 4) - 1,300 = 3,100

Suggestions

The firm should produce and sell 600 units of A and 200 units of B. This combination yields maximum and 200 units of B. This combination yields maximum profit of Rs. 3,100.

Make or Buy Decision (When plant is not fully utilised)

If the similar product or component is available outside, then a manufacturing firm compares its unit cost of manufacture with the price at which it can be purchased from the market. The marginal cost analysis suggests that it is profitable to the total manufacturing cost. In other words the firm should prefer to Buy if the marginal cost is more than the Bought-out price and Make when the marginal cost is lesser than the purchase price. However, the available plant capacity will exert its own influence in such a decision-making.

Example

A radio manufacturing company finds that component No. IST and 3SK which are being manufactured internally can be purchased from the market at a cost of Rs. 17.75 and Rs. 31 per unit respectively with an assured supply.

The structure of cost of manufacture is as under:

	Component No IST	*Component No 3SK*
Raw Material per unit	Rs. 8,50	Rs. 11.25
Wages per unit	5.40	8.15
Variable Expenses per unit	1.10	2.10
Fixed cost per unit	2.75	9.75
Total cost	17.75	31.00

You are required to represent the data in an appropriate form and suggest the management whether they should Make or Buy the products.

Solution

	Component No. IST (Rs. Per unit)	*Component No. 3ST (Rs. Per unit)*
Purchase Price	13.90	24.25
Raw Materials	8.50	11.25
Wages	5.40	8.15
Variable Expenses	1.10	2.10
Marginal Cost	15.00	21.50
Fixed Cost	2.75	9.50
Total Cost	17.75	31.00

1. If purchased — the cost involved will be purchase price plus fixed cost:

Purchase price	13.90	24.25
Fixed cost	2.75	9.50

	Cost to be borne	16.65	33.75
2.	Total cost if manufactured internally	17.75	31.00
	Decision Suggested	To Buy	To Manufacture

Formula to Remember

Firm should buy when PP + FC is lesser than total cost of manufacture

Firm should manufacture when PP+FC is greater than total cost of manufacture

Expand or Buy Decision

In case unused capacity is limited or does not exist, then an alternative to buying is to make by purchasing additional plant and other equipment. The firm should evaluate the capital expenditure proposal resulting out of expansion programme in terms of cash flows and cost of capital. If the installed capacity of the existing plant is partially being used, then it can be utilised by producing more internally. The additional production may necessiate purchase of some specialised equipment and thus involve interest and depreciation cost. It is advisable to expand and produce if the enterprise is able to save some costs by doing so.

Example

Part No. X-293 used in the assembly of product manufactured by your company has during the past three years been a bought-out item. The current price of this part is Rs. 120. Transportation and other delivery costs account for Rs. 15 per piece. Sales tax at 10% is added to the invoice price.

Your company had been manufacturing this part earlier but decided subsequently to discontinue its own manufacture. There is sufficient unutilised capacity which can be used if it is decided to manufacture the part again in its own plant.

Annual requirements of the part are 6,000 units.

Prepare a study to enable the management to come to a decision on a proposal to manufacture the part within its own plant. The following estimates are available:

	Part No. x-293 Estimated cost per unit (Rs.)
Raw materials	96
Direct wages	8
Overheads at 800 per cent of wages	64
Total cost	168
Make up for return on investment	12
	180

In addition, special tools, jigs and fixtures required to manufacture this part are needed to be acquired at a cost of Rs. 1,50,000. These are to be amortised over 5 years.

The overhead rate is the budgeted recovery rate for products manufactured by the company. The variable portion of this amounts to 100 per cent of direct wages.

Make your recommendations.

(C.A. Final, 1976)

Solution

STATEMENT OF BUYING COST
PART NO. X-293 (6,000 UNITS)

Particulars	*Rate per unit (Rs.)*	*Total amount (Rs.)*
Current Purchase Price	120	7,20,000
Add sales Tax at 10%	12	72,000
Invoice Price	132	7,92,000
Add Transportation and other delivery costs	15	90,000
Total cost of buying	147	8,82,000

STATEMENT OF MANUFACTURING COST
PART NO. X-293 (6,000 UNITS)

Particulars	*Rate per unit (Rs.)*	*Total amount (Rs.)*
Raw materials	96	5,76,000
Direct wages	8	48,000
Variable overheads (100% of wages)	8	48,000
Depreciation cost (1/5 x 1,50,000)	5	30,000
Interest on additional capital investment @ 12% (12/100 x 1,50,000	3	18,000
Total cost of manufacture	120	7,20,000

Note: The rate of interest at 12% has been assumed. Fixed costs have not been taken into account because they will remain the same even if the part is not manufactured within the company.

From the above statement it is clear that the company will save Rs. 1,62,000(Rs. 8,82,000 - 7,20,000) if the part is manufactured. The saving per unit will be Rs. 147 - 120 - 27/-.

Thus it is recommended that Part No. x-293 may be manufactured.

Pricing in Home and Foreign Markets

Pricing of a product is governed primarily by its cost of production and the nature of competition being faced by the production unit. Once a price is fixed by market forces, it remains stable atleast in the short period. During short period when selling period, marginal cost and fixed costs remain the same, an entrepreneur is in a position to establish relationship between them. On the basis of such a relationship, it is very easy to fix the volume of sales and selling price during normal and abnormal times in the home market. How far the prices can be cut in case of foreign buyer to effect additional sales is a problem which is realistically answered by the marginal costing technique.

Illustration

A firm is currently producing 20,000 units annually of a product. The cost structure is as under:

	Per unit (Rs.)
Materials	4.50
Labour	3.25
Variable Expenses	1.25
Variable cost per unit	9.00
Fixed Expenses	6,600
Selling Price	Rs. 12/- per unit

The firm is thinking to reduce the selling price due to severe competition to Rs. 10.80 per unit (10% decrease). How much extra should it produce and sell if the previous level of profit is to be maintained?

Solution

MARGINAL COST STATEMENT (20,000 UNIT)

	Per unit	*Amount*	*Cost Reduction Per unit*	*Cost Reduction Amount*
Selling Price	12.00	2,40,000	10.80	2,16,000
Materials	4.50	90,000	4.50	90,000
Labour	3.25	65,000	3,25	65,000
Variable Expenses	1.25	25,000	1.25	25,000
Marginal Cost	9.00	1,80,000	9.00	1,80,000
Contribution	3.00	60,000	1.80	36,000
Fixed Costs		6,600		6,600
Profit		53,400		29,800

As a result of decrease in selling price by 10% the profits of the firm will be decreased to Rs. 29,400 if no effort for additional sales is made. Since the firm has decided to maintain the present level of profit, i.e. Rs. 53,400 it will need additional sales to counterbalance the loss due to price reduction. The number of units required to be sold to maintain the existing level of profit is calculated as under:

$$\text{Number of units to be sold} = \frac{\text{Total Contribution required}}{\text{Contribution per unit}}$$

$$= \frac{60{,}000}{1.80} = 33{,}333 \text{ units}$$

Therefore extra sales required = 33,333 - 20,000 = 13,333 units
Note: The present level of profit can be maintained only if the present contribution could be attained by the price change.

Price Under Recession/Depression

Recession is an economic condition under which demand is declining. During depression the demand is at its lowest ebb, and the firms are confronted with the problem of price reduction and closure of production. Under such conditions, the marginal costing technique suggests that prices can be reduced to a level of marginal cost. In that case, the firm will loose profits and also suffer loss to the extent of fixed costs. This loss will also be borne even if the production is suspended altogether. Selling below marginal cost is advisable only under very special circumstances.

Illustration

Dhining Star Ltd. is experiencing conditions of depression; the demand is declining and the company is forced every time to reduce the selling price. On the basis of following cost information, you are required to suggest to the management the minimum price which they can fix in order to continue production in the short period.

	Existing cost structure		*estimated cost structure*	
Raw materials	4.50	per unit	Rs. 3,85	per unit
Labour	3.25		3.25	
Variable Expenses	1.25		1.25	
	9.00		8.35	
Overheads:				
Variable overheads	0.50		0.50	
Fixed overheads	1.00		1.00	
Total Cost	10.50		9.85	
Selling Price	10.25			

Budgeted Production - 1,000 units for half year.

Solution

MARGINAL COST STATEMENT

Particulars	*Existing cost structure (per unit)*	*New cost structure (per unit)*
Sales	10.25	3.85
Raw Materials	4.50	3.85
Labour	3.25	3.25
Variable Expenses	1.25	1.25
Variable overheads	0.50	0.50
Marginal Cost	9.50	8.85
Contribution	0.75	
Fixed Cost	1.00	
Loss	0.25	

Since the company is under pressure to reduce selling price, it can reduce its price to the level of marginal cost which is Rs. 8.85. By charging this price, it will recover only the variable cost and suffer loss to the tune of fixed cost. Thus the company can fix Rs. 8.85 per unit for its product if it is interested to continue production in the short-run. In the long-run, this price will not work because no firm can afford to operate with zero profits and losses in the long run.

Pricing in Foreign Markets

A foreign market can be kept separate from the domestic market due to many legal and other restrictions imposed on imports and exports and as such a different price can be charged from foreign buyers. Any company which enjoys surplus production capacity can increase its production to sell in the foreign market at lower price if its full fixed cost already stands recovered from the production from home market. Any price in excess of the marginal cost is advisable from the foreign market as shown in the following example.

Illustration

Bright Star Ltd. is operating at 60% of its installed capacity and producing 27,000 units which are sold in the domestic market at a price of Rs. 15 per unit. The marginal cost of production is Rs. 12. per unit and the fixed cost amount to Rs. 15,000.

The company has received a foreign offer to purchase 9,000 units of its product at a price of Rs. 13.50 per unit.

The company has received a foreign offer to purchase 9,000 units of its product at a price of Rs. 13.50 per unit. The Company will have to incur nothing on additional fixed cost. however, it will have to bear Rs. 0.75 per unit as distribution cost in respect of foreign buyer.

You are required to suggest to the management—(a) whether or not the order should be accepted and (b) what will be your recommendations if the buyer is a local one?

Solution

Particulars	*Production and Sales at 60% capacity (27,000 units)*	*Production and sales at 80% capacity (36,000 units)*
Sales	4,05,000	5,26,500
Marginal cost	3,24,000	4,32,000
Contribution	81,000	94,500
Fixed cost	15,000	15,000
Profit	66,000	79,500
Less distribution cost of exports 9,000 units @ Rs. 0.75 per unit		6,750
Net Profit	66,000	72,750

Excess Profit from exports = 72,750 - 66,000 = 6,750/-

The above cost statement clearly shows that the company should accept the foreign offer as it will generate an excess profit of Rs. 6,750/

If the buyer is a local one, the company will have to keep this buyer separate from other buyers for additional supplies of 9,000 units @ Rs. 13.50 otherwise other customers will also ask for price reduction and the company will be put to difficulties.

Production with Limiting Factor

Sometimes, production has to be carried with certain limiting factor. A limiting factor is the factor the supply of which is not unlimited or freely available to the manufacturing enterprise. In case of labour shortages, the labour becomes limiting factor. Raw material or plant capacity may be a limiting factor during budget period. The consideration of limiting factors is essential for the success of any production plan because the manufacturing firm cannot increase the production to the level it desire when a limiting factor is combined with other factors of production. The limiting factor is also called by the name of 'scarce factor' or 'key factor,' 'principal budget factor' or 'governing factor.'

The commodity which contributes maximum contribution per unit or which yields maximum P/V ratio is the most profitable commodity. This is true when there is no limitation or production. In case different products are manufactured with a particular limiting factor, it is not the contribution per unit or P/V ratio which rightly guides in fixing production priorities but the profitability per unit of limiting factor is the proper guiding star. Supposing labour is the limiting factor, the relative profitability will be calculated as under:

$$\text{Profitability} = \frac{\text{Contribution per unit}}{\text{Time required to produce one unit}}$$

Illustration

From the following data which product would you recommend to be manufactured in a factory, time being the Key factor:

	Per unit of product A	*Per unit of product B*
Direct material	24	14
Direct labour (Re 1 per hour)	2	3
Variable overhead (Rs. 2 per hour)	4	6

Selling price	100	110
Standard time to produce	2 hours	3 hours.

(ICWA, India Inter)

Solution

MARGINAL COST STATEMENT

	Product A (Per unit)	*Product B (Per unit)*
Sales	100	110
Materials	24	14
Direct Labour	2	3
Variable overheads	4	6
Marginal Cost	= 30	23
Contribution	70	87
P/V Ratio	70%	79%
Contribution or profitability per hour	70/2=35/-	87/3=29/-

Recommendation: Product B is more profitable if there is no limiting factor. Since labour is the limiting factor, the Product A should be manufactured in the factory as its profitability per hour is Rs. 35 which is more than the profitability of B. If sales is not the limiting factor, all the available labour should be diverted for the production of product A.

A Case of Two Limiting Factors

It is possible that the production is limited by two or more limiting factors. Labour and raw material may be in short supply. The amount of availability of one factor affects the utilization of other factor. Under such a condition the best product mix is one which optimise over-all profits but is achievable under the given constraints.

Illustration

On the basis of following informations in respect of an engineering company, determine the product-mix which will give the highest profit attainable. Do you recommend overtime working upto maximum of

15,000 hours at twice the normal wages (overheads are ignored for the purpose of this question)

	PRODUCTS		
	A	B	C
Raw material per unit (Kg)	10	6	15
Labour hours per unit (Re 1 per hour)	15	25	20
Maximum production possible	6,000	4,000	4,000
Selling price per unit (Rs.)	125	100	200

1,00,000 Kgs. of raw materials are available @ Rs. 10 per kg. Maximum production hours are 1,84,000 with a facility for further 15,000 hours on overtime basis at twice the normal wage rate.

(M. Com., Bhagalpur)

Solution

MARGINAL COST STATEMENT

Particulars	*Product A (6,000 units)*		*Product B (4000 units)*		*Product C (3000 units)*	
	Per unit	*Total*	*Per unit*	*Total*	*Per unit*	*Total*
Sales	125	7,50,000	100	4,00,000	200	6,00,000
Raw Materials	100,	6,00,000	60	2,40,000	150	4,50,000
Labour	15	90,000	25	1,00,000	20	60,000
Marginal Cost	115	6,90,000	85	3,40,000	170	5,10,000
Contribution	10	60,000	15	60,000	30	90,000
Contribution per Kg. of raw material (Contribution per unit) / (-raw material per unit)	1		2.50		2.00	
Contribution per labour hour (contribution per unit) / (- hours per unit)	0.06		0.60		1.50	

Since raw material and labour are the limiting factors, the production of B and C should be encouraged to the maximum level as these products show maximum profitability both per Kg of raw material and per labour hour. Any raw material and labour hours remaining after their use in B and C products should be utilised for the production of A. The consumption of inputs in B and C and the balance available for A is calculated below:

Product	*Unit*	*Raw Material required (No. of Kgs.)*	*Labour required (No. of Hrs.)*
B	4,000	24,000	1,00,000
C	3,000	45,000	60,000
Total	70,000	69,000	1,60,000
Balancing figure for A		31,000	24,000
Total Available		1,00,000	1,84,000

With 31,000 Kgs. of raw materials and 24,000 labour hours, how many units of A can be produced? 31,000 Kgs of raw material is sufficient to produce 31,000 Kgs of A but the labour available to produce 31,000 units is not sufficient. 24,000 labour hours are sufficient just to produce 1,600 units (15 hrs. are required to produce one unit). Therefore, 1,600 units of A can be produced working at current normal conditions. The contribution from the production of 1,600 units of A @ Rs. 10 per unit will be Rs. 16,000.

If the work is done for additional 15,000 hours for which facility exist, the additional 1,000 units can be produced, but at the twice the normal wage rates. The contribution form the total 2,600 units of A will be,

Sales of 2,600 units @ Rs. 125 per unit 3,25,000 Marginal cost of 2,600 units:

(a) Raw material:
26,00 units % Rs 10 — 2,60,000

(b) Wages - 1,600 units
@ Rs. 15 — 24,000

(c) Wages - 1,000 units @ Rs. 30	30,000	3,14,000
Marginal Contribution		11,000

It is clear from the above cost analysis that the production of 1,600 units of a yields of contribution of 16,000 whereas 2600 units of A generates a contribution of Rs. 11,000. Thus the contribution is reduced if additional 1,000 units by working over-time are produced. Therefore, over time work is not recommended. The best product-mix will be,

Products	*Units*
A	1,600
B	4,000
C	3,000

Profits Planning

The process of profit planning involves the calculation of expected costs and revenues arising out of operations at different levels of plant capacity for the production of different types of goods during a given period of time. The cost and revenues at different level of operating are different and a concern has to choose one level at which its profits are maximum. Marginal costing technique help the management by suggesting a suitable product-mix or plant capacity which optimise profits. It also guides the management in selecting the best product mix for attaining a specified level of profit.

Illustration

A manufacturing company operating at its 40% installed capacity produced 12,500 units of a product in involving the following cost was sold at Rs. 28/- per unit.

	Cost per unit (Rs.)
Raw materials	12.00
Labour	4.50

Variable overheads	3.50	
Fixed overheads	2.50	(Rs. 31,250)
	22.50	

The company is planning for profit for 1993. It anticipates a decrease in the selling price by 5% and 10% if it operates at 60% and 90% plant capacity respectively. The supplier of raw materials are agreeing to reduce the price of raw materials by 5% if the order for supplies needed to operate at 90% capacity is made. Wage-rate will remain the same but the fixed overhead per unit will decline according to increase in output.

You are required to estimate the profits at different levels and make your recommendations.

MARGINAL COST STATEMENT FOR 1993

Particulars	*40% capacity 12,500 unit*	*60% capacity 18,750 unit*	*90% capacity 28,125 unit*
Sales	28.00	26.60	25.20
Raw materials	12.00	12.00	11.40
Labour	4.50	4.50	4.50
Variable overheads	3.50	3.50	3.50
Marginal Cost	20.00	20.00	19.40
Marginal Contribution	8.00	6.60	5.80
Fixed Cost	2.50	1.67	1.16
Profit per Unit	5.50	4.93	4.69
Total Profit	68,750.00	92,437.50	1,31,906.25

Thus the profit at 40%, 60% and 90% capacity is recommended that the company should operate at 90% capacity as the profits at this level is maximum provided there is no limiting factor.

ADVANTAGES AND MERITS OF MARGINAL COSTING

After having studied the basic principles, features and application of marginal costing technique, we are now in a position to better understand the advantages of the technique. Main advantages are as under:

1. Avoids Allocation of Fixed Overheads

The allocation of fixed overheads over various products/departments has been a problem with the firms following absorption costing method. None of the methods employed for allocation of overheads is scientific and accurate and as such an arbitrary value of overheads is placed on different products due to which cost and price decisions become unrealistic. The difficulty in the allocation of fixed overheads is avoided by following the marginal costing which separates the fixed and variable costs. Fixed cost is recovered from the contribution of all the products / deptts. If pre-determined overhead costs are used, it is most likely that pre-determined cost does not coincide with the actual cost and give rise to the problem of over-recovery or under-recovery of overheads. Marginal costing also avoids the problem of under or over recovery of overheads.

2. Values Inventory Uniformly

The unsold stock and work-in-progress are valued at marginal cost which remains unchanged, atleast in the short period. Valuation of inventory at marginal cost ensures homogeneity of profits as the reported income is not affected by the amount of production and the differences in the opening and closing inventories.

3. Simplifies Decision-Making

Under marginal costing 'Contribution' forms the basic for marginal costing 'Contribution' forms the basis for managerial decision-making. The management can easily fix selling price, determine production priorities and plan for profits by analysing cost data on marginal costing principles.

4. Facilitates Cost Control

It is possible to control cost more effectively when it is classified into fixed and variable components. Generally fixed costs are the result of policy decisions and these can be controlled by the management by appropriate changes in policies. For example, rent would become payable only when the management takes a decision to acquire a leasehold property instead of freehold property. Variable costs are also the result of managerial decision regarding volume of output and technique of production but here are incurred by all levels of management and operators. J. Batty has rightly observed "the responsibility of variable costs can be traced with substantial degree of certainty and this allows the necessary control to be exercised."

5. Recognises Importance of Selling

Production is meaningless without its disposition at remunerative prices. Marginal costing duly Recognises the importance of selling as it prescribe the calculation of profit on the basis of sales without recognising the opening and closing stocks. The reports for consideration of management are prepared on the basis of sales instead of total production.

DISADVANTAGES AND LIMITATIONS

No doubt, marginal costing is a very useful guide in decision-making but it is not a prefect technique. Following are the main disadvantages and limitations of marginal costing technique.

1. Difficult Separation of Fixed and Variable Cost

The marginal costing is based on the assumption that total costs can be split into its fixed and variable cost Components. In practice it is very difficult to identify and separate the fixed costs and variable costs. Some of the costs are semi-variable and the methods employed to separate the fixed element from the semi-variable cost do not give accurate results. They give rough estimates which reduce the utility of marginal costing technique.

2. Short Period Analysis

Marginal costing provides a short-period analysis of the problems. Fixed cost may remain the same in the short-run but it tends to vary in the long-period. It is not proper to assume that the fixed cost remains the same for all levels of production. After a certain stage in production, new capacity has to be created for which additional fixed costs have to be incurred. Similarly selling price and variable costs remain unchanged only in the short period. Therefore, any decision taken on the basis of marginal cost may hold true in the short period only.

3. Danger of Low Pricing

Since marginal costing does not take into account fixed cost in the calculation of cost for price-fixation, it is most likely that prices are fixed inappropriately to the lower side to the economic disadvantage of the enterprise. Once a lower price has been fixed on the basis of marginal cost, it is very different to raise the same. It is argued that a unit of output benefits from both the variable as well as fixed cost, therefore, it is not the marginal cost but the total cost which is relevant for taking price decisions.

4. Unsuitable for Capital-intensive Industries

In a capital-intensive industry, the proportion of fixed assets to total equal invested is quite large. Such industries carry substantial amount as fixed cost and cannot afford to ignore the same in formulating their production, profit and sales policies. thus, marginal costing technique which emphasis too much on marginal cost is not very suitable for capital intensive industries.

5. Difficult Application

Marginal costing technique cannot be applied adequately in all types of enterprises. Those firms which are engaged in job-work or contract find it difficult to apply this technique to the job or contract costing. The technique has also limited applicability in those industries which have to carry large inventories in the firm of work-in-progress.

6. Under-valuation of Inventories

Under marginal costing, the inventories are valued at marginal cost which is lesser than the total cost. In this way, the inventories are under-stated and the Profit and Loss Account, as per this technique, does not show true profits.

7. Undermines Importance of Production

The marginal costing technique assign too much importance to sales and marginal cost in determining the efficiency of different products / departments. Infact the total production including opening and closing inventories alongwith sales during a particular period should be considered in the evaluation of efficiency of products or department.

Though marginal costing suffers from certain limitations as outlived above, yet it is a very useful technique. Its utility as a managerial tool may be enhanced if it is applied completely with due consideration of the limitations with which it suffers.

COST VOLUME PROFIT ANALYSIS

The industries which use marginal costing as a managerial tool are in a position to establish relationship between cost, volume of output and profits. Once a certain relationship is established, it is continued under the given conditions of production and sales. Sales and marginal cost of sales have a fixed relation as they vary in the same proportion. For example, if marginal cost is Rs. 75 for a sale value of Rs. 100, then for a sale of Rs. 120 (20% increase in Sales), the marginal cost will be 90 (75 + 20% of 75). The proportion between 100 and 75 and 120 and 90 is the same. Profit under marginal costing is not the same as under absorption costing. Profit the former case means contribution which is the difference between sales and marginal cost. Contribution has also a fixed relation with sales and marginal cost. Generally, the contribution is correlated with sales. The ratio of contribution of sales is known as P/V ratio (profit-vólume ratio) which is calculated by dividing the amount of contribution by total sales. Other names given to P/V ratio are marginal contribution ratio, marginal income ratios, contribution-sales ratio and variable profit ratio. Following table shows the relationship between costs, volume of sales and profit.

Particulars	*January*	*February*	*% Change*
Sales	100	120	20
Marginal cost	75	90	20
Contribution	25	30	20
P/V Ratio	25/100 or .25	30/120 or .25	
Percentage P/V ratio	25%	25%	

With the help of the cost-volume-profit relations, the management can understand many production and marketing problems quickly and take decision without difficulty Cost value profit relationship can be expressed in the form of an equation as under:

S-M = C

where S represents Sales

M stands for marginal or variable Cost

C stands for contribution

It may be noted that the contribution is the profit before the recovery of fixed costs. Therefore it consists of profit and fixed cost i.e., C = P + F. The equation expressing relationship between cost, volume and profit may also be written as,

$$S - V = P + F$$

Break - Even Analysis

Cost volume-profit relations may be used to determine the level of output at which a firms will break even i.e. it will neither make profits or suffer loss Break-Even analysis is intimately connected with marginal costing technique. J. Batty considers Break-even analysis as an extension or even a part of marginal costing. Generally, the new firms are interested to know the minimum output / sales which will enable then to just recover the total cost of that output filly. Any output in excess of the minimum or break-even output contributes towards profits of the firms. Break-even analysis is not only deals with the minimum output at which total costs and total revenues are equal but it also facilitate the management in taking decisions on issue such as,

(a) How much to produce to realize given profit?

(b) What will be the profit if a certain level of production is attained?

(c) What will happen to costs, profits if and Break-even output it variable cost changes?

(d) How changes is selling price affect Break-even output and profit?

(e) What should be the price of achieve a desired beak-even output?

Break-Even Analysis

There are two methods of Break-even analysis viz (1) Graphic Method and (2) Algebric Method.

Graphic Method

According to this method, the data of costs and revenues at different levels of output or sales are plotted on a graph paper. This gives Break-Even chart showing a definite level of output/sales at which total costs and total revenues are equal. The graphic representation gives a bird's eye-view of the cost-volume-profit relations.

Construction of Break-even Chart

The construction of Break-even chart is not difficult. Information needed to draw a Break-even chart are,

(i) Variable Cost

(ii) Fixed Cost

(iii) Selling price

Variable Cost: This is the cost which varies directly with production/ sales. Total variable cost for any volume of output can be found out by multiplying the output and variable cost per unit.

Fixed Cost: This is that portion of total costs which is not affected by the variations in the level of activity. It means fixed costs remain the same at all levels of production. The portion of fixed cost has to be separated from total cost carefully for accurate analysis of the problems.

Selling Price: Per unit selling price is determined by market forces of demand and supply and the total selling price at different scales can be calculated at multiplying the scale of production and selling price per unit.

After having ascertained the variables of fixed costs, and total cost for various levels of output, the Break-even chart can be drawn by having the following steps.

1. Fix the scale of production and cost/revenue which shall be shown on X-axis and Y-axis respectively.
2. Locate the point of fixed cost on Y-axis and draw a line through this point parallel to X-axis. This the fixed cost curve (FCC).
3. Draw total revenue curve by locating and joining the points of revenues for different levels of production. The revenue curve starts from point of origin because the revenue at zero output is zero.
4. Draw total cost curve (TCC) by locating and joining the points of total costs for different levels of production. Total cost curve starts from the point of fixed cost because total cost at zero output is equal to fixed cost.

From the chart it will be seen that the total costs curve (TCC) and total revenue curve (TRC) intersect each other at some point. This the Break-

Even point corresponding to which break-even output at OX-axix can be determined. The method of drawing Break-even chart is explained with the help of the following example.

Illustration

A company furnishes you the following data:

Sales Price per unit Rs. 25

Variable cost per unit Rs. 15

Fixed cost Rs. 3,000

Taking imaginary figures for varying sales output volumes, draw Break-even chart to show break-even sales.

COST-VOLUME-PROFIT STATEMENT

Output/ sales	*Fixed cost*	*Variable cost*	*Total cost*	*Sales Revenue*	*Profit/ Lose*
0	3000	—	3000	—	–3000
100	3000	1500	4500	2500	–2000
200	3000	3000	6000	5000	–1000
300	3000	4500	7500	7500	—
400	3000	6000	9000	10000	+ 1000
500	3000	7500	10500	12500	+ 2000
600	3000	9000	12000	15000	+ 3000
700	3000	10500	13500	17500	+ 4000

In the above chart output (units) is shown on OX-axis and cost/ revenue on OY-axis. FCC is the fixed cost curve which is parallel to OX-axis because fixed cost remains the same for all scales of output. TCC and TRC are the total cost curve and total revenue curve respectively. These curves intersects each other at point E which the Break-even point at which total costs and total revenues are equal. Corresponding to E on OX-axis is the Break-even output which is 300 units.

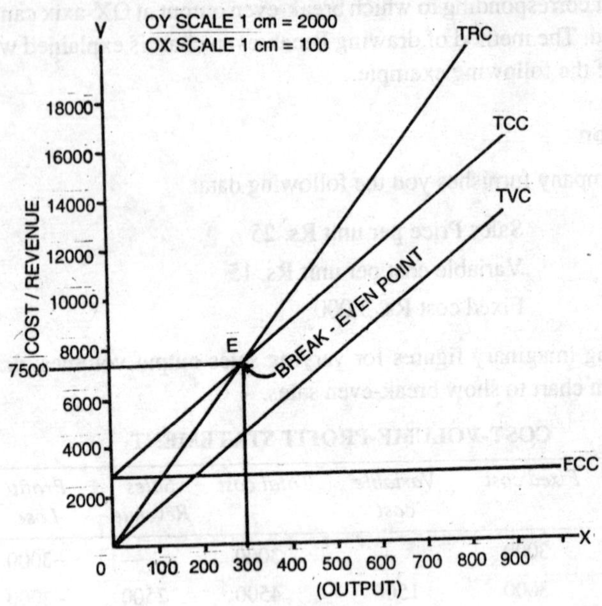

BREAK-EVEN AND X DECISION-MAKING

As pointed out above, Break-even chart can be used to find answer to the following problems:

(A) How much to Produce to Realize a given Profit?

Management may budget profit for certain period. To realize the budgeted profit, some amount of goods has to be produced and sold. This amount of sales can be ascertained from the Break-even chart. Suppose the management desired a profit of Rs. 4000 and wants to know the output necessary for this profit. To know the output, calculate the total cost including fixed costs and total revenue and draw the TCC and TRC in the usual manner and then determine the distance in the profit area which is equal to 4000. In the following diagram this distance is represented by M N which is extended to touch OX-axis in such a manner that it forms right angle at the base line. The extended line touches OX-axis at 700 which is the desired output for a profit of Rs. 4000.

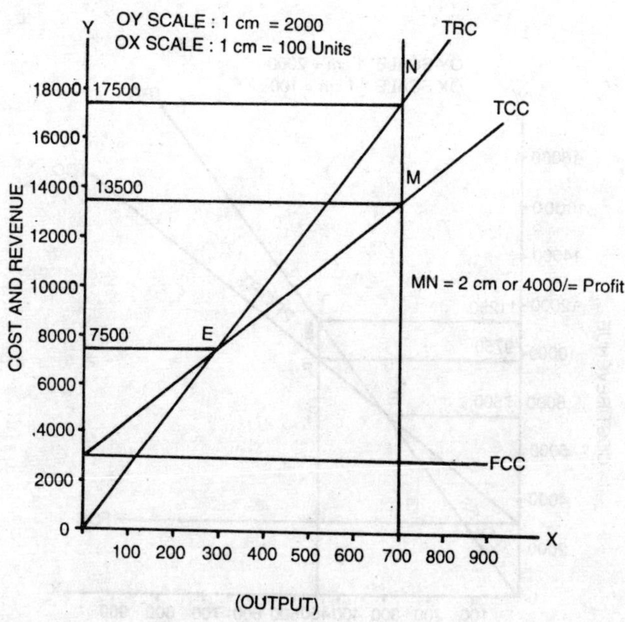

(B) What will be the Profit if Certain Level of Output is Attained

Suppose the management decides to produce 450 units and wants to know expected profits based on costs and revenue as shown in the previous illustration. It can be known by using the chart in the following manner:

(i) Determine the point of output on Ox-axis and draw from this point a line parallel to OY-axis which touches TCC and TRC at some points. In our chart below the line touches the costs and revenue curves at P and T points respectively.

(ii) The vertical distance between P and T is the extent of profits to be generated by the out put of 450 units.

(iii) To know total cost and total revenue for 450 units draw lines parallel to OX-axis from points P and T so that they touch OY-axis to represent total revenue and total cost. Total Revenue and Total costs are Rs. 11,250 and Rs. 9,750 respectively. The difference between the two is Rs. 1,500 which is the expected profit from 450 units of output.

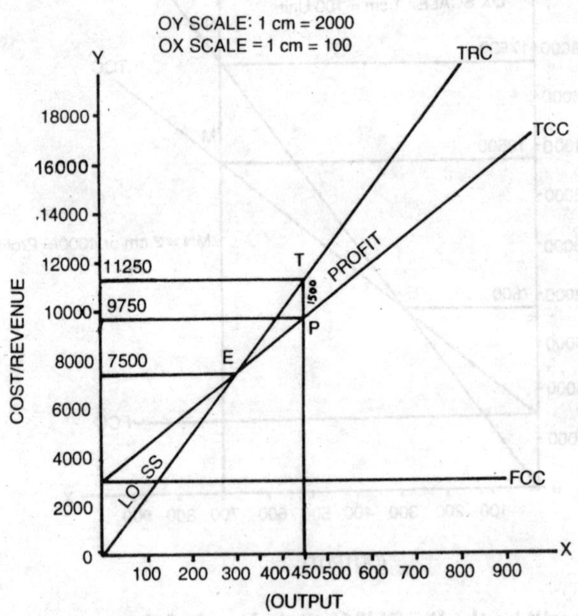

(C) What will Happen to BEP if Variable Cost Per Unit has Changed

Break-Even analysis makes a necessary assumption that variable cost per unit remains the same but the cost of labour and material may change due to changes in market forces and as such variable cost per unit may increase or decrease. The change in variable cost per unit causes the Break-even point to shift according to changes in variable cost. An increase in variable cost causes the Break-even point to shift to the right which means more output or sales is needed to Break-even. The decrease in variable cost pushes Break-even point to the left which means lesser number of units for breaking even. Following illustration shows the position of Break-even as a result of changes in variable cost.

Illustration

From the following cost and sales data prepare a Break-even chart showing the shift of BEP as a result of changes in variable cost.

	Period I	*Period II*
Sales per unit	25	25
Variable cost	15	18
Fixed cost	3,000/-	3,000/-

Production level = 600 units

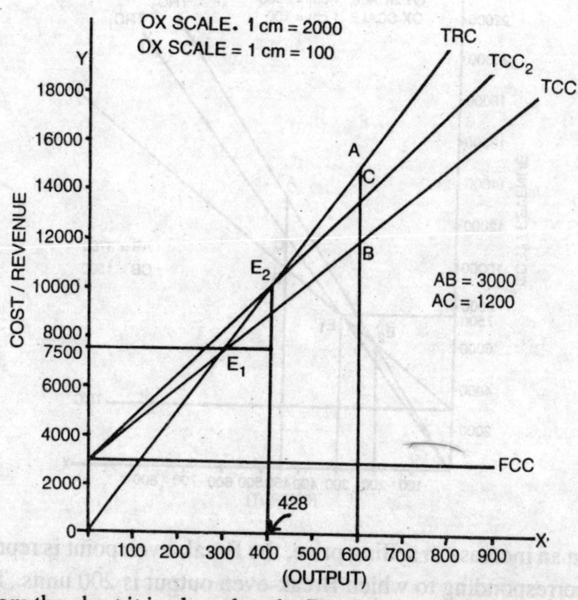

From the chart it is clear that the Break-even point has shifted from E_1 to E_2 on an increase in variable cost from Rs. 15 to Rs. 18 per unit. The New Break-even output is 428 units. It means the firm will have to produce and sell extra 128 units in order to Break-even under the new situation. The profit of the firm will be decreased by Rs. 3,000 CB i.e. AB - AC or the new profit will be AC instead of AB.

(D) How Changes in Selling Price Affect Break-even Output and Profit

A firm may revise its selling policy and fix new price which may be more or lesser than the price being charged presently. If the selling price is raised without any change in the variable and fixed cost, the firm will break even earlier and the Break-even point will shift to the left. The present scale of operation will yield more profit under the new condition.

Illustration

Suppose the firm increases selling price from Rs. 25 to Rs. 30. There is no change in other informations as shown in illustration No. 1. The Break-even chart will assume the following shape.

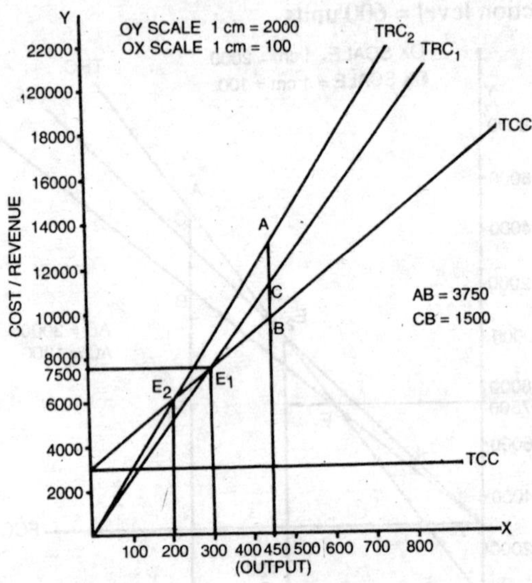

On an increase in selling price, the Break-even point is represented by E_2 corresponding to which Break-even output is 200 units. Thus the increase in selling price without any change in other costs has enabled the firm to break-even at 200 units. If the firm continues to produce 450 units, it is able to even a profit of Rs. 3750 against Rs. 1500 who the selling price of Rs. 25 per unit.

(E) What should be the Price to Achieve a Desired Break-even Output

The management rarely decides the output at which they wish to Break-even. If they have wished so, the selling price per unit which must be fixed to Break-even at the desired level of output, may be determined with the help of the Break-even chart. To determine the price for a desired Break-even output, the steps required tax are, (i) Draw the fixed cost curve and the total cost curve in the usual manner (ii) fix the desired break-even output at OX-axis and draw from this a line parallel to OY-axis so that it touches the total cost curve at some point, (iii) from this point on TCC, draw a line parallel to OX-axis allowing the line to touch OY-axis and read the figure at the point at which the line touches OY-axis. (iv) the figure so read should be divided by the total break-even output desired. It will give the price per unit. This is shown in the following Break-even chart which has been drawn on the basis of the informations as,

Selling price per unit = ?

Variable cost per unit Rs. 15

Fixed cost = 3000

Desired Break-even output = 250 units.

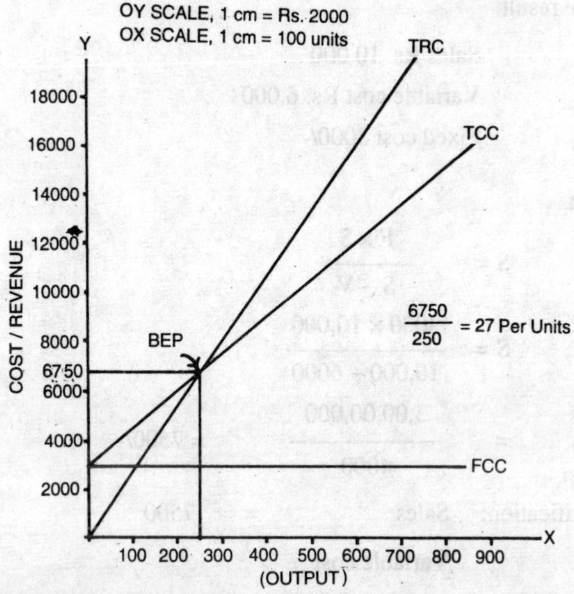

Algebric Method

In order to understand the Cost-Volume-Profit relationship precisely and verify the results drawn from Break-even chart the algebric method may be used. The algebraic equation showing relationship between cost, volume and profit is, S-V = F+P. At Break-even point, there is no profit and the contribution is just equal to fixed cost. Thus S-V = F (at break-even point). We can derive a fundamental equation to find out break-even volume of sales if both sides of the above equation are multiplied by S as shown below.

$$S (S-V) = F \times S$$

$$\text{Or } S = \frac{F \times S}{S-V}$$

where F = Fixed cost
S = Sales volume
V = variable cost

Illustration

Find out Break-even sales from the following informations and verify the result.

Sales Rs. 10,000
Variable cost Rs. 6,000
Fixed cost 3000/-

Solution

$$S = \frac{F \times S}{S - V}$$

$$S = \frac{3000 \times 10,000}{10,000 - 6000}$$

$$= \frac{3,00,00,000}{4000} = 7500/-$$

Verification:	Sales	=	7500
	Variable cost		
	$\frac{6000 \times 7500}{10,0000}$	=	4500
	Contribution		3000
	Fixed Cost		3000
	Profit		0

Other Formulae

According to the information available any one of the following formulae can be used for determining Break-even point.

(i) $$\text{BEP} = \frac{\text{Fixed cost}}{1 - \dfrac{\text{Variable cost}}{\text{Sales}}}$$

(ii) $$\text{BEP} = \frac{\text{Fixed cost}}{\text{Contribution}} \times \text{Sales}$$

(iii) $$\text{BEP} = \frac{\text{Fixed cost}}{\text{Marginal contribution Rate or P/V Ratio}}$$

(iv) $$\text{BEP (units)} = \frac{\text{Fixed cost}}{\text{Sales price percent} - \text{Variable cost percent}}$$

Illustration

Calculate Break-even Units of Sales from the following data.

Sales, Rs. 25 per unit
Variable cost, Rs. 15 per unit
Fixed cost, Rs. 3000

Solution: $$\text{BEP (unit)} \quad \frac{\text{Fixed cost}}{\text{Selling price-variable cost}}$$

$$= \frac{3000}{25\text{-}15} = \frac{3000}{10} = 300 \text{ units.}$$

Proof, S - V = P + F
or S – V = 0 + F (at Break-even-point)
(300 x 25) - (300 x 15) = 0 + 3000
7500 - 4500 = 3000
or 3000 = 3000 Proved

Illustration

Following information has been extracted from the office record of a manufacturing company.

Actual sales, 1500 units @ Rs. 15 per unit

Particulars	*Fixed cost*	*Variable cost*	*Total cost*
Material	—	48,000	48,000
Labour	—	58,000	58,000
Factory overheads	25000	16,000	41000
Administration overheads	8000	6000	14000
Selling and distribution overheads	7000	22000	29000
Total	40000	150000	190000

From the above information, calculate,

(a) Break-even point (BEP)
(b) Profit-volume Ratio (P/V ratio)
(c) Margin of safety

Solution

(a) $$\text{BEP} = \frac{\text{Fixed cost}}{1 - \dfrac{\text{Variable cost}}{\text{Sales}}}$$

$$= \frac{40{,}000}{1 - \dfrac{1{,}50{,}000}{225000}} \qquad \frac{40{,}000}{1 - \dfrac{2}{3}}$$

or Rs. 1,20,000

The Break-even sale of Rs. 1,20,000 is 53/1/3% of actual sales.

(b) Profit-Volume Ratio (P/V Ratio)

$$= \frac{\text{Contribution}}{\text{Sales}} \times 100$$

$$\text{or} \quad \frac{\text{Sales-variable cost}}{\text{Sales}} \times 100$$

$$= \frac{225000 - 150000}{225000} \times 100$$

$$= \frac{75000}{225000} \times 100 = 33\text{-}1/2\%$$

(c) Margin of Safety (MS)

$$= \frac{\text{Sales in Excess of BEP Sales}}{\text{Actual Sales}} \times 100$$

$$= \frac{\text{Actual Sales} - \text{BEP Sales}}{\text{Actual Sales}} \times 100$$

$$= \frac{2{,}25{,}000 - 12{,}0000}{2{,}25{,}000} \times 100$$

$$= \frac{1{,}05{,}000}{2{,}25{,}000} \times 100 = 46\text{-}2/3\%$$

The BEP can also be calculated by using the following formula:

$$\text{BEP} = \frac{\text{Fixed cost}}{\text{P/V Ratio}} = \frac{40{,}000}{33\text{-}1/3\%} = 1{,}20{,}000$$

We have seen how break-even charts are used to understand the problems and take decision. Here we shall deal with similar problems with the help of algebric method of Break-even analysis.

(A) How much to Produce to Realize a Given Profit

Information:	Sales price	Rs. 25 per unit
	Variable cost	Rs. 15 per unit
	Fixed cost	Rs. 3000/-
	Desired profit	Rs. 4000

$$\text{Production for a profit of 4000} = \frac{\text{Fixed Cost + Desired Profit}}{\text{Sales price – Variable cost-per unit}}$$

$$= \frac{3000 + 4000}{25\text{-}15} = \frac{7000}{10} = 70 \text{ units}$$

(B) What will be Profit if Certain Level of Output is Attained

Information: Sales price - Rs. 25 per unit
variable cost = Rs. 15 per unit
Fixed cost = Rs. 3000
Budgeted production = 450 units profit?

S - V = P + F

(450 x 25) - (450 x 15) = P + 3000

11250 - 6750 = P + 3000

P = 11, 250 - 6750 - 3000

P = 11250 - 9750

P = 1500

(C) What will happen to BEP if Variable Cost per unit has Changed

Information

Production	450 units
Sale price	Rs. 25 per unit
Variable cost	Rs. 15 per unit
Fixed cost	Rs. 3000.

Calculate Break-even sales if variable cost per unit-has gone up to Rs. 17 per unit. Also calculate the amount by which the profit will be decreased due to increase in variable cost.

$$\text{BEP (Rs.)} = \frac{\text{Fixed Cost}}{\text{SP} - \text{VC}}$$

$$= \frac{3000}{25\text{-}15} = 300 \text{ units}$$

or 300 x 25 - 7500/-

$$\text{New BEP (Rs.)} = \frac{3000}{25-17} = 375 \text{ Units}$$

or 375 × 25 = 9375/-

Profit if V C is Rs. 15 per unit —

$(450 \times 25) - (450 \times 15) = 3000 + P$

or $P = 11250 - 6750 - 3000$

or $P = 1500$

Profit if VC is Rs. 17 per Unit —

$(460 \times 25)\ (450 \times 17) = 3000 + P$

or $P = 11250 - 7650 - 3000$

or $P - 600$

Decrease in Profit = 1500-600 - 900 (Same as shown by graphic representation)

(D) How Changes in Selling Price Affect Break-Even Output and Profit

Information

Selling Price (original), Rs. 25 per unit

Selling price (Revised), Rs. 30 per unit

Variable cost per unit, Rs. 15

Fixed Cost, Rs. 3000

Output 450 units

Break-even output and value with original selling price = 300 units or Rs. 7500 (as calculated previously)

BEP with selling price of Rs. 30 per unit

$$= \frac{3000}{30 - 15} = 200 \text{ units or Rs. } 5000$$

Profit when selling price is Rs. 25 per unit

$(450 \times 25) - (450 \times 15) = 3000 + P = \text{Rs. } 1500$

Profit when selling price is Rs. 30 per unit

$(450 \text{ x } 30) - (450 \times 15) = 3000 + P = 3750$

Increase is Profit = 3750 – 1500 = 2250

(E) What should be the Price at Desired Break-Even Output

Information,

Variable cost per unit, Rs. 15 per unit

Fixed Cost, Rs. 3000

Desired Break-Even Output - 250 units

Selling Price + ?

Cost of 250 units = (250 x 15) + 3000

= 6750

At Break-even point Cost and revenues are equal. Since the firm desires to Break-even at 250 units, a production and sales value of Rs. 6750 must be obtained by 250 units. The price to be charged per unit should, therefore be 6750-250 = Rs. 27.

Illustration

In trading result of a company for the last years are given below

Year	*Sales*	*Profit*
1994	1,50,000	18,000
1995	2,00,000	30,000

You are required to calculate

(i) P/V ratio
(ii) Fixed Cost
(iii) Profit for sale value of Rs. 1,00,000
(iv) Profit for Sale value of Rs. 3,00,000
(v) Break-even sales
(iv) Variable cost during the two years.

Solution

Substituting of S and P, we get the eq' ,

1995 $\quad$ 2,00,000 — V_2 = F + 30,000 — I

1994 $\quad$ 1,50,000 — V_1 = F + 18,000 — II

50,000 — V = 12,000(Pay substracting II from the I, v = V_2 = V_1)

$-V = 12000 - 50000$

$V = 38000$ or 76% of sales

$$\text{P/V ratio} = \frac{S - V}{S} \times 100$$

$$= \frac{50000 - 38000}{50000} \times 100 - 24\%$$

Again, S - V = F + P

on multiplying S - V by S and dividing by S, we get,

$$\frac{S(S - V)}{S} = F + P$$

We know $\frac{S - V}{S}$ = P/V ratio

S x P/V ratio = F + P

Substituting the value in equation I,

$$200000 \times 24\% = F + 30000$$

$$200000 \times \frac{24}{100} = F + 30000$$

$$48000 = F + 30000$$

$$F = 18000$$

(iii) Profit for sale value of 1,00,000

$S \times$ P/V ratio = F + P

$1,00,000 \times 24\% - 18000 + P$

$P = 6000$

(iv) Profit for sales value of 300000

$S \times$ P/V ratio = F + P

$300000 \times$ P/V ratio = 18000 + P

$300000 \times 24\% = 18000 + P$

$P = 54000$

(v) Sale for a project of Rs. 40000

S x P/V ratio = F + P

S x 24% = 18000 + 40000

$$S \times \frac{24}{100} = 58000$$

$$S = 58000 \times \frac{100}{24} = 241666.66$$

(vi) Break-even Sales - S x P/V ratio = F (because P is zero at Break=-even point)

$$S \times \frac{24}{100} = 18000$$

$$S = \frac{18000 \times 100}{24} = 75000/-$$

(vii) Variable Cost in 1994

150000 – V = 18000 + 18000

V = 1,1,400

Variable cost 1995

200000 – V = 18000 + 30000

V = 15200

Illustration

A company desirės to even a after-tax profit of Rs. 27500 is 1997. The existing Tax rate of 50 % in before=tax income is likely to prevail. Fixed costs in the Company amount to Rs. 5,00,000 the P/V ratio is estimated at 25%.

You are required to compute.

(i) The sales required to earn in after-tax income of Rs. 2,75,000

(ii) Sales required to earn a after-tax income of Rs. 2,75,000 if P/V ratio could be increased to 30%.

Solution

$$\text{Sales to even after Tax income} = \frac{\text{Fixed cost} + \dfrac{\text{After-tax Profit}}{1 - \text{Tax Rate}}}{\text{P/V ratio}}$$

(i) Sales required for a profit of Rs. 2,75,000 if P/V ratio is 25%

$$= \frac{500000 + \dfrac{275000}{1 - 0.50}}{25\%}$$

$$\text{cr} \quad \frac{500000 + 550000}{\dfrac{25}{100}}$$

$$= \quad 42,00,000.$$

(ii) Sales for a profit of Rs. 275000 if P/V ratio is increased to 30%

$$= \frac{500000 + \dfrac{275000}{1 - 0.50}}{30\%}$$

$$= 35,00,000$$

Verification,

	P/V ratio 26%	*P/V ratio 30%*
Sales	42,00,000	35,00,000
Variable Cost (75% of Sales)	31,50,000	24,50,000
Contribution	10,50,000	10,50,000
Fixed Cost	5,00,000	5,00,000
Profit before Tax	5,50,000	5,50,000
Less Tax 50%	2,75,000	2,75,000
After-tax income	2,75,000	2,75,000

Illustration

A manufacturing firm furnishes you the following informations for the production period ended an 31st December 1995.

Fixed overheads	Rs. 3000
Variable Overheads	1400
Direct Materials	5600
Direct labour	3500
Sales	(700 units) 17500

You are required to determine break-even point graphically and shad the curves for each component of Cost

Solution

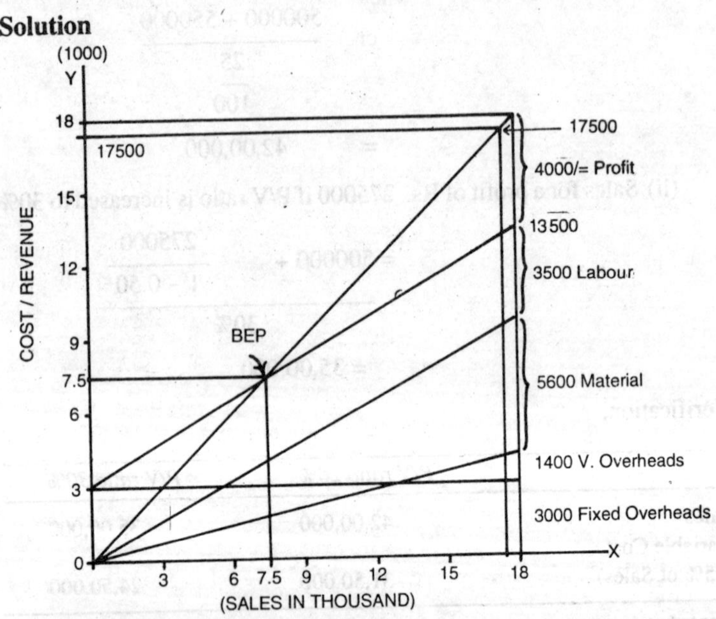

Assumption of Fixed P/V Ratio

Break-even analysis that P/V ratio for all volumes of production and sales remains the same. It means the profit (before recovery of fixed cost) and volumes of production and sales change in the same proportion and the variable cost has a fixed relation which the sales. Under the assumption of constant P/V ratio the total cost curve and total revenue curves in a

Break-even chart assume straight position. In actual practice, the P/V ratio may not remain constant for all levels of output. The variable cost may not change exactly in the same proportion as the change in the volume of production and sales. Sales price depends upon the nature of competition being faced by the manufacturing firm. In general, additional sales after certain volume can be affected only by reducing selling price. Similarly, the price of raw materials and labour undergo change due to changes in the factor market. Break-even analysis separates fixed cost from the total cost and assumes that the former remains fixed irrespective of the volume of production. This assumption may hold good only within small range of production but fixed costs are bound to increase after a certain production capacity. Thus the assumption of constant selling price, variable cost and fixed cost may not hold good in actual practice, particularly in the long-run when all variables change and adapt to the current conditions.

Illustration

A company engaged in the production of an automobile part of a specified standard. At present, it is operating at 70% of its installed capacity and producing 700 units annually. The selling price and variable cost per unit is Rs. Rs. 25 and Rs. 10 10 respectively and the fixed costs amount to Rs. 9,000.

The unused capacity of 30% can be used by the company without incurring any further fixed costs but to produce any amount beyond, 1,000 units it will have to incur additional fixed costs. By incurring additional Rs. 4000 on fixed assets, the company is in a position to raise the output to 3000 units. The market studies have revealed that additional output can be sold only by lowering prices. The demand schedule is as under.

Price (Rs.)	*Demand (units)*
25	300
25	600
25	900
23	1200
22	1500
21	1800

20	2100
18	2400
17	2700
16	3000

Solution

STATEMENT OF COST-VOLUME-PROFIT ANALYSIS

Sales (units)	*Selling Price*	*Sales Value*	*Variable cost*	*Fixed cost*	*Total cost*	*Profit/ Loss*
0	25	0	9000	9000	– 9000	9000
360	25	7500	3000	9000	12000	– 4500
600	25	15000	6000	9000	15000	0
900	25	22500	9000	9000	18000	+ 4500
1200	23	27600	12000	13000	25000	2600
1500	22	33000	15000	13000	28000	5000
1800	21	37800	18000	13000	31000	6800
2100	20	42000	21000	13000	34000	8000
2400	18	43200	24000	13000	37000	6200
2700	17	45900	27000	13000	40000	5900
3000	16	48000	30000	13000	43000	5000

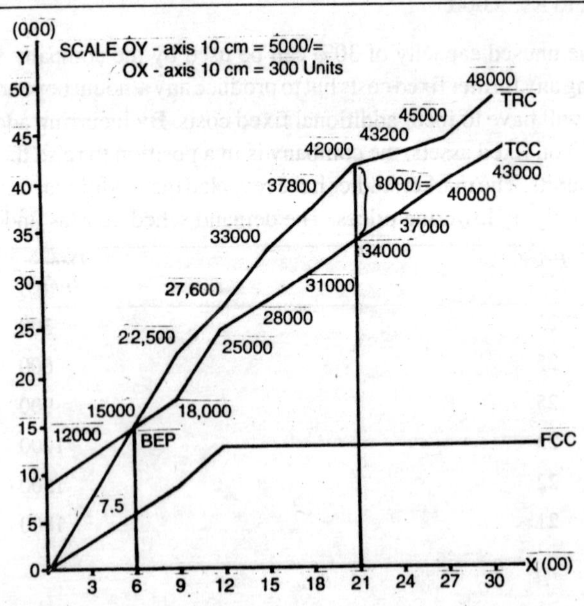

The chart clearly shows that the company breaks even at a production of 600 units and the production and sales of 2100 units is most beneficial as it generates a net profit of Rs. 8000.

Profit-Volume Chart

Profit-Volume Chart may be used if the management desires to know at a glance the profit or loss at different levels of output. The profit-volume charts simply known as profit graphs represent profits at various sales volumes without making use of total cost and total revenue curves. The use of profit graph is necessary if more than one commodity is produced and the profit position of each product has to be shown on a simple graph which is not possible in case of a single break-even chart. Such graphs can be used to forecast profits for budgeted sales or vice versa.

For the preparation of a Profit graph the scale on both the sides of OX-Axis is determined. Sales are shown on OX-Axis. The profit is represented above and the loss and fixed cost below OX-axis. On joining the fixed cost point and the point of profit of the commodity, we get a line which intersect OX-axis at some point which is the Break-even point for the commodity.

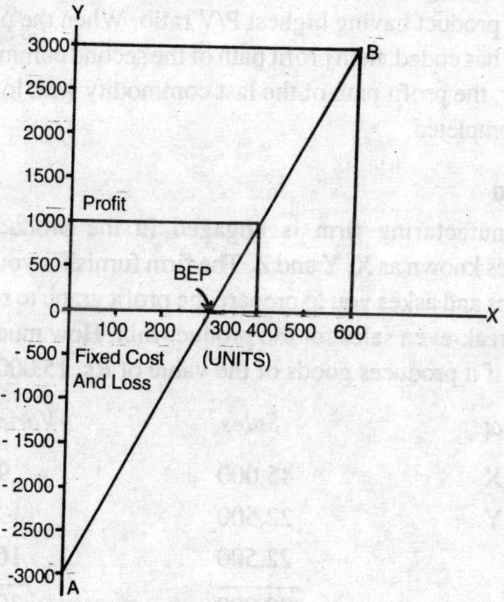

From the following information, draw out a profit chart and find the profit for a production of 400 units.

Sales price	Rs. 25
Variable cost	Rs. 15
Fixed cost	Rs. 3000/-
Output	600 unit

In the above graph the profit for 600 units is Rs. 3000 which is equal to XB. Point A and B have been joined to form the line showing profit or loss at different levels of sales. The line AB passes through the point of 300 units of output which is the Break-even output. The profit for 400 units is Rs. 1000 as shown in the profit graph. Any output below 300 units shows loss.

A Case of Product-Mix

In case two or more commodities are produced, profit graph shows individual profitability of different products as well as over-all or combined break-even point. The graph is drawn in the order of descending P/V ratio i.e. product having highest P/V ratio is own first and the product with lowest P/V ratio is allowed to represent at last. The profit line in such a graph is not a straight line. It starts from the point of fixed cost below OX-axis for the product having highest P/V ratio. When the path of the first commodity has ended, then profit path of the second commodity starts. In this manner, the profit path of the last commodity with lowest P/V ratio is finally completed.

Illustration

A manufacturing firm is engaged in the production of three commodities known as X, Y and Z. The firm furnishes you the following informations and askes you to prepare the profit graph to represent profit path and Break-even sales for the product-mix. How much loss will the firm suffer if it produces goods of the value of Rs. 15,000.

Product	*Sales*	*Variable Cost*
X	45,000	9,000
Y	22,500	13,500
	22,500	16,875
	90,000	39,375

Fixed cost	27,000
Profit	23,625

Solution

MARGINAL COST STATEMENT

Product	*Sales*	*Cumulative*	*Marginal cost*	*Contribution*	*P/V Ratio*	*Fixed Cost*	*Profit*	*Cumulative*
X	45,000	45,000	9,000	36,000	80%	27,000	9,000	9,000
Y	22,500	67,500	13,500	9,000	40%	—	9,000	18,000
Z	22,500	90,000	16,875	5,625	25%	—	5,625	23,625

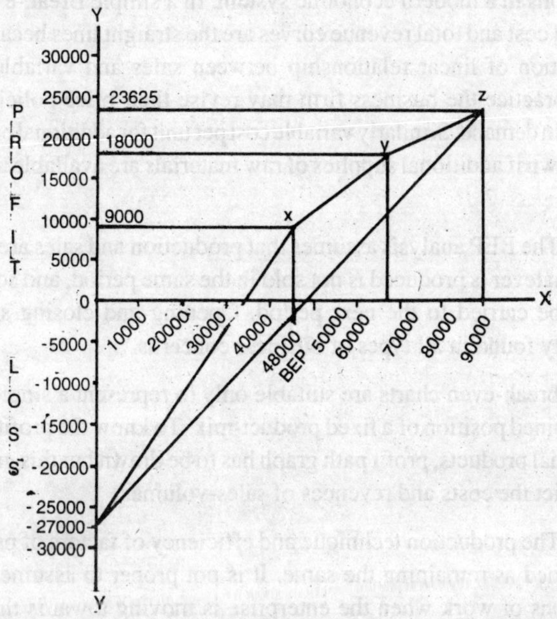

Limitation of Break-even Analysis

From the above explanation of the uses and application of Break-even and profit charts it would appear that they are important managerial tools but they should be interpreted carefully as they suffer from certain limitations as explained below.

1. Break-even and profit charts give only a x bird's eye-view of the cost-volume and profit position. The determination of exact profit or loss for a given output and vice versa requires a lot of care on the part of one

who draws chart. A little deviation may give different result.

2. The analysis is based on the assumption that the total costs can be split into fixed and variable components and fixed costs remain the same for all levels of output. In practice the separation of costs into fixed and variable components is full of difficulties and the component of fixed cost remains the same only upto a certain level of output. Fixed cost is bound to go up if additional capacity of production has to be created.

3. The assumption of linear relationship between sales and variable cost is also not realistic under the varying technological and economic conditions in a modern economic system. In a simple Break-even chart, the total cost and total revenue curves are the straight lines because of the assumption of linear relationship between sales and variable cost. In actual practice the business firm may revise their price policies due to change in demand. Similarly variable cost per unit for additional production goes down if additional supplies of raw materials are available at reduced rates.

4. The BEP analysis assumes that production and sales are equal. In fact, whatever is produced is not sold in the same period, and some stock has to be carried to the next period. Opening and closing stocks are generally found in all types of business concerns.

5. break-even charts are suitable only to represent a single product or combined position of a fixed product-mix. To know the profitability of individual products, profit path graph has to be drawn but this graph does not pepict the costs and revenues of sales-volumes.

6. The production technique and efficiency of factors of production is assumed as remaining the same. It is not proper to assume constant conditions of work when the enterprise is moving towards the path of expansion and development.

Above limitations of Break-even analysis limit the use of the technique in decision-making, specially in the long run when the assumption underlying the analysis do not hold good. However, the economic environment within and outside a firm remains more or less the same in the short-period and the Break-even technique provides an objective basis for decision-making in the short-run.

QUESTIONS

1. Distinguish between Marginal Costing and Total Costing techniques of cost analysis. How are the profit statements under the two techniques are presented?
2. Discuss the methods of separation of Fixed Cost element from semi-variable cost.
3. Write a detailed note on "Marginal Costing and Decision-making."
4. Explain the merits and limitations of Marginal costing as a technique of decision-making.
5. What do you mean by Break-even Analysis? Prepare a Break-even chart using imaginary figures.
6. How is the technique of Break-even analysis used in profit planning? Explain clearly.
7. Write short rules on —

   A. Break-even chart.

   B. Profit-volume chart.
8. "Cost-Volume-Profit analysis is based on unrealistic assumptions due to which it is loosing its utility." Do you agree with its statement? If not, given reasons.
9. Prepare a Break-even chart from the following basic informations:

Sales per Unit	Rs. 15
Variable Cost	Rs. 10
Fixed Cost =	1200

10. From the following information, calculate the Break-even in terms of physical quality at money value.

Selling Price per unit	Rs. 15
Direct Material per unit	Rs. 8
Direct Labour per unit	Rs. 2
Fixed over hands =	1200

    Determine net profit if Sales are 10% and 20% above the Break-even Sales.
11. A company is operating at its 50% installed capacity and produces 2500 units annually. It self the products at the rate of Rs. 8 per unit. The cost of production is as under:

	Cost per cent (Rs.)	Total Cost (Rs.)
Materials	1.00	25,000
Wages	2.00	50,000
Variable overheads	1.00	25.000
Fixed over-heads	0.40	10,000
		1,10,000

The company has received an order for additional supplies of 15,000 units at a selling price of Rs. 13.75 per unit. The increased volume of purchases reduces the material price to Rs. 0.975 per unit. Wage-rate will remain the same but the employment of new workers earns labour efficiency to decline by 5% on all production.

Should the Company accept the order for supply of additional 15,000 units.?

12. A company furnishes the following information :

Sales		1,75,000
Cost of goods sold:		
Variable	70,000	
Fixed	17,500	87,500
Gross Profit		87,500
Selling costs:		
Variable	15,000	
Fixed	8,000	23,000
Net Profit		54,500

You are required to .....

(a) Compute the Break-even point.

(b) Forecast the profits for a Sale volume of Rs. 25,000 and Rs. 3,25,000.

(c) Calculate Sales volume for a net profit of Rs. 1,00,000.

13. The following figures relate to a company manufacturing a variety of products:

	Total Sales (Rs)	Total Cost (Rs.)
Year ended on 31.12.1980	22,23,000	19,83,600
Year ended on 31.12.1981	24,51,000	21,43,200

Assuming stability in prices, with variable costs carefully controlled to reflect pre-determined relationship and an unvarying figure for fixed costs, calculate,

(a) The profit/volume ratio to reflect the figures of growth of profit and sales, (b) Fixed cost per-centage, (a) to sales, (b) Fixed cost, (c) Break-even profit, (d) Margin of safety for the year 1980 and year 1981.

(C.A. Intre Nov. '82)

14. A company is engaged in the production and Sales of 'X' article of which the cost and price date are given below:

Selling price per unit	Rs. 150
Direct Material per unit	90
Direct Labour per unit	15
Variable overheads per unit	10

The company sold 6500 units in the year that ended an 31st March, 1995. It forsee an increase of 5% in the cost of raw materials for the year 1995-96.

You are required to calculate the additional number of units which has to be produced to maintain the same level of profit, or to calculate the rise in selling price to maintain the same P/V ratio.

15. (i) What is Margin of Safety?

(ii) The Profit volume Ratio (P/V ratio) of Solid India Ltd. is 40% and the margin of safety is 30% you are required to without the Break-even point, if the sales volume is Rs. 25,00,000.

16. (A) What should be the considerations in taking a Make or Buy decision?

(B) A proposaly to buy an article which is presently being manufactured at the following costs:

Raw Material per unit	Rs. 75
Wage-cost per unit	25
Variable overheads per unit	20
Fixed overheads per unit	15
Total	Rs. 135

The article can be purchased from the open market with an assured supply for Rs. 110. Should this company buy it? The labour efficiency is likely to decrease by 5% if the production of the article under consideration is abandoned.

17. Jay and Co. manufacturers and sells a single product 'Textile.' It has furnished the following data:

Material	Rs. 20 per unit
Wages and other	
Direct Cost	Rs. 15 per unit
Dealer's Margin	Rs. 5 per unit
Selling prince	Rs. 50 per unit

Fixed Costs: Rs. 3,50,000

Capacity utilisation 50%

The company is contemplating to increase sale of 'Tex it' by following are of the following strategies:

(a) by reducing selling price by 5%

(b) by increasing dealer's margin by 25% over the present rate.

Which one of the strategies would you recommend if the present level of profit is to be maintained.

18. The operating profits of X Ltd. for the half year ending on 31st March 1995. is computed as under:

Sales		2,75,000
Less cost of sales		1,65,000
G rose Profit		1,10,000
Less: Selling cost	25,000	
Administration Cost	10,000	
		35,000
Net Profit		75,000

The cost has been analysed into its fixed and variable components as under:

8

Inventory Valuation

Inventories in case of a manufacturing organisation may consist of raw materials, semi-manufactured goods and finished goods which are held for further processing and sales in the next production and sales budget period. The valuation of inventories possess a problem to the management as it can be valued in a number of ways. Different methods of inventory valuation give different values and this is the area where management may give colour to accounting information by following a method of inventory valuation which serve their purpose. The enterprise which is interested in the computation of true income and depicting correct financial position of its business affairs should rightly value the inventories and follow a consistent inventory valuation policy. Proper inventory valuation is absolutely necessary for correct income measurement and disclosure of financial position as inventories are recorded both in the Income Statement and Balance Sheet External financial analyst should note the method of inventory valuation which has been followed in the past 2-3 years. If there is any change in the method of valuation for the current year, then he should calculate the effect of such a change on the gross profit of the enterprise. Any change in the method of inventory valuation makes a lot of difference if the proportion of inventory is quite large.

We need two information to calculate the value of inventory:

(A) *Physical Quantity.* It is the quantity of raw materials, work-in - progress and finished goods which remain unconsumed/unsold on the date when final accounts are to be prepared. This quantity information can be gathered by physical counting of inventory items.

Physical verification will show the existence of inventory items on the date of final accounts. Other sources of information regarding physical quantity is the costing records which are maintained on continuous basis. Costing records provide detailed information such as opening show purchases and issue of items from time to time and closing stock alongwith their values.

(b) *Unit Price.* It is the price/rate at which the inventory may be valued. The value of inventory can be arrived at by multiplying simply the physical quantities by the unit price.

The accuracy of the valuation of inventory largly depends upon the right calculation of unit-price which is determined by taking into accounts all costs related to purchases and dividing the same by the number of Units brought. The actual cost of raw material inventory shall consist of its purchase price, freight charges, insurance in transit, octroi and cost of buying, receiving and storing. Similarly, the cost of finished goods shall include the cost of raw material and all costs increased in the conversion of raw materials into finished products. In actual practice, a firm may find some difficulties in the computation of cost per unit due to estimation of 'other costs' associated with the inventory items.

Methods of Inventory Valuation

There are different methods of valuing inventors for the purpose of showing the same in the final accounts. The management should clearly understand the implication of each method and follow the one which is most appropriate to its nature of enterprise. International Accounting standard 2 (IAS-2) recommends that the inventories should be valued at the lower of 'Historical cost' and 'net reliasable value.' This standard is based on the conservative principle of book-keeping which ignores expected gains but provides for possible losses. Thus there are primarily three methods of valuing inventories — (i) Historical cost price (ii) Market Price and (iii) Lower of historical cost and market price. In order to facilitate the task of selection of a particular method, a brief explain of each one of them is provided hereunder:

1. Historical Cost Price. Historical cost of inventories is defined as the cost of purchases, cost of conversion and other costs, incurred in bringing the inventories to their present location and condition. It means the inventors of raw materials will not only be valued at the actual price paid for the same but the price will also include the proportionate expenses incurred on acquisition such as freight charges, insurance in transit, octrio and other duties. In case of work-in-progress and finished goods inventories, the wages and other manufacturing cost related to such inventories will also be included. Since inventories an a given date may belong to a particular lot or different lots of purchases the assignment of historical cost to inventories may cause some confusion and difficulty. Following methods based on historical actual cost are used to assign values to material/goods issued or sold and the inventories.

(A) Specific Identification Method

According to this method, each item of inventory is identified with its cost and sum of such costs represent the value of inventory. In other words, the value of inventory on any date is the aggregate cost of all the inventory items valued at their actual cost. In this manner, it is a very simple method but it may cause a lots of problem to the valuer when the number of items is quite large. This method also provides scope for income manipulation when similar lots of items were purchased at different rates. Suppose a firm purchased 200 units of a particular item in four lots of 5050 units each at a price of Rs. 2, Rs. 3, Rs. 4 and Rs. 5 respectively and sold 100 units @ Rs. 6 per unit. In this case the inventory (unsold stock) of 100 units may be valued by the firm at any rate assuming that it pertain to that particular lot of items. If the firm desires to depict higher profits and show current valuation of inventory, then it will value 100 units @ Rs. 5 per unit. If its decides to show a depressed figure of profit and low valuation of assets, then it will certainly value 100 items at a value lesser than 5. This may be a suitable method in case the number of inventory items is few and nature of business is such where purchases are made to meet the specific requirements of the customers.

(B) First-in First-out (FIFO) Method

According to this method, the inventory is valued at the most recent cost value of the unsold stock. It is based on the assumption that the raw materials or goods purchased first are issued first. Thus the inventories constitute the last or most recent purchases. In actual practice, it is not essential that the oldest stock is sold first but it is assumed to have been sold first for the purpose of accounting. However, the general tendency on the part of the seller is to dispose off the old stock first and it is more true in case of less durable and perishable goods. Thus the method is more in true with the business practice. It places the current cost on the value of inventories and thus Balance Sheet of a firm pursuing this method would show current economic position in relation to stock-in-trade (inventory). Valuation of inventory according to FIFO method may be explained by a simple illustration as under:

Illustration—1

From the following information show the value of inventory after each receipt and issue of raw materials:

1993

Jan. 1	Balance 100 @ Rs. 15
Jan. 10	Purchased 500 @ Rs. 20
Jan. 12	Issued 200
Jan. 20	Purchased 200 @ Rs. 25
Jan. 31	Issued 400

Solution

STATEMENT OF INVENTORY

Date	*Receipts*			*Issues*			*Balance*		
	Quality	*Rate*	*Value*	*Quality*	*Rate*	*Value*	*Quality*	*Rate*	*Value*
Jan. 1993	—	—	—	—	—	—	100	15	1500
Jan. 10	500	20	10,000	—	—	—	100	15	1500
							500	20	10,000
Jan. 12	—	—	—	200 [100 100	15	1500	400	20	8,000
					20	2000			
20	200	25	5000	—	—	—	400	20	8000
							200	25	5000
31	—	—		400	20	8000	200	25	5000

The statement is self-explanatory. It is clear that the inventory of 200 units valued at Rs. 5000 is the same which was bought on 20th Jan. at the rate of Rs. 25.

(C) Highest in First-Out (HIFO) Method

According to this method the highest priced material in store is assumed to have been issued first. Accordingly the material issued is priced at the highest price till the quantity of the highest priced material is exhausted. Next issue is made at the next highest price if the quantity of the first highest price material is finished. Thus, the production absorbs the highest cost of materials and the inventory (stock in strude) is valued at lesser than its current cost as is clear from the following statement:

Statement of Inventory
(HIFO Method)

Date	*Receipts*			*Issues*			*Balance*		
	Q	*R*	*V*	*Q*	*R*	*V*	*Q*	*R*	*V*
1995									
Jan. 1	—	—	—	—	—	—	100	15	1500
Jan. 10	500	20	10000	—	—	—	100 500	15 20	1500 10,000
Jan. 12	—	—	—	200	20	4000	400		7500
Jan. 20	200	25	5000	—	—	—	600		12500
Jan. 31	—	—	—	200 200	25 20	5000 4000	— 200		3500

(D) Next-in First-out (NIFO) Method

Under this method the issue price is not the lost price of the materials/ goods in store but it is the price at which the next delivery of material for which an order has been placed, is expected to the received. The issue price under conditions of rising prices will be higher whereas it will be lower than earlier costs when purchase price constantly declines. Accordingly, the book value of unsold stock will decrease and increase.

(E) Last-in First-out (LIFO) Method

This method of inventory valuation is based on the assumption that the materials / goods purchased last are issued first for disposition. Obviously the assumption under this method is just opposite of the FIFO method. Thus the inventory in a firm following this method is assumed to consist of old stock and hence valued at old or earliest rates.

Like FIFO method, it is not essential in LIFO method that the actual flow of materials / goods conferm to the assumption under which the method operates. The chief feature of this method is that it attempts to charge current cost plus profit from the customers but the inventory value is quite different firm its current or replacement cost. Under conditions of rising prices, the cost is in tuve with the market condition but the inventory is under-valued which creates a sort of secret reserve and to that extent Balance Sheet gets window dressed.

Using the cost data of illustration—1, The valuation of inventory may be shown as below:

Statement of Inventory

Date	*Receipts*			*Issues*			*Balance*		
	Q	*R*	*V*	*Q*	*R*	*V*	*Q*	*R*	*V*
1993									
Jan. 1	—	—	—	—	—	—	100	15	1500
Jan. 10	500	20	10000	—	—	—	100 500	15 20	1500 10000
Jan. 12	—	—	—	200	20	4000	100 300	15 20	1500 6000
Jan. 20	200	25	5000	—	—	—	100 300 200	15 20 25	1500 6000 5000
Jan. 31	—	—	—	200 200	25 20	5000 4000	100 100	15 20	1500 2000

Thus the statement shows that the inventory of 200 items consists of 100 units purchased at Rs. 15 and another 100 units which were purchased at Rs. 20. The Last-in purchases of 200 units purchased at Rs. 200 have already been issued to production.

A comparison of inventory value under the FIFO and LIFO methods shows that under the former method the value of 200 units is 5,000 whereas the value of the same inventory under the later method is Rs. 3,500. Value assigned to inventory under the LIFO method is much less than the value under the FIFO method due to the fact that the LIFO method takes into account the earliest cost for the purpose of valuation and the earliest cost under condition of raising prices is lesser than the current prices.

Average Cost Methods

The FIFO and LIFO methods of inventory valuation were based on the assumptions of a particular sequence of issue of materials. In fact, the physical flow of raw material hardly conform to the assumption made. Sometimes, it is, therefore, considered proper to issue raw materials / goods at average cost. For the purpose of issuing raw materials/goods, we may use either simple average cost or weighted average cost.

(F) Simple Average Cost Method

The closing inventory, value, as per this method, depends upon the issue price which is the simple average of prices, which is arrived of by adding the different prices and dividing the total by number of such prices. For instance, if 500 units are purchased at Rs. 20 and 200 units at Rs. 25, then the simple average of prices is 20+25=45÷2=22.50. Issue price and inventory value based on simple average method is represented in the following statement:

Statement of Inventory

Date	*Receipts*			*Issues*			*Balance*		
	Q	*R*	*V*	*Q*	*R*	*V*	*Q*	*R*	*V*
1993									
Jan. 1	100	15	1500	—	—	—	100	15	1500
Jan. 10	500	20	10000	—	—	—	600	—	11500
Jan. 12	—	—	—	200	17.50	3500	400	—	8000
Jan. 20	200	25	5,000	—	—	—	600	—	13000
Jan. 31	—	—	—	400	22.50	9000	200	—	.4000

From the statement, it is clear that the cost of inventory on 10th Jan. 1993 of 600 units is Rs. 11500. On 12th Jan., 200 units at an average price of Rs. 17.50 (15+20/2) have been issued and the balance of inventory (400 units) valued at Rs. 8000. On the last day of the month 400 units at an average price of 22.50 (20+ 25/2) have been issued and thus leaving an inventory of 200 units at a cost value of Rs. 4000.

The average cost method is a very simple method of issue and valuation of inventory. But it suffers from all the limitations with which simple average suffers. Since a simple average is affected to a great extent by extreme values, it is likely that in a certain case, the inventory may be shown at zero or a negative figure, which would be beyond imagination. Supper 100 units are purchased at Rs. 15 and 500 units are purchased at Rs. 5 and 400 units are issued at an average price of 10, then the closing inventory of 200 units would be reduced to zero which is an absurd valuation. Thus, this method is unscientific and generally gives unsatisfactory results.

(G) *Weighted Average Method.* The weighted average method of pricing and valuation of inventory duty recognises the weights or quantities of inventories in stock on the date of issue of raw materials or goods. Under this method, the average price is calculated by dividing the total cost by the total number of units. The materials are issued at the weighted average cost which is calculated after each fresh arrival of materials/goods. This method is a better method insofar as it gives due importance to quantities due to which the effect of large variations in prices is lessened and cost structure reflects true cost of materials / goods issued for production / sales. However, the inventory value under this method, may be very much different from its current value. The operation of the method is represented through the statement given below:

Statement of Inventory

Date	*Receipts*			*Issues*			*Balance*		
	Q	*R*	*V*	*Q*	*R*	*V*	*Q*	*R*	*V*
1993									
Jan. 1	—	—	—	—	—	—	100	15	1500
Jan. 10	500	20	10,000	—	—	—	600	19.17	11500
Jan. 12	—	—	—	200	19.17	3834	400	19.17	7666
Jan. 20	200	25	5,000	—	—	—	600	21.11	12666
Jan. 31	—	—	—	400	21.11	8444	200	21.11	4222

On 10th Jan. the total inventory of 600 units is value at actual cost of Rs. 11500. The average price for a unit is 19.17 (11500 ÷ 600). At this rate the issue of 200 units has been priced. On the arrival of first 200 units, the stock of 600 units cost Rs. 12666 and the average weighted price is 21.11 (12666 ÷ 600). At this rate, the next issue of 400 units has been made. This leaving the inventory of 200 units at a cost of 4222; the average price remaining the same.

(H) Replacement Cost Method

Replacement cost is the market price of materials/goods on the date of issue. It is the price at which the goods can be replaced by purchasing from the market. Under this method the cost of closing inventory will depend upon the replacement cost. In case of rising prices, the replacement cost is always higher than earlier costs. If the inventories are bought in large quantities and issues are made at replacement cost, then the cost of closing inventory will be lesser than the cost of acquisition.

The issues at replacement cost is meant to reflect the current cost of raw materials in the total cost of manufacture. But the valuation of closing inventory at book value arrived at in this manner for the propose of showing the same in the Balance Sheet, will represent unrealistic position as the stock valuation will be at a figure which will be either too low or too high depending upon the condition of rising prices and declining prices respectively. In case the replacement price is not available, then it is based on management's, best estimation which might be different from the real replacement cost and this affects the book value of closing inventory. This method is very simple to follow as issues are made an replacement cost for which information is gathered from the market, as shown below:

Statement of Inventory

Date	*Receipts*			*Issues*			*Balance*		
	Q	*R*	*V*	*Q*	*R*	*V*	*Q*	*R*	*V*
1993									
Jan. 1	—	—	—	—	—	—	100	—	1500
Jan. 10	500	20	10,000	—	—	—	600	—	11500
Jan. 12	—	—	—	200	21	4200	400		7,300
Jan. 20	200	25	5000	—	—	—	600		12,300
Jan. 31	—	—	—	400	26	10,400	200		1,900

The above representation is based on the assumption that the replacement price on 12th January and 31st January was Rs. 21 and Rs. 26 respectively. On comparison with earlier methods, it will be observed that the book value of closing eventory of Rs. 1900 is much less then the book values of the same200 units under other methods.

(I) Standard Price Method

Standard Price is a price which is pre-determined by the costing department for the purpose of issuing raw materials/goods from store to factory/sales depots. The standard pricing system is applied with a view to control cost and follow a realistic price policy. Standard price is neither too low nor too high a price. It is the price which is pre-determined after taking into account the prevailing rates and likely changes in future prices for a particular period of time and revised from time to time in accordance with the changes in the market and other conditions. Thus standard price is not the actual cost price but notional price which is much affected by management's perception about future.

Under standard pricing method, the issues are made at the same standard price. The closing inventory value depends upon the standard issue price.

Using the same data and further assuming that the standard price is taken at Rs. 22, the issue and stock values are depicted in the following statement:

Statement of Inventory

Date	*Receipts*			*Issues*			*Balance*		
	Q	*R*	*V*	*Q*	*R*	*V*	*Q*	*R*	*V*
1993									
Jan. 1	—	—	—	—	—	—	100	—	1,500
Jan. 10	500	20	10,000	—	—	—	600	—	11,500
Jan. 12	—	—	—	200	22	4400	400	—	7,100
Jan. 20	200	25	5,000	—	—	—	600	—	12,100
Jan. 31	—	—	—	400	22	8800	200	—	3,300

(J) Base Stock Method

Base-Stock is the minimum stock of materials/goods which is generally maintained in any firm. According to this method, the Base-stock will be valued at a fixed cost which is generally the cost of the first lot of materials/goods out of which the based stock is assumed to have been created. Any quantity of materials/goods in excess of the Base-stock will be valued by FIFO, LIFO or any other method. In this manner, the

Base Stock Method is not an independent method as it is used with application of any other method.

The merits and demarits of this method depends upon the method used for pricing the issue of materials/goods in excess of the Base-stock.

The Base-Stock is valued at the historical cost and is shown at the same value in Balance Sheet, which is not in tune with showing the current economic position of an enterprise.

2. Market Price Method

Inventories may be valued at market price instead of cost price. Market price means the current market rate at which inventories can be disposed of. It would be appropriate to value inventories at market value if the market price for the inventory items is fairly stable. If the requirements of International Accounting Standard is to be satisfied, then the inventory should be valued at 'Net Realisable Value' which means the current selling price minus selling cost. According to International Accounting Standard (IAS-2), the net realisable value means, "the estimated selling price in the ordinary course of business less costs of compilation and less costs necessarily to be incurred in order to make the sale." If the current market rate is not stable and the management foresee a change in the current rates, then the realisable value may be estimated accordingly. However, minor fluctuations in prices may be ignored. The valuation of inventories at current market price seems quite realistic as it contributes in showing the current economic position of the enterprise but such a valuation gives rise to the problem of unrealised profit/loss.

3. Lower of Cost or Net Realisable Value

It means the inventory should be valued at cost price if it is lesser than the net realisable value and valuation should be done at net realisable value if it is lesser than the cost price. This is based on the conservative principle of book-keeping according to which all expected losses should be provided for but all expected gain should be ignored. If this method of inventory valuation is to be adopted, then the question of comparison of cost price and net realizable value will arise. The comparison can be made in a number of ways. We can compute the total cost price of different items of inventories and compare the same by the aggregate net realisable value of all the items. We compute also divide the total inventory items into homogeneous group and find out the cost price and net realisable value of each group of items separately. It is also possible to compare the cost and realizable value of individual items. Inventory value under different methods is shown below:

Statement of Inventory Valuation under Different Methods

Item		*Cost*	*Market Price*	*Lower of Cost or Market Price*		
				Aggregate	*Group*	*Individual*
Group-I	A	500	750			500
Group-I	B	800	700			700
	(i)	1300	1450		1300	
Group-I	C	1200	1800			1200
	D	2900	1300			1300
	(ii)	3200	3100		3100	
Total Inventory (i + ii)		4500	4550	4500		
		Inventory valuable		4500	4400	3700

Above statement shows different values of inventories under different methods. It may be pointed out that the value of inventories under all the methods will be the same if the market price for all the items shows either constantly increasing or decreasing trend. The fluctuations in the market price of individual items makes all the difference in the value of inventories. IAS 2 has recommended the valuation of inventories either by comparison of cost and market values of group items or the comparison of individual items for the purpose.

Selection of a Method

From the explanation of the different methods as provided above, it is clear that the income determination and asset (stock in trade) measurement is different under different methods of pricing the issue of materials / goods. Which one of the available methods is the best or ideal is a difficult question to answer. The choice of a methods is governed more by the situation faced by an firm. Number of factors such as the need to conform to the physical flow of goods, matching current cost with revenues, degree of price fluctuations nature of inventory items, management policy, etc. are to be taken into consideration while selecting a particular method of valuation. Whichever method the management of a firm chooses for the purpose, should be used consistently till the change has not become inevitable.

QUESTIONS

1. Explain the International Accounting Standard—IAS-2 which deals with the valuation of inventory.
2. Give a critical account of the methods, which can be used for assigning values to raw materials/goods which are issued from store to production /sales?
3. Discuss the impact of a particular method of inventory valuation in Profit and Loss Account and Balance Sheet of a company.
4. What are FIFO and LIFO methods of pricing raw materials/goods? Explain by giving examples. Also make a clear distinctions between the two.
5. Name the various methods of pricing of issue of raw materials and explain with an example the method which you consider to the suitable under conditions of rising prices.
6. The records of a manufacturing firm shows the following position with respect to its purchase and issue of raw materials during the month — July 1993. You are required to show the cost of materials issued for production and the closing cost of inventory on 31st July 1993:

July 1	Purchases	200 units	@ Rs. 35
July 8	Purchases	100 units	@ Rs. 36
July 12	Purchases	300 units	@ Rs. 40
July 25	Purchases	500 units	@ Rs. 42
July 5	Issue	100 units	
July 8	Issue	150 units	
July 15	Issue	250 units	
July 28	Issue	400 units.	

9

Depreciation Policy

Expenditure incurred in an enterprise may broadly be classified into two categories, namely capital expenditure and revenue expenditure. Capital expenditure is concerned with the acquisition of capital assets and other fixed equipments such as land, building, plant and machinery, furniture and fixturs, tools and implements, etc. Such an expenditure is not incurred every now and then but there are special occasions on which the heavy capital expenditure is incurred. On the other hand, revenue expenditure are is done in the usual course of business. The usual items of revenue expenditure the payment for purchase of raw materials, wages and other direct and indirect expenses of running the enterprise in the normal course of business. The whole of revenue expenditure is charged against the profit of the year in which it is incurred. But the capital expenditure needs special treatment in view of its very nature. As we know that a capital asset gives service for fairly long period of time and the amount involved in it is so heavy that whole of it cannot be charged against the profit of a particular year.

Depreciation is something which is concerned with the treatment of capital expenditure in the from of assets in the account books. There is a lot of confusion in so far the causes and method of charging depreciation are concerned. According to J.R. Batlib thad term "depreciation represents loss or diminution in the value of an asset consequent upon wear and tear, obsolescence, effluxion of time or permanent fall in market value." In the opinion of L.C. Cropper. "Depreciation is the domination in the financial value of an asset owing to wear and tear, effluxion of time obsolescence, or similar causes the suggestion being rather that of gradual depreciation than sudden loss or diminition in value." The Institute of Chartered Accountants in England an Wales defines depreciation as "the measure of wearing out, consumption or other loss of value of a fixed asset, whether arising from use, effluxion of time or obsolescence through technology and market changes...." These definition emphasize on the causes of depreciation. The value of a machine goes down as a result of its constant use. The persistent usage also causes the production capacity to decline gradually and after few years it is observed that the machine has been rendered completely unproductiive. This is indicative of the fact that every machine has a production or useful life after which the manufacturing concern has to replace it by a new one. Thus the whole value of the asset is to be charged gradually over its productive life. This change is nothing but, depreciation. Hence every kind of decrease in the value of an asset cannot be termed as depreciation. The loss of a machine due to accident or obsolescence can better be called capital loss but not depreciation. Depreciation is that fractional amount of an asset which is debited to the profit and loss account of a concern according to a pre-conceived plan or schedule of depreciation. It has rightly be recognised that the depreciation accounting is a process of allocation and not of valuation. In other words, the depreciation accounting of a firm is concerned with distributing the cost of assets over the useful life of the same according to a reasonable, method and debeting the Income Statement (Profit and Loss Account) each year with the amount allocated for that year. The accountant has nothing to do with ascertaining exact decrease in the value of the assets or valuing assets annually in order to knew the decrease in their values. In their efforts to show the current economic position, a firm may however, resort to revolution of its assets and show the resultant capital profit and revaluation through Revolution Reserve Account in the Balance Sheet.

How much amount may be charged by way of depreciation on an asset is a problem which may be solved by taking into account the cost value of the asset, residual or scrap value and the productive useful life of the asset. For example, if a machine costing Rs. 45000 has a productive life of 5 years and the scrap value is estimated to fatch Rs. 5000 after the end of its life. In this case the depreciable value is 45000—5000 = 40000. Depreciable value of 40000 divided by the number of years i.e. by 5 years an amount of Rs. 8000 (40000 ÷ 5) what may be charged every year on account of depreciation. There are other methods to spread the cost of assets over their lives.

The fair value of depreciation will largely depend on the accuracy with which the scrap / salvage value and the productive useful life are pre-determined. Truely speaking, it is not possible to exactly forecast these two variables which considerably effect the amount of depreciation. However, the past experience and sound judgement of technical expert can contribute greatly in arriving at the productive life and scrap value and hence fair value of depreciation.

Objects of Providing Depreciation

Charging depreciation periodically throughout the life of an assets serves useful purpose. The managent try to achieve the following objectives through depreciation accounting:

1. Correct Income Determination

Like any other revenue expenditure, depreciation is a charge against profit. Therefore, it has to be debited to the Profit and Loss Account in order to determine correct profit for a year's time. If the depreciation charge is inadequate or no depreciation is provided for, then the Profit and Loss Account would show on inflated profit figure. Similarly excessive depreciation charge would reduce the profit unnecessarily. Thus, both the situation are bad. Reasonable depreciation charge consistently throughout the life of the machine enables us to determine fair profit for further appropriations. The object of showing correct operating performance of an enterprise is achieved only if all the operating expenses including depreciation is rightly calculated every year and shown in the Profit and Loss Account

2. Correct Economic Position

A Balance Sheet depicts correct economic position on a given date if all the assets and liabilities are brought in it at their correct and fair values. Fixed assets form quite a large proportion of total assets in a capital intensive industry. All the assets in a Balance Sheet should be shown at their book values minus depreciation. If the assets are not rightly depreciated, the Balance Sheet cannot be regarded as correct. If the depreciation is not provided or inadequately provided in any year, the Balance Sheet would fail to show the correct picture of the economic position as the assets would get over-valued. Thus the object of depreciation accounting is also to show the assets one their unexpired cost (book value minus depreciation) and thus depict the correct economic position of the enterprise.

3. Replacement of Assets

Every asset has a fixed productive useful life after which it needs to be replaced by the new one so that the production is continued without stoppage. Depreciation charge on a continuous basis during the life of assets enables an enterprise to replace the assets at the end of their lives without difficulty. The amount of depreciation may be invested outside the business or an insurance policy taken for generating adiquate surplus to by new assets.

4. Depreciation as a Source of Finance

If the amount of depreciation is allowed to remain within the enterprise by not investing the same outside the business, it becomes a source of financing the working capital requirements.

5. Fullfilment of Legal Requirements

The companies Act 1956 requires that depreciation must be provided for before the declaration of dividend to shareholders. The provision of depreciation is important to ensure that the dividend is not declared out of capital.

6. Reduction of Tax Liability

Depreciation is allowed as a deduction from total income for the purpose of computing taxable income. If the corporate tax rate is 50%, then tax equal to half of the amount of depreciation can be saved. Thus depreciation can be used a tax-saving device. A company can maximise tax-savings by following a suitable depreciation policy.

Thus the depreciation serves many objects. An enterprise is generally not led by a single object of charging depreciation. A firm attempts to show true and fair view of its business operations and economic position by allowing appropriate depreciation charge but its effort is also to achieve other objectives such as enumerated above.

Methods of Charging Depreciation

We have already observed that depreciation is to be charged according to a pre-conceived plan schedule of depreciation. This implies a particular method which should be used for charging depreciation. There are a number of methods of charging depreciation and a firm can use any one of them which is more suitable to its nature of business and other condition in which it is operating. We shall examine the question of suitability of a method a little later. Let us study the different methods of charging depreciate, which are available to any business concern. The object of explanation is to understand the nature of the methods and their merits and limitation and not the accounting of depreciation.

1. Straight Line Method or Fixed Instalant Method

According to this methods, the depreciation charge is the same for all the years over the life of an asset. If the data of depreciation are plotted on a graph paper, a straight line is obtained, hence the method is known as stright line method. The amount of depreciate is estimated after taking into consideration the cost value of asset, the scrap value and the estimated life of the asset. Cost value minus scrap value divided by the number of years the asset will last give the amount of depreciation. A rate percent can also be fixed for calculating depreciation on original cost value of the asset. Since the instalment of depreciation charge remains fixed, this method is also known as 'Fixed instalment Method' of charging depreciation.

Example: Suppose on 1st Jan. 1985, an asset has been purchased for Rs. 50,000. According to an estimation the asset will last for 5 years with scrap value of Rs. 5,000. (i) Determine the amount of depreciation according to straight line method (ii) Also compute the rate of depreciation, and (iii) Show the treatment of depreciation in the Income Statement and Balance Sheet.

$$\text{(i) Amount of depreciation} = \frac{\text{Cost Value} - \text{Scrap Value}}{\text{Life of asset in years}}$$

$$= \frac{50{,}000 - 5{,}000}{10} = \frac{45{,}000}{5} = 9{,}000$$

$$\text{(ii) Rate of depreciate} = \frac{\text{Amount of depreciation}}{\text{Cost value of Asset}} \times 100$$

$$= \frac{9{,}000 \times 100}{50{,}000} = 18\%\ \text{p.a.}$$

(iii) The profit and Loss account will be debited with Rs. 4,000 every year for 5 years and the Balance Sheet would show at the end of each year the asset at cost less depreciation as shown below. At the end of the 5th year the asset will be reduced to its scrap value.

BALANCE SHEET

31st Dec. 1985		
Asset	50,000	41,000
Less dep.	9,000	
31st Dec. 1986		
Asset	41,000	
Less dep.	9,000	32,000
31st Dec. 1987		
Asset	32,000	23,000
Less dep.	9,000	
31st Dec. 1988		
Asset	23,000	23,000
Less dep.	9,000	14,000
31st Dec 1988		
Asset	14,000	
Less dep	9,000	5,000

Merits

(i) The main merit of straight line method is that it is simple to understand and easy to apply.

(ii) Full value of the asset is written off over the life of the asset. The asset is reduced to zero or scrap value at the end of life of the asset.

(iii) The method is more suitable in case of those assets which loose their value with the passage of time. Leasehold property and patents can be depreciated reasonably by the application of this method.

Demerits

The straight line method suffers for the serious limitations such as—(i) It does not take into account the physical use of the assets. The amount of depreciation remains the same irrespective of the use of an asset.

According to this method, depreciation at the same rate has to be charged even if the asset has not been in use for a single day but such is a rare situation. (ii) The Profit and Loss Account is not unimformly charged with depreciation plus expenditure on repairs and renewals of the asset. The expenditure on maintenance of assets is heavy in the later life of on asset due to high cost of repairs and renewals. Thus the Profit and Loss A/C is over-burdened in the later years which is not fair. (iii) The method does not consider the productivity or operating efficiancy of machine which does not remain the same for all the years during the life of Machine.

(2) Diminishing Instalment Method

Under this method the depreciation is calculated at a particular rate on the Balance of the cost value of the asset standing in the accounts books at the beginning of each year. In this way, the depreciation goes on diminishing or declining year after year. Therefore, the method is also known by the name of reducing or declining instalment method. If an asset costing Rs. 1,000 is depreciated at 10% p.a. according to Diminishing Balance Method, then the depreciation for the first few years would be as under:

I—year on 1000 @ 10% = 100

II—year on 900 (1000–100) @ 10% = 90

III—year on 810 (900–90) @ 10% = 81

IV—year on 729 (810–81) @ 10% = 72.90

Depreciation rate determination under this method is a little difficult problem which can be solved by the application of the following formula:

$$\text{Rate}=1-\left(\frac{\text{Scrap Value}}{\text{Cost Value}}\right)^{\frac{1}{N}}$$

$$\text{Or } 1-\sqrt[N]{\frac{\text{Scrap Value}}{\text{Cost Value}}}$$

Where n stands for the estimated life of the asset in years.

Merits

(i) The method is simple to understand and easy to apply.

(ii) It is equitable and fair in the sense that it attempts to uniformly burden the Profit and Loss Account for various years by recognising the expenditure on repairs and renewals as an important part of depreciation. The burden of depreciation plus cost of repairs in various years is likely to be uniform because the depreciation charge in the initial years is relatively more but the expenditure on repairs is less. As the asset advance in age, the depreciation charge declines but the expenditure on repairs and renewals increases. This is testified by the experience of practioners.

(iii) The method is advantageous from tax point of view. Higher depreciation in initial years saves higher tax also and the amount so saved is used throughout the life of the asset.

(iv) The method is useful in cases where the production capacity of asset declines rapidly and the asset produces more income in the early part of the life of the asset.

Demerits

(i) The value of asset cannot be reduced to zero as the depreciation is charged on the written down value. The method will not be suitable for assets with zero scrap value.

(ii) The determination of rate of interest is somewhat difficult.

(3) Machine Hour Rate Method

According to this method the depreciation is charged according to the number of hours the machine is put to use in a year. For this purpose an hourly rate is estimated by estimating the life of the machine in terms of hours. Depreciation on a particular machine is calculated by multiplying the number of hours by machine hour rate.

This method seems satisfactory as it correlates depreciation with the working time of the machine but its use in actual practice is limited. Actually speaking, reasonable depreciation has to be changed despite the fact that an asset has remained idle for most of the time in a year. In actual practice it may be found difficult to translate the life of an asset in terms of hours.

Example. Suppose an asset has been purchased for Rs. 50000. It is estimated that the asset will enjoy working time of 12000 hours with scrap value of Rs. 5000. Determine the amount of depreciate in any one year the machine worked for 2000 hours.

Solution

$$\text{Hourly Depreciation Rate} = \frac{\text{Cost Value} - \text{Scrape Value}}{\text{Life of Machine in Hours.}}$$

$$= \frac{50{,}000 - 5{,}000}{12{,}000} = 3.75$$

Amount of depreciation = No of working hours x hourly rate

$$2000 \times 3.75 = 7500$$

(4) Production Units Method

This method takes into account the Production Units instead of operating time as the basis for calculating the amount of depreciation. It is considered to be the most suitable method to write off the wasting assets such as mines, quarris, oil-wells, etc. which have fixed production capacity and it is possible to estimate total production content with fair degree of accurracy. The cost paid for the acquisition of such assets is spread over the number of production units the asset is estimated to yield in under to calculate depreciation cost per unit of output. Depreciation charge for a year will be calculated by multiplying the number of units produced in that year by the depreciation cost per unit of output.

Like Machine Hours rate method, the chief characteristic feature and advantage of the Production Units method is that it correlates the amount depreciation with the total estimated production capacity of the working asset. But the correctness of the depreciation is directly governed by the accuracy of the estimation of total production to be yielded by the asset.

Example

A mine is acquired for a value of Rs. 15,00,000. It is estimated value of the mine contains 10,00,000 tons of minerals. In an year 1,50,000 tons of minerals was extracted. How much depreciation be charged in that year.

Solution

Depreciation per unit (Ton) of output =

$$\frac{\text{Cost of Asset}}{\text{Total estimated Production (Tun)}}$$

$$= \frac{15,00,000}{10,00,000} = 1.50$$

Amount of Depreciation = Production of the year × Rate per ton

= 1,50,000 × 1.50 = 2,25,000

It will be observed that the amount of depreciation to be charged during the life of the assets remain fixed or uniform in case of the above three methods of straight line, Machine Hours and Production Units methods. Therefore, these methods may be put under one group of methods which may called by the name of 'Uniform Charge Method.'

(5) Sum of Years Digit Method

According to this method, the calculation of depreciation is very simple. The annual depreciation is in proportion to the ratio of the digit for the years of life remaining divided by the sum of this digits for the total life. It means, the numerator is equal to the number of years including the current year for which the asset will enjoy productive life and the denominator is equal to the sum of the digits of the life of the asset. For example, if an asset enjoy a life of 5 years, then fration for the purpose of depreciation in various years would be as under:

Sum of years digits - 1 + 2 + 3 + 4 + 5 = 15

1st year's fraction = $\frac{5}{15}$

2nd years fraction = $\frac{4}{15}$

3rd years fraction = $\frac{3}{15}$

4th years fraction = $\frac{2}{15}$

5th years fraction = $\frac{1}{15}$

If an asset cost Rs. 50,000 with salvage value of Rs. 5,000, then the depreciation to be charged for various years as per the sum of Years Digits method would be as shown below:

1st Year Depreciation = $45000 \times \frac{5}{15}$ = 15000

2nd Year Depreciation = $45000 \times \frac{4}{15}$ = 12000

3rd Year Depreciation = $45000 \times \frac{3}{15}$ = 9000

4th Year Depreciation = $45000 \times \frac{2}{15}$ = 6000

5th Year Depreciation = $45000 \times \frac{1}{15}$ = 3000

Total Depreciation = 45000

It will be observed that the depreciation charge in the early years of the life of asset is more than in the later year. In other words, the depreciation declines with the passage of time. The method suggests the recovery of cost of asset as early as possible. This will be a suitable method if the management desire speedy recovery of capital cost in fixed assets. It may also be noted that the asset can be reduced to its residual value by the application of this method.

(6) Double Declining Balance Method

Under this method, the depreciation is charged according to the Diminishing Balance method by the application of the rate which is twice the rate charged under the straight line method. The depreciation is charged on the cost value of asset without giving any consideration to the scrap value but adjustment in depreciation in the final year of the life of the asset is made so that the asset is not reduced below the scrap value.

Illustrtation—1

Given : Cost value of asset = 50,000

Life of asset = 5 years.

Scrap value = 5,000

Solution

The annual charge of depreciation without considering the scrap value, as per straight line method would be 50000 ÷ 5 = 10000; and the % rate of depreciation would be $\left(\frac{10000 \times 100}{50000}\right) = 20\%$

This rate of 20% will be doubled under Double Declining Balance Method. Thus a rate of 40% will be used for calculating depreciation as shown below:

Year	*Cost value at the beginning of each year*	*Amount of depreciation @ 40% on Diminishing Balance*
I	50000	20000
II	30000	12000
III	18000	7200
IV	10800	4320
V	6480	1480*
		45000

* In this year, the depreciation at 40% of 6480 comes to Rs. 2592 but a depreciation of 1480 will be charged because asset cannot be reduced below scrap value of Rs. 5000.

The Double Declaning Method is permitted in the U.S.A. under the federal tax laws. Since the depreciation is charged at double the rate, the depreciation in charge in the initial years is quite high. The method provides a speedy recovery of capital cost and attempts to burden the Profit and Loss Account Uniformly over the different years by recognising the fact that the expenditure on repairs in the initial years is low and it goes an increasing with the use of machine in the succeeding years. This method may not find forever with those organisations who want to show a better economic performance in the initial years for which they prefer to show low depreciation charge deliberately.

(7) Inventory System of Depreciation

The usual methods of changirg depreciation are not considered convenient and economical in case of low cost items such as small tools and implements. Such items may be depreciated easily by following the inventory system of depreciation. According to this method, the cost value of assets in good working condition at the end of each year is computed and compared with the cost value of all the assets at the beginning of the year. The difference in cost value is treated an depreciation. Thus, it is a method which is concerned with the revaluation of assets. The loss in the value of assets during the year's time due to usage is termed as depreciation. This method may also be used to depreciate the assets such as live-stock whose life cannot be ascertained with certainly.

(8) Annuity Method

The methods of charging depreciation as explained above recognised the loss in the value of assets due to usage (depreciation) but did not consider the loss of interest on the amount invested in the assets. The enterprise could have earned interest on the amount invested in asset by investing the same in some other form of investment and thus looses interest by commiting the investment in the present form (asset). Therefore, the interest at some reasonable rate should be taken into account. The annuity Method duly considers the interest on balance of amount standing in the asset account at the beginning of the year. The depreciation is calculated with reference to annuity table which gives the annual amount necessary to write off Re 1 at a desired interest rate after a specified time. Total amount of depreciation is arrival at by the multiplication of the annuity factor and the cost value of asset.

(9) Depreciation Fund or Sinking Fund Method

The amount of depreciation charged annually may either be allowed to remain within the enterprise and use it as a resource of financing working capital or other requirements or invested outside the business in some kind of interest-bearing securities. According to Depreciation or sinking Fund method, the instalment of depreciation is invested in outside securities and the interest received on such an investment is also invested alongwith the instalment of depreciation in the subsequent years. The accounting process of charging depreciation and creating the depreciation fund with the amount of depreciation and interest amount and making investments in outside securities is continued till the last year of the productive life of the asset. At the end of the last year, the depreciation is charged but the investment is not made because in this very year the investment have to be sold to realize money for purchase of the new machine.

Depreciation Fund Method is a useful method as it ensures provision of necessary amount which is needed to replace old asset by a new one at the end of a particular period. The only limitation of this method is that it provides for a fixed amount of depreciation whereas the need for money for repairs increases with the passage of time. Thus the Profit and Loss Account is not uniformly burdened with the cost of machine used in the process of manufacture.

(10) Insurance Policy Method

In order to be more certain about the receipt of amount necessary for replacing the old asset by a new one, the management may prefer to take on insurance policy for the required amount instead of making investment in outside securities and selling them at the end of last year of the useful life of the asset. The amount equal to depreciation is paid in the form of insurance premium to the insurance company which is obliged to pay a certain sum at the end of the specified period.

The Insurance Policy method is almost similar to the Depreciation Fund method. The added advantage of the former method is that an undertaking is relieved of the problem of making investment every year and maintaining accounts of interests, etc. There is also no risk which might arise due to decrease in the value of investments when they are sold.

(11) Replacement Cost Method

One of the objectives of charging depreciation is the provision of adequate funds to buy a new asset when the old one becomes unproductive. The traditional methods of charging depreciation simply provide for the recovery of the original cost of an asset and no cognisance is taken of the fact that the replacement requires more money than the cost of the original asset. This is true in a period of rising prices. Under conditions of continued inflation, the replacement of asset is not possible if a firm is absolutely dependent on the recovery of original cost of asset by following any traditional method of charging depreciation. The replacement cost is much higher than the historical cost, therefore, depreciation should be charged on replacement cost if the replacement is to be made without any financial difficulty. The amount of depreciation would be higher than the depreciation on historical cost. Thus, it will put more burden on the Profit and Loss Accounts. It may be pointed out that the depreciation charge on replacement cost is not required under any Act but the business firms may provide for extra depreciation in their own interest of replacement of assets. Since the extra depreciation charge is not permitted for tax purposes, therefore, the industry. in general, do not follow the Replacement Cost method of charging depreciation. The management of some undertakings may not like it when they desires to show better performance as reflected by the profit figure. There are some practical difficulties in following this method. The 'replacement cost' is not certain and a rough estimate can only be made about it and the asset to be acquired in future is different in many respect due to technological changes. The tax authorities do not allow depreciation more than at the specified rates. Owing to these problems the use of the method has got limited application.

Suitable Method

After having stutied so many methods, a pertinent question which arises is — which method of charging depreciation is more suitable to write off an asset and provide funds for its replacement? It is very difficult to answer this question in an unequivocal terms in view of the fact that every method has its own merits and limitations. The question of the suitability or choice of method may be solved after careful consideration of the nature of depreciable asset and the type of industry in which the asset is in use. It may be noted that freehold land is not regarded as a depreciable asset and as such no depreciation is required to be charged on such an asset. Plant and machinery may be depreciated according to Machine Hour Rate method as this method reduces the machines to their scrap values at the end of their productive life. The depreciation on buildings may be charged either by the application of Fixed Instalment method or Diminishing Instalment method. Items such as Loose tools, and live-stock can be depreciated by Revolution Method. Wasting assets such as mines, quarries, oil welb etc. may be written off by Production Units method. The selection of the method of depreciation should be governed by the criterion that the asset is equitably reduced to written down value at the end of its productive life.

Other creterion to be followed in the selection of a method are: (a) Early recovery of the cost value of asset for which accelerated method or depreciation at a higher rate is considered desirable. (b) Deriving maximum tax benefit in the early years of the life of asset for which depreciation at higher rate or Double Declining method is suggested. (c) Generating sufficient funds for the replacement of asset under conditions of inflation the depreciation on the estimated replacement cost is recommended. (d) Earning a uniform rate of return on investment for which a fair matching of expired cost against related income is always desirable. (e) Measurement of true and fair profit for which a reasonable method which avoids under or over-charging of depreciation is to be specified.

There are practical difficulties in the selection of an appropriate method of charging depreciation. There is no particular method which might lead to the achievements of all the objectives of the depreciation policy. For example, the object of early recovery of cost of asset and deriving maximum tax benefit is better served by accelerated depreciation method but it would be against the object of the measurement of true and fair profit.

The sound management practice suggests that the method of charging depreciation should be reviewed periodically and it should be ensured that the assets are being depreciated rightly and the enterprise would be able to replace the existing assets by the new ones. If at any stage, the method of charging depreciation is found unsatisfactory or inadequate and the change has become inevitable, the management is free to switch over to any other suitable method but the effect of such a charge on the final accounts may be calculated and properly reported through the published accounts. Under conditions of rapid rise in price level, the cost of replacement of assets is obviously quite high and the management will have to think of providing for accelerated depreciation on making extra provision for replacement of asset. Similarly, the changes in laws regarding the provision of depreciation will have to be incorporated in the final accounts.

QUESTIONS

1. What in your opinion should be the objects of charging depreciation on fixed assets? Explain clearly.
2. List the methods which are available to a firm for charging depreciation on its fixed assets. Which one of the methods you would recommend for writing off the depreciation on Land, Plant and Machinery Loose tools and Patent rights?
3. What are the components of a suitable depreciation policy? What should be the main consideration in the selection of a method of charging depreciation.
4. Management of an undertaking seeks your advise as to the adoption of a Straight Line Method of charging depreciation .what will be your recommendation?
5. Would you prefer Depreciation Fund Method or Insurance Policy Method for dealing with the amount of depreciation? Give reasons in support of your answer.

10

Emerging Trends in Management Accounting

A. Inflation Accounting

One of the important objectives of maintaining financial accounts is to measure true profit and prepare Balance Sheet which represent true and fair economic portion of an enterprise. This objective can be achieved only if the account books are rightly maintained and any external factor affecting them is duly recognized and its effect is shown in the final accounts. Historical accounting system is based on certain well accepted accounting concepts and principles which guide in the maintenance, preparation and presentation of accounts. Anything which is not consistent with conventional accounting principles is ignored despite the fact that it considerably effects the nature of financial reports and statements which are prepared for internal and external purposes. One such important thing is the 'Inflation' which effect the Final Accounts but its effect is not appreciated by conventional accountants who are attached dearly with the 'cost principle' of historical accounting system. It is only recently that the accountants have started realising the impact of inflation on financial accounts and report the same, in one form or the other, to their users.

Effects of Inflation

Under condition of inflation the price of raw materials, wages, and every other input of production goes an increasing. Similarly, the replacement cost of fixed assets is much higher than their cost values when inflation shows rapid increase in price level. In other words, the inflation pushes down the value of money which can, now buy lesser amount of similar goods with the same amount of money. Since inflation is continuous,

the value of money ever declines with every increase in the rate of inflation
.

Traditional Accounting is based on the assumption of stable value of money which is quite unrealistic under inflationary conditions. The values attached to unsold stock, fixed assets, etc. change with changes in price level; hence the Balance Sheet will fail to show current economic portion if historical values are shown in the Balance Sheet. The profit measurement based on historical valuation of inventory and depreciation charges will also not be fair under conditions of rising prices. Historical accounts may mislead outside uses and the management itself may not rightly interpret the accounts in the absence of inflation accounting as the historical accounts present nothing but a distorted picture of business affairs. The comparison of the one period's performance and economic position with any other period is not proper and fruitful due to distortion in accounts.

Financial analysts should properly understand the manner in which distortions arise in conventional accounts based on traditional concepts and conventions of accounts. Following distortions are notable.

1. Under-valuation of Inventory

Under conventional accounting, the inventories are valued at lower of cost or market value. The closing inventory of the current year becomes opening inventory of the next year. The real value of raw materials purchased for the current year's production is also more than the cost but they are shown at cost values. Thus the cost of goods sold is much less than its real cost. In this manner, the calculated gross profit and hence,net profit is inflated or over-stated. The distortion is caused due to the fact that the cost of sales (at cost value) is matched against the current value of sales.

2. Under Provision for Depreciation

According to traditional costing depreciation is charged on the cost values of assets which are purchased at different periods of time at different price levels. The depreciation change is matched with sales at current prices having low purchasing power. The amount of depreciation is much less than when considered on the real values of assets. It leads to over-statement of profit due to inadequate provision for profits.

3. Capital Erosion

There is always a danger that the capital may be eaten away by the distribution of dividend out of capital when the profits have been overstated. Non -recovery of cost of exhaustion of fixed assets, endangers, the long-term financial stability of the firm.

4. Current Position not Reflected

Fixed assets are shown at cost less depreciation and inventory which form a sizable proportion of working capital is also shown at cost price, or market price, whichever is less. This type of treatment is, not fair when their actual values are much higher. The Balance Sheet based in traditional accounting practices fails to reflect the current economic picture of an enterprise.

5. Different Replacement of Assets

The management may find it difficult to replace the retiring assets by the new ones due to the fact that the amount represented by Depreciation Fund Account is much less than the amount required to buy new assets which obviously cost more due to increasing price level. It becomes almost impossible to maintain capital without recognising inflation Accounting.

6. Loss Gains on Monetary Assets Liabilities

Holding of monetary assets such as cash balances, Bills Receivables and debtors cause loss to a firm as their real value declines due to inflation. Against it, a firm gains on the delayed payment to its creditors. Such losses and gains need to be brought into financial statements if real position is to be conveyed to their users.

Thus, the historical financial accounting suffers from the serious limitations and posses a threat to the very existence of an enterprice in the long-term. Therefore, we need a system of accounting which could contribute in the measurement of true profit and show the true and fair economic values of assets and liabilities in the Balance Sheet. Inflation Accounting is a newly developed technique which is helpful in achieving the desired objectives. It may be defined as an accounting technique which appreciate the impact of inflation on accounts of an undertaking and provides for the same by allowing the assets and liabilities to be shown at current values through adjustments in the Income Statement of that year.

There is a lot of controversy as to the measurement of impact of inflation on an enterprise and method of showing the impact in the Final Accounts. Radical thinking on the subject is that the traditional method of presentation of Final Accounts should be entirely replaced by the current accounting techniques. A large number of academicians and practitioners believe that this type of change will complicate the matter and a greater degree of subjectivity will enter into the accounts. Hence, the benefits of Inflation Accounting may be reaped if the a Final Accounts are allowed to be prepared and reported in the usual manner and the impact of inflation is shown as a supplementary information attached to the historical accounts.

Techniques of Inflation Accounting

Accounting for Inflation has been one of the most controversial subjects. There is no dearth of persons in the accounting profession; who are opposed to the introduction of inflation accounting by the modification of historical accounting system. But nobody can deny the fact that the inflation causes distortions in accounts which need to be rectified by some kind of method which may be of general acceptability.

Partial Price Level Accounting

Since price level accounting is not statutory in case of Indian companies and other organizations, a partial price level accounting may be resorted to neutralise the effect of inflation and produce some degree of improvement in profit measurement. The price level accounting is said to be partial if the accounts are modified along the following lines:

1. Use of LIFO method for valuation of inventory so that the cost of goods sold is valued at the most current cost so as to measure realistic gross profit.
2. Use of replacement cost in place of historical costs of assets for the purposes of depreciation charges, and Balance Sheet figure.
3. Creation of Depreciation Reserve Account out of current year's profits to enable the enterprise to accumulate reserve to facilitate replacement of the retiring assets.

An enterprise can serve its purpose to a great extent by doing the above but the problem of reporting the current economic position of the enterprise still remains unresolved. The partial method does not-specify any method method for the estimation of anticipated replacement cost of assets. It fails to recognize the effect of inflation on monetary assets as a result of change in the value of money as a measuring rod. Thus it does not provide a comprehensive method to deal with Inflation Accounting problem.

Full Price Level Accounting

According to full price level accounting, all the items- monetary and non-monetary is appearing in historical final accounts are recast according to a particular method so as to bring in them the full effect of purchasing power variations. Broadly speaking, two methods to deal with accounting for price level changes have been developed, as explained below:

CURRENT PURCHASING POWER ACCOUNTING (CPPA)

According to CPPA method the historical costs are adjusted by indices in terms of general purchasing power of money at the end of the year. For this reason, this method is also known as General Purchasing Power Accounting (GPPA) or General Price Level Accounting (GPLA) method. Under conditions of rising prices (Inflation), the price Index at the end is higher than at the beginning of the year. The current purchasing power of any item is converted as per the following formula:

$$\text{Current Purchasing Power (CPP)} = \frac{\text{Current Price Index}}{\text{Index at Beginning}} \times \text{Conversion Amount}$$

It may be noted that the historical costs for an item, say, inventory are incurred at different points of time at varying price index. The CPPA method converts the mixed historical costs into an equivalent rupee of current purchasing power and thus makes all the accounting numbers comparable in terms of general purchasing power. General Price Index is fairly a good measure to convent the historical costs into an equivalent purchasing power. It is assumed that the movements in prices of materials, labour and fixed capital equipments, etc., are in the same direction and at the same rates as in case of general price index. The wholesale price index or consumers price Index can also be applied for cost conversion with almost same degree of accuracy. Historical cost multiplied by conversion factor gives the current cost which, if spent, can buy the same amount of goods as could be bought by incurring the cost at the beginning

. The conversion factor is determined as under :

$$\text{Conversion factor} = \frac{\text{Price Index at end}}{\text{PriceIndex at beginning}}$$

Illustration —1

On 1st January 1995, a Company purchased a machine for Rs. 50,000 when the General Price Index was 100. The inflation has pushed up the Index to 120 on 31st December 1995. The Company wishes to show the asset at current cost based on General Price Index. You are required to convert the historical cost into current cost and show how the asset would appear in the Balance Sheet if depreciation @ 20%cost to be changed on current cost.

Solution

$$\text{Current cost} = \text{Historical} \times \text{Conversion factor}$$

$$= 50{,}000 \times \frac{120}{100}$$

$$= 50{,}000 \times \frac{6}{5}$$

$$= 50{,}000 \times 1.2 = 60{,}000$$

Balance Sheet

	Historical costing	*Current purchasing power*
Machine less depreciation	40,000	48,000

Monetary Items

Monetary items are those items of a Balance Sheet which are fixed or otherwise remain unchanged despite the change in the general price Index. For example, Sundry debtors is an item of current asset which is fixed in the sense that a firm will realize neither more nor less than the amount stated in the historical accounts. Other examples of monetary items are the cash balances, Bills Receivables, Sundry Creditors, Accrrued Incomes, outstanding expenses, etc. Since monetary items are fixed by contract or otherwise, they are shown in the inflation Adjusted Balance Sheet as their historical values. However net gains or loss on holding monetary items is calculated and taken into account in determining net income /loss.

There is always loss in holding monetary assets as they loose purchasing power during inflation. On the other hand, there is a gain in holding monetary liabilities which can be discharged by paying the same fixed amount which has lost purchasing power, during inflation. The net gain or loss in monetary items is to be calculated and included in current income or treated as capital item.

Illustration—2

Suppose a firm has a cash balance of Rs.5,000 in the beginning of the current year-1st Jan. 1995 and it holds the same Rs 5,000 on 31st Dec.1995 as there was no transaction during the year. Calculate the loss due to holding this monetary asset if the General Price Index has gone up from 100 at the beginning of the year to 120 at the end of the year.

Solution

The firm must hold cash balance which is more than 5,000 in order to neutralise the effect of inflation. It must hold

$$5000 \times \frac{120}{100} = \text{Rs, } 6,000$$

whereas it holds the same fixed Rs. 5,000. Then there is a loss of Rs. 1,000 (6,000-5,000) in holding cash.

Non-Monetary Items

Non-monetary items include all those assets and liabilities which do not represent a fixed amount to be received or paid. Examples of non-monetary items are equity capital, reserves and surplus, land, building Machinery, etc. There is no gain or loss on non-monetary assets the way it accrues on monetary assets which carry fixed amount. The values of non-monetary items may change over time. This is the reason that the non-monetary assets and liabilities are shown at adjusted values in the CPPA adjusted Balance Sheet. The conversion factor for non-monetary items is determined as under:

(a) Conversion factor for non-monetary asset $= \dfrac{\text{Price Index on date of Balance Sheet}}{\text{Price Index on acquisition of asset}}$

(b) Conversion factor for capital $= \dfrac{\text{Current year's Index}}{\text{Index on date of capital acquisition}}$

(c) Reserve & Surplus (retained earnings) will be the residual figure after restatement of all items in terms of general purchasing power in the year when Inflation Accounting is introduced for the first time.

Adjusted Income Statement

For the preparation of adjusted Income Statement according to CPPA method, the adjustment are required to be made in respect of each item of revenue and expenses which must be converted in terms of the purchasing power equivelent to year-end rupee. The procedure for conversion is almost the same as in case of monetary and non-monetary items as explained earlier. Consider the following in this connection:

Items	*Method of Conversion*
Opening Inventory	$\dfrac{\text{Index at the end}}{\text{Index at Beginning}} \times$ opening Inventory
Purchases	$\dfrac{\text{Index at end}}{\text{Average Index}} \times$ Amount of Purchases
Wages & Salaries and other expenses	$\dfrac{\text{Index at end}}{\text{Average Index}} \times$ Conversion cost
Closing Inventory	Depends upon the method used for issue of inventory for consumption i.e : LIFO or FIFO method
Depreciation written off	$\dfrac{\text{Index at end}}{\text{Index when asset acquired}} \times$ Amount of depreciation

	Alternatingly, the assets may be first restated in terms of current Purchasing power and then the depreciation on such a cost at a particular rate calculated.
Interest and dividend	Interest and dividend paid or received at the end of the year need no adjustment as they represent current purchasing power.

Illustration —3

Balance Sheet of a Public limited company for the year end on 31st Dec. 1994 stood as under:

Liabilities	*1994 (Rs)*	*1995 (Rs)*	*Assets*	*1994 (Rs)*	*1995 (Rs)*
Capital	2,00,000	2,00,000	Land & Buildings	75,000	750,000
Retained Earnings	—	65,000	Plant & Machinery	1,00,000	100,000
Accumulated Depreciation	—	20,000	Monetary assets	65,000	1650,000
Liabilities	1,00,000	1,00,000	Investories –1994 = 4000 units –1995 = 3000 units	60,000	45,000
	3,00,000	3,25,000		3,00,000	32,50,000

The income statement for the year 1995 was as under :

Sales (6000 units @ 50	3,00,000	
Less :		
opening Inventory 4000 units @ 15	60,000	
Purchases - 5000 units @ 20	1,00,000	
	1,60,000	
Less closing Inventory 3000 units @15	45,000	
		1,15,000
		1,85,000

Less Expenses :		
Interest changes		15,000
Administration exp	85,000	
Depreciation	20,000	12,0000
Net Income		65,000

Calculation of Purchasing Power Gains/Loss

	Unadjusted	*Conversion*	*Adjusted*
Net monetary assets on 1-1-1995	(35,000)	180/100	(63,000)
Add monetary receipts during 1995	3,00,000	180/120	4,50,000
Net monetary Items	2,65,000		3,87,000
Less monetary Payments			
Purchases	1,00,00	180/150	1,20,000
Interest	15,000	180/120	22,500
Administration Expenses	25,000	180/120	1,27,500
	2,00,000		2,70,000
Net monetary assets on 31-12-95	65,000		1,17,000
Less Actual net monetary assets on 31-12-1995			65,000
Purchasing power loss			52,000

Adjusted Income Statement for the Year Ending 1995

	Unadjusted	*Conversion factor*	*Adjusted*
Sales : 6000 units @ 50/-	3,00,000	180/120	4,50,000
Loss : Cost of goods sold : opening stock : 4000 units	60,000	180/100	1,08,000
Purchases: 5000 x 20	1,00,000	180/150	1,20.000
	1,60,000		2,28,000

Loss : Closing Inventory 3000 x 15	45,000	180/100	21,000
Cost of goods sold	1,15,000		1,47,000
Gross margin	1,85,000		3,03,000
Other Expenses :			
Interest	15000	180/120	22,500
Admn. Expenses	25,000	180/120	1,27,500
Depreciation	20,000	180/100	36,000
	1,20,000		1,86,000
Net Operating Income	65,000		1,17,000

Reconciliation of Adjusted Earnings

Retaining Earnings 1-1-1995	nil
Adjusted net operating income	1,17,000
Less purchasing power loss	52,000
Net Income transferred to B/S	65,000

Price Level Adjusted Balance Sheet As on 31-12-1995

Liabilities	*Unad-justed (Rs.)*	*Conver-sion*	*Adjusted (Rs.*	*Assets*	*Unad-justed (Rs.)*	*Conver-sion*	*Adjusted (Rs.)*
Liabilities	1,00,000	180/180	1,00,000	Monetary Assets	1,65,000		1,65,000
Capital	2,00,000	180/100	3,60,000	Inventories	45,000	180/100	81,000
Retained Earnings	65,000		65,000	Land & Buildings	75,000	180/100	1,35,000
Accumulated Depreciation	20,000	180/100	36,000	Plant & Machinery	1,00,000	180/100	1,80,000
	3,85,000		5,61,500		3,85,000		5,61,000

Merits of CPPA Method

The chief merits of CPPA method of inflation accounting may be noted as under:

1. This method is conceptually a sound method as it is rightly

concerned with the change in the general level of prices i.e. inflation.

2. The method provides an objective basis for converting the historical costs into current costs as it uses the current price index which is published by a reliable agency.
3. The inter-firm comparison of annual accounts is objective and dependable as the same criterion to represent the current values is used by different firms.
4. The capital of the enterprice is maintainable as the method attempts to provide depreciation on current cost and recognize the loss on holding the monetary assets.
5. Replacement, cost of assets is nearer to the current purchasing power of which adjustments in accounts are made. The management is in a position to replace any asset conveniently when CPPA method is used to incorporate the effect of inflation in account books and accordingly manage the finances.
6. Income measurement is scientific as the matching of revenues and expenses is based on the same value.
7. The CPPA method provides useful information to management to understand the impact of inflation on different firms working with different capital-mix and asset structure and adjust its own policies for optimising income of shareholders.

Limitations of CPPA Method

The method has been criticised due to the following limitations:

1. General price level may not necessarily reflect the current cost of an asset for which we need specific price index. Therefore, the method should be applied with due care.
2. Selection of an appropriate Index Number is itself a difficult task. The result based on cost of living Index Number may be different from that of indices of producers goods. Sometimes, the correctness of available Index Numbers is also doubtful.
3. Calculation of purchasing power loss/gain on monetary items does not serve any tangible gain except that it leads to more confusion in the minds of users of inflation adjusted statements. A highly levered company is likely to show high gains on borrowed funds and over-statement of its profits in a period of inflation

4. Tax authorities do not agree to the method of profit measurement for tax purposes under Inflation Accounting method. This limits the use of the technique for reporting profits on current purchasing power basis .
5. The CPPA is not suitable for small scale undertakings due to its being a costly affair as it requires technical knowledge and other resources for its proper implementation on regular basis
6. Maintenance of operating capability of an enterprise remains unsolved in a period of inflation due to gradual depletion of working capital.

The CPPA method is considered a true Inflation Accounting method despite its limitations for the simple reasons that it offers a simple and objective solution to the problem, specially in a period when an economy is passing through a phase of high degree of Inflation when the prices of all goods move in the same direction.

Current Cost
Or
Replacement Cost Accounting

The basic problem concerning assets management is the replacement of existing capital equipments by new ones at the time of expiry of their life without economic difficulties. This is possible when adequate funds in the form of accumulated depreciation have been created during the life time of assets. Another related problem is the presentation of current cost or replacement cost in the Balance Sheet for rational decision-making by users of Balance Sheet. The Current Cost (replacement cost) Accounting (CCA) for truly reflecting the impact of inflation takes into account the current cost of individual assets by using specific Index Numbers instead of general price indices which are used in case of CPPA method. In order to ascertain current cost of assets, the services of expert valuers may also be utilized. The financial analyst should clearly understood the concept of current cost which is defined as the amount of cash or other consideration which is needed to buy a new asset of more or less similar nature.

Sandiland committee headed by Mr. Francis C.P.Sandiland appointed by the British Government in 1975 to examine various issues relating to Inflation Accounting had recommended the Current Cost Accounting (CCA) to deal with the changes that arise in the economic position of an undertaking as a result of inflation. According to CCA method, the accounts have to be readjusted as under:

1. Preparation of Income Statement for current year to determine current operating income by the application of matching principle.
2. Calculation of holding gains /loss for showing the same in Balance Sheet.
3. Presentation of Balance Sheet on current cost basis.

Following illustration clarifies the redrafting the annual accounts based on current cost Accounting technique.

Illustration—4

Gupta Hosiery Products Ltd. reported the following annual accounts:

Liabilities	*1994*	*1995*	*Assets*	*1994*	*1995*
Capital	80,000	80,000	Land & Building	70,000	70,000
Loans	70,000	70,000	Plant & Machinery	80,000	80,000
Reserve & Surplus	70,000	87,000	Inventives 1994-4000 units 1995-3000 units	44,000	33,000
Accumulated Depreciation	16,000	32,000	Debtors	26,000	46,000
			Cash	16,000	40,000
	2,36,000	2,69,000		2,36,000	2,69,000

Income Statement For 1995

Sales : 7000 units @ 50 per unit	3,50,000	
Less: cost of goods sold :		
opening inventory 4000 x 11	44,000	
Purchases 6000 x 20	1,20,000	
	1,64,000	
Less: Closing stock : 3000 x 11	33,000	1,31,000
		2,19,000

Gross Margin		
Operating Expenses		
Usual Expenses	1,75,500	
Depreciation	16,000	
Interest	10,500	2,02,000
Net Profit		17,000

You are required to redraft the Income Statement and the Balance Sheet for 1995 providing for the following as for the current Cost Accounting method of Inflation Accounting.

1. Replacement cost of land during 1995 was Rs. 130000 and the current cost of Plant & Machinery was estimated at Rs. 1,75000
2. The sales were made at the end of 1995 when the replacement cost of inventory was Rs.25 per unit.
3. The company has used FIFO method of inventory valuation.
4. Plant & Machinery has a life of 5 years.

Solution

Income Statement for the Year 1995 (Current Cost Method)

Sales-7000 units @ 50 per unit		3,50,000
Less cost of sales:		
Opening Inventory 4000 x 25	1,00,000	
Purchase 6000 x 25	1,50,000	
	2,50,000	
Less closing Inventory 3000 x 25	75,000	175,000
Gross Margin	1,75,000	
Less : Usual Expenses	1,75,500	
Interest	10,500	
Depreciation 20% of $\frac{(175000 + 80000)}{2}$	25,500	211,500
		(36,500)
Net operating profit (Before holding gains & losses)		

REALISED HOLDING GAINS

On Inventory :	
(a) Purchases 6000(25–20)	30,000
(b) Opening Inventory 1000(25–11)	14,000
On Depreciation :	9,500
(25,500–16,000)	53,500

BALANCE SHEET
As on 31st December 1995

Equity capital		80000	Land & Buildings	1,30,000
Loans		70,000	Plant & Machinery	
Reserve & Surplus			175,000	
Beginning Balance			Less Accumulated	
	70,000		Depreciation 70000	1,05,000
Operating Profit	(36,500)		Inventories 3000x25	75,000
Realised holding			Debtors	46000
gains	53,500		Cash	40000
Unrealised		87,000		
holding gains		1,59,000		
(Balancing figure)		3,96,000		396,000

Merits of CCA Method

1. Profit is realistically ascertained as the current revenue income is matched against the current cost of earning that revenue.
2. The method suggests the maximum amount which an undertaking can distribute by way of dividend without disturbing productions capability.
3. Segregation of operating income from that of holding gains is important from management point of view. Management can formulate realistic dividend policy when realized and unrealized holding gains are also considered in such policy-making.
4. The method is simple as it can be applied easily in re-drafting the annual accounts.

Demerits of CCA Method

1. The concept of current cost is not rigidly defined. The current cost of an existing asset will be different from the current cost of similar asset with some kind of technical improvements.
2. Ascertainment of current or replacement cost is a difficult problem. Expert valuation, introduces a lot of subjectivity in calculations.
3. The method ignores the gains or losses on holding monetary assets and liabilities.
4. It cannot be used with equal advantage in fixed assets and inventory intensive industries and in industries with few fixed assets and a high turnover of inventory.

Inflation Accounting Standards and Practices

During the last two decades or so, the Inflation Accounting has attracted the attention of professional accounting institutes, and other bodies of accountants and academicians both in developed as well as under-developed countries in the world. In 1969, the Accounting Principles Board (APB)in U.S.A. issued APB statement No.3 which recommended for the disclosure of supplementary price-level changes informations . Since them, the regulatory bodies i.e. the Financial Accounting standards Board and the Securities and Exchange Commission have issued Exposure Draft (1974) and Accounting series Release No. 190 (1976) respectively, which required the firms to furnish supplementary information regarding impact of inflation on their performance and economic position. The Financial Accounting Standard No.33(FAS 33) issued by FASB in 1979 requires mandatory supplementary informations regarding inflationary impact with a view to meeting the users objective of better informations on firms working. In the United Kingdom, Inflation Accounting was favoured by a statement of Accounting Practice No.7 (1974) which required the supplementary informations based on general Purchasing power accounting. Sandilands Committee in 1975 had recommended the Current Cost Accounting method for readjustment of final accounts prepared on historical cost accounting principles. The statement of Standard Accounting Practice-16 (SAP-16) in U.K. presently guides the preparation of accounts which should incorporate the impact of inflation.

The developments in U.S.A and U.K., have encouraged other

countries to think of Inflation Accounting as a means of proper education to management and other users of final accounts for rational decision-making . So far as India is concerned, the inflation accounting is still optional in the absence of any prescribed standard and majority of the Indian Companies publish the accounts based on historical costing. The Institute of Chartered Accountants of India had issued a Guidance Note on Accounting for price level changes in 1982. Few enlightened and progressive companies is private and public sector such as Hindustan Organic Chemicals Ltd., Bharat Heavy Electricals Ltd., Hindustan Machine Tools Ltd., Tata Iron & Steel Co., etc., have started publishing price-level adjusted final accounts for the information of the interested parties. Inflation accounting in India can be made compulsory by an amendment in the Indian Companies Act to the best advantage of companies and other users. The companies will be willing to reconstruct accounts as per the rules provided the tax authorities allow enhanced depreciation on replacement cost.

SOCIAL RESPONSIBILITY ACCOUNTING

Investors and those dealing in companies shares and debentures are directly interested in the operations of such undertakings. The government agencies such as Securities and Exchange Board of India and Board of Industrial and Financial Reconstructive (BIFR) are also keenly interested in the published accounts and other accounting detacts of public limited companies. In the modern time, the consumers and general public has also started taking interest in the economic affairs of large scale business enterprises which effect public life in a number of ways. The people of a particular region in which a large scale factory is set up, cannot ignore its effects on their life. Large scale industrialization brings economic prosperity to the people and effects substantial change in their life style. Simultaneously, it also brings some changes in physical and social environment in which their health and happiness deminish. The disadvantages of unplanned industrialization at a bigger scale are widely known. The welfare governments try to eliminate or minimise the harmful effects of setting up of large scale factories through various legislative measures. Efforts are also made to bring out improvements in the prevailing condition by encouraging public awareness and developing a sense of social responsibility among the industrialists.

The manufacturers and sellers earn a part of profit at the cost of the public. They are not required to pay any extra cost, e.g., for the environmental pollution which the factories create by virtue of the very nature of production. The pollution is injurious to public health and the public has to bear the cost in the form of additional expenditure on medical care and reduced incomes. Therefore, public would expect some kind of compensation against the cost it bears and it would also like to know the policies and programmes of the factories to safeguard the interests of the public. With public awareness and interest taken by the government, the social accounting or social responsibility accounting is a new area in accounting which is emerging fastly with the rapid industrial development in the developing countries in the world.

Social Responsibility Accounting

Social responsibility accounting is not a separate branch of accounting but it is simply on accounting technique which seeks to highlight the social responsibility of business in addition to its economic obligations. Social responsibility of business firms is increasingly being recognised by the government and by all those who feel concerned for public welfare. The enlightened business enterprises realise their responsibility towards the society at whose cost they earn super-normal profits. The public through its elected representatives have started questioning the performance of large scale enterprises in terms of social benefits and the progressive public limited companies provide informations relating to their activities for social good Social responsibility accounting is concerned with identification of the areas of social concern, measurement of social costs and social benefits and reporting the same informations alongwith the published accounts to satisfy public interest and also with a view to show true and fair view of the operations and economic position of business enterprises. The terms such as Social Accounting and 'Societal Accounting' have also been used in place of social responsibility accounting without disturbing the nature and scope of the subject. Therefore, the usage of one term in place of another does not make any difference. However, the term social accounting gives an impression of national accounts and may be avoided in the interest of the clarity of message.

The main objectives of social responsibility accounting are: (a) Creation of public awareness regarding social costs and social benefits of a factory in their locality or regions, (b) Government involvement in safeguarding the health and well-being of the public which is exposed to harmful effects of the industry, (e) Developing consciousness among other social welfare organisations regarding industrial locations and their impact on society, (d) Construction and publication of annual accounts which incorporate social responsibility of business.

The achievement of the above objectives is vital in the interest of the society and enterprisers. With increasing public awareness, the entrepreneurs will be forced to create facilities to neutralise the harmful effects on society of their enterprises and they will also be able to understand realistic economic position of their enterprises and accordingly inform the outside interested parties for their investment decisions. It may be pointed out that in the developed countries, a public limited company which is engaged in large scale business activity is not regarded an economic business entity exclusively for profit-making but it is also required to perform its social responsibility by undertaking social activities for public welfare. In developing countries the social responsibility is also gaining grounds.

AREAS OF SOCIAL RESPONSIBILITY

Social responsibility of business is not only confined to prevent and minimise the harmful effects of pollution but it is extended to other equally important areas such as community involvement, human resource development, product improvements and fair business practices, energy conservation, etc. Each area of social responsibility covers wide range of activities such as mentioned below:

1. Community Involvement

Social performance in this area relates to corporate support to educational institutions, cultural activities, recreational performances, health and welfare activities. Aid in personal problems concerning physically handicapped and child care is considered as a great social responsibility of business in modern times. Encouraging and providing time for employees and to be active as volunteers in community activities is also an important part of corporate social responsibility.

2. Environmental Contribution

A clear, and clear environment is highly important for the health of the society. The establishment of factories in a particular region pollute the environment through the emission of different gases and its waste materials and thus cause harm to the social health. The study of the benefits being enjoyed by the industry and the cost being borne by the society in terms of injury to its health is a subject-matter which form part of the social accounting.

3. Conservation of Physical Resources

Physical resources conservation is considered as one of the important social responsibility of today's manufacturing firms. Energy and scarce raw materials need to be used economically, and new resources developed to meet the industry requirements. Society in general and the investors in particular want that the information on these issues is disclosed in the annual accounts of companies.

4. Product Contribution

It is the social responsibility of business that it does not ignore the interests of the consumers and provide right type of goods at reasonable rates with assured supply and attend to all consumer complaints promptly. Consumers education is regarded as one of the important components of social responsibility of modern entrepreneurs, through the supply of relevant literature and media programmes to keep the consumers informed of the characteristics of product or services.

5. Human Resources

Creation of job apportunities, enhancement of workers skill through education and training, continuity of employment, recruitment in depressed areas, adequate wages, provision of congenial working condition recognition of workers ability and providing equal opportunity for promotion etc., are the vital areas of social responsibility of business enterprises. Provision of education and counselling for employees to prevent or alleviate problems arising out of use of drugs and alcohal by employees is an area of social responsibility which is emerging fastly.

Method of Presentation

The social responsibility of business has been widely recognised and as such the society has the right to be informed of the activities which have been undertaken to compensate it for the cost it bears for the economic benefits of the industry. It is on the basis of such an information alone the society can decide to support or oppose the business programmes of an interprise. The evil effects of an industrial enterprise in a locality are so indirect and slow that the members of the locality pay no attention to it. With an increase in education and knowledge, a lots of awakening is witnessed these days among the ordinary members of the society that they are always prepared to come out openly against the government and industry which may cause harm to their life through the industrial activities in the long-run. Thus the industry cannot ignore the interests of the society while planning their business activities.

So far as the publication of information on social activities by Indian Companies is concerned, the picture is quite grim as majority of enterprises do not care for social good and the publication of such information is not statutory. However, there are some enlightened companies which publish information relating to their social activities for the information of the society. Most of the information provided is in a descriptive form as there is no standard format on which such information could be furnished. Generally, the information relating to social responsibility areas is provided in the Directors Report. Tata Iron and Steel Company one of the premier private sector giant gives sufficient details of expenditure on its social activities for the benefits of employees and the community of the surrounding areas. Some of the public sector companies not only provide social accounts in descriptive form but also in an account from which give a better and accurate idea about their social responsibilities. Public Sector Companies such as SAIL, BHEL, MMTC, IPCL, etc. have been publishing detailed accounts of their social cost-benefits. At present the public sector companies are required to disclose an account of benefits and social overhead costs alongwith the annual accounts.

The Steel Authority of India Limited (SAIL) prepares Social Income Statement and also a Social Balance Sheet. The Social Income statement in divided into: (i) Social benefits and cost to employees, (ii) Social benefits and costs to community, and (iii) Social benefits and costs to General public. The statements also show net social income/cost to employees, community and the general public. The Social Balance Sheet depicts the social funds and the social capital investments on the date of Balance Sheet. The company generates funds through own-equity and social equity contributed by employees. The funds are utilised for purchase of land, residential and other buildings, roads and bridges, electrification, water supply and severage, furniture and fittings, human resources investment, etc.

The social responsibility accounting relating to general public includes various items of social benefits to general public and social cost to general public as shown below:

Social Benefits and Cost to General Public

A. Social Benefits to General Public

(a) Taxes, duties and levies paid to :	
(i) Central Government	—
(ii) State Governments	—
(b) Business generation	—
(c) Foreign Exchange	—
(i) Earned	—
(ii) Saved	—
(d) Research and development efforts	—
Total Benefits to General Public	—

B. Social Cost to General Public

(a) Social services and facilities consumed	—
(b) State services and facilities consumed	—
(e) Foreign exchange spent	—
Total Social Cost to General Public	—
Net Social Income/Cost to General Public	—

The statements in terms of monetary units give a better and accurate idea of the social responsibility of business. But the preparation of accurate quantitative statements is in itself a challenge. It is felt that the quantification of the cost in money value is a very difficult task. It is not possible to exactly calculate the social services and facilities consumed by the enterprise. Similarly it is a complex problem to calculate the damage done to the Wealth of the society (social cost) due to environmental pollution caused by a factory in a particular area. The expenditure which is required to treat the ailments of the community due to environmental pollution is the social cost which should ultimately be borne by the enterprises. An estimation of such a cost is possible and the enterpreneur should either pay the cost to government who provides the medical facilities or make necessary provision for preventive or curative methods of treatment. The social costs payments to government will be in addition to the corporate tax imposed on companies but this showed be a tax deductible item.

HUMAN RESOURCE ACCOUNTING

Human Resource is an important element in any production endeavour though the machines are rapidly replacing labour in the modern scientific age of production. Material resources—machines and materials cannot be put to economic use without human resources which means energies, skill and knowledge of people which are available to a firm for productive purposes. In fact human resources are as good as any other asset as the former actively contribute in the profitability of an organisation whereas the role of the latter in achieving the objectives is quite passive. The importance of human assets in an undertaking may be realized from the fact that all the material resources will be rendered useless or unproductive if they are not attended by trained, experienced and sincere work forces. It is a matter of satisfaction that the importance of human resource as a potent force of production is being realised in almost all the productive ventures in the modern time and this resource is being accorded a high status than that of the consumable physical assets.

The industry practice in the past has been to pay special attention for management of physical resources i.e., inventory management, depreciation policy, amrtization of wasting assets, treatment of capitalized revenue expenditure, etc. Very little attention has been devoted to upgrade human resources through investment in the form of additional expenditure on hiring, education, training, health and satisfaction of people who are the real assets in any organisation. The industrial enterprises have shown more interest to evaluate the performance in terms of total funds deployed for production without any regard to the nature of labour intensity and the role of human resource in total production. Capital-light industries are likely to show a higher Rate of Returns (RoI) simply because the constitution of man-power is much more than the investment in the form of physical assets. Productivity per worker should, in fact, be a certain to judge the performance in such enterprises.

Most of the organisations have no objection in recognising Human Resource as an asset but they do not fully appreciate the significance of this vital asset as it does not find its due place in their final accounts. The only information available with financial accounts is a certain category of labour drawing salary exceeding certain limits. The concept of cost of investment in Human Resources or the value of the assets to the organisation is missing in the conventional accounting system which considers the amount spent an hiring, training and development as usual expenditure of business despite the fact that the implications of such an expenditure are long-term and it is for an asset which is full of life and sensibilities. Disregard to human asset consisting of human energies skills and knowledge results in high labour-turnover and frustration amongst margst the workers which limits the industrial growth. In the absence of adequate data regarding investments in human resources, the management is not in a position to effectively plan and control human resources. Therefore, the Human Resource Accounting should form an integral part of the conventional accounting for generating and reporting information relating to human resources for managerial purposes.

Human Resource Accounting (HRA) may be treated as a process of identifying, measuring and reporting human resources of an organisation. The American Accounting Association has defined HRA as "the process of identifying and measuring data about human resources and communicating this information to interested parties." Thus HRA takes into account : (a) human resource as an asset, (b) measuring the cost of investment in human resources or estimating of the value of human resource to the organisation, (c) periodic evaluation of human asset, (d) reporting of HR investment in Balance Sheet or providing additional information with annual accounts. HRA serve useful purpose. It provides necessary data for decision-making by the management and other interested parties, help evaluation of the contribution of human resource in the performance of an undertaking and assist in reporting the worth of human resource to the organisation.

Accounting for Human Resource (HRA)

The first important step in Human Resource Accounting is the valuation of human resources. There one two methods of accounting for human resources as explained below:

1. Cost Method

According to this method, the costs incurred by an organisation on the acquisition of human assets and its further development through education and training is taken into account. This is the historical concept of cost, which may be substituted by another concept i.e. replacement cost. Thus, the human resource valuation may be done either according to historical costs or replacement costs.

Historical Cost Accounting

Historical Cost Accounting (HCA) takes into account the actual costs incurred on human resources. It consists of the ecquisition cost which is aggregation of cost incurred on recruitment, selection and hiring of people to meet the requirement of the organisation and the development costs which is needed to develop the quality of human asset through education and training. After having determined the historical costs, the next step would be to capitalise it and deal it the way the cost on acquisition of plant and machinery or any other fixed asset is treated. Since the human resource is employed for fairly long-period, the capitalized cost is to be written off during the period of employment of much resource. For example, if an amount Rs. 80,000 has been spent on the specialised training of an employee aged 50 years, then this amount may be written off during the 8 year's remaining service period before the retirement of the employee, by charging every year Rs. 10,000 to income statement. In case the employee leaves the employing firm for any reason, then the unwritten off amount may be written off in the year in which be leaves the firm. Similarly, if the investment in certain category of human resource becomes unproductive due to obsolescence, then also the remaining amount may be written off. Thus, the Balance Sheet on any given date will show the amount which remains invested in human resources.

From the above, it would appear that the Human Resource Accounting based on historical cost is quite simple. The success of this method depends upon the fair and realistic procedure of organisation to write off the human asset which has been consumed during a financial year. However, this is the most difficult task as it is very difficult to predict the human behaviour and the contingencies involved due to typical nature of assets. It is not possible for management to know the stage at which a particular employee or a group of employees will leave the firm as the labour mobility cannot be restricted through artificial means. There is no specified time for death or abrupt changes in the health conditions of employees. Thus, a firm cannot adopt a particular procedure to write off the investments in human resources. The experience of the management would be quite helpful in developing a satisfactory procedure for amortisation of human assets. The procedure, once adopted may be reviewed from time to time in the light of the changes in the health condition of employees and the development of new production techniques which requires further training of industrial workers.

Advantages of HCA

Historical cost-based accounting for Human Resources offers advantages such as, (i) It is simple to understand and apply as it uses the conventional techniques of cost accumulation and cost expiration. (2) It provides useful informations which may be used by personnel managers in planning and control of man-power in the best interest of the organisation. (3) Inter-departmental data with regard to investments in human resource provides useful information which keeps on changing by inter-departmental transfers of workers.

Limitations of HCA

Following limitations reduce the utility of HRA based on historical costs : (1) The measurement of costs which must be capitalised creates some problem. Cost-expiration procedure causes the main problem for which there is no standard solution. There is always scope for subjective valuation which reduces the reliability of human resources. (2) It is argued that the investment in human resources as shown in the Balance Sheet represents nothing more than the unamortised costs which was incurred in past years. It is not related in any way to the contribution of human resources to the total production or profitability of the organisation. The energy, skill and capabilities cannot be represented by the cost spent an human resource and development. (3) Historical cost cannot be used as a basis for decision-making for future under changing business environment. Investment in human resources is undervalued under condition of inflation. (4) This method is least useful to investors who cannot understand the current costs of human resources.

Replacement Costs

Replacement cost is the cost of replacing the existing human resources by the new resources of the same productive capabilities. In other words, it is the current valuation of the historical cost of human resources. Replacement cost can be positional or personal. Positional replacement cost may be defined as the sacrifice which must be incurred to replace a person with another person of the same capability. It consists of three elements i.e., acquisition cost, development cost and separation cost. The concepts of acquisition and development costs are quite clear. Separation cost refers to the cost which an organisation has to bear as a result of leaving the position or job by an employee. On the termination of an employee, three types of cost arise. They are separation compensation cost, differential pre-separation performance cost and vacant position cost. Separation compensation cost is the payments made to the employees leaving the firm. Differential pre-separation performance cost is the cost of lost productivity prior to separation of emplyees whose tendency is to go slow before leaving a firm, and the vacant position cost is incurred during the period the search for replacement is continued. Under Replacement Cost Accounting method, the Balance Sheet will show the replacement cost of investment in human resources instead of historical costs. Replacement Costing method of Human Resource Accounting suggests process of finding out the replacement cost on continuous basis.

Replacement costing method of human resources valuation attempts to measure the current economic values of investment in human assets which make the Balance Sheet a true statement of current economic position of an enterprise. The replacement cost informations are not only useful to management for internal decision-making but they are equally important to outside investors in understanding the real strength of any organisation. The utility of replacement costs is enhanced if it does not vary widely from the economic value of human resources to the organisation to which it belongs. The replacement cost should, however, be used with care keeping in view the difficulties in its measurement. The replacement cost may not be assessed objectively to give colour to Balance Sheet and it will be a fruitless exercise if the organisation is indifferent or unable to replace an outgoing member of the team by a new incumbent of the similar capability.

2. Human Resource Value Accounting (HRVA)

HRVA seeks to measure the value of human resources in terms of its contribution in the benefits which a firm desires from its operations. The calculation of value of human resources on the basis of benefits accruing to a firm is a technical job for which models have been developed by different authors.

Lev and Schwartz have suggested a model which attempts to estimate the human capital value of a person for a firm. According to their Model, the future expected average earnings of different grades of labour upto the age of retirement are estimated and discounted at the rate which is equal to cost of capital. The calculated. aggregate of present values for all categories of employees will represent the value of human capital to the firm. This method is useful in so far as it gives value which can be compared with other non-human capital in order to understand the labour intensity in any firm. It can also be used with the help of the rate of growth in human capital, the structure of labour force i.e. whether the firm has an ageing labour force or a younger labour force. An increasing rate of growth will obviously imply that younger persons are being inducted into the firm. Lew and Schwartz Model has been criticised on the ground that the estimation of a reliable figure of future earnings is not an easy task as the grades of labour keeps on changing and the concept of cost of capital is not always rigidly defined. The utility of the human resources data is reduced due to these limitations.

Another model known as Flamholtz's model seeks to measure the human capital investment on the basis of the contribution of human assets in the total economic value of a firm. The economic value of a firm is to be determined by calculating the present value of future expected earnings. Flamholtz is of the view that an individual is not valuable in the abstract but he is valuable due to personal attributes and in relation to his role and the characteristics of the organisation. He has identified the variables which determine the value of an individual to a firm. The view that the human resource valuation is closely linked with its contribution in the total economic value of a firm seems sound but the problems associated with such valuations make the economic valuation method merely a theoritical proposition.

There is another model Harmanson's model which has developed the idea of super-normal profit (profit in excess of normal profit) as a measure of human resource valuation. The method of valuation of Human Resource as developed by Harmonson is known as Unpurchased Goodwill Method as the super-normal profits give rise to goodwill. According to his model, the human asset valuation may be explained in this manner. Suppose, the average normal return an owned assets (tangible assets) during the last five years has been 10% whereas a firm enjoyed a return of 15% on its owned assets of Rs. 60,000. Total earnings in this case amounted to Rs. 9,000 (15% of 60,000). To earn Rs. 9,000 at 10% normal return, the total assets required are 90,000. Thus unowned assets or Human Resource should be valued at 30,000 (Rs. 90,000 – 60,000). This model fails to explain the existance of human capital in case there is no profit in excess of normal profit.

Advantages of HRA

The advantages of Human Resource Accounting may be listed as under:

1. Information relating to Human Resources is useful in developing man-power budgets.
2. Management is in a position to allocate reasonable funds for the development of human resources in the light of the contribution of human capital in the over-all value of any firm.
3. Incorporation of HRA information and its reporting with annual accounts provide objective assessment of a company's performance for rational decisions. Fair rate of return can be calculated only if the human asset is also taken into account and the Balance Sheet can be made to provide realistic state of economic affairs of the enterprise.
4. HRA is not only useful for human resource planning and, control but it is also advantageous to the investors who can properly value a firm only after having studied its human resources.

Limitations of HRA

1. The problems associated with the measurement of human resources are complex. There is no specific objective method of measurement of human resource due to which subjectivity enters into calculations and the data loose much of their reliability.

2. Some persons do not agree even with the idea of treating human resources as an asset owned by the proprietors.
3. HRA involve costs. Small Scale enterprises do not find it suitable for cost considerations.
4. There is no standard practice for measurement and reporting human resource asset. It is also not compulsory except that the companies are required to show few informations about their employees.

Owing to the above, the HRA has not gained favour with the industry. Only few enlightened companies in India both in the public and private sectors have made attempts to provide detailed informations with respect to their labour force and such an informations has been fund quite useful by the investing community.

RESPONSIBILITY ACCOUNTING

The nature of work in a large scale business enterprise is so complex that it is divided into 'divisions' or 'segments' on some basis so as to effectively carry out the work in each division or department for achieving the over-all objective of the enterprise. Each division enjoys necessary authority to control the business operations under its command to achieve standard performance which forms the basis to evaluate his accountability towards the organisation. The idea underlying such an organisational structure is to achieve over-all efficiency by delegating authority to divisional managers or departmental heads who are held responsible for the results expected of them by the top management. Responsibility accounting is a system of accounting under which responsibility of each divisional executive is established and a system of reporting developed to ensure timely action in cases the responsibility is not being discharged according to the expectations of top management.

Definition

Different authors on the subject have defined Responsibility accounting in different manners. According to Anthony and Reece "Responsibility Accounting is that type of management accounting that collects and reports both planned and actual accounting information in terms of responsibility centre." This definition recognises responsibility accounting as a system of management reporting about responsibility centres. More or less similar view has been expressed by J.A. Higgind who says, "It is a system of accounting which is tailored to an organisation so that costs are accumulated and reported by levels of responsibility within the organisation. Each supervisory area in the organisation is charged only with the cost for which it is responsible and over which it has control." Charles T. Horngren defines responsibility accounting as "a system of accounting that recognizes various responsibility centres throughout the organization and reflects the plans and actions of each of these centres by assigning particular revenues and costs to the one having the pertinent responsibility. It is also called profitability accounting and activity accounting." According to this definition, the Responsibility Accounting is concerned with,

(a) Identification and establishment of responsibility centres. A responsibility centre is a sub-unit under the control of an executive officer who may be called a divisional manager.

(b) Charging each responsibility centre with specific functions or activities to perform and

(c) Evaluating the performance of divisional manager in terms of costs and revenues. Costs represent the values of physical and financial resources in monetary terms and revenues measure the output in money values.

Implementation of Responsibility Accounting

Following steps are required to be taken to implement the responsibility accounting in an organisation:

1. Classification of organisation in suitable responsibility entres is the first important step towards the implementation of R.A. A responsibility centre is a sub-unit under the charge of a manager who is wholly responsible for the operation of that responsibility centre. A responsibility centre may be created in such a manner that it is distinguishable as a separate sub-unit of the organisation for operation and control purposes.

2. Defining the authority and responsibility of heads of each unit division in the organisation is necessary for the success of R.A. system, which, infact, is based on authority and responsibility relationship.

3. Designing an effective reporting system so that the manager of a

responsibility centre receives necessary information in time and there is continuous appraisal system to keep the managers conscious of costs and revenues.

4. Taking necessary corrective action in cases of less than standard performance (adverse variances) and also reporting the same to the responsibility centres for improving efficiency in future.

Objectives

Responsibility Accounting in an organisation may be implementated with the following objectives:

A. To simplify management problems of a large business undertaking.
B. To achieve over-all efficiency through the performance of responsibility centres.
C. To ascertain the contribution of individual responsibility centres with a view to understand their relative importance to the organisation.
D. To measure the performance of divisional managers in charge of responsibility centres. It is possible that a responsibility centre might not show satisfactory contribution towards organisational goals despite best efforts by a responsibility centre manager.
E. To motivate divisional managers to perform well in the interest of the organisation through a system of ıesponsibility accounting which appreciates and provides incentives for efficient discharge of duties.
F. To provide basis for Management By Exception which means focussing the attention of management on deviations which exceed tolerable limits.

Responsibility Centres

A responsibility centre in an organisation is a sub-unit for doing specified activities by a responsible officer who is empowered to control over those activities but is held responsible for the performance of the sub-unit under his charge. The size of a sub-unit (Responsibility Centre) which may also be called a department, division or segment, varies according to the nature of work done therein. It can be as large as the production department or as small as an advertising call in an organisation. On the basis of type of data used to measure performance, an organisation may be classified into three centres viz. (a) Cost Centre, (b) Profit Centre and (c) Investment Centre.

Cost Centre

A cost centre is a responsibility centre which consumes resources or incur costs which is measured in monetary terms. It may be noted that the cost centre is concerned with costs (inputs) only; the revenue (output) is not considered in the measurement of performance, as the costs do not give rise to revenue directly. The cost which is directly traceable to the cost centre should only be brought in the calculation of Cost Centre Indirect Cost which are incurred for the organisation as a whole are not within the direct control of the manager of a Cost Centre; therefore, such costs are excluded in the measurement of their efficiency. These is some controversy over the exclusion of output (revenue) from the measurement of efficiency of cost centre but majority of experts believe that cost is a satisfactory measure of efficiency as output is not measurable in many cases. It would be quite logical to measure efficiency of Cost Centres such as legal department, labour welfare department, advertising division, etc. in terms of costs as the measurement of output (revenue) is full of complexities. The difference between the actual costs and the standard costs specified for the responsibility centre would reflect the efficiency of Cost Centre.

Profit Centre

Profit Centre is a responsibility centre which takes into account both the cost (input) and revenue (output) in the measurement of its efficiency. The difference between revenue and cost is profit which is compared with some profit figures in the past or standard profit, if any, to measure efficiency of the divisional manager in charge of profit centre. For the purpose of measurement of profit, the concept of cost remains the same as in case of cost centre but the concept of revenue (output measurement) is different from its traditional meaning based an accrual principle. Revenue of profit centre will be arrived at simply by valuing the total output at a rate at which output can be disposed off. The surplus of Profit centre is the profit before the recovery of fixed expenses which are incurred for the organisation as a whole and also before income tax which is also payable for the organisation as a whole.

The Profit Centre in an organisation is a better and more effective measure of efficiency as it considers both input (expenses) and output revenue) as against Cost Centre which traces and measures costs only. It generates consciousness to show satisfactory profit and the management is always in a position to safely de-centralize power and authority to the divisional manager in charge of profit centre. However, the Profit Centre encounters the following problems which should be resolved carefully for the proper operation of the centre.

1. Establishment of a responsibility centre as a profit centre is itself a problem. The successful operation of profit centre is also governed by the degree of freedom enjoyed by the divisional manager in deciding about the nature of output. If the authority is limited, the profit centre cannot work as an effective control technique.

2. Measurement of cost is another problem which gives rise to controversy about profit centre. Those costs which are traceable directly to a profit centre should be taken into account in the measurement of efficiency and no other cost should be brought into calculations.

3. Inter-centres transfers of goods and services cause problem insofar as the pricing of such transfers is concerned. Cost and revenues of centres are affected by the method of pricing of goods and services exchanged between the departments. The problem of transfer pricing should be carefully solved so that the measurement of performance is not unduly affected by pricing methods.

There are various methods of pricing the goods which are supplied and received between the responsibility centres. Any one of the following pricing methods may be adopted but no one is without drawback

Cost Price. It is the unit cost of production to the supplying division. The use of cost price for pricing of goods from one department to another is quite simple and convenient but it is not considered suitable for profit centre analysis due to distortions in profits. The profit of the supplying division will not contains any element of profit on the goods supplied whereas the profit of receiving division will be increased to the extent profit is not included in the goods so received.

Cost Plus Pricing. It is the price which includes some amount of profit in the cost price. In other words, the cost plus price is the cost price plus profit at a specified rate which is either the rate which can be realised if goods are disposed off in the open market or a rate which management considers reasonable for transfer purposes. Fixation of profit rate introduces subjectivity in the performance analysis.

Market Price. It is the price at which goods are actually exchanged in the market. Market Price is determined by market forces and as such it cannot be influenced by individual actions of divisional managers, who should normally agree to pricing the goods at the prevailing market rates. In case the market quotations are not readily available, the cost plus pricing which conform to market pricing, should be taken for the valuation of goods exchanged between the responsibility centres to measure their effectiveness.

Negotiated Price. It is the price which is settled between the parties through mutual negotiations. The pricing of goods transferred from one division to another at negotiated price serves the interests of the supplier as well as the receiver of goods. However proper negotiations are possible if the supplier has a choice to sell outside and the buying segment has also a choice to buy from outside where buyers and sellers for similar goods exist.

Investment Centre

Investment centre is that segment of an organisation which is held responsible not only for costs and revenues but also effective utilization of investments in the form of assets. Assets are said to have been effectively utilised if their utilization yields a fair rate of return. Thus, an investment centre is concerned with controlling inputs (cost) output (revenue) and investment (assets utilization) with a view to perform so well that it earns a reasonable rate of return on investment. Return on Investment (ROI) is the proportion of net income to total assets as shown below:

$$\text{ROI} = \frac{\text{Net Income}}{\text{Total Assets}}$$

Actually, the ROI is a function of profit margin and asset-turnover and as such their combined action determines ROI. Therefore, ROI may be interpreted in terms of profit margin an Sales and the proportion of Sales to total assets.

$$ROI = \frac{\text{Net Income}}{\text{Sales}} \times \frac{\text{Sales}}{\text{Total Assets}}$$

The performance of an Investment Centre is reported in terms of Return an Investment (ROI) and is compared with cost of investment or rate specified by management for measurement of performance of the Profit Centre. ROI is fairly a good measure of performance reporting but it involves some practical problems in its calculations due to the problems associated with the assignment of values to different assets and their traceability to investment centre. The determination of net income is also subject to difference of opinion as to the exclusion of interest and taxes from the total income for a year. In view of these difficulties, the concept of residual income may be applied in the measurement of performance of profit centre. Residual income is the excess of income over standard/ expected income of the profit centre. If the excess of income so arrived at is positive, then the performance is considered goods; otherwise the performance is bad for which responsibility of the divisional manager is fixed. It may be noted that the application of residual income' in the measurement of performance is also not perfect as it is not free from the problem of estimation.

Performance Reporting

A CASE OF A COST CENTRE

Items	*Budgeted cost*	*Actual cost*	*Variance*	*% Variance*
Raw Materials	2,75,000	3,00,000	25,000 (A)	–9.1
Labour cost	3,25,000	3,75,000	50,000 (A)	–15.4
Overheads-Directly traceable	50,000	40,000	10,000 (F)	+ 20.0
Total	6,50,000	7,15,00	65,000 (A)	–10%

The performance report of the cost centre has revealed that the costs of materials and labour have gone up beyond the budgeted costs whereas the responsibility manager has been able to save overhead cost. The manager would explain the increase in costs and the future costs will be set up accordingly.

A CASE OF PROFIT CENTRE

Particulars	*Budgeted figures*	*Actual figures*	*Variance*	*% Variance*
Revenue:				
Outside supplies	2,00,000	1,55,000	–45,000	–22.5%
Inter-departmental supplies	6,00,000	6,20,000	+ 20,000	+ 3.3%
Total	8,00,000	7,75,000	25,000 (A)	–3.1% (A)
Costs:				
Raw Materials	3,25,000	3,07,540	+ 17,550	+ 5.4
Labour	2,60,000	3,21,750	–23.75	
Overheads	65,000	85,800	–20,800	–32.00
Total	6,50,000	7,15,000	65,000 (A)	–10% (A)
Profit	1,50,000	60,000	90,000 (A)	–60% (A)

The performance of the profit centre as indicated by a decline of profit by 60% is, obviously, below expectations. According to responsibility accounting, the cause for such a poor state of affairs have to be investigated, responsibility fixed and future plans adjusted. The possible causes for decline in profit may be the increase in costs, decrease in volume of output, decline in selling and supplies rates, wastages in production, etc. A look into the budget would suggest whether the budgeted figures were realistically fixed. The success of responsibility accounting will depend the consideration of all aspects which affect the costs and revenue and the steps which may be taken to improve the position in the future periods.

A Case of an Investment Centre: As we know that a Investment Centre is not only concerned with the costs, revenue and absolute figure of profit but also the rate of return on assets (investment) employed by the centre. Therefore, the profit and the assets employed to earn those profits have to be correlated to determine rate of return. A comparison of budgeted or expected rate of return with actual rate will show the performance of the profit centre. Relevant figures as shown to below show the performance of an hypothetical Investment Centre.

PERFORMANCE REPORT — 1995-96

Items	*Budgeted figures*	*Actual figures*	*Variance (±)*	*% Variance*
Revenue	1,50,00,000	1,70,00,000	+ 13.3	
Costs	1,08,00,000	1,10,00,000	- 2,00,000	- 1.8
Profit	42,00,000	60,00,000	+ 18,00,000	+ 42.8
Total Assets	2,30,00,000	2,50,00,000	+ 20,00,000	+ 8.7
Rate of Return (ROI)	18.26%	24%	+ 5.74%	—

Plus performance of the Investment centre is indicative of its satisfactory performance which is appreciable by the management. However, there is always scope for further improvement in working and the management may explore the possibilities of enhancing profitability by reducing costs which has shown adverse variance.

QUESTIONS

1. "Traditional Financial Statements fail to depict If true operational performance and economic portion of an enterprice." Do you agree with this Statement ? If yes, explain the manner in which the historical accounting causes distortions in the final accounts of a company.
2. What are the different techniques of Inflation Accounting? Explain the disclosure requirements of FAS-33 and SAP-16 by firms in USA and U.K. respectively.
3. Discuss the features, merits and limitations of CPPA method and CCA of Inflation Accounting.
4. What is inflation Accounting? Is there any real advantage of accounting for inflation? Why are the companies in India apprehensive of the use of Inflation Accounting ?
5. What are monetary and non-monetary items? How are they dealt in the price-level adjusted final accounts.
6. How do you decide about a conversion factor for converting items of revenue and expenses in terms of purchasing power equivalent to year-end rupee? Explain with example.
7. A company had 1000 shares of Uniplas India Ltd. @ Rs.60/- per share in the beginning of 1988 when the general price Index was 100. The company sold the whole lot of investment on 31St December 1995 for Rs.90000 when the Price Index was 160. Calculate the gain/loss of the invensting company.
8. Calculate the loss an holding cash balances in respect of the following transactions:

Date	*Particulars*	*Amount (Rs)*	*Price Index*
1-1-1995O	Opening cash balance	1500	100
15-1-1995	Cash sales	5500	110
15-1-1995	Cash disbursement	2000	110
31-1-1995	Closing cashbalance	5000	120

9. A company installed Three different machines with different life span in three different years and charged depreciation at a fixed rate upto the year ending 1990. The details are furnished as under:-

Year of Purchase	*Cost Price*	*Life in years*	*Depreciation Rate*	*Price Index*
1975	30,000	20	5%	100
1980	45,000	15	10%	180
1990	60,000	10	12%	300

You are required to prepare a Statement of Revaluation of assets and depreciation. The company proposes to charge depreciation at 15% on Diminishing Instatment method from the year beginning from 1st Jan. 1996. Pass the necessary Journal entries to record the charges in ledger using Index Numbers to revalue the assets.

10. The summarised Balance Sheet of xyz Ltd., as an 31st December 1995 is given below:

Liabilities	*Amount*	*Assets*	*Amount*
Capital	5,00,000	Plant & Machinery	
Loans	4,00,000	(net of depreciation)	8,00,000
Current liabilities	4,50,000	Current assets	5,50,000
	13,50,000		13,50,000

The Plant & Machinery was acquired at an index of 100 whereas the current index for similar assets is 180. Loans were obtained at an index of 150.

You are required to redraft the Balance Sheet so as to show all assets and equity in terms of current rupee.

11. Following are the Balance Sheets of Prefect Ltd. based on historical cost accounting :

Liabilities	*1994 (Rs)*	*1995 (Rs)*	*Assets*	*1994 (Rs)*	*1995 (Rs)*
Capital	4,50,000	4,50,000	Plant	1,60,000	1,44,000
Reserve & Surplus	30,000	60,000	Building at cost	2,00,000	2,00,000
Creditor for goods	50,000	40,000	Stock	70,000	80,000
Debtors	75,000	90,000			
Cash	25,000	36,000			
	5,30,000	550,000		5,30,000	5,50,000

Prepare supplementary Income Statement and Balance Sheet at current values. Index Numbers prevailing at different timings were as under :-

1. General Price Index in the base year, 1985 was 100; It was 150 and 120 in 1994 and 1995 respectively.
2. Plant was purchased for Rs. 80,000 in 1985.
3. Building was also purchased in 1985.

12. What do you mean by Human Resource Accounting? What are the advantage and limitations of HRA?
13. Describe the methods of accounting for Human Resources in an enterprise.
14. Critically examine either the Historical Cost Accounting (HCA) or Human Resource Value Accounting (HRVA) method of accounting for Human Resources
15. Define Responsibility Accounting and explain its significance in the divisional performance analysis.
16. What is a responsibility centre? Give the classification of responsibility centres in a large scale business organisation.
17. What is a profit Centre? How do you solve the transfer pricing problem in the measurement of performance of a profit centre.
18. Prepare performance reports of Cost, Profit and Investment Centres for consideration of management. Use imaginary figures.
19. Write a detailed note a measurement of segment performance .

Select Bibliography

1. Anthony, R.N. : *Management Accounting: Text and Cases* (Illinois, Irwin, 1980).

2. Anthony, R.N. and J.S. Reece : *Management Accounting and Principles* (Taraporwala, Bombay, 1989).

3. Anthony and Welsch : *Fundamentals of Management Accounting,* Illionis, Irwin, 1981

4. Anthony and Dearden : *Management Control Systems: Text and Cases,* Illinois, Irwin, 1980.

5. Burke, W.L. and E.B. Smith : *Accounting for Management,* Law Book Co. Australia, 1966.

6 Batty, J. : *Management Accountancy,* Plymouth, English Language Book Service, 1975.

7. Betty, J. : *Advanced Cost Accountancy,* Macdonald and Evans, 1978.

8. Bierman, H., Jr. and : A.R. Derbin *Managerial Accounting: An Introduction,* New York, Macmillan, 1975

9. Bierman, Harold Jr. and Thomas R. Dyckman : *Managerial Costing,* Macmillan Publishing Company, New York, 1976

10. Bierman H., Jr. and S. Smidt : *Capital Budgeting Decisions,* Macmillan, London, 1975

11. Brown J.L. and L.R. Howard : *Principles and Practice of Management,* Accountancy English Language Book Society, London, 1975

12. Brock, Palmer and Archer : *Account Principles and Application,* McGraw Hills Book Co. III edition.
13. Carrison R.H. : *Managerial Accounting,* Business Publications, Dallas, 1982
14. Carsberg B. and T. Hope : *Current Issues in Accounting,* Philip Allen, Oxford, 1977
15. Copeland R.M. and P.E. Dascher : *Managerial Accounting,* John Wiley, New York, 1978
16. Chatov Robert, : *Corporate Financial Reporting,* The Free Press, New York, 1975
17. Childs W.H. : *Accounting For Management Control,* Simmonds Boardman Publishing Corpn. New York 1960
18. Decoster D.T. and E.L. Schafer : *Management Accounting — A Decision Emphasis,* John Wily, New York, 1979.
19. Edward J.D. and Others : *Managerial Accounting,* Richards D. Irwin Home Wood, 1978
20. Fregmen J.M. *Accounting for Managerial Analysis,* Irwin, Illinois, 1976
21. Gordon M.J. and G. Shillinglow : *Accounting: A Managerial Approach,* Irwin, Illinois, 1974
22. Gray, J. and K.S. Johnston : *Accounting and Management Action,* Mc Graw Hill, New York, 1973
23. Horace R. Block and Others : *Accounting Basic Principles,* Mc Graw Hells, 1990
24. Horngren Charles T. : *Accounting for Management Control,* Printice Hall, New Jersy, 1978
25. Horngren Charles T. : *Cost Accounting-A Managerial Emphasis,* Printice Hall, N. Delhi, 1977
26. Heitger, L.E. and S. Matulich : *Managerial Accounting,* Mc Graw Hill, New York, 1980

27. Hampton, J.J. : *Financial Decision-making,* Prentice Hall, New Delhi, 1980

28. Ijiri Y. : *The Foundation of Accounting Measurement,* Englewood Cliff, Printice Hall, 1967

29. J.D. Aggrawal : *Accounting for Financial Analysis,* Indian Institute for Finance, Delhi, 1993.

30. James C. Van Horne : *Fundamentals of Financial Management,* Prentice Hall, Englewood Cliffs, New Jersy, 1980

31. Khan M.Y. and P.K. Jain : *Management Accounting,* Tata Mc Graw Hill Publishing Co. New Delhi 1984.

32. Moore, C.L. and P.K. Jaedicke : *Managerial Accounting,* South Western Publishing Co., Ohio, 1980.

33. Porwal, L.S. : *Accounting Theory,* Mc Graw Hills, 1993

34. Robert S. Kaplan, Anthony A. Atkinson : *Advanced Management Accounting* II, edition, Printice Hall of India, Pvt. Ltd., New Delhi 1990

35. Rossed, J.H. and Others : *Managerial Accounting,* Charles E. Merril Publishing Co. Columbus, Ohio, 1989

36. Sizer, J, : *An Insight into Management Accounting,* Pitman, London, 1979.

38. Weston J.F. and E. Brigham : *Essential of Managerial Finance,* Halt, Rhinchard and Windson, New York. 1969

39. William, A.W. : *Accounting for Management Control,* Pitman, London, 1971

Index

APPENDIX

TABLE 1

Present value of Re. 1 payable or receivable at the end of each period

Future Years	4%	5%	6%	7%	8%	9%	10%	11%	12%	13%	14%	15%	16%
1	.9615	.9524	.9434	.9346	.9259	.9174	.9091	.9009	.8929	.8850	.8772	.8969	.8621
2	.9246	.9070	.8900	.8734	.8573	.8417	.8265	.8116	.7972	.7832	.7695	.7561	.7432
3	.8890	.8638	.8396	.8163	.7938	.7722	.7513	.7312	.7118	.6931	.6750	.6575	.6407
4	.8548	.8227	.7921	.7629	.7350	.7084	.6830	.6587	.6355	.6133	.5921	.5718	.5523
5	.8219	.7835	.7473	.7130	.6806	.6499	.6209	.5935	.5674	.5428	.5194	.4972	.4761
6	.7903	.7462	.7050	.6663	.6302	.5963	.5645	.5346	.5066	.4803	.4556	.4323	.4104
7	.7599	.7107	.6651	.6228	.5835	.5470	.5132	.4817	.4524	.4251	.3996	.3759	.3538
8	.7307	.6768	.6274	.5820	.5403	.5019	.4665	.4339	.4039	.3762	.3506	.3269	.3050
9	.7026	.6446	.5919	.5439	.5003	.4604	.4241	.3909	.3606	.3329	.3075	.2843	.2630
10	.6756	.6139	.5584	.5084	.4632	.4224	.3855	.3522	.3220	.2946	.2697	.2472	.2267
11	.6496	.5847	.5268	.4751	.4289	.3875	.3505	.3173	.2875	.2607	.2366	.2149	.1954
12	.6246	.5568	.4970	.4440	.3971	.3555	.3186	.2858	.2567	.2307	.2076	.1869	.1685
13	.6006	.5303	.4688	.4150	.3677	.3262	.2897	.2575	.2292	.2042	.1821	.1625	.1452
14	.5775	.5051	.4423	.3878	.3405	.2993	.2633	.2320	.2046	.1807	.1597	.1413	.1252
15	5553	4810	.4173	.3625	.3152	.2745	.2394	.2090	.1827	.1599	.1401	.1229	.1079
16	.5339	.4581	.3937	.3387	.2919	.2519	.2176	.1883	.1631	.1415	.1229	.1069	.0930
17	.5134	.4363	.3714	.3166	.2703	.2311	.1978	.1696	.1456	.1252	.1078	.0929	.0802
18	.4936	.4155	.3503	.2959	.2503	.2120	.1799	.1528	.1300	.1108	.0946	.0808	.0691
19	.4746	.3957	.3305	.2765	.2317	.1945	.1635	.1377	.1161	.0981	.0830	.0703	.0596
20	.4564	.3769	.3118	2584	.2146	.1784	.1486	.1240	.1037	.0868	.0728	.0611	.0514
21	.4388	.3589	.2942	.2415	.1987	.1637	.1351	.1117	.0926	.0768	.0638	.0531	.0443
22	.4220	.3419	.2775	.2257	.1839	.1502	.1229	.1007	.0826	.0680	0560	.0462	.0382
23	.4057	.3256	.2618	.2110	.1703	.1378	1117	.0907	0738	.0601	.0491	.0402	.0329
24	.3901	.3101	.2470	.1972	.1577	.1264	.1015	.0817	.0659	.0532	.0431	.0349	.0284
25	.3751	.2953	.2330	.1843	.1460	.1160	.0923	.0736	.0588	.0471	.0378	.0304	.0245

TABLE I (Contd.)

Present value of Re. 1 payable or receivable at the end of each period

Future Years	17%	18%	19%	20%	21%	22%	23%	24%	25%	26%	27%	28%	29%	30%
1	.8547	.8475	.8403	.8333	.8265	.8197	.8130	.8065	.8000	.7937	.7874	.7813	.7752	.7692
2	.7305	.7182	.7062	.6944	.6830	.6719	.6610	.6504	.6400	.6299	.6200	.6104	.6009	.5917
3	.6244	.6086	.5934	.5787	.5645	.5507	.5374	.5245	.5120	.4999	.4882	.4768	.4658	.4552
4	.5337	.5158	.4987	.4823	.4665	.4514	.4369	.4230	.4096	.3968	.3844	.3725	.3611	.3501
5	.4561	.4371	.4191	.4019	.3855	.3700	.3552	.3411	.3277	.3149	.3027	.2910	.2799	.2693
6	.3898	.3704	.3521	.3349	.3186	.3033	.2888	.2751	.2621	.2499	.2383	.2274	.2170	.2072
7	.3332	.3139	.2959	.2791	.2633	.2486	.2348	.2218	.2097	.1983	.1877	.1776	.1682	.1594
8	.2848	.2660	.2487	.2326	.2176	.2038	.1909	.1789	.1678	.1574	.1478	.1388	.1304	.1226
9	.2434	.2255	.2090	.1938	.1799	.1670	.1552	.1443	.1342	.1249	.1164	.1084	.1011	.0943
10	.2080	.1911	.1756	.1615	.1486	.1369	.1262	.1164	.1074	.0992	.0916	.0847	.0784	.0725
11	.1778	.1619	.1476	.1346	.1229	.1122	.1026	.0938	.0559	.0787	.0721	.0662	.0608	.0558
12	.1520	.1372	.1240	.1122	.1015	.0920	.0834	.0757	.0687	.0625	.0568	.0517	.0471	.0429
13	.1299	.1163	.1042	.0935	.0839	.0754	.0678	.0610	.0550	.0496	.0447	.0404	.0365	.0330
14	.1110	.0986	.0876	.0779	.0693	.0618	.0551	.0492	.0440	.0393	.0352	.0316	.0283	.0254
15	.0949	.0835	.0736	.0649	.0573	.0507	.0448	.0397	.0352	.0312	.0277	.0247	.0219	.0195
16	.0811	.0708	.0618	.0541	.0474	.0415	.0364	.0320	.0282	.0248	.0218	.0193	.0170	.0150
17	.0693	.0600	.0520	.0451	.0391	.0340	.0296	.0258	.0225	.0197	.0172	.0161	.0132	.0116
18	.0593	.0508	.0437	.0376	.0324	.0279	.0241	.0208	.0180	.0156	.0135	.0118	.0102	.0089
19	.0506	.0431	.0367	.0313	.0267	.0229	.0196	.0168	.0144	.0124	.0107	.0092	.0079	.0068
20	.0433	.0365	.0308	.0261	.0221	.0187	.0159	.0135	.0115	.0098	.0084	.0072	.0061	.0053
21	.0370	.0309	.0259	.0217	.0183	.0154	.0129	.0109	.0092	.0078	.0066	.0056	.0048	.0041
22	.0310	.0262	.0218	.0181	.0151	.0126	.0105	.0088	.0074	.0062	.0052	.0044	.0037	.0031
23	.0270	.0222	.0183	.0151	.0125	.0103	.0086	.0071	.0059	.0049	.0041	.0034	.0029	.0024
24	.0231	.0188	.0154	.0126	.0103	.0085	.0070	.0057	.0047	.0039	.0032	.0037	.0022	.0018
25	.0197	.0160	.0129	.0105	.0085	.0069	.0057	.0046	.0038	.0031	.0025	.0021	.0017	.0014

TABLE 2

Present value of Re. 1 payable or receivable *annually* at the end of each period i.e., for *N* years

Year	1%	2%	3%	4%	5%	6%	7%	8%	9%	10%
1	0.9901	0.9804	0.9709	0.9615	0.9524	0.9434	0.9346	0.9259	0.9174	0.9091
2	1.9704	1.9416	1.9135	1.8861	1.8594	1.8334	1.8080	1.7833	1.7591	1.7355
3	2.9410	2.8839	2.8286	2.7751	2.7232	2.6730	2.6243	2.5771	2.5313	2.4868
4	3.9020	3.8077	3.7171	3.6299	3.5459	3.4651	3.3872	3.3121	3.2397	3.1699
5	4.8535	4.7134	4.5797	4.4518	4.3295	4.2123	4.1002	3.9927	3.8896	3.7908
6	5.7955	5.6014	5.4172	5.2421	5.0757	4.9173	4.7665	4.6229	4.4859	4.3553
7	6.7282	6.4720	6.2302	6.0020	5.7863	5.5824	5.3893	5.2064	5.0329	4.8684
8	7.6517	7.3254	7.0196	6.7327	6.4632	6.2098	5.9713	5.7466	5.5348	5.3349
9	8.5661	8.1622	7.7861	7.4353	7.1078	6.8017	6.5152	6.2469	5.9852	5.7590
10	9.4714	8.9825	8.5302	8.1109	7.7217	7.3601	7.0236	6.7101	6.4176	6.1446
11	10.3677	9.7868	9.2526	8.7604	8.3064	7.8868	7.4987	7.1389	6.8052	6.4951
12	11.2552	10.5753	9.9539	9.3850	8.8632	8.3838	7.9427	7.5361	7.1607	6.8137
13	12.1338	11.3483	10.6349	9.9856	9.3935	8.8527	8.3576	7.9038	7.4869	7.1034
14	13.0038	12.1062	11.2960	10.5631	9.8986	9.2950	8.7454	8.2442	7.7861	7.3667
15	13.8651	12.8492	11.9379	11.1183	10.3796	9.7122	9.1079	8.5595	8.0607	7.6061
16	14.7180	13.5777	12.5610	11.6522	10.8377	10.1059	9.4466	8.8514	8.3125	7.8237
17	15.5624	14.2918	13.1660	12.1656	11.2740	10.4772	9.7632	9.1216	8.5436	8.0215
18	16.3984	14.9920	13.7534	12.6592	11.6895	10.8276	10.0591	9.3719	8.7556	8.2014
19	17.2261	15.6784	14.3237	13.1339	12.0853	11.1581	10.3356	9.6036	8.9501	8.3649
20	18.0457	16.3514	14.8774	13.5903	12.4622	11.4699	10.5940	9.8181	9.1285	8.5136
21	18.8571	17.0111	15.4149	14.0291	12.8211	11.7640	10.8355	10.0168	9.2922	8.6487
22	19.6605	17.6580	15.9368	14.4511	13.1630	12.0416	11.0612	10.2007	9.4424	8.7715
23	20.4559	18.2921	16.4435	14.8568	13.4885	12.3033	11.2722	10.3710	9.5802	8.8832
24	21.2435	18.9139	16.9355	15.2469	13.7986	12.5503	11.4693	10.5287	9.7066	8.9847
25	22.0233	19.5234	17.4131	15.6220	14.0939	12.7833	11.6536	10.6748	9.8226	9.0770

TABLE 3 (Contd.)
The Compound Sum of One Rupee

Year	21%	22%	23%	24%	25%	26%	27%	28%	29%	30%
1	1.210	1.220	1.230	1.240	1.250	1.260	1.270	1.280	1.290	1.300
2	1.464	1.488	1.513	1.538	1.562	1.588	1.613	1.638	1.664	1.690
3	1.772	1.816	1.861	1.907	1.953	2.000	2.048	2.097	2.147	2.197
4	2.144	2.215	2.289	2.364	2.441	2.520	2.601	2.684	2.769	2.856
5	2.594	2.703	2.815	2.932	3.052	3.176	3.304	3.436	3.572	3.713
6	3.138	3.297	3.463	3.635	3.815	4.001	4.196	4.398	4.608	4.827
7	3.797	4.023	4.259	4.508	4.768	5.042	5.329	5.629	5.945	6.275
8	4.595	4.908	5.239	5.589	5.960	6.353	6.767	7.206	7.669	8.157
9	5.560	5.987	6.444	6.931	7.451	8.004	8.595	9.223	9.893	10.604
10	6.727	7.305	7.926	8.594	9.313	10.086	10.915	11.806	12.761	13.786
11	8.140	8.912	9.749	10.657	11.642	12.708	13.862	15.112	16.462	17.921
12	9.850	10.872	11.991	13.215	14.552	16.012	17.605	19.343	21.236	23.298
13	11.918	13.264	14.749	16.386	18.190	20.175	22.359	24.759	27.395	30.287
14	14.421	16.182	18.141	20.319	22.737	25.4[illegible]	28.395	31.691	35.339	39.373
15	17.449	19.742	22.314	25.195	28.422	32.030	36.062	40.565	45.587	51.185
16	21.113	24.085	27.446	31.242	35.527	40.357	45.799	51.923	58.808	66.541
17	25.547	29.384	33.758	38.740	44.409	50.850	58.165	66.461	75.862	86.503
18	30.912	35.848	41.523	48.038	55.511	64.071	73.869	85.070	97.862	112.454
19	37.404	43.735	51.073	59.567	69.389	80.730	93.813	108.890	126.242	146.190
20	45.258	43.357	62.820	73.863	86.736	101.720	119.143	139.379	162.852	190.047
21	54.762	65.095	77.268	91.591	108.420	128.167	151.312	178.405	210.079	247.061
22	66.262	79.416	95.040	113.572	135.525	161.490	192.165	228.358	271.002	321.178
23	80.178	96.887	116.899	140.829	169.407	203.477	244.050	292.298	349.592	417.531
24	97.105	118.203	143.786	174.628	211.758	256.381	309.943	374.141	450.974	542.791
25	117.388	144.207	176.857	216.539	264.698	323.040	393.628	478.901	581.756	705.627
30	304.471	389.748	497.904	634.810	807.793	1025.904	1300.477	1645.488	2078.208	2619.936
35	789.716	1053.370	1401.749	1861.020	2465.189	3258.053	4296.547	5653.840	7423.988	9727.598
40	2048.309	2846.941	3946.340	5455.797	7523.156	10346.879	14195.051	19426.418	26520.723	36117.754
45	5312.758	7694.418	11110.121	15994.316	22958.844	32859.457	46897.973	66748.500	94739.937	134102.187
50	13779.844	20795.680	31278.301	46889.207	70064.812	104354.562	154942.687	229345.875	338440.000	497910.125